MISTRESS

MISTRESS

A History of Women and
Their Country Houses

ANTHONY FLETCHER
AND
RUTH LARSEN

YALE UNIVERSITY PRESS
NEW HAVEN AND LONDON

Published with assistance from the foundation established in memory of Oliver Baty Cunningham of the Class of 1917, Yale College.

Copyright © 2025 Anthony Fletcher and Ruth Larsen

All rights reserved. This book may not be reproduced in whole or in part, in any form (beyond that copying permitted by Sections 107 and 108 of the U.S. Copyright Law and except by reviewers for the public press) without written permission from the publishers.

All reasonable efforts have been made to provide accurate sources for all images that appear in this book. Any discrepancies or omissions will be rectified in future editions.

For information about this and other Yale University Press publications, please contact:
U.S. Office: sales.press@yale.edu   yalebooks.com
Europe Office: sales@yaleup.co.uk   yalebooks.co.uk

Set in Adobe Garamond Pro by IDSUK (DataConnection) Ltd

Printed and bound in the UK using 100% renewable electricity at CPI Group (UK) Ltd

Library of Congress Control Number: 2025939084
A catalogue record for this book is available from the British Library.
Authorized Representative in the EU: Easy Access System Europe, Mustamäe tee 50, 10621 Tallinn, Estonia, gpsr.requests@easproject.com

ISBN 978-0-300-16381-0

10 9 8 7 6 5 4 3 2 1

Contents

List of Plates	vii
Acknowledgements	x
Introduction	1

Part One: Duty, Desire and Discord, 1567–1701

1 Domestic Duties	18
2 Making a Marriage	40
3 The Unhappy Household	62

Part Two: Domesticity and Dynasty, 1702–1836

4 Building the Dynastic House	94
5 The Connected House	115
6 The Affectionate Home	138

Part Three: Deference, Design and Distress, 1832–1918

7 Beyond the Country House	172

CONTENTS

8	The Artistic House	200
9	The Family at War	221
	Conclusion: Defending the Country House	246
	Endnotes	*256*
	Index	*313*

Plates

1 John E. Hoskins, miniature of Lady Alice Le Strange (née Stubbs) (1585–1656). Photo Vault / Alamy.
2 The tomb of Sir Anthony Mildmay and Lady Grace Mildmay showing an effigy of Lady Grace Mildmay lying with hands together in prayer, St Leonard's church, Apethorpe, Northamptonshire. Historic England Archive, DP029426. © Historic England Archive.
3 J.P. Neale, *Apethorpe Hall, Northamptonshire*, 1830. © Victoria and Albert Museum, London.
4 Daniel Mytens (attrib.), Maria Audley, first wife of Sir Thomas Thynne; c.1610. © TopFoto.
5 Lady Brilliana Harley, seventeenth century. Bridgeman Images / TopFoto.
6 The south-east view of Brampton Bryan Castle, in the county of Hereford. Topographical Collection / Alamy.
7 William Wallis, after John Preston Neale, Temple Newsam, illustration in Neale's *Views of the Seats of Noblemen and Gentlemen, in England, Wales, Scotland, and Ireland*, 1822.
8 Sir Joshua Reynolds (after), *Frances, Viscountess Irwin*, oil on canvas, 1755–1758. Major Archive / Alamy.
9 The ceiling in the drawing room, Hatchlands Park, Surrey, photograph from Eileen Harris, *The Country Houses of Robert Adam* (2007). © Country Life / Bridgeman Images.

PLATES

10 Saltram (the seat of Lord Boringdon), engraving, c.1803. Stephen Dorey – Bygone Images / Alamy.

11 Thomas Watson, after Sir Joshua Reynolds, *Theresa Parker (née Robinson)*, mezzotint, published 1773. © National Portrait Gallery, London.

12 Samuel and George Nicholson, Plas Newydd, print in *Plâs Newydd and Vale Crucis Abbey correctly Drawn from Nature*, 1824.

13 Richard James Lane, after Lady Mary Leighton, *The Ladies of Llangollen*, lithograph, 1836. © National Portrait Gallery, London.

14 Satire on the Westminster election, with the duchess of Devonshire canvassing for votes. Library of Congress, Prints and Photographs Division, Cartoon Prints, British.

15 Thomas Rothwell, *Penrice Castle, Glamorganshire, a seat of T.M. Talbot, Esq.*, engraving, 1792. UtCon Collection / Alamy.

16 Orazio (Horace) Manara, *Mary Elizabeth Williams, Mrs George Hammond Lucy*, oil on canvas, 1850. World History Archive / Alamy.

17 Sir Benjamin Stone, photograph of the exterior of Charlecote, the home of the Lucys, Warwickshire, 1900. © Victoria and Albert Museum, London.

18 Lady Knightley, HRH the duchess of Albany and others, Fawsley, Daventry, Northamptonshire, 18 May 1905. Historic England Archive, BB98/05906. © Historic England Archive.

19 The central hall, Wallington Hall, Northumberland. Heritage Image Partnership Ltd / Alamy.

20 William Bell Scott, *The Danes descend upon the Coast and at last possess Northumberland* (one of a series of eight oil paintings illustrating the history of the English border), oil on canvas, 1858. Painters / Alamy.

21 John Singer Sargent, *The Wyndham Sisters – Lady Elcho, Mrs. Adeane, and Mrs. Tennant*, oil on canvas, 1899. Artepics / Alamy.

22 Stanway House, Gloucestershire. Dave Porter / Alamy Stock Photo.

23 Lady Ottoline Morrell, photograph of Arthur James Balfour, first earl of Balfour; Mary Constance Charteris (née Wyndham), countess of Wemyss, 1925. © National Portrait Gallery, London.

PLATES

24 The homecoming after the marriage of Walter Ralph Bankes and Henrietta Fraser taken outside Hillbutts Estate Office, 1897. © National Trust / Simon Harris.
25 Mary Gow (Mrs Sydney Prior Hall), *Henrietta Jenny Fraser, Mrs Bankes, with her elder daughter Daphne*, 1902. Kingston Lacy Estate. © National Trust Images / Derrick E. Witty.
26 Edward Coley Burne-Jones, *Portrait of Frances Graham, Lady Horner*, oil on canvas, 1879. Christie's Images / Bridgeman Images.
27 Mells Park House, gutted by fire, 13 October 1917. Smith Archive / Alamy.
28 Sir Alfred Munnings, equestrian statue of Edward Horner (on a base by Lutyens), Mells church, Somerset. geogphotos / Alamy.
29 Poster advertising Temple Newsam House, colour lithograph, signed by M.A. Brownfoot, c.1929. © Victoria and Albert Museum, London.

Acknowledgements

This project has had a long gestation; therefore, both authors have so many people to thank that a full list of acknowledgements may be as long as the book itself. Many librarians, archivists and information technology specialists have offered invaluable assistance, most notably those at the British Library and the West Yorkshire Archives, Leeds. Curatorial staff and visitor teams at numerous country houses (and not just those that feature in this book) have been an endless source of information and ideas. Past and present colleagues and students at various academic institutions, but especially at the University of Derby, have provided intellectual stimulation and encouragement. Delegates at conferences and attendees at seminars where various ideas that appear in this book were first aired have asked pertinent and encouraging questions. This broad academic community is such a vital resource for researchers, and we are both grateful for the support that it provides.

Some individuals need special mention. The editorial team at Yale University Press have been patient and encouraging, especially Robert Baldock, Heather McCallum and Katie Urquhart. Helen Berry and Elizabeth Foyster played a crucial role in supporting this project. Ruth Larsen would like especially to thank John Saddington for being chauffeur, travel agent, sounding board and cheerful companion on so many country-house visits (as well as being so much more).

Introduction

In the first edition of his *Dictionary of the English Language* (1755), Samuel Johnson gave the reader seven definitions for the term 'mistress'.

1. A woman who governs: correlative to subject or to servant.
2. A woman who possesses faculties uninjured.
3. A woman skilled in any thing.
4. A woman teacher.
5. A woman beloved and courted.
6. A term of contemptuous address.
7. A whore; a concubine.[1]

These definitions cover a wide variety of duties, skills and qualities. From being empowered, knowledgeable and beloved, to the subject of contempt and moral appropriation, this single word captures the complexities of womanhood in the early modern period. The historian Joanne Begiato has recently argued that, in cultural tropes, 'women's lives as wives were undoubtedly constrained within a triptych of virtue, viciousness, and victimhood', and there is no doubting that the pervasiveness of patriarchy dominated the female experience for much of the seventeenth, eighteenth and nineteenth centuries.[2] This was not just a feature of texts written by men; we can see discussions of power and submission in letters between women, too. In September 1771, Fanny

Boscawen wrote to her friend, Mrs Delany, to send her best wishes following the news that Mrs Delany's niece had given birth to her first child, a daughter. She wrote:

> I have always thought it is much better to begin with a girl. The first is generally tant soit peu enfant gaté [a somewhat spoilt child], now it is of much less consequence to spoil a girl than a boy, for he being armed with power will make his caprices be felt, whereas she, being born to obey, will be reduced to submission sooner or later.[3]

This comment reflected the prevailing ideas in Georgian Britain about the relationship between men and women: the men were there to lead, and the women were there to obey. However, both Mrs Boscawen and Mrs Delany were, at this point, widows who had considerable social and cultural power. Mrs Delany, a favourite of the court of George III, was an artist who was also known for her botanical expertise, while Fanny Boscawen was a literary hostess. So, was she right to suggest that elite girls and women would be inevitably 'reduced to submission'?

This book explores this question by examining the role of elite women in country houses from the late sixteenth century to the early twentieth century. It considers their experiences as mistresses of the house and their relationships with their parents, husbands, lovers, children and friends. Unlike many women's history books, this survey does not take a life-cycle approach. Instead, its focus is on how women's lives intersected with the country house and the role of being its mistress. It therefore examines both their domestic responsibilities, including family and home making, and their dynastic duties, such as political and charitable activities. It draws on case studies of women who were from, or became part of, the social class that held significant formal and informal power in Britain. While the case studies include a countess and a wealthy heiress, not all the women were members of the richest or highest-ranked families in the country; many were not members of the peerage, and some, when compared to other members of the upper classes, struggled financially.[4] However, they all, because of their class, held significant social privilege. These women have been selected because they reflect the different ways that elite women fulfilled the role of being a mistress of a country house, or how they faced significant challenges – personally, socially and economically – in doing so. They have also all left behind a range of different primary sources that we can use to understand their lives, loves and losses.[5] These include letters, which vary widely as love letters, gossipy letters to friends and pleas for help. While stylistic conventions – and the fact that we often only have one part of the story – can mean that a historian has to be careful when using epistolary exchanges, letters were places where elite women discussed both the ideals and the realities of their lives. We see this, too, in diaries, journals and autobiographical writings, of which there are a number that were produced by the women featured in this volume. These vary in form, and include appointment diaries, full daily accounts, spiritual memoirs and pieces produced for publication. Again, these need to be used with care, as authors often wished to leave an idealised version of themselves in the texts that they wrote, especially if they were going to be published. There are other materials used which were produced for public view, such as portraits, satires and newspaper reports, as well as the country houses and their contents. Collectively, with the usual caveats that apply to all historical sources, we can use these pieces of evidence to build an (incomplete) jigsaw that allows us a glimpse of the experiences of elite women in and around the country house.

Before we do this, it is important to get an understanding of the different facets of the role of the mistress of the country house. This was a position with considerable responsibility, because the country house was central to the expression of power by the upper classes in this period. Building a family seat was the main way that people could establish themselves within elite society; as the architectural historian Mark Girouard notes, 'people did not live in country houses unless they possessed power or, by setting up in a country house, they were making a bid to possess it'.[6] Following the dissolution of the monasteries there was a significant redistribution of land to secular landowners, which meant that they were able to create their own private estates. This formed a pattern that was followed by multiple generations of the newly wealthy, who acquired land because it was often a requirement, if not a guarantee, of rank in British society. Land ownership was directly connected to political power and, until the 1880s, was seen by many as the most reliable source of wealth.[7] On this land, elites built country houses, and while traditionally this building process was seen as a largely male activity, the role of women in commissioning property, in redesigning the interiors and shaping the gardens has been increasingly recognised by scholars.[8] These houses functioned in a number of different ways. They not only acted as headquarters for the pedigree, from where political activities could be managed, but they also acted as places for the display of cultural capital, by housing the art, libraries and other collections of the family. They were economic centres, as they directly employed large numbers of staff to work within the property, and were also the place where the wider estate was managed. Following the ideas of the ancient Romans, the houses worked as retreats – a place where urban elites could escape the city and retore their minds and their bodies. They were family homes, too, the heart of the elite inhabitants' emotional worlds.[9]

Therefore, running these houses – a task shared by the male and the female heads of the household – was an important role. As Samuel Johnson noted in his dictionary, the main element of being a mistress was overseeing the staff. Household management could be a complex task, especially in large establishments. While there was a distinct hierarchy, with the male head at the top and lower (usually young female) servants at the bottom, the nature of power relations within this structure, and the place of elite women within it, was not always consistent. Many authors of conduct books in the seventeenth century advised women that they should 'keep house'. This could mean that they were expected to take on the responsibility of managing the household, which could give them quite considerable power, at least domestically. However, as we will see throughout this book, elite women did a lot more than just manage the female servants; they were often involved in overseeing a wide range of domestic activities, as well as estate business. A mistress was a woman who 'governed', and her subjects were not just her servants. As the 'lady of the manor', she could have an impact outside the domestic interior – and not just in the local community: she could build connections and influence across the county, country and beyond. As we will see, especially in Chapters 5 and 7, this could involve engagement with local and national politics and leading charitable works both at home and overseas. In this they were active in both the public and the private sphere. During the last forty years, much of the research published on women's history has explored the extent to which the idea of separate spheres shaped women's lives in the past.[10] For the upper classes, these terms do not really work in the same way as they may have done for middle-class families of the Victorian age; and the extent to which they did work in that setting is also debated by historians.[11] In the seventeenth century, while women were associated with the home and men with public roles, these spheres were very flexible, and were not consistently gendered spaces.[12] More widely, elites were public figures with responsibilities to their tenants and local communities; and they were expected to play a role in local, national and international affairs, depending on their relative status. For women of this class, that meant there was also an expectation that they would engage in public affairs on behalf of the family. As historian K.D. Reynolds notes: 'In relation to their own families and, to an extent, their own class, aristocratic women were first and foremost women. In relation to the rest of the world, they were aristocrats first and last.'[13] This meant that women could (and did) act as their husbands' proxies in matters domestic, economic and political, if they supported the concerns of the family.

It is also important to note that elite women were not necessarily disempowered or limited by their association with the private sphere. This is because building and running these houses, and bringing up a family within them, were important facets of creating and maintaining a dynasty. This therefore blurred the distinction between public and private, since for politically active elites 'all politics was family politics'.[14] The family was the central conduit of authority for the aristocracy; their pedigree was the basis of their position as members of the governing class, and every generation of the family was entrusted with furthering the future dynasty. Therefore, events such as births and marriages were family business, as they were necessary to their continuing success – even survival – in the upper echelons of society. The importance of marriage to the dynastic success of an elite family is highlighted throughout the book, but especially in Chapters 3, 6 and 9.

All the women whose lives are explored in detail in this volume formed life partnerships. This is not to suggest that all elite women in the past married; the research of the demographer Tim Hollingsworth suggests that, for the period covered by this book, between 5 per cent and 25 per cent of elite women never married.[15] However, marriage was the main way in which a woman got to be the mistress of a country house; that said, this book includes an example of women who became the ladies of their house by forming a same-sex union. Once married, there was an expectation that there would be children, ideally at least one son. Unlike many of their European counterparts, British elites used the system of primogeniture, where the eldest son inherited not only the title, but also the entire estate. This did mean that there were times when the birth of a girl was bemoaned, and some women acknowledged and internalised this idea that they were to be 'reduced to submission'. However, daughters and younger sons (the 'spares') were not perceived as inconveniences: by forming effective marriages or having successful political careers they could also play an important role in shaping and enhancing the dynasty. Occasionally, women could become the head of the dynasty, and thus become, in Johnson's phrase, 'a woman who possesses faculties uninjured'. Approximately a tenth of estates were owned by women; this included women who inherited property directly and widows who became custodians of the estate while the heir was still young. This meant that they could claim prestige from their own wealth, through consumption and through the ownership of land.[16] However, in the majority of cases, the role of a woman was to support the male head of the household, whether it was her father, brother or husband, in the management and advancement of the dynasty.

Being a mistress of a house was not usually shaped by the joyless fulfilment of dynastic duties. We should not see elite women as uninterested incubators of future aristocrats, for they often took great delight in motherhood. There are numerous examples of close parent–child relationships among elites, and there is clear evidence that, once the future of the pedigree was assured, daughters were a welcome addition to the family.[17] In recent decades, historians have rejected the idea that, in Shulamith Firestone's words, 'the heart of woman's oppression is her childbearing and child rearing roles'. Instead, they have highlighted the power and pleasure that women could gain from motherhood.[18] Part of this was because of their educational role: the term mistress could mean a woman teacher. While this use of the word was usually reserved for the professional classes, the educational role of the lady of the house, in terms of both her children and her staff, was an important one. This is not to say it was always an easy role: parent–child relationships could be problematic, and a combination of childhood diseases, accidents and warfare meant that many mothers buried more than one of their children. Their sadness in these circumstances often reflects the great importance of being a mother, as well as the significant emotional investment that usually accompanied it.

Marriage could also be a place of joy and affection. Parents often played an active role in finding a spouse for their adult children, because of the importance of such unions to the success of the dynasty. Many parents began thinking about possible spouses when their children were still quite young. However, they did not want them to marry too soon: in 1774, Countess Spencer was worried that her daughter may be 'snatched from me before her age and experience make her by any means fit for the serious duties of a wife, a mother, and the mistress of a family'.[19] Also, while parents often had strong ideas about suitable in-laws, children frequently had a certain degree of freedom in choosing their future spouse. This did not mean that they were happy to marry anyone. Although there are some examples of marriages across the socio-economic divide, many children were also aware of the benefits of marrying someone of a similar status; and daughters, in particular, appear to have acknowledged the problems they would face by marrying a poorer husband. Women had considerably more to lose than their brothers by marrying someone of lower social status, as wives assumed the rank and the wealth of the husband.[20] This would have had an impact on their ability to fulfil the role of mistress of a country house. This may, in part, have promoted the endogamy of elite marriages, since in purely practical terms there was little to stimulate marriage outside a narrow social circle. Once married, husbands had the legal power within a marriage; until the late nineteenth century, the property of a wife technically became her husband's property on marriage, and he usually had custodial rights over the children, too.²¹ However, this does not necessarily mean that these unions were loveless, or that women would inevitably fall victim to viciousness. While there were some unsuccessful matches involving cruel or unfaithful husbands, many spouses wanted the partnership to be a success. Because most marriages were between similar people who often shared similar ideals, women were able to develop their own place in the union, and they were commonly relationships shaped by care and affection. This included partnerships that did not lead to the production of heirs; while motherhood was important, it was not the only thing that led to affection and companionship. Couples often had shared interests, and could work together in developing their homes, their networks and their legacies. Samuel Johnson described a mistress as a 'woman beloved and courted'; and while this was often associated with extramarital affairs, many women sought, and found, love in their marriages.²²

Marriage, maternity and managing a property were all central elements of being mistress of a country house. In balancing these different roles, a mistress would often become, in Johnson's phrase, 'a woman skilled in any thing'. This could include accounting, the production of medicines, or cooking – all traditional areas of female knowledge. It could also encompass the arts, whether literary or pictorial – something that helped in the formation of country-house collections. Similarly, a woman may have been an expert in networking, in leading philanthropic works or in acting as a political agent. In all of these activities, managing people was crucially important, as it was central to maintaining domestic harmony within the family and household. The knowledgeable, generous and caring Lady Frances Horner, who lived in Mells, Somerset, was remembered in 1939 as 'the perfect mistress of perfect houses'.²³ The qualities that earned her that accolade were ones that were valued through the period covered by this book, although their form and expression was subject to change. In order to examine these ideals, their realities and how they changed over time, this book is split chronologically into three parts. The first considers the early modern elite household, with a particular focus on the seventeenth century. This period is traditionally regarded as a time of change in familial and domestic relations, as the patriarchal family model came increasingly to be questioned. There was also a heightened emphasis on privacy, and a shifting language that emphasised how elite buildings were familial homes.[24] The extent to which these changes shaped the lives of women in the country house is explored in these first three chapters, which examine the experiences of women managing households, forming marriages, and defending themselves and their homes from destructive forces from both without and within.

The second part focuses on the eighteenth century, the so-called 'aristocratic century'.[25] This was a period when there was both growth in the power and influence of elites and an increased celebration of the home and domestic ideals within the art and culture of the age. Again, there were shifts in gender ideals, and a developing focus on sensibility and politeness that encouraged a growing sociability and open expression of emotions.[26] The degree to which these shifts shaped the lives of elite women is explored by examining both their familial activities as wives, mothers and household managers, and their roles in building both houses and dynastic networks in order to gain and maintain elite power.

The final part considers the period after 1832, when the elite 'great world' (to use the novelist Thackeray's phrase) was growing in both size and influence. While the successors of the Georgian period's *beau monde* could still be found in London's fashionable society, *nouveaux riches*, artists, churchmen and intellectuals all intermingled within an expanding elite society.[27] It was also a period of considerable change, with industrialisation, political and social reform, and the expansion of empire impacting life within Britain. This did not mean that old models did not continue to exist: there were some continuities in the relationship between landlords and tenants, and many of the elite responses to the First World War were shaped by medieval ideals of chivalry.[28] These ideas of the old and the new are seen through the three chapters in this part. They consider, in turn, the paternalistic duties of elite women both on their estates and beyond the country house; the ways in which they shaped the artistic worlds of the stately home; and conflict within the family and how war shaped the country house and its communities.

This idea of old and new shows how, although there were notable social, cultural and legal changes in this time period, there were surprising continuities in the lives of elite women. The ideals and realities of the role of mistress may have changed, due to shifting economic, cultural and religious expectations and norms; but the essential focus of the role – to manage the household, lead the family and represent it externally – remained the same. Continuity was an important facet of elite women's status and their class identity. Therefore, the emphasis on dynasty among elites, and the importance of the endurance of family and familial ideals, often encouraged conventional (as opposed to new) behaviour. It was a role that women could shape for themselves; by examining this extended time period, it is possible to chart how mistresses were able to adapt changing social expectations both of their class and of their gender to forge their own place within the country house and in wider society. This includes their political, philanthropic and economic activities in their local, national and international communities. We can also see the significant roles that these women played in country houses as designers and managers, and how their domestic responsibilities could bring them both joy and sorrow. While some were praised for their morals and others suffered from marital cruelty or significant emotional hardship, their lives were not enclosed by 'virtue, viciousness and victimhood'. They were not usually the equal of their partner, and most did not have the same rights and privileges as their brothers. However, they were not usually 'reduced to submission', as they were often central in enabling their husband and their own family to be successful in their duties and ambitions as elites. Therefore, although they were not always the ones who were completely in charge, they did have significant influence as mistress of their estate.

Part One

DUTY, DESIRE AND DISCORD, 1567–1701

The early modern period was a time of significant instability for the inhabitants of the British Isles. The impact of the Reformation and the Counter-Reformation continued to be felt, and emerging forms of Protestantism jockeyed for acceptance and influence. Through the sixteenth and seventeenth centuries there were outbreaks of disease, and it was a period of social and political turmoil, both at home and overseas. It has been estimated that 190,000 people died directly or indirectly as a result of the Civil War in England. With the associated destruction of property and crops, financial hardship, disease and insecurity, there was significant human suffering in this period of conflict. Therefore, it is no surprise that this was the period during which philosopher Thomas Hobbes wrote that life in time of war was 'nasty, brutish and short'.[1]

While the impact of all this was most harshly felt by the poorest in society, the elite classes were also subject to social and economic changes. They benefited from some elements. The dissolution of the monasteries had led to a notable increase in the amount of land and building materials that the wealthier classes could access. This meant that more landed estates were established, and there was a move away from the castle to the country house. The 'great rebuilding' (to use Hoskins' – debated – phrase) of the later sixteenth century was of particular importance to the gentry; and throughout this period, many families that wished to establish themselves as members of the elite classes were building new properties or improving existing ones. The Renaissance fascination with invention, the fashion for ornamental brickwork and the increasing popularity of classicism shaped the houses of this period. Internally, there was an increased emphasis on privacy and comfort, with the general withdrawal from the medieval-style 'great hall' to smaller spaces that were connected by corridors, which segregated the family from the servants. This reflects how, over the course of the seventeenth century, while elites shared a common culture with one another, this culture became more exclusive. However, the communities that lived on the estates that gave the landed classes their power continued to be important. While there may have been a growing emphasis on displays of refined taste, which was primarily for the benefit of their peers, elites also needed to display and reassert their status within the regional community, too.[2]

It was not a time of peace for the upper classes, as they were directly impacted by the instability of the period. As many held positions that meant they oversaw the management of social order in their region (or the nation more widely), they were often drawn into responding to conflicts and protests, such as those organised by the Levellers.[3] There were also significant political changes in the role of parliament and the court during the seventeenth century. The cult of the monarchy, which had led to the growth in the power of the Tudor royal court, was disrupted by regicide and revolt in the seventeenth century.[4] The British Civil Wars and the interregnum were especially difficult for elites: local gentry power was subverted, and lower orders threatened rebellion. Those who had supported the royalist cause faced having their land sequestered and being obliged to pay the 'Decimation Tax'; some were even made to pay compensation to those who had suffered damage during the conflict. More generally, landowners' incomes were severely limited, as few of their tenants could pay rent; many of them also suffered from looting and the impact of high taxation on agricultural income. Therefore, this period felt like a time of social revolution for many elites; and while, by the end of the century, there was an increase in peace and prosperity for many members of this class, the legacies of the Civil Wars were long-lasting for some families.[5]

While there was not a lasting social revolution, there were conservative changes in the ideas about the roles of women during the seventeenth century. In the Tudor and Stuart period there was a growth in the production of conduct literature, much of which delivered complex and contradictory views of the ideals of femininity. Some presented a very binary view of women: those who married and followed biblical teachings were seen as paragons; those who were not under the control of a man were seen as shrews. Therefore, there was a strong emphasis on patriarchy, and the family was seen as a mirror of society.[6] As the family defined gender ideals, there was real concern when these were disrupted. At the start of the seventeenth century, women who killed their husbands – like servants who plotted the death of their master – were regarded as guilty of treason, for which the punishment was to be burnt alive.[7] The patriarchal model was reflected in marital laws, as wives were *femes covert*, which meant a wife was not a legal person under common law, as she was subsumed under her husband's legal identity.[8] However, there were places where female authority was accepted. Some advice books written by women, such as Elizabeth Jocelin's *The Mothers Legacie, to her unborne childe* (1624), were reprinted frequently throughout the seventeenth century, reflecting the way in which female expertise on appropriate topics could be welcomed.[9] Throughout the period some women used their domestic and spiritual authority to address political debates in their writings, especially during the middle of the seventeenth century, when the disruption to the social order meant that women had greater opportunities to engage with these ideas. The close connection between gender and order meant that when the world was turned upside down, social norms could be questioned; some argued that if a tyrannical king could be overturned, so too could a tyrannical husband.[10] Despite the great predominance of women among those convicted of witchcraft in this period, the complete ostracisation of females was unusual. While some questioned whether women had souls, generally in the seventeenth century this was seen as ignorant, and most thought, like William Austin (1637) that 'in that the soul there is neither hees nor shees'.[11] This reflects a change in how gender ideals were formed, and there was an increasing focus on medical understandings of female subservience. By the later seventeenth century, although a handful of writers acknowledged that female subordination was cultural rather than biological, there was an increased emphasis on the bodily differences between men and women. However, the idea that men were just women 'with their insides out' – to quote the popular sex manual, *Aristotle's Masterpiece* (1684) – remained widespread into the eighteenth century.[12]

This all had an impact on elite women and their role as mistresses. In order to explore this, this first part of the book focuses primarily on the lives of six women. The first of these is Lady Grace Mildmay (c.1552–1620). Born Grace Sharington, she married Anthony Mildmay in 1567, and they lived in his parents' house of Apethorpe, Northamptonshire. An excellent cook and medical practitioner, Lady Mildmay produced one of the earliest existing autobiographies written by an English woman in her own hand.[13] Another woman who had medical expertise was Lady Alice Le Strange (1585–1656). Daughter of the lawyer Richard Stubbe, she and her husband, Sir Hamon, successfully managed their estates in North Norfolk that were centred around their house in Hunstanton. She kept detailed account books, from which it is possible to explore the nature of life in a Jacobean household, with its feasts, jests and music making.[14] Maria Thynne (c.1578–1611) likewise worked in partnership with her husband in managing his estates at Longleat, Wiltshire. The daughter of George Touchet, later earl of Castlehaven, her clandestine marriage to Thomas Thynne in 1594 resulted in a lengthy legal case and was at the heart of the discordant relationship between the couple and Thomas's parents. Maria's surviving letters to her husband reveal a passionate and companionate marriage, and reflect her willingness to talk openly about her emotions, her worries and her desires.[15] While the Thynnes faced a legal fight to have their marriage recognised, Elizabeth Wiseman (1647–1730) was threatened with legal action after she rejected a suitor. The widow of Sir Robert Wiseman, she was part of the North family and found herself the topic of London gossip when she became an unwilling participant in a claim for breach of a marriage contract. To explore the nature of courting in the late seventeenth century, we use the various letters that were collated by her brother in anticipation of a court case. These reflect how different familial influences could shape, or limit, a woman's choice of spouse.[16]

Conflict lay at the heart of the lives of the last two women in this part. Brilliana, Lady Harley (c.1598–1643), daughter of Edward Conway, first Viscount Conway and first Viscount Killultagh, was the third wife of Sir Robert Harley. Brilliana and Robert had a shared commitment to puritanism and, subsequently, the parliamentarian war effort. Well educated and highly literate, her letters reflect her dedication to her faith, her family and their home, Brampton Bryan Castle, Herefordshire.[17] Brilliana's writings provide vivid details of the external threats to her family and house during the Civil War; in contrast, the letters of Anne Dormer (c.1648–1695) tell the tale of the threats to her from within the home. Born into a royalist household – her father, Sir Charles Cottrell, was a master of ceremonies under Charles I, Charles II and James II – she married the widower Robert Dormer in 1668. This was a deeply unhappy marriage, and her letters from her home in Rousham, Oxfordshire, to her sister set out her husband's mistreatment of her and how his actions meant that she could not fulfil the expected role of an elite mistress.[18] Across the next three chapters we explore how the lives of these six women reflect the varied models of duty that the mistress had to negotiate during the seventeenth century, and how they dealt with discord both within and beyond the home.

CHAPTER 1

Domestic Duties

In 1567, Sir Walter Mildmay, resident at his magnificent home of Apethorpe in Northamptonshire, was determined to persuade his son to marry Grace Sharington. Grace later recalled Walter's 'extraordinary love and favour . . . towards myself in my tender youth, which love was such that he desired me of my father to marry with his eldest son'.[1] The boy, Anthony, hesitated, being, in Grace's words, 'more willing to travel to get experience of the world than to marry so soon'. Sir Walter asked his son: 'Doest thou distrust me, Anthony? . . . [I]f thou marry with this woman, I shall give thee all that I have and whatsoever else I can procure shall be thine.' Sir Walter was moved to tears and Anthony's mother 'wept also'. So Anthony yielded to his father, 'upon the trust of his fidelity and good hope that he would never alter his mind nor break his said oath and vow, the consummation of that marriage being the seal of that bond.'[2] Grace did as she was bid; this was an entirely patriarchal marriage.

It seems that Sir Walter saw Grace, at seventeen, as a paragon, and so ideal for his son. This was in part due to her education. Her governess had taught her with a curriculum that included needlework, casting accounts and varied reading, including Dr Turner's *New Herball* (1551) and a recent work on surgery. Grace believed her governess sent her 'furnished into the world . . . that I should ever carry with me a modest eye and a chaste ear, a silent tongue and a considerate heart, wary and heedful of myself in all my words and actions'.[3] Her father had an equally careful eye on her. Grace recalled that:

he could not abide to see a woman unstable or light in her carriage, to hold her head one way and her hands another and her feet a third way, her eyes tossing about in every place . . . [H]e liked a woman well graced with a constant and settled countenance and good behaviour throughout her whole parts, which presenteth unto all men a good hope of an established mind and virtuous disposition to be in her.[4]

Her mother, Grace explained, 'taught me her meditations and prayers by heart and how I should fear and worship God in spirit and truth'. She censored Grace's reading and would not allow her lavish clothes or jewels 'until I were furnished with virtue in my mind and decked inwardly'. She counselled her never to weep, 'but for my sins'.[5] In choosing to highlight these elements of her upbringing, she was presenting herself as fulfilling the ideals of the virtuous woman that appeared in much of the didactic literature of the period. Similarly, in writing about her relationship with her husband, she noted:

I carried always that reverend respect towards him, in regard of my good conceit which I ever had of the good parts which I knew to be in him, that I could not find in my heart to challenge him for the worst word or deed which ever he offered me in all his life, but in silence passed over all such matters betwixt us.[6]

This silence reflected biblical teaching, which encouraged women to remain silent in the presence of their husbands.[7] In her autobiography, Grace described how she spent 'the best part of my youth in solitariness . . . first in divinity as my leisure would give me leave . . . also every day I spent some time in playing my lute and setting songs of five parts thereunto.'[8] Stable, modest, silent: these were the characteristics associated with the ideal elite woman in the early seventeenth century.

In writing her own life story, Grace Mildmay was clearly keen to show herself as fulfilling these ideals; but to what extent was she unusual for her class, in terms of the virtues that she claimed to embody? In Norfolk, Alice Le Strange was also celebrated for her virtues. In his will, her husband, Sir Hamon, wrote of his wife:

I thank thee for the great measure of days wherewith thou has filled my glass of time and abundantly for that comfortable union and blessed harmony which for many years enjoyed with that life of my life [sic] my dear wife . . . And further moved by long experience of her ever dear esteem of my life and person and care in the education of my children, those olive branches wherewith God hath pleased to bless our table, and to propagate my name and family and her ever incessant industry in strayness of knowledge above her sex to the just faithful and laudable advancement of my estate.[9]

Hamon and Alice had been married for over fifty years when he died in 1654. Together they had rebuilt the house and fortunes of the Hunstanton estate and weathered the physical and financial deprivations of the Civil Wars.[10] To Hamon, Alice was his ideal life partner; he left a note in one of the household account books that Alice oversaw, commenting: 'who shall find a virtuous woman for her price is above pearls, the very heart of her husband trusteth in her'.[11] Both these women played an important role as the mistress of a country house. As we show, Alice was far more proactive than Grace (and many women of her social standing) in the practical management of her house and estate. However, they both, in different ways, fulfilled the ideals of the didactic literature of the period of what made a good wife. This literature often portrayed the ideal wife as a submissive and obedient woman, whose main goal was to be 'godly'.[12] Grace Mildmay drew on religious teachings in her understanding of the duty of women, something that she shared with her parents-in-law; when she looked back on twenty years of living at Apethorpe, she noted that 'I thought myself in the house of God.'[13] Many didactic texts drew on Proverbs 31:10–31, which celebrates the wife of 'noble character', who is motivated by concern for the welfare of her husband and children, and who effectively applies her skills to household management. It was from this text that Hamon Le Strange concluded his note in the household book, adding: '[S]he overseeth the ways of her household and eateth not the bread of idleness.'[14] This reflects how being a good wife was also closely connected with being an effective mistress of the house. Many of the spiritual memoirs written by Stuart women, including the texts written by Grace Mildmay, indicate that they generally perceived domestic duties as being part of their spiritual duties.[15] We can see this, for example, in William Gouge's *Of Domesticall Duties* (1622), a popular husbandry manual of the early modern period. In this text he encouraged husbands to empower their wives if they were 'conscionable and wise'. He said a husband should give his wife the freedom to manage some of the duties of the effective housewife without having to seek his consent. These specific duties were:

1. To order the decking and trimming of the house.
2. To dispose the ordinary provision for the family.
3. To rule and govern maid servants.
4. To bring up children while they are young.[16]

These duties were based on biblical texts, but also on a practical understanding of the nature of married life. For Gouge, the virtuous wife and the effective mistress were not contrasting models of ideal femininity, but were instead to be seen as complementary to one another.[17] Using Gouge's text as a guide, this chapter considers how elite women managed and ran the country house and the estate, in their roles as chatelaines, wives and mothers. By drawing on the lives of Grace Mildmay and Alice Le Strange, we explore how elite women were central to running the household; to the development and promotion of their family's dynasty; and to upholding its reputation and standing within the local community.

Being part of a well-run household was central to the life of the mistress of a country house. The household was like a miniature state; Grace Mildmay wrote that the 'private household of family (which may resemble a whole commonwealth) consist[s] of the master and mistress, the husband and wife, children and servants, all of one mind in love, fear and obedience, being all well-chosen, instructed and governed with true judgement'.[18] The male head of the household was the governor of this 'commonwealth', and Sir Walter Mildmay had advised his son that his 'example is a guide to thy wife, children and family'.[19] As seventeenth-century gentry households were strongly patriarchal, many conduct books, such as Gouge's *Of Domesticall Duties*, stressed the subservience of wives to their husbands. They were, though, second in command in a household, and so were not without influence.[20] The role of the housewife was celebrated in some country-house poetry of the seventeenth century. This includes Ben Jonson's poem 'To Penshurst', which first appeared in 1616 and which describes the Sidney family seat as an idealised country house, estate and household.[21] One of the elements that make this an 'ideal' house (in the poem at least) is Lady Sidney. Jonson praises her fertility, her chastity, the godly education of her children and, especially, the effective management of the household; as literary critic Hugh Jenkins notes, it is the body of Lady Sidney that underpins the integrity of the estate.[22] The poem describes an unexpected visit to the house by James VI and I, and notes:

> . . . and what praise was heap'd
> On thy good lady, then! who, therein, reap'd
> The just reward of her high huswifery;
> To have her linen, plate, and all things nigh,
> When she was far: and not a room, but dressed,
> As if it had expected such a guest![23]

It is notable that it was the lady of the house who was praised, not Lord Sidney; the effective running of the home, and how it was perceived by guests, was seen as very much part of the duties of the mistress. The term 'high huswifery' reflected the status attached to this role, as well as the supervisory nature of the chatelaine's activities. We see examples of this beyond the literary world. Apethorpe had become established as a place for royal visits in the late sixteenth century, and Grace Mildmay entertained James VI and I on his journey from Scotland in 1603, and again in 1612, when he came to Apethorpe with a hunting party.[24] A contemporaneous history of the royal progress in 1603 noted:

> Dinner being most sumptuously furnished, the tables were newly covered with costly banquets, wherein every thing that was most delicious for taste, proved more delicate by the art that made it seem beauteous to the eye, the lady of the house being one of the most excellent confectioners in England.[25]

Following his return visit, the monarch gave the Mildmays timber to thank them for their hospitality.[26] While, traditionally, the domestic sphere, and by association the mistress of the house, has been seen as 'private', for elites the home also had a public function. Therefore, the successful demonstration of domestic virtues to these guests was an important duty for elite women.

Thus, in theory, household management could be a source of prestige for elite women, and so 'high huswifery' was not considered beneath them.[27] However, in practice, managing the household was frequently a difficult role. A new bride was often uprooted from her childhood home while she was still young, and had to negotiate the different traditions and expectations of a new establishment. For example, Alice Le Strange was just seventeen when she married Hamon, who was only two years her senior.[28] It was not always the case that a bride would be able to take up the role of mistress of the house straight away; for example, it was only when Sir Walter Mildmay, the patriarch, died in 1589 that Anthony and Grace took charge at Apethorpe of his ten servants – twenty-two years after her arrival. This would have been a long apprenticeship for the adult children, and their household roles would have been uncertain in a multigenerational establishment. While Sir Anthony travelled a great deal in the 1570s and 1580s, including a brief period as ambassador in France, his wife seems to have primarily remained at Apethorpe. Grace later reflected on how relations between the young couple and Sir Anthony's parents were not always smooth: she noted that 'many afflictions and contrary occasions fell out between us and them'.[29] Being both a wife and a daughter (in law), but not a mistress, in a household meant that Grace held a liminal position. Therefore, she seems to have drawn on her religious faith; this, along with her forbearance, was especially tested.[30]

When women were able to take up the role of mistress, there were opportunities for them to fulfil their godly duties, as well as to shape the household in line with their own needs – and those of the marital dynasty. The elite woman's responsibilities often ran parallel to those of her husband. While in grander households there would have been professional staff to run the home and estate, in more modest establishments both the husband and wife needed to be more proactive. This meant that they might be involved in all aspects of household management, such as hiring and training servants, overseeing the production of goods for domestic consumption and managing the accounts.[31] Even in the wealthiest of households, elite women were rarely 'ornamental', and would have overseen the staff, even if they did not have to engage with tasks directly.[32] This meant that they had significant influence: the household was an important social unit in the early modern period, a place where social rules and culture were developed, expressed and challenged – including those governing gender and class.[33] Therefore, the way in which the household was run was very important – and not only to the happiness of the family and to the future successes of the dynasty: it could also have a wider impact on shaping social norms within the local community.

This hands-on approach is especially visible in the case of the Le Stranges at Hunstanton. Although they were members of the social class that would normally employ a steward and/or other elite servants, Alice and Hamon took control of the direct management of the household. This was quite an undertaking, as it became a fairly large establishment: whereas until 1613 the household – family plus servants – consisted of around ten people, from around 1622 to 1654 it grew steadily to include between twenty and thirty members. Although Sir Hamon usually agreed the terms for male servants, and Alice those for female servants, the Le Stranges exceeded the boundaries of Gouge's guidance that wives should 'rule and govern maid servants', since Alice directly managed most of the staff and oversaw their pay.[34] Managing the servants was often a complex role, as households were rarely static communities: large numbers of different people moved in and out of the typical early modern household. Female servants often changed employer within a year of taking up their post, and most household staff did not expect to stay long in service. This was because service was seen mainly as a feature of an individual's teenage years: it was used by parents to ensure that their children developed a strong disciplinary framework during adolescence and learnt how to run their own households when they married.[35] At Hunstanton Hall there was a notable turnover of servants: between 1613 and 1628, the Le Strange family employed eighty-nine servants in all. However, well over half of those had had some previous contact with the household.³⁶ This suggests not only that Hunstanton was seen as a house to which servants were happy to return, and to which families were happy to send their children to work, but also that the Le Stranges were keen to have staff whose background they knew. This is because, within the intimate society of the gentry house, trust was important. This was not just the family needing to rely on their servants; the staff also needed to trust their master and mistress. Therefore, in order to attract and keep good staff, it was important for the employers to have a good reputation. Sir Walter Mildmay advised his son, Grace's husband, to live 'so as thou mayest deserve good report'.³⁷ As the elite family was so dependent on the staff, it needed to ensure that they were appropriately rewarded. This was not just through pay. In 1617, the lower servants at Hunstanton (i.e. those not in livery) were paid between one and three guineas a year, and also enjoyed the benefits of living in, which included having feather beds. They were also well fed – though not to the same standards as those enjoyed by the family: we can see that when the family was away, food purchasing patterns for Hunstanton Hall altered, with goods such as chicken, turkey, currants and fresh fish all coming off the menu. It is clear that while the servants often ate leftovers from the family meals, in general there was one diet for the family and another for the household when they were left alone.³⁸ While the Le Stranges could be generous, they recognised the importance of prudence in the management of their employees – especially when the house was not on public show. However, long-term service was more richly rewarded: in their wills, Sir Hamon left gifts for twelve of his servants, while his wife rewarded six personal servants.³⁹ The staff were an integral part of the household, and so gaining and maintaining mutual respect was important in creating a harmonious home.

The supervisorial duties of the mistress were not necessarily contained within the domestic space: some ladies of the house also played an important role in managing the wider estate. For example, Elizabeth Hotham of Scorborough managed 10,000 acres in the East Riding of Yorkshire during her husband's exile and death in the late seventeenth century.⁴⁰ While some of the women who managed properties did so because of the absence of a husband, in other cases it was because the woman had a particular talent for the role. This was very much the case with Alice Le Strange. She was engaged in such duties from 1613; at first she was responsible for receiving rents, and then she started managing the accounts for the sheep that she and her father had given her children. Following her father's death in 1620, she inherited his estate of Sedgeford and turned her existing systematic approach to household expenditure to the management of this estate, keeping detailed accounts for both. Then, from the 1630s, she was managing large parts of the Le Strange estate, including Hunstanton.[41] While this work may have fallen into the category of 'husbandry', which was more usually associated with men, Alice's skills in the area meant that her husband probably saw her, in Gouge's phrase, as 'conscionable and wise' in household accounting, and so this degree of delegation was appropriate.[42] As Barbara Harris notes for the period 1450 to 1550, there was no substitute at that time 'for competent wives who shared their husbands' interests and on whose loyalty they could count'; this was certainly the case for the Le Stranges in the seventeenth century, too.[43]

Her expertise in accounting also helped Alice Le Strange in another area of responsibility for the housewife – as Gouge put it, 'to dispose the ordinary provision for the family'. Alice oversaw both the kitchen and the garden accounts, thus directly managing food production. However, she did not just oversee activities within Hunstanton Hall, but also managed the large numbers of 'outside' day labourers that the family employed. They were responsible for producing a wide range of goods, including barley, peas, hemp, saffron, clay and reed for thatching. Collectively, these goods both met the needs of the household and provided some of its income through their sale at market. In addition to the day labourers, her accounts show that there were forty-one locals who worked for them as craftsmen or specialist workers between 1615 and 1624; others based in King's Lynn and Norwich were also in the employ of the Le Stranges, including shepherds, carpenters, weavers and nurses. The family was the largest employer in the district and the biggest consumer of locally produced goods. This reflects the high number of local contacts that Alice needed to maintain in order to run the farm and 'provision' her home.[44] Therefore, the networks of patronage were considerable, reflecting the significant economic impact that the Le Stranges had on the local community.

In many ways, both the Mildmays and the Le Stranges were quintessentially country gentry in their aspirations and way of life. However, they were deeply ambitious and looked to develop their links beyond the region. Hamon Le Strange took rooms for himself and Alice at Westminster during the 1614 parliament. They were back in London in 1617, when they sat for their portraits by John Hoskins, a rising miniature painter, in the characteristic ruffs of the period.[45] Similarly, the Mildmays were also a family that was trying to establish its relatively newly acquired gentry status, building on its connections to the royal court. They emphasised their medieval lineage and were granted heraldry in 1583 that displayed their associations with noble families. However, while both families spent some time in London – the Mildmays visiting twice a year, with a large retinue of servants – it was the country life that they preferred. A family friend of the Le Stranges said that London would be 'a marvellous fine sweet place . . . if it stood but in the country', a sentiment with which both Alice and Grace would probably have concurred.[46] Therefore, having a country house enabled them both to confirm their status and to retain their rural roots.

Sir Walter Mildmay was one of a number of government officials or courtiers who acquired land in the sixteenth century, and he quickly became a leading figure in Northamptonshire. He led major alterations and additions to Apethorpe Hall during the 1560s, which may have been completed specifically for the visit of Elizabeth I in 1566. This was just before Grace arrived at the property. The next major set of building work was led by her daughter and son-in-law after her death.[47] While Grace enjoyed a newly restored home, Alice saw her house of Hunstanton being rebuilt around her. On a moated site, the Le Stranges' Elizabethan wing of their manor and their fine brick fifteenth-century gatehouse sat apart. Hamon's notebooks reveal his supervision of extensive building works to connect these two separate buildings. He used both his architectural knowledge and his network of skilled labourers and suppliers to oversee the work, employing masons such as Thomas Thorpe (who also worked at Apethorpe in the 1620s).[48] It is not clear whether Alice played a direct role in the building process at Hunstanton, although she reportedly encouraged the construction of a summer house, where her husband could play his viols, rather than in the main property. However, she did manage the costs of Hamon's projects; her detailed accounting meant that he could predict his income with some certainty, allowing the Le Stranges to engage in a continuous programme of building works from 1620 until Hamon's death in 1654.[49] The ownership of land and of a property that could be passed down through the generations enabled a family to maintain its place in society. Therefore, the combination of a longing for social esteem and of a desire to leave a legacy led to elite families engaging with the disruptive, expensive and often lengthy work of building or enlarging a house.[50]

While Grace and Alice do not (unlike some other women) seem to have been directly involved in the building of their houses, they did engage with its interior decoration, reflecting Gouge's guidance that part of housewifery was 'To order the decking and trimming of the house'.[51] Grace wrote: '[E]very day I spent some time in works of my own invention, without sample of drawing or pattern before me, for carpet or cushion work and to draw flowers and fruits to their life with my plummet upon paper.'[52] Although many professional embroiderers were men, women also actively engaged in needlework for their own homes.[53] This was often seen as a pious activity, but it could also be used to express power. For example, the high-quality needlework that Elizabeth, countess of Shrewsbury (Bess of Hardwick) produced to decorate her houses contained both overt and covert political messages.[54] Alice Le Strange seems to have been more engaged with the purchasing of goods than with the making of them. She and her husband undertook extensive shopping trips to London between 1614 and 1628 to complete a programme of furnishing the new rooms in the Hall. This included a new black four-poster bed, for which they gave the upholsterer precise directions about its painting and gilding, packing and delivery to Hunstanton. On the 1628 trip, purchases covered nine sides of entries in the household accounts, with 308 individual items that cost a total of £492; these included glassware, basketware, earthenware and silverware.[55] The purchasing of these goods directly enhanced the quality of the accommodation at Hunstanton. There were rugs on beds, carpets on tables and cupboards, and some rooms had window curtains, which was rare in this period. Following the general trend among the Jacobean gentry, many walls were decoratively painted, often with religious images; and luxury items were bought to complete the rooms, such as looking glasses and clocks. In furnishing their house so richly, the Le Stranges were part of a wider consumer trend that encouraged expenditure on consumer goods and that reflected the Stuart elites' aspirations for domestic splendour.[56]

Decorating the house was part of this conspicuous consumption. Owning the right goods and being seen to be engaging with the right activities meant that a family could distinguish itself from other social classes. The Le Stranges lived well, with lifestyle expenses running at 8 per cent of their income as early as 1610–1619, rising to 14 per cent in the 1620s and not dropping much below that until 1653. Expensive furnishings, books, scientific instruments, hawks and hawking equipment were all significant items in the accounts before the Civil Wars; in the library collection were philosophical, mathematical and religious texts, alongside husbandry manuals, including Gouge's *Of Domesticall Duties*. Sir Hamon encouraged serious music making in his sons and arranged for travelling musicians to play at the Hall; the composer John Jenkins was based there during the 1640s.[57] However, it was important for the family to demonstrate its wealth and cultured tastes beyond Hunstanton. Hamon and Alice stayed in Norwich eighteen times between 1614 and 1628; Norwich was becoming a genteel town in this period, with a summer assizes week and public promenading.[58] Between 1606 and 1626, the couple frequently visited their closest friends across the county, attended christenings in the Knyvett family and acted as godparents to the Townshend family of Raynham. Horses and travel brought joint delight to Hamon and Alice, and the Le Stranges spent lavishly on coaches, so that they could make Norwich and London trips in style, sometimes taking the children with them.[59] These urban elite and rural gentry social circles were quite distinct from the tenantry community of the King's Lynn district, and so through this visiting and travelling they were able to demonstrate their status to a wider and more influential audience.

However, they needed to continually develop and enhance these networks, both locally and nationally, and strategic consumption offered them a way of doing this. Sir Hamon and Lady Alice ran an establishment that exemplified early Stuart gift exchange. Gift giving and hospitality were closely linked in the early modern period, as they helped to form and maintain bonds, especially with immediate neighbours. The vast majority of the gifts the Le Stranges received were food based: almost 1,500 entries in their kitchen accounts for the twelve years from 1613 to 1625 record food gifts to the family, including turkey, damsons, cheese, cakes and marmalade.[60] Thirty per cent of the gift givers were women, often handing over produce of their own labour. This echoed certain themes within Jonson's 'To Penshurst':

> But all come in, the farmer, and the clown:
> And no one empty-handed, to salute
> Thy lord, and lady, though they have no suit.
> Some bring a capon, some a rural cake,
> Some nuts, some apples; some that think they make
> The better cheeses, bring them; or else send
> By their ripe daughters, whom they would commend
> This way to husbands; and whose baskets bear
> An emblem of themselves, in plum, or pear.
> But what can this (more than express their love)
> Adde to thy free provisions, far above
> The need of such? whose liberal board doth flow,
> With all, that hospitality doth know![61]

The Christmas season was the peak time for the exchange of gifts with associated hospitality, since this was when the family feasted its tenants. At Hunstanton, this exchange was sometimes the gift of uncooked food for a cooked meal; the accounts show that expenditure on food at Christmas at Hunstanton was below average, because the household received so many food gifts.[62] The exchange also sometimes involved money. Alice's practice was to offer the giver a payment broadly aligned to the cost of purchasing the gift at market. Some asymmetry was acceptable here: proverbs of the time stressed unequal exchange and the acceptability of the smallest gift from the poor and weak. Therefore, Alice Le Strange often used her discretion: according to historians Whittle and Griffiths, 'the presentation of a reward appears as an assertion by Alice of her household's social superiority and right to give and choose favours'.[63]

This social superiority was also asserted when elite households held feasts – occasions that enabled them to maintain links with more exclusive guests, as well as with their tenants. Beyond the events at Christmas, family celebrations could be times for show. For example, the wedding feast at the marriage of one of the Le Strange daughters was spread over two weeks in October 1636. Forty-nine rabbits, ten turkeys, three swans and peacocks graced the tables of Hunstanton Hall at the making of an auspicious alliance between Sir Hamon and Lady Alice's twenty-three-year-old daughter Elizabeth and Sir William Spring of Pakenham in Suffolk.[64] As well as feeding their guests lavishly, the Le Stranges could also accommodate them in comfort: by the reign of Charles I, they had acquired a sequence of guest chambers that, in terms of the quality of their personal facilities, probably equalled anything that middling country gentry could boast anywhere in England. The best rooms for favoured guests each had a fireplace, multiple upholstered chairs, at least one table, and an 'inward chamber', furnished with a close stool.[65] Such facilities exemplify a family completely and proudly up with the times. This all suggests that the Le Stranges were engaging with the type of hospitality that Jonson celebrated in 'To Penshurst', and which was seen as being the result of the 'high huswifery' of the lady of the house.

The dinners and feasts to which these guests were invited appear to have been lively affairs. Nicholas, Sir Hamon's heir, compiled a family jestbook, in which he recorded 611 jests. These included jokes about bodily indiscretions and misunderstandings about common turns of phrase. So many of them relied on the speaker's rhetorical gifts for them to work effectively that the family and their guests were clearly confident jesters. The jokes often reflected the preoccupations of those who were credited with telling them originally. Among the forty-three attributed to Alice was one which reflected concerns about managing servants and another that was based around a minister who was in debt to a butcher; evidently her domestic duties were on her mind even while she was jesting.[66] Humour was clearly an important part of family life and entertaining, because the Le Stranges also had their own resident fool – first in 1615, when the children were growing up, and then again from 1624 onwards. This, alongside the presence of apes in the household, suggests that an older (and coarser) sense of humour was enjoyed at Hunstanton than was increasingly being promoted among more fashionable elites.[67] Generally, there appears to have been a degree of tradition and nostalgia shaping the hospitality at Hunstanton, as the family continued practices that had been established on the estate in the early Tudor period and that others of a similar class had long since given up.[68] Tradition was an important facet of creating and maintaining the dynasty, and seems to have been central to the Le Stranges' way of life.

The most crucial element of maintaining a dynasty, though, was parenthood. Children were needed to ensure the future success of the pedigree; motherhood was therefore one of the core expectations of the country-house mistress, as it enabled her to fulfil both her domestic and her dynastic duties. For women, it was often a responsibility that they had for most of their adult life. As they tended to marry earlier than women of other social classes, elite women often also had more pregnancies (although the nineteen children borne by Elizabeth Savage between 1603 and 1630 was an extreme example).[69] Not all elites had a large family. While Alice and Hamon Le Strange had eight children, Grace and Anthony Mildmay had only one – a daughter who arrived after fifteen years of marriage. This was unusual in terms of both the size of the family and the lengthy wait, and again reflects the fact that Grace spent her early years at Apethorpe in a sort of 'life-cycle limbo': although she was a wife, she was neither the mistress of the house nor a mother. In her spiritual meditations, Grace lamented her long period of childlessness, as she described motherhood as a 'natural and necessary employment', and so hailed the delivery of a child as a blessing from God.[70] As it enabled the fulfilment of one of the main duties of an elite wife, motherhood offered women status within the country house; correspondingly, in line with scripture, those wives without a child were thought to have suffered one of the greatest misfortunes that could befall a woman.[71]

While motherhood could give women status, it came with significant responsibility, as they wielded considerable authority over both male and female offspring. Grace Mildmay believed that children were governed by 'the terror of punishments', and there was an expectation that both parents would chastise their children if they misbehaved.[72] Mothers also often took an active role in the education of their children, thereby fulfilling the fourth area of Gouge's advice, 'To bring up children while they are young'. Alice Le Strange ensured that primers were bought for each child, so that they could all learn to read before they were four years old; and the boys were also bought 'accidences' or grammar textbooks. Children were also prepared for their adult lives, in terms of the duties befitting both their class and their gender. The eldest of the Le Strange sons spent more time at home in his early years than his brothers, so that he could develop an understanding of the estate that he would run; his notebooks from this period show how much he learnt from his mother about account keeping.[73] Likewise, while we know relatively little about Grace's experiences as a mother, in her will Lady Mildmay entrusted her medical papers to her daughter, showing how keen she was to pass on her expertise to the next generation.[74] In both cases, we can see how the preparation of children for their adult roles did not necessarily entail a limited education: it could be both practical and intellectual.

While elite parents were responsible for the discipline and education of their children, this task was by no means always undertaken without sentiment. For many years, historians argued that most elite fathers (and some mothers) showed little affection for their children, especially before 1750; however, more recent research has uncovered significant evidence of caring parent–child relationships in the seventeenth century.[75] Elizabeth Grymeston wrote in 1604, for example: 'There is no love so forcible as the love of an affectionate mother to her naturall childe', and there was a belief among physicians that women who did not love their children were mentally unwell.[76] Although the practice of wet nursing has been used by some scholars to suggest parental lack of interest, it was very much the norm in the seventeenth century, when it was often seen as a mark of extraordinary commitment for an elite mother to breastfeed her own child. So, while the Le Stranges sent their babies out to be wet nursed for extended periods – their children were often away from home for far longer than those of many of their gentry neighbours – this should not be seen as evidence of emotional detachment.[77] The health, clothing and education of her children were all chronicled in Alice's account books, and the details suggest a degree of care. The Le Strange boys, Nicholas and Hamon junior, received toys such as bows and arrows, tennis balls and shuttlecocks. Lady Alice also enjoyed treating her eldest daughter Jane to new and pretty clothes. There were hose, stockings and petticoats from three months onwards; then ribbon, laces and furred gloves were added. At the age of six, Jane had her first gown using silk, and expenditure rose as she began to wear a bodice and a ruff.[78] In many ways, these were children who were loved and cherished by parents who wanted to do the best they could by their offspring.

Similarly, although Grace wrote very little about her daughter, Mary, in her autobiography, it is clear that she cared deeply for her wellbeing.[79] As the Mildmay property was entailed on a male heir, there was insufficient money to provide a decent jointure for Mary to attract a suitable spouse. This was the subject of a legal dispute and, fearing that it would not be settled quickly, Grace risked an impoverished widowhood by paying for Mary's jointure with her own inheritance.[80] As their daughter was the focus of the Mildmays' dynastic hopes, a successful marriage for Mary was more important to Grace than her own comfort in older age. It proved a sound decision, as Mary's husband became the earl of Westmorland and eventually, after Sir Anthony successfully broke the entail in his father's will, the estates at Apethorpe descended from her.[81]

The successful establishment of her children was important to an elite mother on an emotional level, as well as being important to the dynasty as a whole. Therefore, the death of a child was often a time of significant grief. There were not only close affectionate ties between the parents and their children, but the parents also grieved for the future that they could have shared together, and for the role the children could have played in establishing the pedigree. Four of the children of the Le Stranges died when young; while written emotional responses to the death of their children have not survived, there are some hints attesting to the parents' grief. Eight-year-old Jane Le Strange was given a paved grave following her untimely death in 1620, and her funeral was attended by the whole household in mourning clothes.[82] By the time Mary was born the following year, the Le Stranges had already lost three children, and there seems to have been a decision to celebrate her christening in style.[83] Sadly, she lived for only three months. She and two of her siblings died while still in the care of the wet nurse. While this might suggest that their wet nursing was in some way inadequate, the evidence of the accounts is that these children were very carefully tended: the wet nurse, who continued to live in her home, not at Hunstanton Hall, was given a new cradle for each child, costing up to six shillings, and her pay was above the average for a woman in this period. Also recorded in the Hunstanton account books was a payment to the woman who watched young Mary when she was ill.[84] Like Jane, these babies were buried in Hunstanton church; this either suggests that the wet nurses were local or that there was a desire for the children to be brought to the family burial site, since it was common for children who died in the care of a wet nurse to be buried in her parish. While the evidence from the account books suggests that these burials were much simpler affairs than Jane's funeral, this is not unusual. Jane would have spent a great deal of time with Alice; as we have seen, she was treated to a variety of clothes and would have been under her supervision in terms of her education, and so the loss may have been felt more deeply. We can see from the writings of other parents how devastating such a loss could be. Following the death of her nine-year-old daughter in 1654, Lady Ann Fanshawe, who had already lost three children, noted that she and her husband 'both wished to have gone into the same grave with her'.[85] Being a mother was an important role for the mistress of the house, and so the loss of a child could be a time of real sorrow.

In their responsibilities for caring for their children, as well as for their husbands and the wider household, many elite women developed expertise in making medicinal cures. In a published marriage sermon from 1591, the puritan preacher Henry Smith argued that a woman should, in her duties as her husband's helper, be a 'woman physician'.[86] As we have seen with Grace Mildmay, medical knowledge was an important part of the education of many young women, and expert texts often featured in country-house libraries. For example, the Le Strange library catalogue lists thirteen medical books printed in English before 1626 – texts that focused on avoiding illnesses, simple diagnoses and recommended treatments for ailments.[87] Although neither Grace Mildmay's will nor an inventory of 1604 names any books, we know from her autobiography that she carefully studied texts on herbal medicine and surgery.[88] She appears to have used these in the development of her own medical writings; these included two bound collections of medical papers, as well as a collection of apothecary accounts and letters.[89] From these it is possible to see how she was part of a wider network of medical practitioners; but unusually for a woman at this time, her correspondents were mainly men. She attributed some of her cures to these male physicians, and this, along with her choice of ingredients, reflects the fact that she was seeking out and engaging with new remedies. Across her 270 recipes she employed over 350 different ingredients, some of which were from the 'New World', such as sarsaparilla and sassafras, and had only recently begun to appear in collections of medicinal cures within the British Isles.[90]

In order to make these medicines – whether concocted from guidance in a published book or from self-devised recipes – some equipment would have been needed. While much of this could be found in the country-house kitchen, some more specialised utensils were needed for more complex cures. Included in her apparatus, Grace Mildmay had furnaces, crucibles and different stills; Alice Le Strange also had stills and a 'limbeck with a brass bottom'. In both houses there were clearly defined spaces for the medical work; we know a glazier was paid for work 'on the stillhouse' at Hunstanton Hall in 1615, and a stillhouse appears in the 1629 inventory of Apethorpe, just nine years after Grace's death.[91] There would also have been some storage space required: as well as the chest that contained some of her ingredients, Grace would have needed somewhere to keep the 10 gallons of aqua vitae or metheglin that she made in batches.[92] The making and sharing of cures was an important part of the work of the mistress of a country house, and so it needed to be appropriately accommodated. Whenever possible, doctors were not called in when someone fell ill, and so the household needed to be self-sufficient in treating ailments. From her accounts, we know that ninety-one different medicines and medical ingredients were used by Alice Le Strange between 1606 and 1626. These were not just for the human members of the household: some were designed for the Le Strange horses and dogs.[93]

Sometimes, though, doctors were needed. Among the local medical practitioners that the Le Stranges employed between 1606 and 1626 were local apothecaries and various physicians from Norfolk and London, including the royal physician Dr William Harvey. However, these were mainly for the family. Although there is some evidence of servants being seen by external medical experts – such as the unlicensed bonesetter who was employed to cure a servant's leg – generally Alice treated her own staff.[94] As with caring for children and trimming the house, medical work was closely aligned with 'high huswifery'.

Although by the later seventeenth century active housewifery and the provision of 'cures' was seen by elite writers as dull and laborious, it was not necessarily enclosing. It was through her medical expertise that Grace Mildmay escaped the isolation of Apethorpe, as it gave her opportunities to create epistolary networks and to apply her knowledge in the local communities. On many estates, the elite woman was often the only one who had the expertise, the household equipment and the financial means to produce home remedies, and so offering these cures to tenants was part of her local charitable work.[95] Lady Mildmay was well aware of how the local community relied on her, and when she was unwell, she had her housekeeper deputise for her.[96] She did not use her talents for self-aggrandisement, though; for Grace, her medical knowledge was closely aligned to her Christian and elite duty to serve the people of the local community, and it was their care that she focused on. She was therefore willing to let others help, especially if she thought them more expert. Richard Banister, a famous oculist, praised her in a treatise of 1622 in terms which stressed her care for others. 'The right religious and virtuous lady, the Lady Mildmay, of Apethorpe,' he wrote, 'had herself good judgement in many things; yet when the poor came to her for help . . . in cases of physic she would use the approbations of a physician; in surgery, the aid of a surgeon and for the eyes the assistance of myself.'[97] While she had significant mastery of medical knowledge, she also knew her place within society. Her devotional writings testify to her belief that her medical activities were part of her doing God's work, and the ideals of elite paternalism meant that there was a strong sense of duty to those who lived and worked on the estate. This was also reflected by some of the provisions of her will, which provided funds for the religious education of the children on the estate, work for the poor and care for the elderly.[98] There were limits to women's charitable activities, though. When Alice Le Strange treated a stranger for an injured hand, she subsequently related the story to her husband, as she thought it was odd that someone in such poor clothing had such good manners. Sir Hamon was at once suspicious, and it was discovered that the patient was a Catholic priest who had escaped from captivity in Wisbech. Although Alice pleaded for the man, Hamon had him committed to Norwich gaol, and he was condemned at the next assizes.[99] While Alice had a commitment to serving those who were in need, the familial desire to promote the Protestant cause remained strong. The duty to God and one's husband underpinned many of the decisions made by the elite women in the early seventeenth century.

Through their commitment to their households, the care of their children and their community, and through their efforts to promote the family name, both Grace Mildmay and Alice Le Strange fulfilled key elements of the domestic duties that elite women were expected to undertake during the seventeenth century. Theirs were very different households, though, and the historical records suggest that they were very different women. Hunstanton was a place that seems to have been full of gifts, guests and jests. It was certainly livelier than Apethorpe, which was portrayed by Grace Mildmay as a quiet and isolated place, and in her autobiography she stressed her solitude and piety, rather than jests with her neighbours.[100]

This shows how different models of elite womanhood could exist at the same time. But both women could be seen as meeting, in their own way, the expectations of their families and their peers. In both cases, the responses to their death reflect how they met these ideals – and how those ideals were often connected to acts of charity, hospitality, piety and maternal love. The monument to Sir Anthony and Lady Grace Mildmay in Apethorpe church depicts them in effigy, with four life-size figures of Piety, Charity, Wisdom and Justice, key ideals that shaped Grace's actions. She herself is shown with her hands clasped in prayer, demonstrating in stone her dedication to her faith. This monument was built on behalf of their daughter and son-in-law, who inherited the estate and maintained the dynasty. Likewise, on Alice Le Strange's tombstone in Hunstanton church Proverbs 31:29 is cited: 'Many daughters have done virtuously, but thou excellest them all.'[101] Hamon

Le Strange attributed his family's prosperity firmly to his partnership with Alice, and she had a long-lasting influence on the family's estate management, as her notebooks were in use right up to the start of the eighteenth century. Both Grace and Alice were perceived to be virtuous mistresses, and they show how these ideals could be broadly understood and how they encompassed a wide variety of activities. Therefore, virtue was not a trope that simply enclosed them; rather, it could be employed in different ways to enable them to play a crucial role in shaping familial, household and estate lives – and to leave a lasting legacy for their marital dynasties.

CHAPTER 2

Making a Marriage

On a spring evening in 1594, Thomas Thynne, the sixteen-year-old heir to Longleat, then a student at Corpus Christi College in Oxford, rode out to the Bell Inn at Beaconsfield. There he attended a supper held by some members of the Marvin family. Although the Marvins were, like the Thynnes, part of the Wiltshire elite, this was unusual behaviour, as there was a long-standing feud between the two families.[1] At this supper, Thomas met for the first time sixteen-year-old Maria Touchet, the granddaughter of Sir James Marvin.[2] They talked together and then, urged on by Maria's mother, Lucy Touchet, they agreed that a priest who was present at the inn should marry them on the spot. This man, who was on his way to London, performed the ceremony in an upper chamber of the inn by candlelight. The couple spent the night together, and a new chapter in the Thynne dynasty was begun.[3]

This was not the expected way for elites to make a marriage in the early modern period. The secretive and hurried nature of the union would have been seen as especially problematic. This is because the choice of spouse was usually quite the family affair, and 'suitability' was a significant consideration for adult children and their parents. It was a topic that the wider family and friends discussed; as historian Rosemary O'Day notes, it 'is certainly a mistake, at least when discussing the English aristocracy, to assume that the making of marriage was a matter simply for the parents and children'.[4] In her study of the 1692–1717 collection of letters from the gentry Verney family, Susan Whyman found that marriage was the second most discussed topic after finances; in the epistolary networks the writers were 'obsessed with matrimony' and it was a central focus of their 'news'.[5] Marriage was seen as the key building block of social life in Protestant teachings in the early modern period, and its success or failure could bring joy or misery to the individuals, households and dynasties involved.[6] Therefore, a hurried arrangement between two warring families, with no legal or financial agreement in place, was clearly not just unconventional: it risked the reputation and fortunes of all parties.

This chapter examines how marriages were made in the seventeenth century by looking at both the process of finding a spouse and the nature of married life in the country house. It considers the ideals and the realities of courting, and examines the role of love – not only for a potential spouse, but also for one's parents – when forming a marital union. It not only looks at the origins of successful unions, but also considers why a woman might decide not to marry someone, drawing on the peculiar courting experience of Elizabeth Wiseman. This case highlights the role of familial influence, and the extent to which elite brides (and grooms) had a degree of choice regarding their future life partner. The nature of married life and the extent to which it could be a loving partnership are also examined through the experiences of Alice Le Strange, Grace Mildmay and Maria Thynne. It highlights how, despite the unusual start to their married life, the Thynnes were able to form an affectionate and intimate partnership. Marriages were central to the dynastic success of an elite family, but life within the country house did not need to be loveless. A wife could be the mistress both of the house and of her husband's heart.

Courtship was a critical life stage for young women, as it could determine the rest of their lives. While women of all classes shared many of the same expectations in terms of their prescribed roles at this stage of their life cycle, gentry and noble women usually had less privacy and fewer opportunities to follow their personal feelings than did their plebeian counterparts.[7] However, this did not mean that they were unable to shape their own path through the courting process. While the literary model of women 'being on top' during courtship was not the experience for many in practice, during the seventeenth century English elite women had more input into their choice of spouse than did many noble Catholic women in continental Europe.[8] This is because English women were statistically more likely to be older (19–23 years of age) than their European counterparts and, following Protestant teachings, there was an expectation that love should form the basis of a marriage. Therefore, affection was not completely absent from the usual courting process. This meant that the parents faced a balancing act of finding a spouse who would enhance the dynasty and of ensuring their child's happiness. The ideal in this period was that the bride should have some say in who her husband was to be. However, her choice was normally aligned with her family's wishes, as their support and approval were usually important to her.[9] For example, when, in the 1650s, William Thornton sought to marry Alice Wandesford, a Yorkshire gentlewoman, she agreed because it was a match that suited her family and her friends, despite the fact that she was reluctant to change her 'happy and free condition'.[10]

If a child married well, the parents and the wider dynasty could benefit significantly. Marriage allowed networks to be formed and consolidated, political ties to be strengthened and familial prestige to be gained.[11] Sometimes this could be a risky business. When, in 1602, Richard Stubbe arranged for his daughter, seventeen-year-old Alice, to marry Hamon Le Strange, the young man had 'neither household stuff nor stock'. However, while his home was 'half built', Hamon's lineage and connections made him very desirable, especially for a woman from a modest gentry family: an ancestor was a veteran of the Battle of Crécy, and Hamon was knighted in 1603 for riding to Scotland to inform James VI of the death of Queen Elizabeth.[12] Crucially, the Le Stranges were long established within the same North Norfolk region as the aspirational Stubbe family: they had been based in Norfolk (and had been christening one of their sons Hamon) ever since the Norman Conquest.[13] Dynastic networks mattered throughout the seventeenth century; but the focus of these connections changed during this period, shifting from building up regional support and protection to making connections associated with Westminster, especially after the 'Glorious Revolution'.[14] Therefore, throughout the century, who was chosen as a spouse was critical – not just for the couple, but also for their wider kin.

The complexities of these choices can be seen in the life writings of some elite women. Among Stuart gentry women, the prospect of marriage was often a cause of anxiety, and some women, such as Mary Boyle (later the countess of Warwick), even had an 'aversion to marriage'.[15] However, it was a step that the majority of women took: it has been estimated that at least four fifths of elite women in the seventeenth century married.[16] Following the ideals of the period, most also had some choice over their spouse. In her study of Stuart women's diaries, Sara Mendelson found that of the thirteen marriages where she had evidence of the courting process, although six were forced or arranged unions, in two of these the bride had the option of vetoing the union. She also noted that those marriages where either the child concerned or the parents did not give consent (i.e. forced marriages or elopements) were more likely to be unhappy.[17] For both parties, having a shared acceptance of the union meant happier familial relations, and in turn greater opportunities for a more companionate marriage. This reflects how influential parents were in their adult children's lives; they were keen to impart their wisdom to their children about what made a happy marriage, and to support them at times of marital discord.[18]

However, the case of Elizabeth Wiseman highlights how there could be conflicting familial interests about what made a good match. The daughter of Dudley, fourth Baron North, she had married Sir Robert Wiseman in 1672; but her husband died twelve years later. As a widow, Elizabeth would have expected to have a greater degree of control over who her second husband would be – if indeed she decided to remarry at all.[19] But she was an heiress with a £20,000 fortune and brothers who had differing ideas about how her status could be used for their own dynastic gain, and so she did not have complete freedom of choice. In a written report of events that took place in 1686, Elizabeth Wiseman claimed that her brother, Lord North, manoeuvred her into meeting a man she disliked on three distinct occasions.[20] North thought that his sister and his friend, Robert Spencer, were an ideal match and he presented Spencer (in the words of their cousin) 'to her every way the most accomplished in the world, but she herself thought far otherwise'.[21] At the second of these meetings, which took place in Lord and Lady North's garden at Tooting, Elizabeth and Spencer were left alone.

Elizabeth claimed that she was so annoyed at being placed in this situation that she returned to her brother and sister-in-law's house the following day to complain. During this visit, Spencer arrived at the house, and they were left alone together; both Elizabeth and a witness claimed that she was unable to leave the room she was in with Spencer for several hours. Following this, Spencer claimed that Elizabeth had accepted a proposal of marriage; while Lord North and his wife supported this claim, Elizabeth strongly denied accepting Spencer.[22]

The fact that Elizabeth could have been thought to have assented to marry a man for whom, in her cousin's words, she had 'rather an aversion than love' shows how the expectation of affection promoted in some didactic texts was an ideal that was not shared by all. In this case it was Elizabeth's sibling, rather than her parents, who was keen to make the match; Lord North boasted to his cousin about 'how many happy matches he had made in his life before and hop't this would be the best of all'.[23] However, his other siblings did not agree, and they did not support this arrangement. It is unclear why Elizabeth's other brothers aligned themselves with her, but they – and especially Roger – remained key allies even when she remarried in 1687, becoming Countess Yarmouth.[24] The networks of family support were powerful: in his letters to Elizabeth, Lord North proclaimed his hurt at the suggestion that he and his wife had conspired against her; there was an expectation that siblings would not act against each other's best interests. What did unite all parties, though, was that they did not want a long-running public legal dispute; family honour was a shared concern.[25]

However, although it was problematic for families, litigation did happen. Records from legal cases provide a great deal of the evidence that historians draw on when seeking to understand courting practices. Although they were much less common in the seventeenth century than they had been in earlier periods, these cases can be used by historians to assess the different notions of what constituted a commitment to marry or a valid union. This is because many of these cases focused on the central transactions of courtship, including the exchange (or not) of words, gestures and gifts.[26] These words could include the plighting of troths, which was when a clear intention to marry was publicly sworn; this promise could therefore prevent either party marrying another, as this was a recognised pre-contract. The Elizabeth Wiseman case charts some of the 'expected' steps of a betrothal. As historian David Cressy notes, while there were no secular or religious rules to follow, courting was a 'deeply patterned activity', and there was usually a sequence of enquiries, meetings and rituals before an agreement of marriage was made.[27] In Lord North's version of events, Elizabeth willingly went through many of these stages. He claimed that not only did Elizabeth encourage him to set up meetings for her and Spencer, but that at the meeting in Tooting 'after a short dinner and a long wo[o]ing, [there were] many expressions of mutual delight, and genial salutes were openly in the balcony'.[28] North also noted that she received a gift from Spencer in the form of a handkerchief.[29] By including these details of a 'mutual' embrace and a gift, North was arguing that Elizabeth and Spencer adhered to commonly understood customs of courting. In relation to the final meeting, North also noted that he and his wife were 'much dissatisfied by the liberties she took with one not then her husband', adding that when they did open the door, the behaviour of Mr Spencer implied

> intimacies which I cared not to inquire further of, I joyn'ed hand in hand, and telling them I was for the country on Monday following, added God bless you both, and since 'tis thus, pray marry as soon as you can.[30]

This suggests that North thought that the relationship had become 'intimate' and that there was therefore a full mutual betrothal between Elizabeth and Spencer.

Lord North's account suggests that his sister had willingly gone through the standard courting process. However, there was a key element that had not been properly discussed: finances. It was usual during courting for legal matters and money to be considered, including jointures and dowries.[31] While the absence of these discussions did not make a marriage invalid, nor did it indicate whether the courting had been mutually embraced; the lack of a formal financial agreement could cause long-lasting problems for the families concerned. For example, Sir Walter Mildmay did not secure a written marriage settlement at the union of Sir Anthony and Grace in 1567, which meant that there was no agreed provision for Grace's widowhood. Sir Anthony had to request an act of parliament in order to break the entail on the Apethorpe estate. This meant that he was able to provide for his wife and daughter, by leaving his estates to them rather than his brother Humphrey.[32] Likewise, one of the reasons given by Thomas Thynne's parents for their frustration over his clandestine marriage was the lack of a dowry – something that Maria's genteel but cash-poor parents may have welcomed.[33] For all gentry families, the absence of a decent jointure was problematic, as it had an impact on the financial stability of the family as a whole.[34]

As well as planning for the wife's future, the financial stability of the husband was also important, as it reflected his social credit and status.[35] Many of the discussions in the letters and statements collected following the disputed Spencer–Wiseman proposal revolved around Spencer's fortune. Lord North had noted of him that

> [£]600 a year is his present fortune, [he] has a grant certain as may be of [£]1500 a year more from this king, he is heir declared to Lady Shaftesbury of £30,000 by every one's estimate, as also to his godfather my Lord Teviot. On May next [he] shall have a lease for 30 years of 1000 a year more. These are great matters.[36]

However, contained within the evidence collected by Elizabeth's brother Roger, in anticipation of a potential court case, was an account given by a North family retainer that included gossip about the Spencer family being 'poor', despite being related to the second earl of Sunderland.[37] There was also a different report that Spencer had wooed another woman who, after he claimed to have a significant fortune, had 'inquired and found his estate but £500 per annum' and so 'totally declined the proposition'.[38] Spencer's credit, both in terms of his fortune and his honesty, was directly impugned, and this attack on his reputation was one of the reasons why he threatened three of Elizabeth's brothers with legal action.[39] The ongoing debate became public and so was seen as injurious to Elizabeth Wiseman's reputation; therefore there was some discussion about whether she also had a legal case against Spencer.[40] In the end, it was her new husband, Earl Yarmouth, who took the action that led to Spencer writing a document that confirmed he did 'release and forever quit claim' against two of Elizabeth's supporters in 1687.[41] Her economic value as a wealthy widow made her, in Lord North's words, 'one of the good things . . . to be got'; but thanks to the support of her wider family, she was able to escape a union that she did not desire, and instead formed one that enhanced the family's prestige.[42]

Once the courting was complete and finances discussed, assuming the betrothal was accepted there then needed to be a wedding. Although it could be a modest event, if all parties were happy with the union the nuptials could involve a large celebration. In 1630, the Le Strange family saw the marriage of their eldest son Nicholas. Alice Le Strange took a great deal of care to prepare not only for the wedding, but also to provide the rooms and all things necessary for the newly married couple to live at Hunstanton Hall; it was not unusual for the heir and his wife to live, at least at first, with his parents. The total cost of the wedding, including the new furnishings, was £272. The groom arranged for some of the local costs to be paid, including for music by the Norwich 'waits', for bell ringers and for 'dressing up' the church of St Gregory's in Norwich, which was probably chosen so that he could invite the county elite to be there; this was not just a display of wealth and connections, but also saved guests from having to travel to the Hunstanton estate in the north-west corner of Norfolk. He also spent almost £20 on gloves for guests and £2 on garters for his wife's two bridesmaids.[43] Dressing up for the ceremony was a feature of many of the descriptions of Tudor and Stuart weddings; and for gentry families their costume reflected their status – as well as marking the day out as a special occasion.[44]

The wedding in Norwich was a profoundly celebratory occasion, designed above all to honour the Le Stranges in the eyes of the county society. Although we do not know what involvement Alice had in the celebrations themselves, the accounts show that Nicholas's teenage sister was supplied with a very expensive gown for the event. There was also the display of wealth through gift giving. The bride, Anne Lewkenor, was given silver domestic ware, including a basin and a candlestick, which together cost £24 3s.[45] Marriages were important markers not only in the lives of the new couple, but also in the histories of the dynasty, and so they were ideal times for conspicuous consumption and celebration of the family's status.

However, not all weddings were major family events. Some, such as the Thynne union, were clandestine affairs. This did not necessarily mean that the marriages were either invalid or rejected by the wider family. For example, in the early part of the seventeenth century, when Margaret Bagot married a member of her household, her father – part of the Staffordshire gentry – had to accept her new husband, as a way of maintaining a relationship with his daughter.[46] However, John and Joan Thynne were less welcoming of the union between their son, Thomas, and Maria. It was at least a year after the events at the Beaconsfield inn before Thomas's parents knew about the marriage.[47] In the intervening period, the feud between the families had worsened when one of the key allies of the Thynne family was killed by associates of the Marvins.[48] It was also deeply problematic that the union was between the children of John Thynne and Lucy Touchet. For in 1574 there had been early negotiations for John and Lucy to marry, but the Thynnes had thought that Lucy's father, Sir James Marvin of Fonthill, was trying to cheat them by offering as a dowry lands that were entailed to the Marvins. As he was threatened with disinheritance, John called off his relationship with Lucy and married Joan instead.[49] Thomas could not have made a more problematic choice of bride.

It is therefore no surprise that the Thynnes tried to get the marriage 'remedied'; while they used the language of divorce, this was not an option – annulment was the only possible solution.[50] Although there had been a very public 'bedding' of the newlyweds, the couple had not consummated the marriage; as they had spent the night together clothed, it was hoped that the marriage could be declared void.[51] However, in their private letters both Joan and John acknowledged that this was going to be difficult.[52] This was because a marriage was legal if both parties committed themselves to one another in the present tense or in the future tense; the agreement was then made binding following consummation. While these 'simple unions' could be challenged through the courts, the presence of a cleric at the Thynnes' marriage made a significant difference. If a cleric officiated over a union outside of a canonical house, or if the ceremony did not take place in a church, it was a clandestine marriage. However, clandestine unions were not necessarily invalid: although the parties may have broken canon law, if the cleric was ordained and the couple freely gave their consent, it was a legal union. Therefore, although they were sometimes challenged in courts, and the legitimacy of any children from such a union could be questioned, clandestine marriages continued through the seventeenth century. Following the interregnum, when the centrality of a church wedding was challenged, there was a tendency towards private marriages among the wealthier classes, which could have been classified as 'clandestine' despite them being widely accepted.[53]

Although the ceremony could be a private one, the fact that a couple had married could not remain secret forever, especially if both parties desired to live as husband and wife. Although relatively few people knew of the Thynne–Touchet union at first, by November 1595 it was a matter of public comment. One contemporary wrote: 'Mistress Touchet hath catched Mr. Thynne's son and heir, and married herself unto him, to his father's mislike, for with her shall he have nothing, but those virtuous qualities she brought from court.'[54] The Marvin and Thynne families were too well known nationally for this union to remain secret, and gossip, or 'news', was an important form of exchange in elite circles. Also, as Maria was a member of the royal court, her marriage soon became subject to scrutiny, as Elizabeth I liked to control the marriages of her ladies-in-waiting.[55] Because of these royal connections, Alison Wall suggests that the secret marriage may have prompted William Shakespeare to write *Romeo and Juliet*, drawing on the well-known accounts of feuding among the gentry in Wiltshire.[56]

There was also considerable real-life drama. Although witnesses said that Thomas Thynne was joyful about the union, and wrote to Maria a few months later calling her his wife, he was not completely consistent in his loyalty to her. This led to Maria Thynne, encouraged by her family, taking him to court so that he would recognise her as his wife.[57] Maria was in a difficult position: she had lost the protection of the monarch, as she had married without her blessing, and was neither single nor married in the court of public opinion. Thomas's parents managed for as long as possible to prevent him from attending the case, but eventually he had to testify. At first, possibly swayed by parental pressure, he claimed that he'd been too drunk to give consent to the marriage. However, by 1601, when he was examined under oath in private, Thomas 'confessed the marriage'.[58] Maria's mother appears to have taken care to ensure that all the crucial elements of a marriage not only took place, but were also witnessed. This, when combined with the exchange of gifts and letters between the couple, meant that the key signifiers of a legitimate union were all in place. Crucially, after a long-drawn-out legal process, both parties eventually admitted that they had freely consented to the union; it was a marriage that they both desired. Seven years after their meeting in the Bell Inn, Thomas and Maria were finally recognised as husband and wife.[59]

This did not mean, though, that cordial familial relations were restored. Maria needed to fight for her place within the Thynne family. We know that she tried to make connections with her mother-in-law, Joan, soon after the legal status of the union was confirmed, in an attempt to heal the rift. In 1601 she wrote:

> If I did know that my thoughts had ever entertained any unreverent conceit of you (my good mother), I should be much ashamed so impudently to importune your good opinion as I have done by many entreating lines, but having been ever emboldened with the knowledge of my unspotted innocence, I could not be so great an enemy to my own happiness, as to want your favour for want of desiring it.[60]

It is interesting that she used the language of mother and daughter, and this letter to conciliate her mother-in-law still bears her family seal, with a lock of deep-red hair underneath it, reflecting the emotions of the situation.[61] As Gary Schneider notes, letters were stages for emotional expression; but because of the distance between sender and recipient, the writer had to use direct and rhetorical means to create a sense of intimacy, such as sending one's hair.[62] Maria wrote several more letters, which were often pleading in nature, including 'many entreating lines'. In July 1602, she wrote to Joan: '[M]ost earnestly I have desired your favour, with promise to perform any kindness that might deserve it, and God who knows the heart, best knows that my desire in that respect is as great as ever.'[63] In these letters she was employing the 'rhetoricalities of sincerity', a feature of epistolary conventions in this period, by using words such as 'earnestly', 'respect' and 'desire'.[64] Maria appealed to the ideals of motherhood in her letters as a way of forming a bond. She asked Joan to listen to the petitions made by her own son (Maria's husband) on Maria's behalf; and she enlisted her own mother's support in the dispute – a brave decision, considering that Maria's mother was blamed by the Thynnes for the marriage taking place.[65] This all shows how important close family ties were, as the connections that a marriage brought were not just political: they were also important in creating emotional bonds.

However, Maria's bold letter from three years later, which is riddled with examples of sarcasm and mock politeness, shows that she eventually gave up any attempt at conciliation with her mother-in-law. Throughout this letter, Maria asserted her own status and power, as a wife, as the new mistress of Longleat and as a member of the elite. As her mother-in-law did not write her own letters, she criticised Joan's use of a scribe, saying it was 'to little purpose': the use of a secretary did not impress Maria, as she thought it highlighted the fact that Joan lacked the skills required to write her own letters. She added:

> Now, whereas you write your ground put to basest uses, is better manured than my garden, surely if it were a grandmother of my own and equal to myself by birth, I should answer that odious comparison with telling you I believe so corpulent a Lady cannot but do much yourself towards the soiling of land, and I think that hath been, and will be all the good you intend to leave behind you at Corsley.[66]

She was responding to Joan's criticisms of Maria's gardening prowess in a previous (non-extant) letter. It seems that Maria was stung by this, and so suggested that Joan was going to use her own manure (i.e. human excrement, and maybe even her own body) to fertilise her land at Corsley, where Joan had moved after being ousted from Longleat by her son and daughter-in-law. Maria clearly thought that she was Joan's superior morally, intellectually and socially, and her rudeness in her letters reflects her defiance.[67] This breakdown in relations had been exacerbated by the fact that John Thynne had died intestate in 1604, leading to a difficult legal dispute between mother and son over property and provision for her and the younger Thynnes. In one suit, Joan claimed that John had intended to disinherit their eldest son because of the clandestine marriage, although Joan persuaded him against it.[68] She also claimed Thomas

> married and took to wife the daughter of a Noble man, with whom the said Sir John Thynne had not any portion of money or land, so as Sir John lost all benefit of his eldest son's marriage, and his daughters lost money which by this means was intended to be provided for them.[69]

The hurried nature of the union had ongoing legal implications not only for Maria and Thomas, but also for the wider Thynne family. The dowries of Thomas's sisters remained unsettled after he inherited (something that concerned Joan a great deal) and Joan's financial status, as the dowager Lady Thynne, was uncertain. From the surviving letters, it seems that it was not until Maria's unexpected death in 1611 that a positive relationship between Joan and her son was restored.[70] While a marriage was primarily a union between two people, it was also the entanglement of two families.

Despite the legal difficulties that they faced, Maria and Thomas appear to have had a loving marriage; the desire which meant that they fought for their right to be together sustained them into married life. While the circumstances of the Thynnes' marriage were unusual, during the sixteenth and seventeenth centuries there was a growing focus on marital love. Protestant teachings emphasised that love was central to marriage, and so it was an expected part of why a couple would choose to marry. While children were expected to obey their parents, a purely dynastic match where one of the parties found their future spouse repugnant was criticised in Lutheran teachings.[71] The importance of affection and respect was also seen in secular writings. Contrary to the main arguments of many didactic texts, the countess of Bridgewater thought that a woman should not act like a servant and see her husband as a master, but 'have an affection, and love to him as to a friend ... [I]f the wife be so meek, and low in spirit, to be in subjection for every word, she makes him fear he is troublesome ... this is far from a companion's way.'[72] The 'companion's way' can be seen in the marriage between Alice and Hamon Le Strange, reflected in their partnership that was examined in Chapter 1. This was an arranged marriage, but it seems to have been shaped by a real sense of affection. By contrast, the affection in the Mildmay household was more muted, and the feelings were shaped by duty rather than desire. In her autobiographical writing, Grace Mildmay described her mother-in-law as 'a virtuous woman and dutiful to her husband ... and she instructed me likewise to become a faithful wife unto her son'.[73] Neither in her autobiography nor in her spiritual meditations did Grace refer specifically to love for her husband, or to love for her parents and parents-in-law. These were duties that she never questioned, founded as they were on her deep faith.[74] It is notable that her wedding ring had the inscription 'maneat inviolata fides' – 'let faith remain inviolable'.[75] It seems as though Grace's desires were focused on fulfilling her religious duty, rather than on meeting her own personal needs. In the 'meditation on the corpse of her husband' that she wrote in 1617, Grace was at her most candid, but also at her most forgiving:

> ... he never carried malice in his heart towards any. He was charitable and of a compassionate mind ... every rash word which he spake in anger was not from his heart or of evil meaning. He loved hospitality and bounty. He was of a free heart and good nature. He was not treacherous but faithful in all things. He was more sincere in his own heart before God than he made show of to the world.[76]

This was not a passionate marriage, but she did care for him and for maintaining their relationship.

However, for others, passion was an important feature of the relationship. This was encouraged, because of the centrality of procreation to most elite marriages. Desire was also seen as central to fertility, as it was believed that mutual orgasm was essential for conception. Therefore, if either party was repulsed by the other, it could be used as strong grounds for vetoing a partnership, as it may have resulted in a barren one.[77] It was not just about fertility. While signs of fecundity could be important markers of whether a match was suitable, female infertility was not seen by didactic writers as being a legitimate cause for marital breakdown, as it did not prevent sexual intimacy. However, male infertility was regarded as more problematic, as it was associated with impotence and, therefore, a lack of marital sexual pleasure.[78] During the seventeenth century, various texts, such as Robert Burton's *Anatomy of Melancholy* (1621), explored sexual desire, conception and the power of love; and other authors, such as William Gouge, depicted marital sexuality not only as a 'domestic duty', but also as a source of pleasure for both husbands and wives. He used the phrase 'due benevolence' to describe sexual intercourse; it was seen as a marital obligation that should 'be performed with good will and delight, willingly, readily and cheerfully, so it is said to be due because it is a debt which the wife oweth to her husband, and he to her'.[79] This reflects the way in which Protestant teachings, especially Lutheran interpretations of the Bible, had moved away from the idea of Eve as a sexual temptress, and so rejected the model that any form of female sexuality was sinful.[80] As the historian Patricia Crawford notes, 'good sexual relations were thus a central part of married life'.[81]

While sexual desire within marriage was encouraged, it can be difficult to find evidence of it. In many cases, the only evidence of sexual relations is the presence of children, which are not necessarily proof of mutual attraction. Although the historian Ralph Houlbrooke notes that the greater epistolary freedom that women enjoyed during the seventeenth century means that they were able to show more evidence of affection in their private correspondence than writers in previous centuries, there is relatively little written evidence of female sexual desire between a wife and her husband.[82] However, Maria Thynne is famous among scholars of early modern epistolary cultures for the sexual assertiveness of her letters. Even in this case, the evidence is fleeting: although Maria's letters are full of protestations about her concern to keep Thomas fully informed of life at Longleat while he was in London, there are only four extant letters to him, and they are hard to date or even put in the correct order.[83] Despite this, we can use her letters to get a hint of a close and flirtatious union between a husband and wife.

As was not uncommon among gentry couples, the Thynnes spent protracted periods of time apart. Thomas was an MP and had a house in Canon Row, London, so he just paid occasional visits to Longleat, where Maria effectively deputised for him as manager of the estate.[84] It is clear that she did not like being left at Longleat by herself. Unlike Alice Le Strange and Grace Mildmay, Maria did not prefer life in the country; as a young woman, she had enjoyed London life as a member of the court of Elizabeth I. In a letter to Thomas sent in c.1604, she bemoaned rural life, noting 'when my sisters will be in London at their pleasure, I am talking of foxes and ruder beasts at home'.[85] Bored and frustrated, in her letters she subverted the gender norms associated with scatological humour: she wrote about how she was in need of a 'strong purgation' and how their neighbours 'strive till they stink'; and she indicated that she was going to encourage the dogs to defecate in her husband's bed, so fed up was she. Elsewhere in the letter, she joked about patriarchal power, sarcastically noting that Thomas had given her 'authority to care' about her role as a housewife – something that she clearly felt was in her own gift.[86] Maria was clearly not a quiet, submissive wife.

She was also intellectually sharp in her letters. She played with the language of didactic literature, while refusing to comply with its advice, thus showing how women could defiantly subvert the model of the good wife in order to gain their own power in a marriage.[87] However, we should not see this as evidence of the Thynnes enduring an oppositional relationship; rather, the playfulness suggests compatibility and companionship.[88] Maria finished this letter with the following lines: 'Well do but make much of thy Mall when thou dost come home. I will not be melancholy, but with good courage spend my life and waste my spirits in any course to please thee, except fighting . . .'[89] This was very flirtatious, indicating that she knew that Thomas would not mind her complaints and lack of complicity, but would find it attractive; to cite a saying of the period, 'better a shrew than a sheep'.[90] In Maria's letters to her husband, she felt able to show her own feelings. She was clearly literate, and she had received sufficient education to be fluent with the pen and to have some understanding of Latin. While we do not know the details of her education, Maria's sister became a successful writer, suggesting that care was taken with the education of daughters in the Touchet household.[91] As we have seen, Maria disliked it when others used scribes to write to her; she not only highlighted it to criticise her mother-in-law, but she also bemoaned her husband's use of a scribe to write to her, as it made her think that he was angry with her because the letter felt impersonal.[92] As she wrote her own letters, she was able to use them not only to reflect her own emotions, but also to try and provoke them in her husband.

We can see this in action in a letter from c.1607. She began thus:

> My best beloved Thomken, and my best little Sirrah, know that I have not, nor will not forget how you made my modest blood flush up into my bashful cheek at your first letter, thou threatened sound payment, and I sound repayment, so as when we meet, there will be pay, and repay, which will pass and repass, *allgiges vltes fregnan tolles*, thou knowest my mind, though thou dost not understand me. Well now laying on side my high colour, now in sober sadness that I am at Longleat, ready and unready to receive thee, and here will attend thy coming. Remember that your last day's journey will be the longer by five or six miles, and therefore determine accordingly. Your horses are taken up, and I will take thee up when thou comest home for staying so long from me.[93]

Historian Faramerz Dabhoiwala notes that this intimate, frankly sexual, language from a female hand is extremely rare – especially when it is about the writer's own sexuality.[94] In this letter, Maria was toying with her husband, as he seems to have done with his wife in the (now missing) letter that prompted this response. He had aroused her passion, but also her propensity to tease; linguistic scholar Graham Williams notes that the use of the 'contemptuously diminutive *sirrah*' was a brand of verbal irony, using mock (im)politeness, a rhetorical device that allowed early modern women to express desire through their letters.[95] Maria did this to full effect: she played the role as the bashful but willing wife. There are many parallels in her language in this letter to dialogue in Shakespeare's *Romeo and Juliet*, showing that there was a shared discourse about female desire in this period. In Act II, when the nurse tells Juliet the news that Romeo desires her and awaits her at Friar Laurence's cell, she says:

> There stays a husband to make you a wife.
> Now comes the wanton blood up in your cheeks
> They'll be in scarlet straight at any news.
> Hie you to church.[96]

This description of a blushed cheek suggests enjoyment, as well as bashfulness. This combination can be seen in Maria's phrase 'bashful cheek', as well as in her (mis)use of Latin: the phrase *allgiges vltes fregnan tolles* can be translated as 'you will collect frequently: you will rise up'.[97] This garbled Latin may have been her playing the role of a bashful wife, who was too coy to be precise about her feelings; while it could be a genuine mistake, it may have reflected her struggle to express their mutual orgasms. However, she also could have been teasing her husband: she appears to have been his intellectual superior, and this wordplay could be another part of the power games in their relationship. The comment 'thou knowest my mind, though thou dost not understand me. Well now laying on side my high colour, now in sober sadness that I am at Longleat' may also have been part of this teasing. She was telling him that she was aroused, but as he was away, he could not 'understand' her. To ensure that he grasped what she was suggesting, she declared herself to be as 'ready and unready to receive thee, and here will attend thy coming'. Likewise, the comments about the horses may again be seen as metaphorical allusions to the pleasures that she was promising on his return. After a section on estate business, she concluded the letter with:

> I salute thy best beloved self with the return of thine own wish in thy last letter, and so once more fare ever well, my best and sweetest Thomken, and many thousand times more than these 1 000 000 000 000 000 000 000 000 00 for thy kind wanton letters. Thine and only all thine. Maria.[98]

This use of numbers is especially playful. Not only was Maria using the language of accounting, showing that there was a payment and repayment of the marital debt, but the use of the zero may have been deliberate. It was sometimes used as a euphemism for female genitalia, as reflected by a bawdy pun in the title of Shakespeare's *Much Ado About Nothing* (1598–1599).[99] Maria here was reflecting both the financial and personal nature of marital relations, thus showing that while marriages had pragmatic elements, this did not necessarily exclude desire.

These expressions of sexual desire reflect the close and intimate ties that could be formed within elite marriages. However, this did not necessarily mean that the relationships were equal, and the possible consequences of this inequality are explored further in Chapter 3. In accordance with Lutheran teachings, there was an expectation that marriage would be a patriarchal institution.[100] This was clearly the case in the Mildmays' marriage, which in many ways illustrates, to use Faramerz Dabhoiwala's term, the 'extraordinary' nature of the Thynne union.[101] However, even though keeping her silence was the main way in which Grace maintained a happy marriage for over fifty years, Sir Anthony Mildmay recognised his wife's capabilities by naming her, and not his son-in-law, as his executor.[102] Also, although the Le Stranges' marriage worked as a partnership, Hamon made many of the choices regarding the management of the household and estate.[103] There were relatively few marriages where the husband and wife regarded each other as complete equals, but this was something that Maria Thynne demanded in her letters.[104] This equality was particularly sought in relation to her role in running the estate. While Thomas was in London, she ran everything at Longleat for eight years, until her early death in 1611. Her letters are stuffed with references to her energetic pursuit of estate business. She fell out with her steward George Halliwell – not surprisingly, since her assertive management of the Thynne lands challenged his rule and her energy put him in the shade. Eventually she described him as 'weary of his office', but confessed that, from her experience of having to cope with the role herself, 'I do not know whom to place in it.'[105] She did not wholly trust the staff at Longleat. Although stewards appear in the accounts in April to July 1609, and again the next year, Maria received rents herself and made up the accounts. In the spring of 1610, she put together a list of money paid in and, at about the same time, noted money borrowed. It seems that she struggled to form positive relationships with the senior household staff, who may have remained loyal to Joan Thynne. Therefore, Maria had to take charge. She acquired a detailed knowledge of the family's estates, her tenants and neighbours, and so, as letters and the account books suggest, she played an active role in the management of the family's financial affairs.[106]

The difficulties of this complex role can be seen in her letters to Thomas. As we have seen, Maria could be passionate, and this sometimes turned into frustration. In a letter sent after her father-in-law's death in November 1604, she felt that her opinions about how to run the household were not being taken seriously:

> It is but the effects of a very disquieted mind, for I cannot grieve a little to find that I, who have been a willing companion in and partaker in your hard fortunes, should now be made so great a stranger to your proceedings in your better estate. But I see my hopes to find it otherwise were built upon a very weak foundation, when they were grounded upon my conceit of your good opinion and love towards me. Well, Mr Thynne, believe me I am both sorry and ashamed that any creature should hold such a contempt of my poor wits, that being your wife, you should not think me of discretion to order (according to your appointment) your affairs in your absence, but if you be persuaded that it is most for your credit to leave me like an innocent fool here, I will the more contentedly bear the disgrace.[107]

Maria insisted that she was his 'loving wife howsoever', reflecting that despite her frustrations, she wanted to show that she cared for him.[108] There may have been only a short gap between this missive and the next one, when Maria was sharper and even more scathing:

> I will not entreat too earnestly because I know thou art choleric with me ever in these cases, but though thou doth many times call me fool for yielding to the enticing of fair words, yet if you mark it, I

have never yet craved anything of such great importance as hath ever been prejudicial to your reputation or profit. If so (as it is too true it is so) name me any man that hath a wife of that rare temper. No, in good faith this age will not help you to an equal, I mean for a wife. Alas I sit at home and let thy dogs eat part with me, and wear clothes that have worn out their apprenticeship a year and a half since.

'Thine, Maria Thynne', she signed herself. What a tirade this was! The postscript confirmed, though, that she was still the efficient and conscientious wife he expected her to be: 'I will say nothing of any business, for I have this last night written you a whole sheet of paper and given you knowledge, according to your appointment, of all your affairs.'[109]

These letters show that Maria was keen to appear as his equal in running the estate, as she appears to have been keen to be his equal in matters of intimacy. However, she also knew that she needed to be seen not to be claiming power that would potentially be 'prejudicial' to his 'reputation or profit'; and so she was aware of how her demands for a full partnership could not always be seen to be played out in public. What was crucial, for her, was their affection for one another. She wrote in c.1607:

I will be a careful officer in your absence, and even so God in Heaven preserve thy health as long as I live, and continue thy love to me, as I may have cause to love thee no less than I do, which is yet as my own soul.[110]

She desired both him and her role as his companion. Although few of his letters to her survive, we get a sense that this desire was reciprocated. In the last extant letter from Thomas to Maria, he signed off with the line 'I mean shortly to be at home with thee and then fare thee well.'[111] The following year, Maria fell pregnant again. Family tradition claims that she feared she would not survive the birth; she told Thomas that if he wanted a portrait of her made, it needed to be done swiftly.[112] Whatever the veracity of this story, we know that she did die in childbirth in 1611; her mother-in-law Joan died the following year.

During the early modern period, for most women, their ideal of marriage was a partnership based on respect and affection.[113] The form that this respect and affection took, though, was not the same for all members of the elite. Some, like Maria Thynne, were able to make marriages that brought them both power and pleasure. They could play with the language used by didactic writers to define their own place within the relationship and as mistress of the house. Other women quietly endured more patriarchal marriages, drawing – as Grace Mildmay did – on a sense of duty, rather than personal desire. The ideal of the 'companion's way' was a reality in many unions, like that of the Le Stranges, although husband and wife were rarely wholly equal. Marriage was an important mechanism for creating and enhancing dynastic connections; but this did not mean that women were excluded from discussions about their future spouses. Elizabeth Wiseman's rejection of her brother's choice of a suitor shows that personal desire was an important consideration, running alongside concerns about pedigree and patronage. This was because marriage was recognised as being a personal union – one that was shaped by religious teachings, but that could also be at the heart of an individual's long-term happiness. Despite the ongoing feuding with relatives, and the feistiness of their epistolary exchanges, Maria and Thomas Thynne appear to have had a happy marriage, even if it had an unconventional beginning. These happy unions were important in enabling the woman to be the mistress of the house and oversee a peaceful household. However, as we will see in Chapter 3, this was not a good fortune that all elite women enjoyed, especially during the period of the Civil Wars.

CHAPTER 3

The Unhappy Household

> I think a Bad Husband is far worse than No Husband, and to have Unnatural Children is more Unhappy than to have No Children, and where One Husband proves Good, as Loving and Prudent, a Thousand prove Bad.
>
> Margaret Cavendish, *Sociable Letters* (1664)[1]

The lives of the women we have examined so far were predominantly happy. While Grace Mildmay appears to have been driven by duty rather than desire, she claimed in her autobiographical writings that she gained pleasure by serving her husband, the community and, crucially, God. Alice Le Strange's relationship with her husband was one shaped by a sense of partnership; and so, while she endured hardship – especially the death of some of her children – she did so in a household where there was a strong community spirit. Likewise, while the Thynnes argued with one another and with their relatives, they seem to have had a happy marriage, which they fought to defend. This, though, was not the experience of all elite women in this period. While they had many advantages over their less-wealthy counterparts, especially in terms of comfort and social influence, they did not necessarily live blissfully happy lives. There were many causes of unhappiness. Some wives could be victims of viciousness on the part of their husbands. For elite families with strong dynastic ambitions, childlessness could be a real source of unhappiness.[2] For those who had children, as Margaret Cavendish remarked, their behaviour could cause significant sorrow. There were also intra-familial conflicts, as we have already seen, which could be prompted by a combination of legal disagreements and a drive to defend either individual or dynastic honour.[3] The death of a loved one could similarly be the cause of real despair. On the death of her husband in 1666, Lady Ann Fanshawe wrote 'See me with my soul divided, my glory and my guide taken from me, and in him all my comfort in this life.'[4] These words reflect what was often at the heart of an unhappy home: an absence of comfort, or a threat to the dynastic future of the family. Both were central to the ideals of elite life in the country house, and when these were removed – or at risk – women often faced real distress.

This chapter looks at the experiences of two women who endured an unhappy home. We look at the ways in which Brilliana, Lady Harley fought for her home during the conflicts of the Civil Wars, and how the happiness that she had previously enjoyed, through her love for her husband, children and God, was at the centre of her defence (quite literally) of Brampton Bryan Castle. First, though, we look at a woman who was fighting an enemy within. This chapter examines the cruelties faced by Anne Dormer at the hands of her husband, and considers how her sister and the local community played a crucial role in supporting her. In the case of both women, the root of their unhappiness lay in the fact that they were not able to feel 'at home' in their houses. In his history of the idea of 'home', Witold Rybczynski identifies three key elements to the modern bourgeois ideal of home: privacy, domesticity and comfort. Although these were newly developing ideas in the seventeenth century, they were becoming increasingly popular among the gentry classes.[5] However, in Brampton Bryan Castle and at Rousham, the residence of the Dormers, these ideals were not met. In both cases, the image of the elite country residence as a 'retreat', as described in Ben Jonson's 'To Penshurst', was not a lived reality. This caused both women great sadness and directly challenged their ability to be mistress of their respective country houses.[6]

As we saw in Chapter 2, the expectation of love between husband and wife was widespread in gentry families in the seventeenth century. Therefore, unhappy marriages often reflected expectations of affection that were not met in reality.[7] By exploring unsuccessful unions, we can see both what could go wrong in a marriage and also what the norms were that the unhappy husband or wife felt were missing. The letters between Anne Dormer and her sister Elizabeth Trumbull chart the miseries that a wife could endure when the expectations of comfort, care and control of herself were denied. Anne and Elizabeth were daughters of Sir Charles Cottrell and Frances West; their mother died in 1655 and they were brought up in the care of relatives and then later by their father and his mistress. Anne married Robert Dormer (c.1628–1689) in 1668, aged twenty. He had properties at Dorton (Buckinghamshire) and Rousham, Oxfordshire. It was his second marriage, and he had a son already, Robert junior, who was ten. Anne bore Robert eleven more children, eight of whom reached adulthood.[8] In many ways, this may seem to have been a successful union: many of the medical and conduct treatises of the period make an association between fertility and felicity.[9] In contrast, Anne's sister Elizabeth did not have any children with her husband William. This did not mean it was an unhappy marriage: Elizabeth's husband was a virtuous man, and their union was a love match.[10] Sir Charles Cottrell wrote to William Trumbull in Constantinople:

> Since I must want your company and my daughter's [i.e. Elizabeth], your happiness in each other is my greatest comfort, & I could be glad her sister [i.e. Anne] were as far of another way, with her husband, if he could be made thereby as kind a one as you are.[11]

However, this was not to be the case. Anne's life was made a misery by her husband Robert, who could not be 'made' kind. Anne charted his abuse in the letters she sent her sister between 1685 and 1691, while Elizabeth was accompanying her husband during his diplomatic work overseas.[12] They not only reflect the experiences she faced during the period when she was writing her letters, but they also include her reflections on earlier incidents. As historian Sara Mendelson argues, she used the epistolary space both to chart her marital difficulties and to find a way of enduring them.[13]

In these letters, Anne claimed that her marital problems had started early. Robert Dormer was infatuated with Anne when they wed.[14] She recalled how, during their courtship, Robert showed 'such a passion for me he could not rest till he had got me'.[15] Anne's father and his mistress, Lady Salkeld, encouraged Anne to get married. She later reflected that she worried that she was going 'to be packed off' if she remained single, and recalled that her father had become unkind, telling her that 'he kept house only for me, and often complained of the charge'.[16] This suggests that, despite her ill ease at Robert's passion, Anne felt compelled to form a union with him. She was right to feel uneasy: for two or three years after her marriage, Robert limited Anne's opportunities for going home to London to see her father, despite the fact that Sir Charles and Robert were royalist allies.[17] This action was reflective of his controlling behaviour. Anne later told her sister that:

> Pride makes him think a Wife can not be kept too much a slave; and for jealousy . . . one of the first maxims he laid down to me was, that if he had a Wife [that] was either handsome or anything else that was agreeable, he would have it all to himself; and that it would not trouble another man more to see his wife in bed with another man then it would him if his wife were pleasing to any but himself.[18]

This jealousy and passion made Anne's life miserable, as Robert wanted her to be simultaneously both virtuous and responsive to his sexual desires. For example, he insisted that she welcome him home with a kiss whenever he returned from London. However, if she did, he ignored her. If she did not kiss him, he bemoaned her behaviour and saw it as evidence that she no longer loved him.[19] Such was the impact on her self-esteem that Anne continuously felt that he was ridiculing her; she was suspicious of his desire, especially as she became increasingly unwell. She hoped that he would 'leave telling me I am extra ordinary handsome, and truly that now looks so much more like a jeer than a commendation that I shall be glad to be freed from hearing anything that I do not believe'.[20] She so disliked his attentions that she welcomed illness, as she hoped it would mean he would bother her less.

However, as much as she distrusted him, his jealousy meant that he distrusted her more. It was not until 1688, the year before her husband died, that Anne managed to tell her sister the whole story of Robert's deepest suspicions of her, which dated back to an incident before they married. Robert noticed that when he came to London to marry her, she had a scratch on her arm 'and he asked me how it come and he was not satisfied with my answer and had thought of it many times since, and did believe there was something in it'.[21] Although it had been caused by Anne catching herself on some gilt leather as she rushed through a doorway, he did not believe her and thought it proof that she was not chaste. Many years later he was still asking her about the scratch. She wrote to her sister that she told him

> I was alone when I did it, and that was the truth. If he pleased I would not only take an oath it was so, but another that not only then, no man was rude to me, as he fancied, but that in my whole life I never had any rudeness offered me, nor no kind of affront put upon me throughout the whole time I have lived.[22]

It seems that Robert's fury with Anne was ignited by this premarital fantasy of a sexual alliance that never occurred.[23] Chastity was closely connected to honour, and sexual misconduct dishonoured a woman's father and husband; and so by questioning her virtue, he was undermining her status.[24]

Robert not only doubted her status as a virtuous woman, but was also critical of Anne in her role as mistress of Rousham. A husband had significant control over how successfully a wife could fulfil her duties within the household, because he could determine the degree of power she held within the structure. While most husbands recognised that they should work in partnership with their wives, some men, like Robert, undermined their spouse's ability to run the household.[25] He managed the finances tightly, meaning that she could

> scarce allow myself necessaries, so I am poor in the midst of abundance. I have at least thirty servants and not a creature to send on an errand, and my own maid is so sickly that she is rather a continual care than a help.[26]

However, while he limited her ability to run the household, he did not take on the responsibilities himself. She complained that he spends his time as he used to do, loiters about, sometimes stews prunes, sometimes makes chocolate, and this summer he is much taken with preserving, but between whiles he has sometimes a frump, and sometimes a kiss, in readiness for me.[27]

These activities were not seen as helpful; the making of these products was especially associated with women, and while preserving was usually seen as an aspect of prudent femininity, sugar-based goods were also associated with luxury.[28] Instead, Robert seems to have been doing it as a conspicuous display of leisure. It also shows us that, as he had no career, Robert appears to have spent his time tormenting his wife. This was not always done privately. During a visit to Rousham in 1687, Anne's father witnessed Robert chastising Anne, who told Sir Charles that 'he would make her fear him'.[29] The outburst in question was in front of not only Anne's father, but the servants, too, showing just how comfortable Robert was in undermining his wife in her role as mistress of the house.

Therefore, however hard she tried, Anne could not really make the house a home, nor enjoy the status that she should have held within the household. She noted 'I am in the eye of the world a man's wife, reputedly worth several thousand pounds a year', but in private she was suffering 'the solitude of the country without the quiet'.[30] She had so little agency in the home that she felt constricted in terms of the spaces of the house that she could use. Anne clung to her closet as a retreat. Often, she would cry in there, when writing letters to her family, and it was a place she could hide. She recalled that on one occasion

> he had been half an hour in the house before I saw him being in my closet; there I stayed till I heard him pass the door and say where is my wife, then I came out and met him as I always do with a cheerful face.

Other spaces were less welcoming to her: the claustrophobic feeling of airlessness in the marital bedroom made her describe it as a 'torture chamber'. Moreover, this was aggravated by her husband cluttering it with 'trinkets'; his love of luxury meant that she felt overwhelmed by his possessions, and she struggled to find a place for herself. She started escaping the bedroom at night, finding it unbearably hot, sleeping in a separate room for some peace.[31] However, during the day, Robert tried to exercise total control both indoors and outdoors. She told her sister,

> now I am grown so grey, so lean and so hagged [sic] that I might justly hope I might now be trusted in the garden, without the fear of anybody running away with me but no, my Lord has as constant watch over my steps as ever and can tell exactly how many will carry me from my chamber to the garden and if I happen to stop one minute I am sure to be asked the reason.[32]

There was little comfort, little privacy and few opportunities for domestic bliss for Anne at Rousham.

Robert also had power over Anne in her role as a mother. The legal frameworks of the period meant that, as father, he had overall disciplinary power over the children, as well as the household. Therefore, it is no surprise that she wrote 'I must not exasperate him, for I and my poor children are in his power.'[33] Robert's jealousy spread to when she was caring for their youngest children. She recalled:

> in the nursery if I stay half an hour he is in fury and once this winter broke the door and made it fly across the room when he fancied I was there, but I was not, nor no creature but Clem [their son] and his maid. His jealousy is a sort of madness I think.[34]

Anne sought to content herself by caring for and educating the children, although she found it difficult. She thought that Clem and Fanny were 'all the pleasure that two sweet natured ... children can be, but then teaching comes in, which is a toil to me now'.[35] It was clearly a household that was aware of the instability of its patriarch. For example, Anne described how Robert was

> after his way mighty fond of Clem, who has a vast deal of wit and [is] just such an entertaining child ... and when he cries 'Clem I love thee', 'do you?', says the bratt, 'then what will you give me?',

and then he'll fetch him something to look upon a little while, and so lay it again. But the boy will never be fooled, for when he takes it, 'truly', says the child, 'I love my good Mammy she will give me things to be my own. You shew me something now and then and so take it away from me again . . . nobody loves me that ever cozens me.'[36]

In her reporting of her youngest son's words, Anne was setting out Robert's nature: he toyed with affection and was insincere in his love of both her and her children. Although she attributed the line 'nobody loves me that ever cozens [i.e. tricks] me' to her son, it seems that these were (also) Anne's thoughts. However, she had always considered Robert to be faithful. Therefore, she was shocked to discover in 1688 that her husband was directing his passions towards other women, following the death of her friend Elizabeth (Betty) Vernon. She discovered 'by his lamentations with abundance of tears many days together . . . he had a very raging passion for her, which truly he did not spare to set out before me by all manners of expressions'.[37] Robert's infatuation with Betty appears to have been unrequited, as Anne 'heard many things since she died that confirm her kindness to me and much to the contrary for my lord', showing that it was not just his wife who could be subject to Robert's unwanted attentions.[38] This discovery changed Anne's view of the marriage: whereas previously she had seen him primarily as patriarchal and jealous, she now saw him as not only cruel, but also deceitful.

However, Anne did not wish to leave Robert, as she considered that her vows and duties meant that she was tied to him. She expected that she would care for him in his old age, writing:

> I now have given him quite over, and tho' nothing shall take away the care I will still take to do my duty yet I will concern myself no farther and whether he frowns or smiles it shall be no more to me than the changes of the weather.[39]

This sense of duty might have been shaped by pragmatic realism. If she had wanted a separation, Anne would have faced a number of difficulties, as the formal opportunities to end a marriage were relatively limited in the seventeenth century. While couples could gain an annulment if they could demonstrate that the original union was invalid, unless they secured the successful passage of a private act of parliament there was no opportunity for them to separate and remarry. Instead a couple could only gain a separation *a mensa et thoro*, which allowed a husband and wife to live apart.[40] The grounds on which these separations were granted show a distinct gender divide. As Laura Gowing notes: 'Men sued their wives for adultery; women sued their husbands for extreme cruelty.'[41] This shows how there were different expectations about the role of each partner in a marriage: he had a duty to protect her, and she had to be faithful to him in order to retain that protection. In Anne's case, she also did not explicitly mention details of physical abuse in her letters, although she wrote in 1688 that 'I tell him he can but hurt my body but he ruins his own soul.'[42] Instead she focused on how the emotional cruelty made her ill. Proving cruelty in court was difficult: since obedience was an expected part of marriage, what was understood as reasonable behaviour by a household patriarch – and what went beyond the bounds of decency – was often subjective.[43] Therefore, for women like Anne, often the only option was to find ways to bear the abuse.

One mechanism for coping with this 'viciousness' was gaining the support of family, friends and neighbours. In the case of the Dormers, it is interesting to note that many neighbours and relatives did support Anne; while Robert saw himself as fulfilling the ideals of the patriarch, his reputation within the local community and her family was not so positive. Anne noted that the men of the community 'cursed' Dormer because his cruelty to his wife undermined the ideals of marriage as a partnership, with the wife in a subordinate role.[44] There was an acknowledgement that her situation was caused by her husband not fulfilling the ideals of his gender, rather than by any failure of her own femininity. As Anne argued:

> If many Husbands should take that liberty he allowed himself with me, to lay aside as he doth, conscience good manners reason and justice in all their conversation with their wives, in a few years no woman of understanding or consideration would ever venture upon

Marriage, then Men would get no wives but such impertinent Gossips as were fit for such usage.[45]

However, Anne was not always able to access networks of support. Robert not only prevented his wife from visiting her father, but also refused to allow her to use his coach and servants, or to travel significant distances alone.[46] In addition, the geographical location of the house meant that she was not able to call easily on neighbours for some respite, and so was extremely isolated unless someone came to visit her.[47] She welcomed these visits, and noted that she was 'glad when they step in, it doth a little revive me'.[48] She also welcomed paper visits, and it was through her letters to her sister that Anne received the greatest support.

She did not start writing the letters straight away; it appears that for many years she silently accepted Robert's torments, and while she did write a private account of his actions, Robert destroyed it.[49] It seems as though her sister's departure triggered the epistolary recording, as a way for her to converse about her feelings – 'all my joys and all my sorrows' – and to find a way of managing them.[50] As she could not stop her husband from reading any letters she dispatched from the house, she used neighbours to send letters that she wrote covertly, or else waited until he was away from home.[51] The dialogical nature of the letters seems to have given Anne some strength and allowed her to try and improve her health and her self-esteem.[52] Robert had described her as 'the most abject pitiful creature in the world' and argued that 'as one values themselves they shall be valued'.[53] She was therefore grateful for the love of her sister and friends, and started to take care of herself physically, so that she could fulfil her promise to her sister that she would still be alive when Elizabeth returned from Constantinople.[54] She wrote that she was worried that all of the efforts and care of her friends would be in vain, so

> therefore I strive to cheer up my self but it is so unnatural to me . . . then comes a new supply of some good thing as the other day a vessel of rare wine from thee, the kindness of which gave me a greater joy than if I had had it full of pearl[s] some other way.[55]

Collectively, the visits from her neighbours and the letters to and from her sister gave her a sense of hope, as she knew that those people cared for her. This seems to have given her the strength to start resisting her husband. She therefore promised herself to be a rational wife, but also to challenge his behaviour. She reported to her sister a speech she delivered to Robert. She told him,

> 20 year is long enough in conscience to have been a tool and now I am resolved if you will have my kindness you shall deserve it, I am weary now of playing the monkey any longer, and if I cannot deserve your friendship I do not desire your fondness.[56]

Anne went on to explain that she hoped she would be 'less sensible of his anger'; she had tried many years to be kind to him, to little effect, and so had decided that it was time to feel his scorn less. However, despite these accounts of bravery, it was clear that twenty years of abuse had had its impact.

It is therefore sad, but not surprising, that following her husband's death in 1689, Anne had difficulty in escaping the memories of the marriage, and the behaviour his abuse had inculcated in her. Friends now believed she had 'cause to rejoice' and expected her to 'fly out as soon as the cage was broken'.[57] But she remained under Dormer's domination for a good while. Although some of his property was now legally hers, she felt uneasy when she looked in boxes and trunks that he had kept locked. She knew that her emotions were irrational, but felt that 'using such things as he would scarce suffer me to look upon, I am like one haunted by an evil spirit or who has committed some crime'. She was unwilling to turn into the lively urbanite and showy gentry woman that her father hoped she would become once widowed; instead, she commented 'I have done with the world . . . Sweet Retirement is all I covet.'[58]

Anne was reluctant to put herself first or to spend money that she hoped would be used for her younger children's portions, noting that 'it is torment to me to have so much spent for show'.[59] In this retirement she wanted to regain her health and continue to fulfil her duty as a mother. She wrote to her son, Jack, in 1691:

> I bless God I am better now, not though well for I lived so many years with very little sleep that I had such a languishing indisposition of body as I find will not soon be removed . . . my spirits are very low and my body weak.

Anne then implored Jack: 'Oh my dear child mayst thou never afflict a wife that loves thee nor suffer what I have undergone.'[60] What Anne wished for her daughter-in-law, and for her son, was a partnership based on love and respect. She was not unusual in wanting this; what is unusual is how detailed she was in recording the failures of her marriage. She was not able to fulfil, as she had wished, the key roles of the elite mistress: chatelaine, mother, partner and member of the community. Rousham was not a place of comfort; her only retreat was a closet, showing her utter lack of privacy. During her married life she was not able to enjoy domesticity in a loving home or to have a strong sense of her own self-worth; it was these deprivations that were at the heart of her unhappiness.

In many ways, Anne's relationship was ill-fated from when the marriage was originally formed. However, some other women who had more promising unions still spent some of their lives in unhappy homes. This was not necessarily because of a lack of love; some women were able to have full affectionate lives, but outside factors shaped their emotional worlds. This was especially the case in the mid-seventeenth century, when civil wars were experienced across the British Isles. Brilliana, Lady Harley, was one woman whose prodigious letter writing – and the careful archiving of those letters by later generations – means that we can chart the journey into conflict. Born Brilliana Conway, she married Sir Robert Harley in 1623, when he was in his mid-forties and she was in her mid-twenties. It was his third marriage, and, through her father, the match offered Robert a valuable personal connection with the royal court.[61] Their union was therefore very much a political one; but it was not the links with the monarchy that became the heart of the relationship, but rather their shared enthusiasm for the parliamentary cause.[62] This shift away from court to parliament was, in many ways, influenced by the Harleys' shared religious beliefs. They were part of the growing puritan movement, and this shaped their networks both before and during their marriage. The importance that they placed on keeping company with the godly meant that the early Stuart puritans had much in common with the Protestant Scots, French Huguenots and members of the Dutch Reformed Church.[63]

Brilliana's unusual Christian name was taken from the town of Brill (Brielle) in the Netherlands, where her father was governor, and it appears that Brilliana's upbringing in this Protestant Dutch town had a significant influence on her spiritual development and inculcated the Calvinist beliefs that she later shared with her husband.[64] As a couple, they promoted the international community of religious dissenters; in 1624, Harley family prayers were dedicated to 'the good estate of God's church everywhere, the defeating of the plots of all the enemies of it, the distressed churches of Bohemia, France, the Palatinate, Low Countries, in the k[ing's] Dominions'.[65] Across Europe, it was a time of rising uncertainty, both religiously and politically, and the Harleys engaged closely with the changes and the associated debates. Just before they married, Robert Harley had drawn up his own definition of 'puritans', describing them as those who looked only for what God's word warrants in the worship of God and the course of their lives.[66] He disliked religious superstitions, such as the sign of the cross and kneeling in church. In the 1626 and 1628 parliaments, Harley spoke against what he deemed to be 'offensive images'. However, while Robert Harley rightly had a reputation for his dedication to puritanism, it is important that we do not think of Brilliana as just a loyal wife who followed his religious lead. In 1633, a puritan lecturer wrote about Sir Robert:

> you shall find a worthy, Religious, and loving Patron and friend of Sir Robert, and such as I have not found many like in all these respects . . . Sweet and humble in his consideration for your comfort and converse and free of his heart and purse and I hear his Lady (for I know her not but by report through those [who] had experience of him as my parishioner and next neighbour) rather transcends him.[67]

It is clear from the commonplace book that she created just before she married that Brilliana's own religious beliefs were sophisticated, drawing on both Protestant and classical traditions.[68] As a married woman, she was recognised for her beliefs; Robert Horn, the puritan incumbent at Ludlow, which is geographically close to Brampton Bryan, dedicated his text *The History of the Woman of Great Faith* (1632) to her.[69] Her family also recognised her intellect: her brother was amused that the letters that he received from Brilliana were about scholarly matters, and those from her husband on the domestic, leading him to note to Robert that 'in your house the order of things is inverted'.[70] However, it was a partnership. As historian Jacqueline Eales notes, there was a 'deep religious sympathy' between the couple, and this helped them forge a union that enabled them to fight for their beliefs.[71] In 1639, their daughter, another Brilliana, recounted to her brother Edward that when their father had broken up a painting of 'the great God of Heaven and Earth', found in a stable on their estate, their mother had then thrown 'the dust of it upon the water'.[72] Puritanism brought them together.

The Harleys' marriage was not just one driven by politics and religion; there was evidence of affection, too. Brilliana sent numerous letters to Robert, and many of these, in Eales' words, 'testify to the depth of her emotions for her husband' and reflect the warmth within the marriage.[73] In 1626, Brilliana gave birth to her second boy while Sir Robert was away, attending parliament. She told her husband 'I chose that name I love the best it being yours.'[74] During his absences, she wrote to him about their young children and entreated him to return to her. In December 1629, for example, she wrote: 'I should be glad if you would but write me word, when I should hope to see you.'[75] It seems that she needed reassurance of her husband's affection for her. In one letter, written when she was heavily pregnant, Brilliana begged Robert to 'grant me my request, that you answer my love with yours, and where yours comes short mine shall supply in excusing the failings'.[76] Robert's letters to his wife do not survive, and so it is difficult to fully understand his feelings.[77] However, from her letters it seems that he was not quite as demonstrative in his emotions as she was. She wrote: 'I know I love you much, but I find it no trouble, nor cannot think that with all your arguments you can persuade me to love is a trouble. I desire much to see you which I know you believe.'[78] However, despite this apparent coolness, Sir Robert often spoke of his wife as 'my dear Brill' or 'my dear heart', suggesting that they cared for one another.[79]

So, although they were probably not equally besotted with one another, there was real affection in the household. Collectively Brilliana Harley's letters demonstrate, in historian Susan Wiseman's words, 'the affective bonds of a seventeenth-century family'.[80] The couple had six children by 1631: three sons, followed by three daughters. It appears that Brilliana took a proactive role in their upbringing, especially that of their eldest son Edward, or Ned.[81] Once Ned left for Oxford, aged just fourteen, she wrote to him regularly, giving him advice on a whole host of topics. Discussions of key works filled her letters, including religious texts, conduct literature and humanist treatises. She guided Ned in becoming a young man, and produced a small didactic book in which she encouraged him to 'labour to live a holy life' and to avoid the 'pernicious sin' of drunkenness. Among other things, this text was full of advice to him on what he should wear, as she felt that clothing was important in the creation of her son's political and religious identity.[82] She was not only happy shaping her son's intellectual and sartorial worlds, but was equally comfortable in sending advice to her husband. Her letters to him show how they developed their beliefs that put them and their family in opposition to the Crown during the Civil Wars.[83] Together the Harleys shared a strong sense of what a better future would look like, and they hoped that they and their children could play a role in creating it.

Preparing their children for this future was therefore important to both Brilliana and Robert – not just because of their status as members of the gentry, but also because of their religious views. Due to their belief in the doctrine of predestination, Sir Robert and Brilliana thought they were distinct from the rest of society, as they believed themselves and their family to be 'the elect' or 'God's children'. Correspondents in their circle referred to Lady Brilliana as 'that elect lady', and the attributes of an 'elect wife' were a key theme in the speech delivered at the Harleys' wedding.[84] The dedication to this doctrine shaped the way they ran their household. Brilliana's commonplace book focused on religious and moral teaching, including passages from the Bible and from writers such as William Gouge.[85] In her letters to Ned, when he was a young man, she presented herself as a 'rational godly thinker', and encouraged him to become the same.[86] In November 1639, Brilliana sent her son detailed instructions on the introspection required of him: 'My dear Ned, keep always a watch over your precious soul; tie yourself to a daily examination.'[87] The Harleys' beliefs shaped their private and public actions, as their faith was central to everything they did.

It is no surprise, therefore, that for the Harleys the religious and the political were closely entwined. They believed that the struggle between the antichrist and the people of God was actively taking place around them in the 1620s and 1630s. Brilliana wrote to Ned that 1639 was 'the year in which many are of the opinion that the antichrist must begin to fall. The Lord say amen to it.'[88] Therefore, there was considerable excitement generated by the calling of parliament in the spring of 1640.[89] Brilliana told her son that she prayed

> God give a happy success to this Parliament; if not we may fear worse effects than has been yet. You and myself have great reason to be earnest with our God for your father. I believe this week will shew what they will do, as all our expectations are upon the Parliament.[90]

She was not misguided in putting her faith in her husband, alongside God. Sir Robert was a very active MP, especially on religious issues, and had a long record of working tirelessly for further reform in public morals, including relating to swearing, adultery and drunkenness.[91] He was unusual in his devotion to his religion, especially as a member of the elite classes, and therefore was seen as one of the men in parliament who could lead religious reform.[92] While the changes around them were increasing in speed, they were in line with views that both Brilliana and Robert had held for some time. In her commonplace book, written when she was just twenty-four, Brilliana had articulated justifications to resist a ruler; for both husband and wife, the time was now.[93]

However, although there was some excitement, the family was aware of the emerging factionalism that surrounded them. In the first weeks of the Long Parliament in November 1640, the unity of the Herefordshire gentry was remarkable. Sir William Croft, who soon became a great enemy of the Harleys, approved the attack on 'ship money', an unpopular tax.[94] However, the differences between the

Harleys and the rest of the gentry in the county soon became more marked. Within Herefordshire, the Harleys were the only major gentry family both to be puritans and to fully support the parliamentarian cause.[95] From the start of the century, the Harley family had installed puritan preachers in the parish at Brampton Bryan; as it was situated in the extreme north-west of the county, remote from the diocesan centre of Hereford, the Harley family was able to run things as it wanted.[96]

Despite a general reluctance in Herefordshire for church reform, Robert Harley adopted the 'Protestation' of 1641, in the hope of encouraging the community to the cause.[97] On 16 May 1641, Brilliana reported the taking of this oath at a number of towns and villages in the area. Those who took the oath swore to defend 'the true reformed religion expressed in the doctrine of the Church of England, against all Popery and popish innovation within this realm'.[98] That autumn, Robert led an iconoclastic drive in Herefordshire; when writing to the churchwardens of Leominster he listed crucifixes and 'scandalous pictures of the persons of the Trinity' as things to be destroyed, following the orders of the committee that he sat on in the House of Commons.[99] Members of their household also shared the Harleys' beliefs. At least two of the medical professionals that they used had Calvinist or puritan leanings, and one of them, Dr Nathaniel Wright, was also a political ally.[100] While their household was increasingly united, their neighbours did not share their enthusiasm.

Therefore, like Anne Dormer, Brilliana began to find herself isolated. During the 1640s, Robert spent most of his time in parliament, which meant that Brilliana was running the household, alone, in an increasingly hostile environment. In November 1641, stories of papist plots created anxiety in Brampton Bryan; Brilliana described how the household 'were all in arms upon the top of Sir Robert's castle and took up provisions with them and were in great fear'.[101] Brilliana became convinced that Brampton could not withstand a siege and asked Robert whether she and their family should not seek refuge in a nearby town. Whenever she repeated this request, Robert always urged her to stand firm. Despite her husband's reassurances, she remained concerned and so turned to her faith for comfort. She wrote to Robert in late 1641 'I thank you for giving me warning not to be afraid . . . if I suffer anything in professing His name, I hope I shall never be sorry for it, but rather rejoice that I am counted worthy to do so.'[102] By the following spring, Brilliana knew that Brampton Bryan was encircled by royalists, and that she lacked allies. The Harleys had been ostracised by families that they had once counted as friends. This led to an absence of visitors that would have hit Brilliana hard, as it meant that she had no audience for her public role as mistress of the house: in previous years, she had been keen to make her home a place that people would want to visit. In her letters to her teenage son, she often asked Ned to purchase items from Oxford for her and for Brampton Bryan, showing that she was keen to have a fashionable house that reflected the changing tastes of an increasingly consumer-conscious society.[103] However, they no longer had guests, and the hospitality that was such a key feature of gentry networks was now replaced with fear. Brilliana became isolated from the rituals of gentry life and the politeness associated with such visits in peacetime; instead, the Harleys increasingly felt the threat of war.[104]

At first, the threats were feared, rather than felt. Brilliana told Robert in August 1642 that local royalists 'say they maintain the true religion, but they shamefully use all that profess it'.[105] By the following February, she was worried that the servants were going to have to be dismissed, as she had nothing to offer them to make them stay. She thus feared that she might become a victim of looting, as the household was becoming too small to provide protection to the family.[106] She also wrote to her son about her feelings:

> Since your father thinks Herefordshire as safe as any other country, I will think so too; but when I considered how long I had been from him, and how this country was affected, my desire to see your father, and my care to be in a place of safety, made me earnestly desire to come up to London. But since it is not your father's will, I will lay aside that desire.[107]

As it was for Anne Dormer, Brilliana's home was no longer a place of safety. While her husband did not cause the fear, neither did he protect her. Therefore, for comfort, Brilliana wrote to her son instead. In a letter sent to Ned on Christmas Day, she poured out her heart:

They are in mighty violence against me; they revenge all that was done upon me ... My dear Ned when it is in your power show kindness to them, for they must be overcome so ... I pray you advise with your father whether he thinks it best I should put away most of the men who are in my house and whether it is best for me to go from Brampton or by God's help to stand it out. I will be willing to do what he would have me do. I never was in such sorrows as I have been since you left me, but I hope the Lord will deliver me; but they are most cruelly bent against me.[108]

Historian Diane Purkiss argues that Brilliana's emotional life was centred on her son, Ned, rather than her husband; and it is notable that she often asked her son to ask Robert for things on her behalf.[109] It is therefore not surprising that it was in her letters to her son that she increasingly articulated her sense of local isolation and fear, along with the 'sorrows' that these caused her.[110]

Despite this, and the geographical distance between them, her loyalty to her husband was strong. She wrote to her son in July 1642:

At first when I saw how outrageously this county carried themselves against your father, my anger was so up, and my sorrow, that I had hardly any patience to stay. But now, I have well considered, that if I go away I shall leave all that your father has to the prey of our enemies, which they would be glad of; so that, and please God, I purpose to stay as long as it is possible, if I live ... I have received this night the hamper with the powder and match, but I have not yet the muskets, but will enquire after them.[111]

It is clear that, despite her own nervousness, she wanted to protect the castle, as it reflected the Harleys' – and therefore her own – dynasty.[112] Protecting her home and its household was part of her duty as its mistress. However, the castle's role was shifting away from being a home: it was reverting to being first and foremost a fortress. Parcels that had previously brought fashionable goods to the property now brought items of war. It was also expensive: she noted that the 'mending of the house will cost a great deal'.[113] A few days later, she told her son that 'we are a despised company'; and another letter set out the plans of the locals to starve her out of her house by withholding rent and driving away her cattle.[114] This plan would impoverish her and oblige her to send away her servants:

> For the contentment of this country they do their utmost against me, my servants are taken and the horses they ride upon. Antony Child was set a liberty but bound not to come into my house ... Griffiths they keep a whole month in prison because he would not say that he would not come to Bromton [sic]. Now they have set him of liberty, they kept him in a dungeon ... Mr Cumings has forbid the rents to be paid and they at Kingsland swear to take those that come to redeem them. I am daily threatened to have forces sent against me, but yet it has pleased God to restrain them and I hope he will do so ... But Deare Sir do not think that I am yet weary of the hand of my God and it is my comfort that I share with the servants of god in their troubles and I hope I shall in their comforts.[115]

Her worries about her household being slowly depleted were coming true, meaning that she again feared that 'a few rogues' might seize their house and kill them.[116]

Brilliana's greatest fears were realised in spring 1643. In March, royalists entered the park at Brampton, took four oxen and shot dead a Harley tenant.[117] The safety of their home and estate was directly under threat. Alarmed, she wrote to her husband, asking again whether she should stay and how she should gain supplies. This letter, sent in April, physically shows her concerns: unlike her other letters, her handwriting is cramped and she has used a scrap of paper, having had to forgo her normal epistolary conventions.[118] By July 1643, Sir William Vavasour had the castle surrounded by a 700-strong force of horse and foot. Brilliana was fortunate that this was a 'proper' castle, rather than a property that was just a castle in name. Inside this fort, Brilliana had command of fifty musketeers, with some fifty civilians, men, women and children, including some of her own. She wrote that they 'threaten poore Brompton [sic]; but we are in the hand of our God, who I hope will keep us safe.'[119]

However, it was Brilliana who was central to keeping her household safe. While an effective mistress of the domestic sphere, it appears that she had not been active in the management of the estate in times of peace; however, she was able to effectively converse with the representatives of those who now threatened it.[120] Throughout 1643 she used her intellectual skills when responding to the summons sent to Brampton Bryan, helping to take control of the 'paper wars'.[121] After a request from Fitzwilliam Coningsby in March 1643 to deliver Brampton Bryan 'with all arms, munitions . . . and all warlike provisions' to the royalists, her reply was firm and carefully phrased. 'I know not upon what ground,' she declared, 'the refusal of giving you what is mine (by the laws of the land) will prove me or anyone that is with me traitors.'[122] It is interesting that in many of these letters she used the language of 'my' and 'mine' to describe the property; she was clearly defending the castle for herself and her children, not just for her husband.[123] However, while Brilliana's letters justified her role due to her status, the royalists who wrote to her consistently referred back to her sex.[124] During the siege there was continual negotiation with local royalist gentlemen, who warned that if 'your ladyship should be obstinate we cannot promise and expect those conditions for you that are fit for your quality . . . neither any quarter for those that are with you'.[125] They stressed her femininity and her need to be treated like a lady – a courtesy which, they claimed, the royalist Katherine Stuart, Lady d'Aubigny, had not received from the parliamentarians.[126] However, Brilliana simply repeated 'I have the law of nature, of reason and of the land on my side and you none to take it from me.'[127] She insisted to Sir William Vavasour that she and her family were faithful subjects of the king, but that she wanted to protect her home and household:

> Those gentlemen you write of seemed in their letter so far to befriend me as to let me know you had sent soldiers before my house to reduce it. I know nothing I can be reduced to but to poverty, and it is endeavoured as much as can be, for all my cattle and sheep are taken by your soldiers. I wrote the gentlemen word I would endeavour to keep what was mine as long as I could and I know that does not make me an ill subject, nor give anyone warrant to take it from me.[128]

In this letter she again used the language of 'my house'; however, in a letter a couple of days later, she did not claim the house as her property, but rather as her responsibility. This shows how 'house' could be used to mean 'household' – and she was indeed mistress of that.[129] She wrote in response to Vavasour's request for her to accommodate a royalist garrison at Brampton Bryan:

> Sir, for me to yield that you should place a garrison in my house, I can not find out any reason for it, and under what notion you would do I know not; but this I conceive, I should become a prisoner in my own house, which I cannot yield to . . . [M]y dear husband hath entrusted me with his house and children, and therefore I cannot dispose of his house but according to his pleasure, and I do not know it is his pleasure that I should entertain soldiers in his house; and surely, Sir, I never will voluntarily betray the trust of my husband.[130]

In these letters she was showing that it was her duty to protect her children's and husband's property as its mistress, and she played with the language associated with the ideals of marital deference, in order to assert her right to defend her home.[131]

Throughout this period, she remained stalwart, even when the attacks moved from the epistolary to the physical. Her bravery was recognised by those who were supporting her. Priamus Davies, a parliamentary captain who helped defend the castle against the royalist attack when it came in July 1643, recorded how she 'commanded in chief, I may truly say with such masculine bravery, both for religion, resolution, wisdom and warlike policy, that her equal I never saw'.[132] During the six weeks of the siege, cattle, sheep and horses were plundered, while the mills and houses in the village were all burnt. Sieges were difficult for those who had to endure them. As the historian Charles Carlton notes, sieges were 'the most brutal and prolonged experience of the British civil wars', accounting for nearly a quarter of the deaths in the conflicts.[133] At Brampton Bryan there were very few casualties, but the war did have an impact on the household: with provisions scarce, they feared starvation.[134]

The siege also invaded the domestic space. When describing the events of Monday, 7 August, Priamus Davies noted a 'very great gun' made three shots, one of which

> came in at the window and shattered the wall by the clock, broke the bell and hurt in the lobby at the parlour door the Lady Colebourn, struck out one of her eyes. Mrs. Wright, Dr. Wright's wife, was also hurt, but thanks be to God, neither of them mortally.[135]

This description shows how the war had come to the Harleys' home: their friends and their domestic goods were damaged by the conflict. Davies noted that in another exchange of shots, some Venice glasses were broken that had 'formerly entertained some of those gallants who had now unmanned themselves in offering violence to so noble a lady'.[136] The sociability of the previous age was forgotten, as were the gender ideals. In the end, despite entreaties from Charles I directly to Brilliana, she remained steadfast and refused to surrender. She was aware that parliamentary forces were on their way; and eventually, when Fairfax reached Gloucester, the royalist forces left Brampton on 9 September 1643.[137] With the siege over, Brilliana wrote to her husband: 'This is indeed the day of our deliverance, a day to be remembered, and never to be forgot throughout our generations.'[138]

Although Brilliana found her role difficult, she told her husband on 24 September 1643 that

> God has made me (though an unworthy one) an Instrument to keep possession of your house that it has not fallen into the hands of spoilers, and to keep together a handful of those such as feared the Lord together so that his word has yet had an abiding in these parts ... In this work I have not thought my life dear, neither shall I.[139]

She had fought to protect her home and household – the main duties of a mistress. However, the end of the siege was not the end of their difficulties. Brilliana fell ill. It seems that the siege had weakened her, and we can see this in her handwriting which, in the later letters that she wrote, was uncharacteristically unsteady.[140] She died after three days 'in great extremity with admirable patience'.[141] Captain Priamus Davies, keen to show her having a 'good death', wrote that she looked 'death in the face without dread and the Lord Jesus with joy and comfort to whom she resigned her soul . . . Never was a holy life consummated and concluded with a more heavenly and happy end.' He thought that Brilliana was an 'honourable lady, of whom the world was not worthy, as she was setting forward the work of God'.[142] In the end, it was this work, along with her defence of her home, that cost her her life.

In a text based on a speech delivered at the wedding of Brilliana and Sir Robert Harley, Thomas Gataker said that

> The wife indeed is an assistant to her husband: one that may either help to relieve and release him, or bear part of his burden with him, or comfort and cheer him up in the bearing of it, yea, or that may but bemoan him, and weep together with him.[143]

Brilliana fulfilled this ideal to the last. In her final years her home lost the comfort and domesticity that she would have enjoyed there in the earlier years of her marriage. Instead, it became a place of conflict. But the attack was one that she was able to resist, all for a cause she was dedicated to. In contrast, Anne Dormer was only able to enjoy domesticity at the end of her life, and even then she did so warily. After many years of unhappiness, though, she was able to start planning for the future. When she died in 1695, in her will she ensured that all her children were provided for.[144] The experiences of both these women show that there was a gap between the ideals of familial and domestic life and the lived realities. Like Maria Thynne, Grace Mildmay and Alice Le Strange, they had to negotiate a path through social and religious expectations to find a way of life that best suited their duties and desires. Whether their lives were shaped by joy or fear, peace or war, jests or jibes, all these women had a strong commitment to their role as mistress of the house, to promoting the family name and to ensuring that it survived for future generations.

Part Two

DOMESTICITY AND DYNASTY, 1702–1836

Although the popular understanding of eighteenth-century life often presents it as being a period of prosperity, while some indeed became very wealthy, it was not a peaceful age. The eighteenth century saw the most sustained period of warfare in British history: between 1689 and 1815, the British state was either officially or unofficially at war for no fewer than sixty-five years. There were not only notable international conflicts that drew in combatants from across the social spectrum, but also conflicts at home, in the form of violent uprisings, riots and even attempted invasions.[1] In terms of domestic politics, it was a period of growing strength for parliament following the passing of the Bill of Rights in 1689, when some of the features of modern government – such as the concept of a 'prime minister', party politics and 'new' political satire – began to emerge. This did not mean authority moved away from the wealthier classes. Due to their close involvement in both the House of Commons and the House of Lords, they had significant influence.[2] Thus it was an age when they could consolidate their power.

There were growing numbers of wealthy families, and the old aristocracy increasingly merged with a new plutocracy to form a larger upper class. Industrialisation and empire meant that there were new ways, aside from agriculture and landownership, to become wealthy. Some were very rich indeed: when Robert Clive, who made his fortune in India, received the title Baron Clive of Plassey in 1762 he was worth about £300,000, having bought a 7,500-acre estate for £70,000 the year before. However, for the 'practical men of enterprise', entering the formal circles of the social elite was more difficult. While the landed classes enjoyed the benefits of the national wealth and the services that merchants and manufacturers provided, members of this latter group – however rich they were – were often socially excluded from elite circles because of their involvement in precisely those activities. Wealth alone was not enough, and those aiming to join the peerage were carefully judged; the aristocracy recognised the benefits of maintaining the family interest and upholding the traditions of dynasty. As historians Stone and Fawtier Stone argue, it was not an 'open elite'.[3] While there was upward mobility across the lower social orders, access to the upper echelons was relatively limited. However, political networks, elite friends and a country estate could all help the socially ambitious, and this period saw a significant growth in the building and rebuilding of country houses. The classical world was a strong source of inspiration to painters and architects, and this can still be seen in the design of most Georgian buildings. Many of them were influenced by the writings of Andrea Palladio on the architecture of antiquity, and the growing popularity of the Grand Tour reinforced the connections between the age of enlightenment and the classical world. This was the golden age of the 'power house', to use Mark Girouard's phrase, and this combination of classical taste, the celebration of the rural ideal and the display of wealth meant that these properties helped to reinforce the elite status of their families.[4]

While this was the age of enlightenment and revolution, there was not a dramatic change in the freedoms granted to women. There were significant debates about the nature of gender roles during the period, and didactic literature and periodicals, especially *The Tatler* and *The Spectator*, were central to the creation of ideals of masculine and feminine behaviour. While, in practice, there was not a single form of hegemonic 'masculinity' or 'femininity', common ideals appeared in these texts. While the Jacobean idea of the 'shrew' declined, the connection between femininity and virtue remained, and generally it was presumed that women exerted a positive impact on men. This was especially notable from the mid-eighteenth century, when there was a rise in heterosociability. This shaped male and female roles in polite society;

sensibility and politeness were both encouraged, as they enabled sincere and easy social interactions. While for most of the eighteenth century there appears to have been a relatively tolerant attitude towards 'deviant' expressions of gender, such as foppery and cross-dressing, there is some evidence that in the later part of the century there was a 'gender panic'.[5] This led to increasingly conservative views about how men and women should behave, and included the growing popularity of the model of gendered separate spheres. However, while the public/private dichotomy was one that was used by contemporary commentators, recent historical studies have found that the actual separation between the spheres was often indistinct and subject to personal interpretation.[6] This was especially the case for members of the wealthier classes and, as we explore in Chapter 5, some elite women were actively involved in the most public arena: politics.

There was a female monarch at the start of this period, and Mary Astell mused in 1706 that if Queen Anne followed didactic writings, she would have to obey her footman.[7] It is important to remember that it was not until the passing of the Great Reform Act in 1832 that women were formally disenfranchised in parliamentary elections. Previously, in most constituencies there had been nothing that stated that the electorate had to be male: the vote was usually granted on the basis of property ownership, which would have included some women. Therefore, when property-owning women were excluded from voting, it was purely on the basis of custom and practice.[8]

In terms of the private sphere, men were often concerned with the domestic and the familial, involved with their children's upbringing and wellbeing. Domesticity was celebrated in art, novels and didactic texts of the period, and the home was seen as a place of comfort and affection that could be enjoyed by all members of the family.[9] However, although they had a great many opportunities to go beyond narrow gender boundaries, the expectations placed on elite men and women were high, and they were under significant public and familial scrutiny. Their roles as wives, mothers, daughters and sisters, or fathers, husbands and public servants were often shaped by culturally specific expectations, and so they were still expected to fulfil the ideals of masculine and feminine behaviour.

The extent to which country-house mistresses of the Georgian age fulfilled these ideals is explored over the next three chapters by drawing on the experiences of seven women. These include three women who played an important role in shaping their country houses. The first is Fanny Boscawen née Glanville (1719–1805), who married Edward Boscawen, son of the first Viscount Falmouth, in 1742. Together they built a new property, Hatchlands Park, Surrey, although Edward was usually involved at a distance, because, as an admiral, he was frequently away at sea. We can chart their plans for their home from the charming and often witty letters that they sent to one another.[10] Fanny Boscawen was widowed while still relatively young, as was Frances Ingram, ninth Viscountess Irwin (c.1734–1807). The daughter of Samuel Shepheard MP, she brought a £60,000 fortune to her 1758 marriage to Charles Ingram, later Viscount Irwin, who inherited the title and Temple Newsam, Leeds, in 1763. Following Charles' death in 1778, she not only remodelled the house, but also played an active role in managing the estate and its political interests. Her letters, especially to her friend Susan Stewart, later marchioness of Stafford, show how much Lady Irwin enjoyed her life as a country woman, and embraced her duties as the mistress of a country house.[11] Frances was painted by the leading portrait painter of her age, Sir Joshua Reynolds, as was the third mistress we examine here, Theresa Parker (1745–1775). The daughter of Thomas Robinson, first Baron Grantham, she was well connected to networks of artistic patronage through her natal family, and she brought these to her marriage in 1769 to John Parker, who had inherited Saltram House, Devon, the previous year. Together, she and John reshaped the property's interior, as well as playing an influential role in the landscaping of the park.[12]

These three women had happy marriages; but that was not the universal experience. Therefore, we also look at the lives of two women who were reluctant brides. Mary Talbot (1776–1855) was the daughter of Henry Fox Strangways, second earl of Ilchester; he encouraged her marriage in 1794 to his friend Thomas Mansel Talbot, who owned Penrice Castle, along with the Margam estates, both in Glamorgan. Her letters to her sister reflect her ill ease at this union, and her desire to remain at her favoured childhood home of Redlynch.[13] This connection to the childhood home is also seen in the writings of Mary Elizabeth Lucy (1803–1889), who was very fond of Bodelwyddan Castle and her parents, Sir John and Lady Williams. Her reflections on her anxieties before she married George Lucy, owner of Charlecote Park, Warwickshire, in 1823, feature in her memoirs, which she compiled in her old age.[14]

Not all the mistresses of country houses were married, and in this part we look at the lives of Lady Eleanor Butler (1739–1829) and Sarah Ponsonby (1755–1831), also known as the Ladies of Llangollen. After they fled from Ireland in 1778, where they grew up, they formed a home together at Plas Newydd in Llangollen. Their lives are captured not only in their own life writings, including a journal, but also in the reports and sketches created by their many visitors.[15] The home of the Ladies of Llangollen does not fall within the traditional understanding of a country house, as the cottage of Plas Newydd and its gardens were only modest in size – especially compared to the larger country houses of the Georgian period. The Ladies are included here to illustrate the 'pull' of the country house and how, despite lacking the fortune of many elite families, they were able to create a place that enabled them to fulfil the ideals of being elite mistresses.

All these women shaped their homes and their family lives, engaging with the language of dynasty and inheritance, as well as using new forms of expression in relation to domestic affection. However, they were not just mistresses of their homes; they were also well connected to the growing elite society that became increasingly important in this period. By looking at their roles in building the houses, in managing the networks that shaped elite life and in forming – with different levels of success – domestic relationships, we can see the ways in which they were able to synthesise the ideals of femininity and of their class to define their own place in Georgian society.

CHAPTER 4

Building the Dynastic House

> I amuse myself wonderfully and I may say prodigiously for I have attacked a huge wing of Temple Newsam – have pulled down walls as thick as the Tower for the sole pleasure of building them up again and here I am now in the midst of desolation created by my own nonsensical self.
>
> Frances, ninth Viscountess Irwin, 1795[1]

At the time that she wrote this letter to her friend, Frances Irwin was a widow and mistress of Temple Newsam, near Leeds, the house that she had lived in with her husband following their marriage in 1758. When her husband died twenty years later, they had five daughters but no son. However, thanks to a clause in their marriage settlement, Frances was able to take over custodianship of the property. She was free to change the house and its environment as she wished; she did not have to gain permission from a husband, but could knock down the walls of her home for pleasure.[2] The language she uses in this letter suggests a degree of playfulness; and in a great deal of writing about architecture from the eighteenth century, it was considered to be a 'gentlemen's sport'.[3] However, men were not the only players. While male heads of the family were normally credited with 'building' the houses (even though they did not usually design them or get physically involved with the work of the actual builders), a number of women were also active participants in major building projects during the eighteenth century, including Marchioness Grey at Wrest Park and the duchess of Marlborough at Blenheim. This was not a new phenomenon: in the late sixteenth century, for example, Elizabeth, countess of Shrewsbury, shaped two houses at Hardwick, and Joan Thynne, Maria's formidable mother-in-law, was central to making Caus Castle a more comfortable home. While their role in 'decking' houses was acknowledged by didactic writers, the role that women played in shaping the design of country houses and their gardens has traditionally been overlooked. As researchers have shown, women could be active in this process and so, as Amy Boyington has highlighted, they were important, but often 'hidden', patrons.[4]

This chapter looks at six women who shaped their houses and gardens in the Georgian period: Fanny Boscawen at Hatchlands, Frances, Viscountess Irwin at Temple Newsam, Theresa Parker at Saltram, Mary Talbot at Penrice and, as a partnership, Lady Eleanor Butler and Sarah Ponsonby at Plas Newydd. It considers the roles that they played in the many different steps that needed to be followed in order to start to build a house, including finding a site, arranging the finances and then planning the project. It also explores how they shaped the interior of the properties, and how they were able to integrate their own taste and individuality into these dynastic buildings. It was not just the houses; women played a role in shaping their gardens, too. A woman could bring her organisational skills, along with her taste, knowledge, networks and enthusiasm, to co-create a property that was central to her family's pleasure and pedigree: a place where she could be the mistress of the house.

Finding the right location to build a home that could also act as a seat for their dynasty could be a difficult decision for those members of the elite who did not already have a country house of their own. Younger sons of aristocrats, the newly monied, or more established elites who wished to have a new property in a more convenient or fashionable location, would have had to find somewhere that was both suitable and available for them to acquire. This was a challenge that the Boscawens faced from the start of their marriage in 1742; Edward and Fanny were an ambitious couple, but they had no country house of their own. They lived in Audley Street, London, at first, and although their letters from the early years of their marriage show how their young family brought them joy, they both desired a more rural location for their home.[5] As Edward was often away at sea, climbing the ranks in the navy, this responsibility fell to Fanny. After she moved their family to Enfield Grove in 1748, she wrote to Edward to tell him that

> I am pretty positive that you would approve my resolution of hiring this place ... not withstanding it almost ruins me, for the gardens will cost me £50. But then, I have such a lawn for my babes to skip on when 'tis shady, and such a wood to hide 'em in when 'tis sunny, that 'tis worth all the money.[6]

However, she was not fully settled there, and she began to travel around the country looking for something more suitable. In her diary of 1748, which she wrote for her husband to read, she made various mentions of how she liked Hatchlands, a country estate with a Tudor house near Guildford, and how she thought of it regularly. Although Edward agreed with her, purchasing the property was not straightforward, and they did not acquire it until 1750. One of the reasons why it appealed was its location: being near to both London and the south coast of England, it was ideally placed between two main locations of naval business. As Edward's career in the admiralty developed, he spent an increasing amount of time in the capital, and so a property where he could return home to his family for long weekends would have been attractive. He was very fond of domestic life; despite his high standing, in one letter Edward admitted 'I am happier at home in the arms of my darling Fanny.'[7] This underpinned his desire for them to have a shared retreat, a place that was a home but that also reflected his status. They felt that Hatchlands was the perfect spot to build such a property.

Like the Boscawens, a new home was often on the minds of Lady Eleanor Butler and Sarah Ponsonby. However, they had to take considerable risks to find a place of their own. Brought up as members of the Anglo-Irish upper classes, they both experienced familial conflicts as young women. Perceiving her to be 'unmarriable', Eleanor's mother wanted to send her to a convent to live there permanently, a plan that Eleanor resisted. At Woodstock, County Kilkenny, Sarah was subject to sexual advances from Sir William Fownes, who raised her together with his wife Elizabeth, Sarah's cousin.[8]

Both Eleanor and Sarah were unhappy and, despite a significant age difference, they formed a close friendship. They corresponded secretly for some eighteen months and planned their escapes. Their first attempt was on 30 March 1778, when the pair of them fled from their homes and made for Waterford, disguised as men and armed with pistols. On this attempt their plans were unsuccessful: they were found and returned. A family friend of the Fownes wrote that the

> [r]unaways are caught and we shall soon see our amiable friend again whose conduct, though it has an appearance of imprudence, is I am sure void of serious impropriety. There was no gentleman concerned, nor does it appear to be anything more than a scheme of Romantic Friendship.[9]

However, this was a serious relationship, and again Eleanor escaped her home of Kilkenny Castle, this time going to Woodstock to join Sarah. Eventually, they persuaded their relatives to give them permission to travel together. They headed to North Wales, and when travelling around the region, they discovered Llangollen; they climbed Dinas Brân, the conical hill to the north of the town, and gazed from the top over 'an extensive prospect ... of the Beautifullest Country in the World'.[10] While 'society' as they had known it in Ireland simply did not exist in Llangollen, that did not put them off. In fact, they longed for retreat, and they were determined to live a rural but landed way of life, even if it had to be on a smaller scale than most members of their class. They had the freedom, if not the finances, to select their own property, choosing a plain stone square cottage, with a slate roof, in the fields on a hill outside the village of Llangollen. They called it, as it is still famously known, Plas Newydd. From this 'new house' they were able to shape their own home, and they became so closely connected to the place that they came to be known as the Ladies of Llangollen.

It was not enough simply to find a location for a country house. For those who were designing somewhere new, as well as for those who took on renovating an existing property that had long been in the family, finances had to be secured. Women were not necessarily silent bystanders in this process. In many cases, the opportunity to rebuild was realised by a woman bringing money into a family when there was a marriage. For example, two marriages were of significant importance to the architectural history of Saltram, Devon. While George Parker had bought Saltram in 1712, it was not until his death in 1743 that members of the Parker family began to shape the house. His daughter-in-law, Catherine, made changes to the house while her husband was ill, thinking that she would soon be widowed and that it could be her dower house. However, he recovered, and so they shaped it into their home. The supervision of the project has traditionally been attributed to Catherine, and, as the daughter of the former chief minister to Queen Anne, it seems that she wanted a suitable property firstly for herself, and secondly for her family.[11] Crucially, it was her dowry that paid for the development of the property, and a surviving presentation drawing of a proposed elevation for Saltram is inscribed to her, not her husband.[12] The marriage of her son to his second wife enabled the further development of the property at Saltram. John Parker was wealthy in his own right: when his eccentric father died in 1768, he left 135 money bags with some £30,000 in cash in various places, including in Saltram's wainscot toilet. However, these finances were enhanced further when he married Theresa Robinson in 1769, as her marriage portion was £6,000. As historian Ronald Fletcher notes, 'she brought wealth and titled connection into an already substantial and well-connected estate; one which could give her the station and security to which she was accustomed'.[13] This union meant that together they had the finances and the opportunity to continue Catherine's work and complete the decoration of one of the great treasure houses of the south-west of England.

Similarly, the 1758 marriage between Frances Shepheard and Charles Ingram, later ninth Viscount Irwin, was an ideal match for the Irwin family. Burdened by costly mortgages and the debts of a succession of viscounts who died intestate, the dynasty needed a rich heiress. Frances, the illegitimate daughter of Samuel Shepheard MP, was independently wealthy, as her father had left her his fortune, to be released on her marriage.[14] It is not clear how the couple met, but their relationship caused some concern to her trustees, as there were various stipulations in her father's will, including that she was not to marry a peer. However, while it may at first seem that this was a courting shaped by the needs of the Irwins, it is clear that it was Frances who was determined to marry Charles. She continued to visit his home of Temple Newsam, although she was told not to by her trustees, and she was (understandably) welcomed there by Charles and his sisters.[15] It took two years of negotiations and a private act of parliament for her to be able to marry Charles and still inherit her fortune; this meant that a long and detailed marriage settlement was produced that protected the interests of Frances's inheritance. This gave her direct control of the estate when her husband died and allowed it to be passed down the female line if the couple had no sons; as the five children of Frances and Charles were all daughters, this became an important clause. From 1774, Frances owned Temple Newsam in her own right, and it was then inherited by two of her daughters. For ninety-six years in the period 1774–1904, the house was owned by women, who played a significant role in the building's history.[16]

For other women, finding the finances was more difficult. As women without significant landed estates of their own, Lady Eleanor Butler and Sarah Ponsonby had no secure form of income. Eleanor described themselves as 'two poor spinsters with something less than nothing' in 1782.[17] While Eleanor's father had provided a £200 annuity for her when they left Ireland, this ended upon his death in 1783. Financially, his death dealt Eleanor a double blow, as she also did not receive the inheritance that she thought she was entitled to. It was not until the following year that her brother agreed to give them £200 a year and £500 to pay their debts. This modest income (in aristocratic terms) was enhanced in 1787, when Eleanor was added to the Irish Civil List, giving them £100 per annum. However, while they were far wealthier than the Welsh labourers who lived in their neighbourhood, they did not feel financially secure. They were dependent on gifts from relatives and friends, and while they made some money from the sale of produce, their income was erratic, as the Irish pension was not always paid regularly.[18] This insecurity was compounded by the fact that, despite their limited income, they lived an elite way of life. They called it a 'system', which they believed was both romantic and realistic. Elizabeth Mavor, their biographer, has delineated its main elements, noting that it 'bound them never to leave home, to devote hearts and minds to self-improvement, to eschew the vanity of society, to beautify their surroundings and to better, in so far as they could, the lot of the poor and unfortunate'.[19] Despite this performance of an elite way of life, for many years they failed to meet one of the usual criteria for being regarded as an aristocrat: they were not landowners. Eleanor and Sarah were tenants at Plas Newydd, and this compounded their sense of economic vulnerability. These fears were made real when their landlord threatened them with removal in 1800. However, this storm was weathered and in January 1819, Eleanor's first entry in the new journal noted 'we this day completed the purchase of our house'.[20] It is probably the case that one of the main sources of the monies which allowed them to buy the property was the bequest left to them by their housekeeper, Mary Carryl. When she worked for them, most of her income came from the large tips from the visitors she showed around Plas Newydd, for the Llangollen Ladies became a tourist attraction for those travelling to Snowdonia or Holyhead. When Carryl died in 1809, the size of her fortune – at least £500 – caused Eleanor and Sarah some surprise, as it made them realise how they had been sold as curiosities. Also, by the time of her death Carryl was a landowner, having purchased the field adjacent to Plas Newydd, where the Ladies grazed cows; she bequeathed this land to Sarah, as it was the younger lady who managed the couple's finances. Their gratitude to Carryl was significant, and they erected both a monument to her and an avenue of beech and lime trees.[21] Through her dedicated service to the women as their housekeeper and her generosity to them at her death, Carryl was central to enabling Sarah and Eleanor to be perceived as, and then to become, mistresses of their own home.

While some elites struggled financially, generally the gentry and aristocracy became increasingly wealthy during the eighteenth century. This, alongside the greater availability of loans, led to a growth in the total number of country houses in England and Wales, and the size of these properties increased significantly, too. Two of the main sources of new income in this period were warfare and the empire, and recent research has shown how many Georgian country-house estates were interconnected with colonialism.[22] This was the case at Hatchlands: its purchase and design were made possible through naval prize money awarded to Edward Boscawen for his successes in wars that focused on defending and expanding the empire. He noted in one letter: 'I flatter myself to make the French pay for this building this summer. I have got at least one-fifth of it already, and another trip to the southward will bring three or four sugar ships more in our way.'[23] The family were well aware of their global links, and on the admiral's tomb it was noted that it was erected 'at the expense of the enemies of his country'.[24] While country houses seem quintessentially 'British', their financing and contents were often the result of an increasingly global economy.

Once the land and money were in place, the next crucial step was to identify an architect and the key personnel that would lead on the project. It was important for landowners to make sound choices, as balancing the costs and dealing with the different elements – especially if it was a full new build – could be difficult. There were workforces to find and accommodate, building materials to source and store, as well as the unforeseen problems caused by weather, war and personal woes to manage. They also needed someone who could help them with the design of the property. While some of the 'gentlemen architects' of the eighteenth century, such as Lord Burlington, may have felt confident in managing such complexities themselves, for many patrons they had to rely on a clerk of works and/or the family steward. During the eighteenth century it was increasingly usual to hire an architect for large private projects; but the type of service that they provided and the degree of 'project management' that they delivered varied greatly.[25] Therefore, some women played a role in ensuring that the lengthy process of building a house continued successfully.

This was especially important for the Boscawens. As Edward was often away from home, either working in London or at sea, he could not always directly manage the project himself. However, the idea of building a house dominated his resting thoughts. In one letter he admitted that he had 'the plan of the building every day in my head'.[26] This plan was based upon a design for Lady Essex's dower house at Russell Farm, Hertfordshire, and Edward drew up a version of it for his own amusement while at sea. This pleased Fanny a great deal, who told her husband that she was not just keen to see the plan, but also wanted it implemented on their own land. Therefore, it was no surprise that they selected Stiff Leadbetter to be their architect, as he had produced the original design for Lady Essex.[27] However, Edward did not just leave Leadbetter in charge at Hatchlands. Instead, his letters to his wife are full of instructions. In his guidance, he drew on his expertise in military logistics. In May 1756 he wrote:

> I have been this morning hoping you have seen Mr. Ledbeater [sic], as I think when I am so sent away in the summer it will be the best time to build, and fancy the middle of the third summer you would get into it. I have even been thinking what to do with our goods, and have settled as thus. The ordinary chairs and tables in the water house, the bedding, blankets etc. and chests, in the room by the laundry, the china, glasses, etc., packed up in boxes and sent to Mr. Weston's. He would give us house room for a cartload at least. Our parson surely would take in some odd things. How do you like this kind of stowage? And when you have no better engagement, and have a mind to see how the works go on, what think you of going to Levels Grove for a few days or weeks? . . . I think the Grove would do best, as you would be near enough your own garden to have the use of it, and look at your walk and improve it, and see that things are not totally neglected.[28]

This extract from a lengthy letter shows that he trusted Fanny with the day-to-day supervision of their building project: from overseeing storing the goods, to managing the workforce and getting clear answers from the architect. Another letter to her set out his notion of their joint responsibility and mutual dependence: 'I am very sensible of your condescension in letting me have the direction of our buildings and much more so for your owning you do not understand it.' He believed he was very lucky in having her, since 'most wives meddle with all concerns, understanding or not'.[29] This shows that he wanted to retain control of the management of the building of the house, but was going to do so through her, as he trusted that she would follow his wishes and not interfere, since she was aware of the limitations of her own knowledge. Although it was not a wholly equal partnership, they worked together to fulfil a shared ambition.[30]

In the early stages of the project, Fanny had to oversee some of the practical challenges of house building. In June 1756, Edward advised that his 'present scheme is to buy brick, lime and sand, but to work them up by contract. As to the carpenters' work, that must be entirely by contract, with agreement to make use of all our old stuff that will be serviceable.'[31] She was able to respond to these plans and put his ideas into practice. For example, the following year Fanny wrote to her husband to tell him that she had arranged for 50,000 bricks to be brought to Hatchlands. She added that, at 25 shillings per thousand, they were a shilling cheaper than she had expected, showing that she was well aware of financial concerns.[32] It also shows that Fanny was not always completely dependent on Edward's instructions. Despite what Edward's letter of May 1756 suggested, she understood, to some degree, the realities of a building project, as she had previously overseen the work undertaken at their London house in Audley Street. When she described the work she was leading there in a letter to Edward in 1748, it was clear that she felt a sense of ownership of the project and the property:

> My house is an hourly expense to me, as you may imagine. The job of repairing the sluices in the back houses, making the pump etc., was £9, and now I am paving the street with broad stones, the vault underneath having threatened 'twould fall in, if we did not repair gutters worn between the pavement and where the rain settled. Then, my furniture, which is now pretty complex, costs many a penny. So elegant am I, that my fender is a Chinese rail.[33]

This experience was used to shape Hatchlands. For example, the choice of a Chinese rail was an unusual one, but it was a design later repeated in their country house.[34] Her husband was cognisant of her experience in interior decoration, and so when he wrote to Fanny to thank her for allowing him to lead on the building of the house, he added that in 'return you shall have the principal hand in furnishing, that is in directing all that is new'.[35] This was not a division of labour on simplistic gender grounds: it was not unusual for men to shape the purchasing of furniture for a household, and often it was an area of responsibility that was shared between husbands and wives.[36] Nor did it reflect lack of interest: while Edward was away at sea, his new home often dominated his thoughts. So, while he was happy to let her lead, he did have his own ideas. He wrote:

> I own I have a plan for the disposal of the furniture we have and for putting up the china, taffeta, and paper, as well as the chintz. The latter I propose for our own bedchamber and dressing room. I don't forget the inlaid ebony doors for a cabinet for the best dressing room, which is to be on the ground floor, and serve for a drawing room, or a fine dressing room on grand occasions . . .
>
> The large room, one pair of stairs, and that under it, will be entirely at your discretion as to furniture, though I own I have thought of Cornish marble for the table below stairs, and a fine but plain white marble chimney piece.[37]

So, although Edward was keen to share his ideas, he seems to have felt some guilt about interfering in a sphere in which he had already told his wife she was the mistress, and he was keen to let her discretion shape the furnishing and decoration of the house.

However, even when Edward let Fanny guide the choices regarding the interior decoration, there was another crucial contributor to the design of some of the rooms: Robert Adam. Adam became one of the leading country-house architects of the eighteenth century, but Hatchlands was his first commission to work on a country house's interior.[38] The selection of Adam was rooted in Edward's naval connections: the young architect had been introduced to the Boscawens by Edward's fellow lord of the admiralty, Gilbert Elliot of Minto, who had commissioned him to design the Admiralty Screen, Whitehall.[39] These naval connections shaped Adam's original designs for the drawing room. It celebrated Admiral Boscawen's role in the Seven Years' War through its inclusion of nautical and military images – for example, dolphins alongside the figures of Neptune, Victory, Justice and Fame. There were also marine motifs on the ceiling of the great dining room, similar in style to those used by Adam on the Admiralty Screen.[40] Many of the choices in these designs followed guidelines given by Edward in his letters. However, we should not see patriotic and military designs as an exclusively male taste. Fanny actively oversaw this work and so had opportunities to alter them: as with other naval wives, when her husband was away, she became the de facto head of the household, and thus had the power to be both mistress and master of the estate. She also had a good knowledge of architectural design and later was a subscriber to Adam's *The Ruins of the Palace of the Emperor Diocletian at Spalatro in Dalmatia* (1764).[41] She was proud of her husband and her role as an admiral's wife, and these designs reflected her husband's successes that were central to their shared status.

After his work at Hatchlands, Adam became much sought after as a designer of country houses and interiors. One of the properties that he worked on was Saltram, the marital home of Theresa Parker. Born Theresa Robinson, she was brought up at the court in Vienna, where her father, the first Lord Grantham, was British ambassador. She acquired there a deep and informed sense of architectural and artistic values.[42] She had much in common with her elder brother, Thomas Robinson, who was an amateur architect, and their letters to one another reflect their shared interest in design. Theresa put this knowledge into practice when helping to shape the interior at Saltram. When Theresa arrived, following their marriage in 1769, John Parker had already employed the now fashionable Robert Adam to design a new saloon and library.[43] As with Hatchlands, Adam did not shape the spaces alone; the Parkers knew what they wanted, and they did not accept their patronage role without asking their own questions. The collective nature of the project can be seen in the saloon, for while it was shaped by Adam, it was based on the collaborative work of many hands and utilised both the architect's and the patrons' networks. Adam first produced a full set of drawings for the wall elevations, ceilings and chimneypiece. However, the Parkers rejected the plan for the fireplace and, based on his interest in field sports, John chose a bold ceiling which had medallions by the painter Antonio Zucchi and a central image of the goddess of the hunt, Diana. Adam himself designed the carpet that echoed the ceiling design, which was made by Thomas Whitty at Axminster, while Theresa selected some of the smaller objects to decorate the room, including a set of four ormolu and Blue John candle vases from Matthew Boulton and John Fothergill.⁴⁴ Her siblings shaped her taste. She had admired a set of vases that had been made for her brother, Lord Grantham, and she used him to get some samples of blue damask, 'as we shall soon write to Genoa and wish to fix upon the best blue for setting off the pictures'.⁴⁵ Collectively, these design choices shaped the interior that cemented the reputation of Saltram and the Parkers as leaders of taste. It is a testament to their work that in August 1789 there was a royal visit to the property, with George III and Queen Charlotte in the party.⁴⁶ Although Theresa Parker did not live long enough to see this, dying aged only thirty-one in 1775, it was clear that she was active in reshaping the house into a property worth visiting.

Hatchlands and Saltram were neoclassical buildings that can be seen to embody the idea of the 'power house'. In the case of the Ladies of Llangollen, Plas Newydd was more a retreat, which was shaped by the emergence of Romantic ideas. However, while their budget (and their property) was more modest, they were as keen as their wealthier counterparts to create a house that was fashionable and reflected their own ideals. Eleanor Butler's diary made continuous references to what she called their 'delicious and exquisite retirement', and although they had many visitors, they preferred each other's company; for them, a quiet day spent reading and working on a map was, in Eleanor's words, 'a day of strict retirement, sentiment and delight'.⁴⁷ This desire for fashionable retreat was reflected in their design choices for Plas Newydd, which embodied the new taste for *cottage ornée*, a celebration of idealised cottage life that frequently ignored the realities of rural poverty. For example, in his *Rural Architecture* (1796), John Plaw included cottages that had rooms usually associated with elite lifestyles, such as withdrawing rooms, smoking rooms and music rooms, instead of the spaces used by the usual occupants of rural cottages. From about 1800, Eleanor and Sarah poured money and time into making Gothic additions to their home. Many of the features of the house were gifts to the Ladies, and a complex gift-exchange network enabled them to design a fashionable property; while they were not able to afford an Adam or a Leadbetter, they could use their knowledge, taste and networks to design their home. They delighted in what they created, with Eleanor noting in her diary that it had 'an appearance of Content and cheerfulness never to be found but in a cottage'.[48] Others celebrated their taste, too. The poet Anna Seward described the Ladies as the 'celebrated recluses of Llangollen Vale' and wrote that the house was 'a little temple, consecrate [sic] to Friendship, and the Muses, and adorned by the hands of all the Graces'. Similarly, newspaper reports described their home as 'the sylvan-like retreat of those ornaments of their sex'.[49] At Plas Newydd they created a space that was both renowned and a retreat.

It was not just the Ladies of Llangollen who desired homeliness: many country houses managed to balance being 'power houses', retreats and homes. This can be seen in the design choices made by Frances Irwin at Temple Newsam. When she first arrived at her new marital home in 1758, she brought a pair of Chinese cabinets with her. These objects not only reflected her independent wealth, but also gave her a direct connection to her own past within her husband's house. It soon became *their* home; because of the wealth that Frances brought to the family, many of the changes that were made to Temple Newsam were undertaken in her name, even before Charles' death. Her early redesigning of the house's interior was mainly to make it more fashionable; for example, she redecorated her bedroom with Gothic-style 'pillar and arch' wallpaper. When widowed, her work continued. She demolished most of the south wing, which featured an old, medieval-style hall and kitchens, and rebuilt it with a series of reception rooms, dressing rooms and, most importantly, bedrooms for her five daughters. Frances was not simply a figurehead for the building work, but took an active role in the decisions and appears to have managed the building accounts herself.[50] Her work at Temple Newsam was centred on making the house a home – a comfortable, domestic location, ideal for bringing up her five daughters. As married women, four of Frances's daughters lived at the refurbished Temple Newsam, each with her own bedchamber and dressing room. Informal dining spaces were created, as well as a parlour. As historian J.S. Lewis notes, there was no withdrawing room in the new design: 'perhaps in a household so dominated by women there were rarely enough men from whom to withdraw'.[51] However, while Frances was interested in comfort, she was also aware of the dynastic role of the house. She appreciated the importance of a fashionable house and landscape in order to attract suitable suitors for her daughters, and later her grandchildren, and so she matched the desire for comfort with style, thus enabling Temple Newsam to be both a show-house and a home.

It was not just the interior of the house that women shaped: they also played a crucial role in designing the gardens and the wider landscape. Despite the fact that traditional scholarship on the country-house estate is dominated by the works created for and by men, more recent research has shown that some women were active in this area, too.[52] Gardening, in particular, was seen as a suitable activity for women, as it was considered to be an extension of their domestic duties, and botany was an increasingly popular area of science for women to engage with. By demonstrating their appreciation of the benefits of the country-house garden, women could highlight their moral virtues and their aristocratic sensibilities. In his *Ichnographia Rustica* (1718), Stephen Switzer praised the dowager duchess of Beaufort for spending time in her garden at Badminton, rather than on 'the tiresome pleasures of the town'.[53] As leisure and retreat were indicators of elite sensibility, the enjoyment of the rural landscape could be seen as a marker of an individual's status.

However, gardening could also bring joy, as reflected by the gardening life of Mary Talbot. She was active in tending the garden of her childhood home at Redlynch; her grandmother, Elizabeth, countess of Ilchester, had also played a significant role in shaping those gardens, and so there was a long tradition of female horticultural involvement.[54] Mary's father encouraged her love of gardening, and their shared interest is evident in a letter he sent her when she was in London in 1791:

> I shall write you two or three lines to tell you how garden matters are. Every thing looks vastly well in general, but I think there will [be] no good hyacinths at all. There will be, I believe, some very good auriculas, and we are making a stand for them and the carnations under the portico, which will be [a] very good place for them ... Every thing looks delightful, the grass coming on, the birds singing, and the bushes coming out very fast. I have been planting, that is, filling up, a good deal. I am not certain, but I rather think you would prefer the gloomy horrors of this poor country life to the sunshine through a Claude in Burlington Street.[55]

Like his father and mother before him, Lord Ilchester had previously worked on the gardens with his wife; after her death he shared the role with his teenage daughter. When Mary married and moved to Penrice in South Wales, her aunt noted that while Mary's sister Harriot 'will succeed you in many pursuits and, I hope, practices, yet I think she does not shew any great taste for gardening or flowers'.[56] Sadly, her aunt was correct and the gardens at Redlynch had become overgrown by 1804.[57]

As Mary's father knew, she preferred the country life to 'sunshine through a Claude in Burlington Street'; it was 'real' rural scenes that she loved, rather than relying on the glowing skies that featured in the paintings of Claude Lorrain. At Penrice, the gardens were at the heart of her daily life. Mary had her own botanical chronology, which included 'the crocus and harebell seasons', 'wood anemone time', 'lilac time' and 'honeysuckle time'. She kept careful records of her plants and she made the most of the growth of the facility to order plants and seeds by mail. Her notes in her pocketbooks reflect how much she loved the garden. For example, in October 1798, after two months away, she wrote: 'Home. Walked to my garden the minute I got to Penrice.' She did not just give orders to gardeners, but spent long hours in her garden. She even owned a 'whittle', a loose-fitting cloak of red flannel, which the local countrywomen wore. She recommended horticulture to her female friends, believing that the physical effort of gardening would be beneficial to them, and she knew that it was good for her own mental health.[58] She did not enjoy a happy marriage, and so gardening was her form of solace. Her son Kit wrote in his memoir of the family:

> had it not been for the garden, that never ending still beginning subject of interest it would have been impossible to have endured for nineteen years such as my mother was subjected to. Gardening was her passion not her employment for employment's sake, and I do not believe that all the gaieties of London would have induced her to forgo seeing the snowdrops or the crocuses in blow for one single day![59]

In a letter to a cousin in 1827, Mary summed up why gardening was so important to her:

> I have a rose tree at the garden gate, which was dug up by my dear grandmother herself out of her garden at Cappercullen, which with other memorials of the same kind make my garden more engaging to me than any other spot in the world, and I spend all the time I can in it, as it mends my health, as well as soothes my heart.[60]

The continuity with her grandmother's garden at Cappercullen meant a great deal to Mary; it was how she could continue her dynastic responsibilities, while finding peace and repose.

This focus on retreat can also be seen in Plas Newydd; but for Lady Eleanor Butler and Sarah Ponsonby, the gardens were not a place to escape to, but rather acted along with the cottage as a combined site of retirement. In their drawing room there were numerous landscape sketches and paintings which not only brought the outside in, but reflected their celebration of the idealised natural world.[61] This love of nature can be seen in the inscription on the title page of the journal used by Eleanor in 1788, where she wrote:

> Society is all but rude
> To this delicious solitude
> Where all the flowers and trees do close
> To weave the Garland of repose.[62]

These ideals of retreat were reflected in their daily life. On one of the pages of this journal Eleanor described how they

> rose at six, enchanting morning, my beloved and I went the home circuit – the morning so heavenly could not leave the shrubbery till nine ... breakfast, reading, drawing then went again to the shrubbery ... there: dinner, roast breast of mutton, boiled veal, bacon and greens, toasted cheese ... half past three till nine ... blue sky with patches of cloud scattered over it ... so picturesque ... planted out one hundred carnations in different parts of the borders.[63]

The 'home circuit' was a carefully crafted walk for both themselves and their visitors, and many of the latter were suitably impressed.[64] Anna

Seward extolled the talents of her two friends who had, by 1795, converted two and a half acres of 'turnip ground' into 'a fairy place amid the bowers of Calypso'.[65] In creating a series of wavy and shaded gravel walks, they drew on the ideas of the botanist Henry Phillips, who thought that shrubberies should always lead to a particular object: a kitchen garden, dairy, mushroom hut or poultry house.[66] Underpinning this was the notion of the picturesque, which meant that they saw their garden as a series of pictures, where, as Mavor notes, variety in 'tone, texture and position of objects' was the essence.[67] Flowers were not neglected: Sarah's journal for 1789 listed forty-four different kinds of rose. The Ladies also engaged in 'wild' gardening, by renting the land on either side of the Cyflymen stream, which bounded their property. Here they placed a font that they had obtained from the nearby Valle Crucis Abbey and encouraged ferns and mosses to grow around it.[68] In doing so, they were directly engaging with fashionable ideals in order to create a space to which to escape from the fashionable world.

The picturesque and the importance of a good walk also shaped the developments made by Lady Irwin at Temple Newsam. In 1767, she wrote to her friend Lady Susan Stewart:

> I have come out of a wet fog to regale myself with writing to you, who I question not are sitting by the fireside and saying to yourself that it is really too bad to stir, but I have not only been out, but actually standing still while Col. Pitt and my husband have been brownifying my dear Gravel Walk, his little wife carried the stakes for them to mark out places for Shrubs and I stood by to give my gracious approbation.[69]

As we saw at Plas Newydd, although on a smaller scale, walking across a landscaped garden was a particularly celebrated pleasure. Therefore, the paths that allowed people to explore the grounds were important.[70] Lady Irwin wrote several letters to Susan about her work in the garden; it seems that while her husband and friends did some of the work, Frances preferred to oversee activities, rather than get practically involved.[71] Therefore, it is no surprise that in some of her letters she rather idealised the labour, describing it as like working on a painting.

In one she wrote: 'I apply myself to my beauteous Claude where the scene always enchants me, the trees are Green, the Water placid and serene and the air has a warmth which is very comfortable.'[72] The appeal of the good weather of the Italian Renaissance landscape of a Claude Lorrain painting was in stark contrast to the realities of a Yorkshire park undergoing hard landscaping. In another, more realistic, letter she noted that as the weather had been good, she was 'out of doors all day long'. She added that while 'Mr Brown has put us in a woeful dirty pickle', she was grateful for the gravel walk that was being constructed using a design from Lancelot 'Capability' Brown.[73]

These walks were important in opening up the grounds for polite visitors to explore. We see this at the Boscawens' house at Hatchlands. In July 1755, Elizabeth Montagu wrote during a visit to see Fanny Boscawen that she had

> walked round the park this morning. It does not consist of many acres but the disposition of the ground, the fine verdure and the plantations make it very pretty. It resembles the mistress of it, having preserved its native simplicity, though art and care has improved and softened it and made it elegant.[74]

This simplicity and elegance had taken some work. As with the house, the landscape was a project that Edward and Fanny Boscawen planned together. In one letter Edward wrote to Fanny about the near 700 plants that were ready to be moved to Hatchlands:

> They will go a great way in planting the new part that I have planned, but it must be two years before they can be moved, for they must recover their vigour they had before transplantation and if we have success with those sown in the boxes they will complete the walk. I don't intend Mr. North [the gardener] shall have anything to say to it, and ten to one he won't like it, but I think you will and that is sufficient for me.[75]

As with the building of the house, Fanny received instructions about the management of the estate from Edward while he was at sea. In April

1756, he encouraged her to have a trench made either side of her walk at Hatchlands so that it would be dry, passable and in good order for the following year.[76] In some of his letters, Edward would repeat instructions that he had already given regarding the management of the land. He was aware of this, adding 'I hope my dear will excuse my giving her these long directions and repeating them so often.'[77] It was clear that he wanted to be an active participant in shaping their house and gardens, even though he was not physically there. However, it is notable that he often described the walk as *her* walk, as did later visitors.[78] It was a place where he imagined her and their children. It was her space, and it became a place where she could present her house and home to guests and friends – just as the Ladies of Llangollen did at Plas Newydd and Frances Irwin did at Temple Newsam.

At Saltram, following the role that she played in shaping the interior of the house, Theresa Parker was especially interested in the architectural features that were central to the design of country-house gardens in the eighteenth century. After only two years of being at Saltram, she reported that the 'Hot houses, Kitchen Gardens are just finished. The Castle, the other lodges and a Green House employ the next year, and after that we turn farmer and make such improvement in Land, Estates and Ploughs that Posterity shall bless the day.'[79] As she did with the interior of the house, she used her networks to design garden buildings. Her brother had promised a plan for the summer house that she wanted at the end of the avenue to the west of the mansion: she wrote in 1772 that something 'must be done upon that spot', to take advantage of the view over the estate and towards the sea.[80] She also consulted with Lord Grantham about her greenhouses, in which she wanted to house a collection of citrus trees. He was concerned about the decision to construct them using wood – 'because it cannot last forever' – but approved of the design.[81] By 1774, Theresa was asking him for ideas about how they could decorate the interior of the space; and in July 1775 she wrote him a letter from the 'Saltram Green House' which began: 'I inhabit this beautiful Room comfortably, I long much to shew it you, and think it would meet with your approbation.'[82] She died later that year, and so both the interior of the house and the gardens now stand testament to the role that she played in shaping a 'power house' that helped make the Parkers an influential dynasty in the late Georgian period.

Whether in partnership with male relatives, with other women or independently, mistresses of country houses were able to shape their homes and gardens during the eighteenth century. Some of these projects were major rebuilds, as we saw at Hatchlands, or enhanced an existing property and estate, as at Penrice and Saltram. Others were more concerned with making a house a home, as was the case – although on very different scales – at both Temple Newsam and Plas Newydd. Elite women could take a role at every stage of the process – from finding a location and financing the process, to shaping the designs and helping to manage the projects. They did not do this work alone, even when – as was the case with the Ladies of Llangollen and the widowed Lady Irwin – there was not a male head of the household. They were all reliant on the work of many designers, craftsmen and builders, as well as on their effective networks of friends and family who could help them to find goods, provide them with advice or shape their ideas. However, it was often women who helped to form these connections, and how they built these, alongside building their houses, is the central question of the next chapter.

CHAPTER 5

The Connected House

> The unaccountable knowledge those recluses have of all living books and people and things is like magic, one can mention no one of whom the private history is unknown to them.
>
> Hester Thrale Piozzi[1]

Hester Piozzi's comments about the Ladies of Llangollen reflect how important information was to polite society in the eighteenth century. Despite their rural location and their attempts to retreat from society, Eleanor Butler and Sarah Ponsonby remained well informed and well connected. This is because 'news' was an important currency, as it could be exchanged for other news and allow connections to be gained and maintained; and it helped reduce the chances of social or diplomatic *faux pas*. This was critical because the elite classes were at the heart of many important networks of power during the eighteenth century. They not only had significant influence in Westminster politics, but they also played a crucial role in the royal court. Elites likewise had an impact on the shifting of social norms, the circulation of knowledge, and the emergence and acceptance of ideas. The combined impact of enlightenment thought and the rise of the ideals of 'politeness' and 'sociability' meant that the gentry and the aristocracy were able to shape the cultural hinterland of the period. Patronage networks for artists, writers and thinkers were as important to 'soft' power as they were to political power.

These were not exclusively male networks. Women were also able to play a central role in making themselves, their houses and their families well connected. This chapter considers the roles that they played in traditional political power, drawing particularly on examples from the Irwin family of Temple Newsam, especially in relation to the parliamentary seat of Horsham, Sussex. It shows how elite women were important patrons not just of architects (as we have seen), but also of artists and writers, by highlighting the importance of the Parkers at Saltram to artists such as Joshua Reynolds, and looking at the role of Fanny Boscawen in encouraging the work of the writer Hannah More through her connections within the bluestocking circle. It also explores how the networks of gift exchange that permeated the lives of Eleanor Butler and Sarah Ponsonby shaped their home in Llangollen and underpinned their 'magical' knowledge. How these networks helped women to form friendships that could provide both comfort and prestige is also discussed. Women were central to networks of influence in elite circles, and this gave them power both within and beyond the country house.[2]

One of the most important places for forming and maintaining effective networks was in relation to politics. During the eighteenth century, as with previous centuries, there was a close relationship between politics and property. Voting rights were property based, as was entry to both the House of Lords and the House of Commons. This meant there was a close relationship between landownership and political influence. Those who were peers had places in the House of Lords, which meant that they were central to decision-making processes. Their power was not limited to the 'upper house', as the aristocracy had significant influence in the House of Commons, too: many elites directly controlled parliamentary seats. Landowners commonly selected candidates for constituencies, who then often stood unopposed. If there was an election, there was an expectation that tenants would follow their landowner's political wishes and support his or her candidate. This influence was so significant that the historian John Cannon estimates that peers controlled about one fifth of the seats in the Commons at the start of the century, and this increased significantly in later decades.[3]

This political influence was not just held by the male members of the family. Although the statesman George Canning wrote in 1795 that a 'woman has no business at all with politicks, or that if she thinks at all about them, it should be at least in a feminine manner', generally there was a presumption that elite women not only could, but actually would interfere in political issues.[4] They were important figures in maintaining the 'family interest' in politics, and thus helped to form wider connections within the political world. They were sometimes gifted politicians, and some wives were better than their spouses in acts of diplomacy. For example, Anne, fifth Viscountess Irwin, noted that when the Catholic duke and duchess of Norfolk attended court in 1733, after publicly disavowing all allegiance to the Pretender, it was the duchess who represented the views of the couple. Anne commented that the duchess, who 'is a sensible woman, and must act the man where talking is necessary, behaved much to her credit; she reassured the Queen though she and the Duke were of a different religion, they had as much duty and regard for the King as any of his subjects'.[5] Through proactive electioneering, being key players in social politics and engaging in patronage networks, women could be important figures in the political life of the elite family.

Engagement with elections was one of the most direct ways that elite women were seen to be active in politics. While there were small numbers of female voters before 1832, generally elite women's involvement was less about casting and more about directing votes. As peers were formally disbarred from taking an active role in elections to the House of Commons, they needed someone else to fulfil this role on their behalf. While this duty may have fallen to younger sons or political agents to complete, wives often took on the role, and it was commonly part of the expected duties of the female head of a political family. They often co-hosted, with their husbands, 'Public Days', when the local gentry and some senior tenants gathered together for entertainment.[6] These gatherings were usually held at the country house, showing how it could be used as a 'power house'. The rural setting also helped with the entertainment, as, along with dancing, hunting was often part of the activities included. Inviting the right people to these events was important, as it allowed connections to be seen and formed. Those women who were most politically engaged were sometimes very proactive. It was noted that Georgiana, fifth duchess of Devonshire, 'really is a very good Politician. As soon as ever any young man comes from abroad he is immediately invited to Devonshire House and to Chatsworth – and by that means he is to be of the Opposition.'[7] As well as these rural parties, events were also hosted in a family's town house, and were often important for the formation and maintenance of political allegiances. By hosting balls, acting as a 'lady patroness' to local groups and attending events at assembly rooms, a great deal of a woman's socialising was tied up with political duties in influential families.[8]

These were duties that the two Viscountess Irwins took seriously. Although their main seat was in Yorkshire, their political influence was in the constituency of Horsham, Sussex; property in this borough had come to the family through the marriage of Isabella Machell to Arthur Ingram, who later, in 1688, would become the third Viscount Irwin. Horsham was a double-member borough, despite there being only about eighty voters, meaning that it returned two members to parliament. It therefore gave landowners in the constituency the opportunity to obtain some notable political power, and the Ingrams had gained ownership of the majority of burgages – and their votes – by 1743.[9] Following the death of the ninth Viscount Irwin, his widow, Frances, took over the interest in the seat. At first, she passed this over to the Tory administration, which selected candidates who were elected unopposed. This lack of direct engagement was not altogether surprising: as a younger woman, she had written to a friend about how she enjoyed a rural life where she was not 'tortured with political Horrors'.[10] However, later she settled into the role and wrote proudly to the same friend to tell her that her 'little Horsham business went on Flourishingly and my vanity is flatter'd at the idea of being personally well with the Burgesses'.[11] This influence was soon challenged when the lord of the manor, the eleventh duke of Norfolk, began to buy up properties so that he could control their votes; in 1788, there were reports that some houses which had votes attached to them had increased in value by 1,000 per cent. This led to there being a full contest in 1790 – the first since 1715. This soon became costly, with both parties not only buying properties, but also spending money on 'treating' the voters. Frances, for example, provided a venison feast at a public house; and when similar repasts were offered by the Whig Norfolk, one newspaper asked: 'Who would not be a burgess of Horsham when cobblers are treated like kings?'[12] As Norfolk threatened to undermine Frances's influence in Horsham, she was given financial support by the administration to ensure that the Irwins (and therefore the Tories) kept control of the borough. Although Norfolk had incredible influence and wealth, spending £70,000 on the borough, it is a testament to Frances's determination and petitioning skills that he had to rely on his wealth to win the election. However, Frances knew that it was her dynastic duty to maintain control of the seat, and so she showed her defiance by successfully petitioning against the result. This meant that although his men formally won at the ballot box, because Norfolk was deemed to have used corrupt methods, it was Frances's candidates who took their seats – not only in the 1790 contest, but also in 1806, when she again challenged the result. It took twenty years and the death of Frances for Norfolk to gain control of the borough, when he bought the Irwin interest for the record sum of £91,475 from Frances's daughter and heir. Frances's determination to keep Horsham under her family's control reflects how important issues of inheritance and maintaining political power were to some elite women.[13]

As well as engaging with electioneering, some women gained and maintained influence through patronage networks. Most political positions (if not all) were obtained through patronage in the eighteenth century, and critics argued that favouritism was at the heart of government in this period.[14] Because senior political positions were mainly in the gift of ministers of state or of the Crown, those patronage networks were dominated by men. However, as Elaine Chalus notes, the majority 'of eighteenth-century patronage remained in private hands, where it could well be controlled by women'.[15] This included the decision about who would be parliamentary candidate in a seat that was in the gift of a landowner. These positions were often awarded to family members; the House of Commons became increasingly elite in nature, and by the late eighteenth century over half of the MPs were from titled families.[16]

We can see evidence of this at Horsham. Various members of the Ingram family held the seat, including – before he became the viscount – Frances's husband, Charles. In 1790, with no sons or brothers of her own, one of Frances's candidates was her son-in-law, Lord

William Gordon.[17] However, finding a candidate for the second seat was more difficult. This was the type of situation where landowners may have received patronage requests from other elites who were keen to find positions for themselves, a friend or a relative. While men often lobbied for themselves, women also made approaches on behalf of their relatives. Therefore, patronage requests could appeal to personal relationships, and some women, such as Frances's friend Lady Stafford, made requests of politicians who were guests at their country houses. It was not unusual for women to 'play up' their femininity in these requests. As they were able to act more helpless and in need of assistance than their male relatives, they were sometimes encouraged by husbands and fathers to be the ones who sent requests.[18] However, for those who had control of a political seat, there may have been practical, as well as political, factors to consider, and sentiment did not always shape decisions. In 1790, Lady Irwin sold the second seat at Horsham for about £5,000. Reflecting her Tory, pro-slavery views, the recipient was a West Indian merchant; for both men and women, politics and economics could be as important as personal ties.[19]

Therefore, being well connected and well informed was important. Patronage networks were not just about parliamentary candidates, but spread far wider. They could therefore help to provide financial security and/or enhanced status for families. Through good networks, a family could access those who granted livings in Church of England parishes, who appointed people to government offices, who promoted individuals in their military careers, or who nominated the governors of the Bank of England, to name just a few opportunities.[20] For both men and women, one of the most important sources of income, and possibly status, was the Civil List. This was under the ultimate control of the monarch and contained various diplomatic and political posts, as well as those relating to the monarch's household. It was also an important source of royal charity, often in the form of pensions. As, in E.A. Reitan's words, the 'Civil List was the fountain from which all blessings flowed, a great cornucopia with something to please every taste', there were regular petitions sent to the court for funds.[21] These were sometimes forwarded through intermediaries: Lady Yarmouth, the mistress of George II, received many requests from people who thought she could persuade the monarch to support them.²² Records suggest that at least half of those receiving pensions were women. These included Sarah Ponsonby, one of the Ladies of Llangollen, who in 1829 was granted an annuity of £200 from the English Civil List by her friend – and the prime minister of the day – the duke of Wellington.²³ Therefore, having good networks was economically imperative for financially constrained elites.

While being awarded a pension was a 'blessing' for those who were in straitened circumstances, gaining a position in the royal household could bring a family both financial and social benefits. Generally, the royal household was a large and amorphous body, with different departments, including that of the lord chamberlain, who presided over the upper household and the ceremonial role of the court. The bedchamber, which became increasingly separate from the lord chamberlain's department, was presided over by the groom of the stool; and it was in that department that women had particular influence, especially during the reign of Queen Anne (1702–1714).²⁴ Posts at Anne's court gave women status (thanks to the associated prestige) and power, as they often heard important 'news' that could be politically advantageous. For example, Sarah Churchill, duchess of Marlborough, held three of the most important posts at the court of Queen Anne, giving her considerable influence over the monarch, as well as a direct income of £5,600. Her closeness to the queen also promoted her family interests; it led not only to her husband being named captain-general of the army, but also to the Churchills' political ally, Sidney Godolphin, being awarded the role of first lord of the treasury.²⁵ But the position secured need not have been in the household of the monarch: as in previous centuries, any royal connection could be advantageous to a woman and her family. Lady Susan Stewart, who was one of the thirteen children of the sixth earl of Galloway and a close friend to Frances, Lady Irwin, found that her position in the household of the sister of George III allowed her to form political networks. This enabled her to secure good positions for her siblings, and to develop the skills she later used when she married the marquis of Stafford and became more personally involved in parliamentary politics.²⁶

While the court gave women experience of political networks, gaining access to the political spaces of the Palace of Westminster was often a little trickier for them. They were not completely excluded:

until 1770, women were able to sit in the 'Strangers' Gallery' in the House of Commons to listen to debates; and noblewomen had some access to the House of Lords for events such as the Opening of Parliament.[27] They also may have attended on business. Fanny Boscawen wrote in a letter to Mary Hamilton in 1785 that she was 'obliged to go down early to the House of Lords expecting to be called upon to swear, in relation to a Bill my Son had before a Committee of their Lordships'.[28] However, while they had some access to the spaces, they could not hold political office. This included the small number of women who were peeresses; while they had the right to sit in the House of Lords, they all passed this privilege on to male heirs in this period.[29] This did not mean that women were fully excluded from political conversations and debates. Although parliamentary politics was formally based within the Palace of Westminster, it was supplemented by informal social politics that took place in private houses, clubs, coffee houses and assembly rooms. Elite women could enter many of these spaces where politics were discussed in order to promote their own familial and community concerns. They sometimes led these events, and hosted dinner parties, afternoon teas and salons. Political assemblies in town houses were usually run by the hostess, not the host, and those could be important political spaces.[30] These events could therefore enhance, or possibly damage, the reputation of a family; Fanny Boscawen was much relieved when a 'drum' (private assembly) she held while Edward was away in 1755 was not only deemed to have been successful, but was also seen to have reflected positively her status as a 'polite' mistress of a fashionable town house.[31] Women without husbands – either through widowhood or because their menfolk were away fulfilling military or diplomatic service – often felt that they had to proactively 'do their duty' by taking a full part in the parliamentary season, and to act as the family's representative in the socio-political worlds of eighteenth-century London.[32]

The mixing of the social and the political enabled women such as Georgiana, fifth duchess of Devonshire, to have considerable political influence. For over twenty years she managed one of the most influential political salons of the age, campaigned tirelessly for the Whig party and showed herself to be a skilled propagandist. However, she could also be the subject of propaganda, as the cartoons attacking her political influence and her role in the controversial 1784 Westminster election show. In some of these she was accused of immodest behaviour, such as kissing butchers for votes; although other women were politically active, the duchess of Devonshire received particularly personal and unpleasant criticism. While she refrained from campaigning for votes on the street after 1784, Georgiana continued to host parties and acted as an unofficial party whip to the Whigs in the late eighteenth century; the novelist Frances Burney described her as 'the head of the opposition public'.[33] While Georgiana was unusual in possessing political influence that was far greater than that held by nearly all other non-royal women (or indeed most men), she was not alone in being a politically active woman. For most elites, it was part of their life, especially when living in London. The social and the political were closely aligned, especially during the parliamentary season. This not only involved attending the Palace of Westminster (for peers and MPs), but also morning levees, political dinners and events at royal court.[34] Research by Hannah Greig and Amanda Vickery has shown that regular attendance at court events was the norm for London elites.[35] This is because at these events they could signal to other attendees their social prestige, especially through engagement with rites of passage; for women, these included being presented to the monarch as debutantes or following their marriage.[36] For those families that needed to establish their position in society, as they did not have a title, this was especially important. Although the Boscawens had peers as relatives, Edward Boscawen's position in society was only settled once he gained the title of lord of the admiralty and he had built a country house to cement his status. Therefore, it is not surprising to find that in Fanny Boscawen's diary of 1763 she reported that she took her daughters regularly to court, following a year of seclusion after Edward's death in 1761.[37] She needed the family to be seen again, so that the connections they had developed as a couple could benefit their now fatherless children. For the upper classes, there was an expectation that there would be at least some engagement within the political networks of court and Westminster. The ability to use these networks in the 'family interest' was an important skill for all elites, men and women, as it could help to secure their status and support the dynastic ambitions of their families.

It is important to note that not all connections were about traditional forms of power. Elite women could use their networks to support others as patrons of the arts, as well as to form links for their own benefit, such as finding intellectual companionship and friendship. One of the most notable female networks in this time period was that of the 'bluestockings'. Originally used as a term of abuse against puritans in the 1650s, the name was revived in 1756, when a male guest at one of Elizabeth Montagu's assemblies wore blue worsted stockings, a garment usually worn by working men. It was subsequently used to describe visitors – male and female alike – who attended Montagu's gatherings, and Admiral Boscawen used the term 'bluestocking circle' to describe his wife's network of friends.[38] Fanny Boscawen, Montagu and Elizabeth Vesey were leading hostesses among the bluestockings, and they used their London homes to provide spaces for discussion and debate from the 1750s through to the end of the century.[39]

These gatherings were distinct from the afternoon teas, featuring card playing, that women of the elite classes generally attended; instead, they encouraged intellectual and polite conversation. Nicole Pohl and Betty A. Schellenberg argue that there was a shared endeavour for 'intellectual improvement, polite sociability, the refinement of the arts through patronage, and national stability through philanthropy'.[40] These values were celebrated in a poem by Hannah More, 'Bas Bleu, or Conversation' (1786). This poem championed the importance of conversation as a mechanism for improvement, as it enabled women to act as a civilising influence and to highlight their feminine values of sympathy and compassion.[41] Unlike the conversations among 'gentlemen of the club', described by writers such as the third earl of Shaftesbury, the gatherings of the bluestockings tended to be less socially exclusive and to include both men and women. The guests included aspiring authors, which meant that Elizabeth Montagu's house, in particular, became something of a literary headquarters. By drawing on her income from mining in the north-east of England, she was able to provide annuities to authors such as Hester Chapone and Sarah Fielding. In many ways, for writers and thinkers these assemblies were like the court of the 'Queen of the Blues', as Samuel Johnson described Montagu, and so a place where favour and patronage could be sought and provided.[42]

Fanny Boscawen regularly hosted gatherings of these well-connected women at her London home on Audley Street. The guest list regularly included Elizabeth Montagu and Elizabeth Carter, who had both developed public profiles as writers, which delighted Fanny.[43] She teased Montagu about this in a letter that she wrote in 1753:

> As I never in my life addressed a Muse till now, I have had some doubts whether there is not an Ancient Rule still in force that obliges One to invoke them in Rhyme or at least blank verse; but then I consider again that my beloved Muse is very reasonable, and that if such a thing had been expected she would have taken care to furnish me with materials, and not require me to make brick without straw.[44]

The date of this letter is revealing. Generally, Carter and Montagu were not widely regarded as muses until after the production (and reproduction) of Richard Samuel's painting *The Nine Living Muses of Great Britain* in 1778.[45] This shows how closely connected Fanny was to these women, and how much she admired their work and ideas even when they were relatively unknown in wider elite circles.

Although Fanny Boscawen was not celebrated in the same way as the 'Living Muses', she was recognised by her friends as an accomplished correspondent and hostess. Her letters were greatly admired, and they were compared favourably to those written by Madame de Sévigné, a seventeenth-century French noblewoman whose epistles were widely read by literary females of the eighteenth and nineteenth centuries.[46] She was also good company: in 1789, George Selwyn described 'old Mrs Boscawen' as 'an admirable companion for such an old story teller as I am'.[47] Fanny used these skills to connect her bluestocking circle with aspiring writers.[48] These included Hannah More, a writer and philanthropist, who was active in setting up charity schools and in the campaigns first against the slave trade, and later for the emancipation of slaves in the British West Indies. It is not clear when Hannah first met Fanny, but we know that they were part of the same circles in London by 1774.[49] More wrote that 'Mrs Boscawen came to see me the other day', with her daughter, Elizabeth, fifth duchess of Beaufort, 'in her gilt chariot with four footmen... I read my own books, see my friends and, when I please, may join the most polished and delightful society in the world.'[50] More found Fanny 'polite, learned, judicious and humble', and in 1774 she dedicated her play *The Inflexible Captive* to Mrs Boscawen, whom she described as 'a Lady possessed of every quality and accomplishment'.[51] More became part of the bluestocking circle and enjoyed the meetings at Boscawen's home in Audley Street. She recorded in 1775 that they 'spent the time, not as wits, but as reasonable creatures, better characters I trow. The conversation was sprightly but serious. I have not enjoyed an afternoon so much since I have been in town. There was much sterling sense.'[52] After a similar 'conversazione' in early 1776, More reported 'what a comfort to me that none of my friends play at cards'. With simply 'a few sensible ladies' present, it was 'a very enjoyable day, until the world broke in on us'.[53] This reflects a desire for quieter meetings, and the bluestockings increasingly favoured the small and intimate gatherings that became characteristic of their later socialising.[54]

It was at these gatherings that Hannah More made important connections, such as meeting Mrs Delany at Fanny Boscawen's home. Mrs Delany was an artist who was well known for her political and royal networks. Fanny was one of Mrs Delany's regular correspondents; they shared news about friends and family, as well as updates on political gossip.[55] Fanny was keen to promote More's writings, and so she encouraged Delany's support of her younger friend's talent. In 1777 Fanny wrote:

> I am very glad you approve of Miss More's Essays, such an imprimatur does her and them honour. I believe her to be a worthy and religious woman of exceeding good principles, and then one may hope that whatever she writes may do some good; at least we are sure it can do no harm. She wrote me that she had had the honour of a very polite card from Mrs. Delany, and was much flatter'd with her notice.[56]

It was clear that More appreciated Fanny's support and friendship. She delegated to Fanny the ultimate decision as to whether she should publish the poem 'Bas Blue', and she also dedicated the poem 'Sensibility' to her in 1782.[57] More used this friendship when she, in turn, became a patron of other writers, including Ann Yearsley, known as the 'milk-maid poet'. She used her 'network of literary talent', which included Fanny, Elizabeth Montagu and Horace Walpole, to raise the necessary financial support to put Yearsley's poetry into print.[58]

As well as being formal patrons, the bluestocking women were active readers of books, and they liked to share their opinions on new works in their letters. This helped to promote the works of key writers, and created a shared ideological and literary identity among the correspondents.[59] Fanny Boscawen discussed editions of the works of Alexander Pope and William Shakespeare in her letters to Elizabeth Montagu.[60] While she found a new edition of the work of Pope frustrating, with little edifying in the commentary, she later particularly praised the work of Edmund Burke, saying of *Reflections on the Revolution in France* (1790) that 'we may talk down the Sun and then talk down the Moon, so ample is his wonderful book . . . I was highly entertained with it and it will do a great deal of good.'[61] She was not, though, immune to the temptations of a good novel. In one letter she confessed that she had given up on Milton because she was so engrossed in reading Samuel Richardson's *Sir Charles Grandison* (1753). She wrote that *Grandison*

> was introduced to me while I was writing; I laid down my pen (that was but civil) but I had no notion that it would have been anything more than a short introductory Visit, just to give me time to ask a few formal questions, but how dangerous is it for some women to trust themselves with a young man, and a handsome man, especially in the absence of their husbands. I protest to you that I never was sensible of this danger in my life before but if I own the truth on this occasion I must confess that the Gentleman and I were inseparable for the best of the Evening, and that I even suffered him to keep me up [a] great part of the night.[62]

This delight in reading was not limited to just the London bluestockings. There are numerous bills for books ordered by Frances, Lady Irwin, while her daughters were growing up. These were for a combination of books for herself and for her children, including Aesop's *Fables* and Thomas Boreman's *A Description of Three Hundred Animals* (1730), both traditional educational texts.[63] She also supported writers more directly. Ann Gomersall, a novelist from Leeds, dedicated the first of her didactic novels, *Eleonora* (1789), to Frances, thanking her for her patronage and for her 'favourable opinion . . . of the productions of my Pen'.[64] For other women, reading was a central part of their life. It was a shared interest in reading that had brought Sarah Ponsonby and Eleanor Butler together, and in their home in Llangollen they read aloud to one another, enjoying not only the works of Spenser and Milton, but also texts on botany and works by philosophical writers such as Rousseau.[65] They especially enjoyed his *Nouvelle Heloise*, which was fashionable among elite women; Lady Irwin was among those who pre-ordered it in 1761.[66] The pursuit of an Arcadian philosophy by Sarah and Eleanor drew admiration from many far and wide, including notable literary figures such as Sir Walter Scott and William Wordsworth.[67] They also developed epistolary connections with writers. One of their regular correspondents was Anna Seward, a poet from Lichfield. She had first met them at the house of mutual friends, and she swiftly developed a great admiration for the women, writing to a friend that they were 'women of genius, taste and knowledge'.[68] They must also have seen something in Anna, as they invited her to a dinner hosted by one of their friends in the ruins of Valle Crucis Abbey. They became regular correspondents, and their letters explored the importance of friendship, as well as their shared interest in Milton. This friendship led Seward to write the poem 'Llangollen Vale' (1796), which celebrated the history of the region and connected Ponsonby and Butler to that history. Others were inspired to write their poetry during visits to the cottage, including Robert Southey.[69] Once Plas Newydd had come to be seen as a site of idealised sensibility, and a visit to the Ladies had come to be an accepted part of the itinerary for the fashionable romantic traveller, writers wanted to mark their time there more formally, through their published works, which meant that their visits were noted by a wider audience.

Part of the appeal of Plas Newydd was its library – remarkable both in its design and in its contents. The library was central to the daily life of Eleanor and Sarah, and so it is not surprising that it should have been one of the first spaces that they changed.[70] Reading was important to them, and they created a library known as the 'saloon of the Minervas', an 'evocative Gothic chamber' filled with books and portraits, and lit by stained-glass windows.[71] However, there were some challenges in acquiring the volumes for their collection. Obtaining books in rural North Wales was not straightforward: they needed access to networks of booksellers and, as they were financially limited, they relied on gifts. These included gifts from relatives and friends. Frances Anne Crewe noted in 1795 that many of the books owned by the Ladies were the 'finest editions, not collected regularly but at different times for them by their Friends who have taken the opportunity of making them such presents of Choice Editions'.[72] They also sometimes passed books on: for example, Eleanor Butler gave their friend the duke of Wellington a Spanish prayer book that had probably come from the collection of her relative, the duke of Ormond. Some authors gave their own work to the Ladies; as the Ladies' library was so well renowned and as they were recognised for their excellent literary taste, writers wanted to feature in the Plas Newydd collection. This reflected wider patterns of gift exchange, where authors gifted their work in order to gain associated status.[73] This meant that despite their rural location, Eleanor and Sarah had excellent access to the latest news, ideas and writings, as reflected by the comment by Hester Piozzi that started this chapter.

While the library at Plas Newydd was distinctive, it needs to be remembered that many other elite women bought books and developed their own libraries. These often reflected their distinct interests. For example, Fanny Boscawen owned a forty-volume edition of the works of the Jansenists that she bequeathed to Hannah More, while Sabine Winn at Nostell Priory owned books reflecting her interests in religion, health and medicine, echoing some of the patterns of book ownership that we saw at Hunstanton and Apethorpe in the previous century.[74] Other women had much more extensive collections. For example, at the death of Lady Mary Wortley Montagu in 1762 her library had 1,500 books.[75] However, as many libraries were multigenerational, reflecting the interests of various family members, it is often difficult to identify from historic library catalogues and inventory lists which of the books were bought and/or read by the mistress of the house.[76] The library spaces were also important to women. Though traditionally seen by some scholars as a 'masculine space', country-house libraries were also places of heterosociability, as well as repositories of knowledge.[77] The Saltram library was a family collection, which was used by the Parkers to find inspiration for the design of objects for the house and to provide books for visiting guests; so while Theresa's brother thought it looked like a 'snuff box', it was a practical, as well as beautiful, library.[78] Libraries were an important part of many country houses, and it is no surprise that elite women, and their networks, were central to shaping their collections and spaces.

Women were not just collectors and consumers of the literary arts. They were also active patrons of both art and architecture, and their choices were often followed by their friends and admirers. For example, Elizabeth Montagu followed the Boscawens' lead and used Robert Adam for her country house at Sandleford.[79] Also, because Queen Charlotte was interested in the *cottage ornée* style (of which Plas Newydd was regarded as a fine example), in 1785 the Ladies of Llangollen received a request for them to send her a plan of their cottage. However, they were alarmed to discover that the perfume that they used to scent the letter was 'obnoxious to Royal Personages', which caused much panic in North Wales.[80] Elite women could also use art to cement their friendships. Fanny Boscawen commissioned John Opie to paint a portrait of her friend, the writer Hannah More.[81] More was a reluctant sitter, noting that 'I hope you will not think me ungrateful when I say that I have such repugnance to having my picture taken that I do not know of any motive on earth which could induce me to it, but your wishes'.[82] In Plas Newydd, many of the sketches and prints that featured in both the drawing room and the library were gifts from friends. Some of the others were portraits of those who had visited the property; Prince Pückler-Muskau of Prussia commented, following his visit in 1828, that 'there is scarcely a remarkable person of the last half century who has not sent them a portrait or some curiosity or antique as a token of remembrance'.[83] In the same way that authors wanted their work to appear in the library, especially if it had been inspired by the place, other visitors wanted to leave at Plas Newydd a permanent reminder of their visit.

Such gifts were not always completely welcome, either at Plas Newydd or at other properties. For example, Anne, duchess of Grafton, gave a portrait of herself to her friend Frances, Viscountess Irwin. As Anne was the wife of the prime minister, this gift was laden with additional meaning, made more complicated when the Graftons divorced a few years later and the Irwins' support moved to the new North administration.[84] Sometimes the political significance of an object meant that it would not be admitted into a house: Eleanor Butler's loyalty to the Bourbon cause led her to refuse the gift of a lock of Napoleon's hair. What was on display in one's country house could closely reflect personal and political networks.

We see this especially at Saltram, where, alongside their work with Robert Adam in redesigning the interior of the house, the Parkers were also involved in commissioning new art for the property. While it is now not always clear whether it was Theresa or John Parker who commissioned any specific individual item, it is possible to get a good understanding of the wider patterns of the purchasing of art at Saltram through their account books. These show payments to various artists, including one of £1,000 to Sir Joshua Reynolds in 1780. Reynolds, one of the preeminent portrait painters of the late eighteenth century, was the first president of the Royal Academy of Arts, and so his connections to the family reflected well on Theresa and John.[85] Born in nearby Plympton, Reynolds had a long-standing connection to the Parker family: Lady Catherine Parker was reported to have presented Reynolds with his first drawing pencil.[86] Traditionally, the relationship between Reynolds and the Parkers, and the collecting of art for Saltram more widely, has been seen as something that was led by John Parker.[87] However, this is to overlook the importance of his wife, Theresa. We know that Reynolds regularly visited Saltram, and the names Parker and then later Boringdon (Sir John's title after 1784) feature in Reynolds' appointment books more than any other. However, while it is clear that some of those appointments were with John (since Reynolds painted a portrait of him that was shown at the Royal Academy in 1773), others must have been with Theresa and their children.[88] He painted Theresa on a number of occasions. One of the paintings was a full-length portrait to feature in their newly designed saloon, reflecting Theresa's centrality to the future of the

Parker dynasty.[89] This painting soon acquired additional importance. First, before it was sent to Saltram, it was shown at a Royal Academy exhibition; and then secondly, the family arranged for a print to be made of it. This meant that the image could be seen by a much wider audience than just those who visited Saltram or the Royal Academy. While Theresa felt some awkwardness about the discussions of the painting among visitors to the Academy who were keen to judge the president's artwork, there is no doubt that both the exhibition and the print raised the profile of the Parkers.[90] As her brother, Lord Grantham, noted, the cost of getting the print made would have been offset by its advantage to John Parker's political career: 'The Expense is a Trifle, and indeed a Knight of the shire, should have it, to please his voters with.'[91] The connections to the artist – and the presence of a beautiful wife – were very much in the 'family interest' of an ambitious politician.

Although she knew that being connected to Reynolds could raise the status of the family, Theresa did not appear to submit passively to the artist's decisions. When Reynolds painted a half-length portrait of her, Theresa told Lord Grantham:

> I have some thoughts (that is) Mr Parker talks of having the little boy put into the half length of Sir Joshua's, which remains just as you left it, only in bright yellow, which he is very fond of at present but I do not approve of.[92]

This letter is revealing. It shows that she was confident in telling Reynolds that she wanted to be depicted as a mother, and that if she disliked something, such as the bright yellow, she was not willing to just accept it. The letter also suggests that she was keen to ascribe decisions to her husband, even when they were her own. The phrase 'I have some thoughts' is quickly balanced by 'Mr Parker talks'. While she knew how she wanted to be portrayed in the painting, she also knew that she needed to be seen as a submissive wife, so that her husband's status was not undermined.[93] Her confidence in directing Reynolds' work did not sour their relations: following her death in 1775, Reynolds wrote an obituary for Theresa Parker that was published in the *Gentleman's Magazine*. After describing her beauty, he noted that in so exalted a character as hers, it is scarce worth mentioning her skill and exact judgement in the polite arts. She seemed to possess by a kind of intuition that propriety of taste and right thinking, which others but imperfectly acquire by long labour and application.[94]

This obituary was published anonymously, and the fact that he was willing to take the time to write such a piece, despite the risk of not enjoying any associated prestige, shows his close connection to Theresa. This text reflects how he admired her taste and indicates that the relationship between Reynolds and Saltram was not solely through John, but that Theresa was central to it, too.

Because of this close friendship, the Parkers were able to make use of Reynolds' networks. Reynolds encouraged them to use other painters, such as the American artist Gilbert Stuart. Theresa was impressed by Stuart's portraits, noting that 'they are very strong and good likenesses'.[95] Reynolds also tried to help them find other works of art; but his suggestions were not always accepted, especially by John Parker, who seems to have thought some of his recommendations were too expensive. Historian Rosemary Baird suggests that, as the art collection did not include paintings of dogs and horses, John Parker was not 'overly involved in building it up'.[96] Instead, it seems that Theresa used her own family connections to find old masters, possibly at more affordable prices than those Reynolds was suggesting. In 1771, while he was in Spain, Theresa's brother Lord Grantham was well placed for purchasing. She reminded him: '[R]emember if you meet with anything abroad of pictures, bronzes etc. that is valuable in itself, beautiful and proper for any part of Saltram . . . you must not lose an opportunity of procuring it for us.'[97] Grantham later sent back prices for pictures by Rubens and Veronese, and commissioned some by Murillo.[98] Theresa also brought art by Angelica Kauffman into Saltram. Swiss-born, Kauffman studied in Italy before moving to London, where she became one of only two female founding members of the Royal Academy.[99] Among the collection at Saltram are a number of paintings that Kauffman presented at a Royal Academy exhibition in 1768; in letters to her brother Frederick, Theresa claimed to have been responsible for bringing these and other

Kauffman paintings to Devon. As Ellis Waterhouse notes, some of these paintings do not appear in the account book that starts in 1770, suggesting that Theresa may have acquired them either before her marriage or in her first few months as a wife. Kauffman went on to undertake work for the Parkers at their London property in Sackville Street, and they bought her bound copy of old master prints in 1772.[100] Theresa clearly thought a great deal of Kauffman's work. In a letter to Frederick in 1775 she described the subjects that Kauffman had painted for them, and noted that 'the prettiest and I think the best she ever did, is the painting of Hector and Andromache'.[101] It appears that Kauffman was grateful for the support; art historian Angela Rosenthal suggests that Kaufman may have gifted the Parkers the portrait she made of Theresa in 1773, in recognition of their patronage.[102] Through her connections and taste, Theresa was able to enhance the collection at the house, and, in turn, enhance the family's standing more generally.

For other women, their networks were crucial sources of comfort and friendship. As well as intellectual engagement, the bluestocking circle provided companionship for Fanny Boscawen. As we can also see with other naval wives, such as Betsey Fremantle, a strong network of female friends was an important source of support during the long absences of a husband who was away at sea.[103] These became even more crucial to Fanny after her husband's death. One of the first people who came to visit her was Elizabeth Montagu, and she invited Fanny to stay with her at Tunbridge Wells in the period immediately after the admiral's funeral.[104] Even before this time of crisis, it was clear that these two women had a very close relationship. Fanny's ability to tease Elizabeth for her status as a muse suggests that this was a connection that was not just based upon show and strategic alignments. They also talked about shared values; they often discussed matters associated with the Church, and their Anglican faith bound them together.[105] It was an enduring union: like many of the bluestockings, Elizabeth and Fanny lived long lives.[106] In a letter sent in 1794, Fanny reflected 'so long Dear Madam have I enjoyed the Honour and Pleasure and Advantage of Your Friendship'.[107] It remained good-humoured, too; in a letter sent in November 1798, Fanny reflected that if her friend had found her recent visit to the Boscawen household dull, she needed to remember that 'it was the fault of the fog, not mine, since, but for its impenetrable texture we might have mix'd in the Society of French and English beau Monde at Lady Onslow's'.[108] The idea of the seventy-nine-year-old Fanny Boscawen and the eighty-year-old Elizabeth Montagu living it up with the fashionable London society would surely have amused both women greatly.

In Llangollen, the intellectual, aesthetic and domestic life of Sarah Ponsonby and Eleanor Butler was shaped by their friendships and the associated gift exchange. While this included offerings from those who wanted to be associated with the Ladies for their own prestige, they received gifts from close friends, too. Although they welcomed some gifts – such as a hare sent by the dean of St Asaph – a gift of fish from Lyon, France, led to Eleanor noting 'I hate culinary presents.'[109] In return, they sent produce from their land or created their own artistic and knowledge-based gifts: engravings were copied, satin portfolios were worked and transcriptions were made. For example, during a visit, one Mrs Tighe (a friend from Ireland, who remained in contact with them after they moved to Wales) was presented with a copy of the entire manuscript of Lady Ann Fanshawe's seventeenth-century memoirs.[110] While the Ladies had a strong sense of reciprocity, they rarely visited their friends at their own properties – their visits to the Piozzi household at Brynbella, also in North Wales, being a rare exception.[111] Instead, they relied on people coming to them (which they did frequently) or on 'paper visits': as with other elite women, much of their network was maintained through letter writing. They often appreciated letters as gifts in their own right, and so judged them for their worth. While they especially enjoyed the letters received from Anna Seward, they were disappointed by those from Hester Piozzi. They seem to have thought that, as a writer, her epistles would have focused on the aesthetics of the local landscape; instead, she reported on the price of meat, the marital fates of her friends, her endless lawsuits and, inevitably, the misdeeds of her daughters.[112] The Ladies did not feel these notes offered a fair exchange for their own missives.

This sense of reciprocity, their biographer Mavor notes, was not confined to the letters and to their friends; they also developed a complex 'great web of obligation and counter-obligation, which entrapped willingly, and sometimes not, man, woman and child to a radius of several miles'.[113] While they were not as charitable as they claimed, the Ladies did create within Llangollen 'a true sense of community, of shared experience'.[114] Their visitors were not only good for the Ladies' own networks, but they also helped the town develop its own domestic tourism industry. Their complex gift exchange with their visitors, friends and the local community enabled the Ladies to fulfil the (increasingly anachronistic) ideals of rural hospitality, of a sort similar to that celebrated by Ben Jonson in 'To Penshurst' and that we saw in seventeenth-century Hunstanton.[115] Despite their more modest income, the Ladies' connections, patronage and community helped them to maintain an elite way of life that was central to many (more traditionally sized) country houses. In short, the Ladies of Llangollen were women who used their networks to adorn their table and their house, and to improve their knowledge. When they first settled into Plas Newydd, their focus was very much on retreat. However, while they took the ideal of retreat to heart, this did not imply total isolation from the world. They not only had many visitors – prestigious guests, close friends and unwelcome tourists – but they also depended on the local community, where their patronage was an important part of their elite duty. Collectively, these encounters were the 'magic' at the heart of their knowledge and networks, and so shaped their role as mistresses of their house.

This 'magic' was not exclusive to the Ladies of Llangollen: their networks embodied the importance of connectedness that shaped elite society in the eighteenth century. Knowledge, access and companionship were crucial elements of the influence held by the upper classes. Knowledge was also at the heart of the bluestocking circle that not only brought Fanny Boscawen close friendships, but also meant she could assert her own place in society and enabled her to encourage others in sharing their talents, especially Hannah More. Likewise, Theresa Parker used her networks not only to adorn her house, but also to support the work of artists such as Reynolds and Kauffman. These connections provided additional prestige to the family and to the house at Saltram. Similarly, the political activities of Frances, Viscountess

Irwin placed her within the networks of social politics that were central to elite life in the eighteenth century. As the mistresses of 'power houses', women played a crucial role in gaining and maintaining their family's influence and status without transgressing the gender ideals of the period.

CHAPTER 6

The Affectionate Home

In the mid-eighteenth century, Frances, Lady Irwin, wrote a letter to a London-based friend, in which she commented on a recent fashionable marriage:

> I think Miss Lowther and Lord Buckingham a very proper match as the world goes, where fine equipage and fine clothes are esteemed essentials in happiness, but I don't suppose they have those sentiments for each other that will give them very delicate sensations. You fine folks may despise us homely ones as you please, but think if you will without the extremist envy on a party my husband and I had yesterday evening by moonlight, we harried in pursuit of Nightingales and to our inexpressible happiness heard the tuneful lags of the little animal.

She added that when moonlight and nightingales do not have the power to please, 'no wonder that operas are thronged and loo tables crowded. But when they have, they have the sort of happiness one perceives is really what makes life desirable.'[1] Frances's comments reflect her delight in her domestic life; it was at her Yorkshire home of Temple Newsam that she could feel truly contented. Her letter reflects her preference for rural attractions over those of the city: she suggests that urban dissipation reduced sensibility and prevented one from feeling true happiness. She clearly separated herself and her family, 'the homely ones', from the 'fine folks' of fashionable society; her joys were her husband and nature, not opera and gambling.

This idealisation of the home as the centre for sensibility and simplicity was a theme that appeared in many letters through the eighteenth and early nineteenth centuries. Often, those who were based in their country houses would write to their London friends with tales of domestic bliss, while mocking the rushed and hectic lives of the *bon ton*; when they were not in Westminster, elite women could distance themselves from the 'fine folks' and emphasise their happiness in the countryside. However, these letters were often written with a knowing smile, as the authors were normally fashionable women, too. Also, the countryside was not completely restful. The Ladies of Llangollen had a stream of visitors to Plas Newydd, and in Devon, Theresa Parker complained to her brother in 1772 that they expected 'a great deal of Company this week . . . half the County. You may guess how agreeable it will be; how far I shall think so, I may as well keep to myself.'[2] Following the ideals associated with the Roman villa, they wanted the country house to be a retreat, and a place where they could happily be with a family that they cared for.[3] In short, they wanted it to be a home – a theme we see regularly in elite women's writing. For example, in her memoir Mary Elizabeth Lucy described the 'beautiful and dearly loved family seat Bodelwyddan' as 'the home that I so loved'.[4] This reflected the idea of the home as a place of comfort, but also a place for the family, following the eighteenth-century idealisation of domesticity.[5] However, were eighteenth-century country houses homes? Affectionate familial relations were often at the heart of idealised domesticity, and so it is important to consider the nature of married life in this period. Accordingly, we look at a number of marriages, including those of two young women who were 'encouraged' into marriage by their fathers: Mary Elizabeth Williams (later Lucy) and Mary Fox Strangways (later Talbot). This chapter then examines how duty and domesticity shaped the roles of women as wives and mothers, drawing especially on the examples of Fanny Boscawen and Lady Irwin. So as to understand how women were able to use the ideals of the age to shape their own place within society, we examine the relationship of Eleanor Butler and Sarah Ponsonby. The household duties of the mistress are also considered, and the importance to creating a happy home of maintaining a good relationship with the servants is highlighted. As we saw in the seventeenth century, domestic duties were not necessarily joyless; and in this period, for many women their stately homes could be places of comfort, care and affection.

This was because affection was seen as important to family life in this period, especially in relation to marriage. As we have seen, while there were unhappy marriages, there was clear evidence of marital affection in earlier periods, including the relationships of the Thynnes and the Harleys. However, many historians argue that during the eighteenth century the emphasis on domesticity led to a focus on companionate relationships, and there was also an increase in the use of the language of romantic love. Within Georgian Britain, the term 'love' was used frequently by elites to describe their own emotions, although marriages were usually patriarchal.[6] For example, Fanny Boscawen reminisced with her husband about their early courting, reflecting on 'when you and I loved one another and told it only by our eyes'.[7] The nature of this love took many forms, and different ideals were expressed by different writers. Pragmatic love was considered the ideal basis for marriage by commentators such as Samuel Richardson, the author of *Sir Charles Grandison*.[8] In many didactic texts, love was seen as encouraging both partners to accept their complementary roles within the marriage, and to serve as a guard against husbandly authority turning into tyranny.[9] It was also regarded as what made marriages happy. In one conduct book, a fictional letter writer commented to a new bride: 'Do not be shocked at being counted a *fond* Wife; you have, I am sure, too much Good-Sense to be ashamed of what must now not only be the Essence of your Happiness, but your highest Glory.' This reflects the sense that not only was there a desire for affection, but that it was expected. However, the fictional letter continued: 'It is your Duty to love your Husband with unalterable Affection.'[10] If the positive feelings did not come naturally, there was a sense that it was the woman's duty to make them appear for both her husband and herself; the language of duty was not just confined to seventeenth-century didactic texts.

This sense of duty was also felt by women in relation to their natal families. As we have seen for earlier time periods, families could form new networks and consolidate land ownership and political ties through marriage; and this remained important in the Georgian age. So although there was a real desire for a married couple to be happy, it was also hoped that the union would help to maintain, or enhance, the family's status. Therefore, many parents took an active role in identifying suitable spouses for their children – a partner who would fulfil the dynastic and emotional desires of both parties. This would have included helping their children navigate the formal courting practices of the period. As people increasingly married into families whose rural seats were a great distance from their natal homes, the London 'marriage market' was important and was a central feature of the Season. This included 'coming out' balls, the presentation to court of debutantes and other assemblies.[11] At family-arranged parties, possible suitors who were particularly favoured would be advantageously seated and privately encouraged, so that the parents could engineer a relationship without the daughter being fully aware of their involvement. Across these events, some women attracted a number of suitors. For example, Mary Fox Strangways, daughter of the second earl of Ilchester, was presented to court in spring 1793. During this London Season she received marriage proposals from two 'young smarts'.[12] However, not all young women were so fortunate, and so may have faced consecutive seasons full of balls, assemblies and parties, which some women engaged in more willingly than others.

The capital's marriage market was not the only way to find a suitor. Although Mary Fox Strangways received two proposals during her London visit, she was reluctant to commit herself, as she had already received a proposal before the trip. This was from her father's friend, Thomas Talbot, who had inherited the Penrice and Margam estates in 1758, when he was ten years old. Thomas had remained a bachelor for many years, but the visit of Lord Ilchester in 1792 seems to have prompted him to look for a wife. Ilchester was accompanied on his trip to Glamorganshire by two of his children – Harry, only five years old, and Mary, who was nearly sixteen.[13] Mary's letters and pocketbook suggest that although she found rural Wales blissful, the visit was a period of immense internal turmoil for her. It is unclear what happened, but it seems that Mary became the object of Talbot's attentions, and that this unsettled her. She noted in her pocketbook 'Let the 6th February never be forgot.' It is not clear what should not be forgotten, but it is probable that she was referring to Thomas's proposal of marriage. On 10 February she wrote 'far from happy', and the following day 'My birthday, oh what a day!'[14] Despite her ill ease, she did not reject Talbot completely; like the fictional Elizabeth Bennet with Pemberley, there was something about the house, particularly its gardens, that meant that she felt she could dream about being mistress of the place.[15] She also knew that marrying Talbot would please her father, and so she accepted his proposal in late 1793.[16] This decision appears to have been shaped by a sense of duty, as she does not seem to have been the most enthusiastic of sweethearts. We can see this in a letter Talbot wrote to her after she formally accepted him. He started the letter 'My Dearest Love' and wanted some clarity regarding when they would be able finally to marry:

> May I entreat you, in compassion to me &, if I may be allowed the expression, in atonement for all the sad delays I have felt, to think of the day when we may be united. I have also requested your father's intercession on that point, & have myself named the 28th to be at Melbury, for I am there & can be nowhere else till you make Penrice my home . . . Your dear father will be kind enough to intimate your determination, and remember you have not yet favoured me with one line or - ! But let the day be in this year, & I forgive.[17]

The phrase 'make Penrice my home' is of particular interest here. Although he had overseen the rebuilding and decoration of the house, it seems that he felt that it would not be his home until he was there with Mary. However, Mary already had a home, as she was very attached to Redlynch, where she had grown up, and so married life did not have the same appeal to her as it did to him. Talbot seems to have been aware of this, and so, while he was appealing to Mary, he also knew that he needed her father to be a willing participant in the planning, or there may never have been a wedding. He was right to be concerned: in the period following the proposal, Mary's letters show she was anxious and unhappy, and was saddened by the idea of living away from her sister.[18]

In the end, the date was selected by her father; Lord Ilchester and Talbot very much drove both the courting and the wedding, with the bride being something of an observer.

Again, it was the father of the bride who was instrumental in shaping the marriage between George Lucy and Mary Elizabeth Williams. In 1822, Mary Elizabeth's elder sister met George Lucy, the squire of Charlecote, during the London Season and confided to Mary Elizabeth that 'she thought she had made a conquest'.[19] When George came to visit the Williams' family home at Bodelwyddan in August 1822, the family arranged music; but it was Mary Elizabeth whom George asked to dance 'much oftener than any of my sisters'.[20] When he visited again in October that year, it was with intent: he asked her father for Mary Elizabeth's hand. This caused Mary Elizabeth great consternation, as it was the second time that she had been proposed to by a man who had been the object of one of her sisters' affections.[21] As with the first proposal, she knew the upset that this would cause, and so she pleaded with her father to reject George's request: 'I fell on my knees and implored him to refuse', she related in her memoirs. But her father, Sir John, was far too astute to miss this opportunity to marry his daughter into a well-respected family. The first unwanted proposal had been refused, as Mary Elizabeth was too young; but she had now 'come of age', and so forming a union was an expected part of this stage in her life cycle. She later recalled that 'Papa insisted on my submission so my tears were in vain . . . I felt I dared not disobey him.'[22] The sense of duty is notable here; while she wanted to be loyal to her sister, she knew that she had a responsibility to please her father, too. After the proposal from George, Mary Elizabeth

> rushed out of the room and flew upstairs to my own darling precious Mama, weeping bitterly. She kissed me and kissed me again and again and said all she could to comfort me, adding 'My sweet Mary, love will come when you know all of Mr Lucy's good qualities.'[23]

It is interesting that Mary Elizabeth's mother used the language of love here; however, as Mary Elizabeth was recording her memories of the event over sixty years later, it is not clear whether she was using the language of the high Victorian period or accurately reporting the words used by her Regency-era mother. Nevertheless, the idea that love was an important facet of a marriage, and the sense that happiness and companionship would come with time, were common sentiments in the Georgian age.

Therefore, because of this emphasis on love, it was usual for parents to hope that their children would find emotional companionship, even in marriages that were strategically important. For the eighteenth century, it is not really helpful to see 'love matches' and 'arranged marriages' as the only two models for finding a partner. Most betrothals fell between the two; and, as we see in Lady Williams' comments, the practical and the affective functions of the partnership were usually considered by both the parents and the adult children.[24] In both of the examples above, despite first appearances, it can be argued that the parental decisions were driven by a degree of kindness. It seems that during all the procrastinations that almost drove Thomas Talbot to the brink of despair, Lord Ilchester was moving carefully in dealing with Mary, judging his steps as an affectionate father. He bought her a Welsh dictionary before the wedding, which Mary confessed to 'studying all morning'.[25] Ilchester wished his daughter's life to be happy; but he also wanted her to marry his friend, as it was a good match in terms of status and cementing existing connections. Duty and affection did not have to be incompatible.

Whether the union was encouraged by the parents or the couple found each other, everyone was keen to see evidence of affection both during the courting period and into the early stages of marriage. Although Mary Elizabeth Williams was a reluctant fiancée at first, George Lucy began to win her over through his active courting. In a love letter sent by George three days after the proposal, he declared: '[Y]ou are the delight of all circles and the idol of your own. Indeed I shall never cease to style myself the most fortunate and happiest of mankind.'[26] Historian Sally Holloway notes that during the early nineteenth century, love letters were increasingly seen as sentimental items worthy of preservation, and so the fact that George asked Mary Elizabeth to keep his missive – and that she did so – shows how, at the early stages, this had the potential to be a sentimental marriage.[27] As we saw in unions from the early modern period, the exchange of gifts was an important element of courting, too. So when George Lucy returned to Bodelwyddan in November, bringing magnificent presents for his fiancée's twentieth birthday, including 'a complete set of rubies and diamonds set in massive gold', his serious commitment to the union must have settled the nerves of both Mary Elizabeth and her parents.[28]

However, some brides remained nervous. Marriage was a rite of passage, and a woman's social status was significantly altered during the wedding ceremony; she moved away from the authority of her father and became a wife.[29] This shift in identity could be unsettling for some brides. Mary Fox Strangways was clearly anxious about her new role in the run-up to the wedding. Only sixteen years old, her wedding and the family's attitude to it hung over her. She dreaded going to the family seat in Dorset, noting that: 'The formality of going down to Melbury is terrible but my motto is "Do as you would be done by when your *fatal day* is at hand".'[30] As well as items for the wedding day itself, in the weeks beforehand new clothes and goods were bought for the bride to support her in her shift to being a wife. A reluctant shopper, Mary was happy to report from London when she was able to 'see all my fineries completed; I like my day apparel very well, but . . . – perhaps you may guess what I mean, if not I will explain it to you'.[31] As it was so laden with symbolism, she could not say anything to her sister about the actual wedding dress. In another letter to Harriot, she reported that

> I feel so great a mixture of pleasure and pain that, tho' accustomed to examine myself daily for these two years past (you know I never thought before that) I can hardly unravel my anxieties. I feel great joy to leave this hateful town (which, you know, never suited either my body or mind), but I feel great pain to think it accelerates my departure from all that I once loved best.[32]

She reported having 'grown very morose' at the thought of the forthcoming changes in her life. One of Mary's anxieties was undoubtedly sex. Her father seems to have been rather clumsy in his attempts to prepare her for her marital duties. He showed her a letter which included the phrase 'the ice is broken, the frost of her prudery is beginning to thaw'. Embarrassed, she told her sister 'my face is all in a glow with shame and resentment . . . I tried to misunderstand it but my confusion was too evident to be mistaken.'[33] However, she knew that when she had inevitable but 'disagreeable' things to face, she had the courage to face them. The phrase 'Pity me, my dear Harriot', though, encapsulates her lack of enthusiasm for her wedding day – and night.[34]

Mary Elizabeth Lucy also found the marriage celebrations quite overwhelming. Recounting the day of her wedding (2 December 1824), she later recalled that when the

> solemnisation of matrimony [was] over, as I rose from my knees, I fainted away . . . my poor husband in agony, looking at his bride and not knowing what on earth to do, whilst darling Mama and old Nurse, weeping, chafed my hands and sprinkled water . . . over my face.[35]

This description shows quite how emotionally tumultuous a wedding could be for a reluctant bride. It is important to remember that these were not necessarily big weddings; although there could be a certain degree of pomp about the events, most Georgian weddings saw only a modest number of guests invited. Once the legal details, such as the marriage settlement, were agreed, the couple often married swiftly, and so it was only practical to invite the close relatives of the bride and groom. However, once married, the new couple needed to declare their married status publicly, and they would be involved in a round of parties, visits and celebrations.[36] The former Mary Fox Strangways, now Mary Talbot, reported to her sister that she 'was welcomed into Wales with acclamations'.[37] Similarly, the newly married Mary Elizabeth Lucy was welcomed to Charlecote with a torch-lit procession by the tenants and the ringing of church bells as the new mistress of the property.[38] In the weeks following the wedding, there was a series of dynastic duties for the couple to fulfil, including visiting important relatives, friends and contacts. It was also expected that they would be able to demonstrate to observers that they were happy. Therefore, young brides would often write to their family to reassure them of their marital felicity. In receipt of such news, Mary Elizabeth Lucy's mother wrote:

I should have felt keenly disappointed had your situation in life turned out contrary to my expectations, so I may be allowed to indulge in heartfelt gratification on the receipt of every letter that arrives from Charlecote testifying the domestic bliss that already reigns there. Old Nurse came in to hear your letter, her apron up to her eyes, wiping away tears of delight which were chasing each other down her furrowed cheeks at the mention of her dear Mrs Lucy's happenings.[39]

It would appear that after her fainting fit at the wedding, concern for Mary Elizabeth was felt across the household, and so there was collective joy in her new happiness.

Similarly, the relatives of Charles Ingram were concerned about whether he and Frances were happy following their wedding. Although it seems to have been a match shaped by affection, it had been beset by legal complications in the months before the union. When Charles visited his sister after the marriage, she noted how he was 'much pleased with his wife . . . and both in his Conversation and Behaviour appears what his best friend would wish him'.[40] This affection continued beyond the first few months of the marriage, as, although no known letters between Frances and her husband survive from this period, it is clear from her correspondence with others, and from their relatives' descriptions, that they were a devoted couple. Frances's former guardian noted her devotion, writing that her 1759 letter to him 'has convinced me that you are not to be reckoned amongst Modern Wives but are in Love after more than 12 months of Marriage'.[41]

This comment is very similar to one written by Fanny Boscawen in 1756 to her husband: ''Tis not that I prefer you to solitude, but that I prefer you to all the world. A strange, old-fashioned sentiment this, to confess to a fine gentleman, but it escaped me, and you must not betray me.'[42] Both these letters reflect the way in which an association was perceived between those who voiced their feelings of romantic love and those who were unfashionable.[43] However, many texts highlighted the importance of affection. One didactic book contained a model letter that wished a new wife that her

Spouse's Affection, instead of decreasing with Time, ripen into that soft Esteem, that tender Complacency, which are the natural Attendants of Love and Merit, and the highest Summit of all sublunary Happiness![44]

Being old-fashioned was, in a way, fashionable.[45]

To what extent did elite women have marriages that featured these ideals of esteem, felicity and happiness? As with twenty-first-century society, there were Georgian marriages that were unhappy, where the couple were ill-suited to one another. However, some marriages that appear to have started unhappily became stronger partnerships. In her memoirs, Mary Elizabeth Lucy recalled that 'On Christmas Day [1823] we went to Charlecote church and words cannot describe my inward thoughts as I prayed to God that I might be ever mindful of my duty as a wife and be diligent of such duties as His providence should allot me.'[46] In these early days of the union, she missed her childhood home and natal family, and so had a strong focus on the marriage as a duty, echoing sentiments expressed by Grace Mildmay over 200 years earlier. However, Mary Elizabeth wrote that, despite their unsteady start, 'my whole life became as fondly devoted to my husband as if he had been the object of my earliest affection'.[47] This seems to have been, in part, because she was able to fulfil the model of the 'incorporated wife', where the bride took on some of the duties of her new husband, as well as his identity.[48] Mary Elizabeth Lucy supported George in his work as an MP. She recalled: 'I became his secretary and he would say to me "you are the Mary after my own heart".'[49]

Similarly, the working relationship between Edward and Fanny Boscawen when they were overseeing the building of Hatchlands shows how couples could act in partnership. But Fanny and Edward were not just joint project managers, as they were an affectionate couple, too. Although they spent a great deal of time away from one another, they both clearly enjoyed each other's company, whether it be in person or in epistolary form. They wrote to each other about 'home affairs'.[50] It seems that Edward wanted to imagine life at Hatchlands while he was away at sea, so important were his wife and family to him and his happiness. There was a playfulness to their relationship, too. For example, in their letters they discussed a naughty cow that opened gates on the estate at Hatchlands whom they christened 'Saucy face'.[51] However, the distance did sometimes make Fanny anxious. Fearing that her looks were fading as she approached thirty, she told Edward that

> beauty and I were never acquainted. But may I not hope dear husband that you will find charms in my heart, the charms of duty and affection, that will endear me as much to you as if I were in the bloom of youth and beauty. But I must return to my trifles, for talking thus from my heart kills me, and tears blot my writing![52]

This sharing of emotions and the desire to be loved reflects how this was an affectionate union. This was especially in evidence following Edward's death in 1761. After spending so much time at the centre of naval conflict, there was something especially distressing about his death, at the relatively young age of fifty, at home.[53] Fanny commissioned Robert Adam to build a memorial monument to her husband at the church of Saint Michael Penkivel, Cornwall, and she took great care to ensure that it reflected not only his military role, but also his domestic one. The epitaph that Fanny wrote for her husband concluded with the line: 'His once happy wife inscribes this marble – an unequal testimony of his worth and of her affection.'[54] This was not just a dutiful public expression of emotion, but was reflective of their privately expressed feelings, too.

One of the strongest partnerships in the long eighteenth century that this book explores is the one between Eleanor Butler and Sarah Ponsonby. Not only did they significantly risk their reputation and their income by leaving Ireland, but by living together, as two women, they also defied many social norms. The ideals of marriage and motherhood, especially for families where dynastic succession was a central feature of their identity, shaped the life course for many women. However, not all women became wives, and during the eighteenth century nearly a quarter of aristocratic women never married.[55] Many unmarried women continued to live in their childhood home, with their parents and, in later life, with their eldest brother, and maybe even with their nephews. Two unrelated women setting up home together was less common, although not unheard of, as the well-documented case of Anne Lister and Ann Walker at Shibden Hall reflects.[56] Affectionate female relationships were not wholly discouraged; and widely read works, such as Rousseau's novel *Julie, ou la nouvelle Heloise* (1761), idealised female friendships, which were depicted as more faithful and beautiful than heterosexual passions.[57] These relationships came to be known as 'romantic friendships', which were seen as 'sentimental' or increasingly 'spiritual', and were made distinct from 'Sapphic sexuality', which was viewed with more concern.[58]

It is clear from Eleanor Butler's diary that she and Sarah Ponsonby were in an affectionate relationship. She recorded exquisite moments of private bliss in those first years. For example, on 24 September 1785 she wrote 'Read Madame de Sévigné. My Love drawing. From seven till nine in sweet converse with the delight of my heart, over the first. Paper'd our Hair.'[59] The Ladies demanded, as Mavor puts it, 'to be taken seriously as exponents of an ideal manner of living; that way of life which they insisted was the true reason for wanting to live together'.[60] By the late 1780s, they felt happy with their way of life as the Ladies of Llangollen, and the ideal of romantic friendship meant that they were largely accepted by others. However, there were critics. In July 1790, Eleanor noted in the journal their decision for instant cancellation of the *General Evening Post*, normally received for 'essential reasons'.[61] The newspaper had contained a personal attack on the Ladies, under the suggestive heading 'Extraordinary Female Affection'. As was common at this time, almost identical versions were reprinted in the *St James's Chronicle* and the *London Chronicle*.[62] The *St James's Chronicle* version read:

> Miss Butler and Miss Ponsonby now retired from the society of men, into the wilds of a certain Welch [sic] vale, bear a strange antipathy to the male sex, whom they take every opportunity of avoiding . . . Miss Butler, who is of the Ormond family, had several offers of marriage, all of which she rejected. As Miss Ponsonby, her particular friend and companion, was supposed to be the bar to all matrimonial union, it was thought proper to separate them; and Miss Butler was confined . . .

> Not many months after, the ladies concerted and executed a fresh elopement ...
>
> Miss Butler is tall and masculine, she wears always a riding habit, hangs her hat with the air of a sportsman in the hall and appears in all respects as a young man, if we except the petticoats which she still retains. Miss Ponsonby, on the contrary, is polite and effeminate, fair and beautiful ... Two females are their only servants ...
>
> Miss Ponsonby does the duties and honours of the house; while Miss Butler superintends the gardens and the rest of the grounds.[63]

There were two main criticisms in this piece. The first was that there was something concerning about Eleanor's avoidance of men and marriage, and the fact that Sarah was the cause of it. The second was that they had formed a pseudo-heterosexual union because of the ways in which they dressed and divided their household work. The women turned for advice to their friend, the philosopher Edmund Burke, seemingly out of concern that not only could their reputations suffer, but so also could those of their families and benefactors. In his response, Burke wrote about his feeling of indignation that he believed was felt 'by every worthy mind', but also encouraged silence in response to slander.[64] While they did not pursue a legal case, in their response to this piece and more generally, Sarah and Eleanor strove to distinguish themselves from those (much criticised) women, most notably Marie Antoinette, who were alleged to have engaged in 'Sapphic' activities.[65] The Ladies of Llangollen formed alliances with writers who celebrated their lifestyle using the language of friendship, classical ideals and natural imagery, all of which legitimised the Ladies' relationship.[66] This meant that they could shape the narrative of their lives so that it highlighted that they engaged in the activities expected of women of their class: good works, self-improvement, reading, gardening and hospitality, all from their miniaturised country house. These narratives also highlighted that their dedication to one another followed the emotional, rather than sexual, ideals of a happy marriage, thus conforming to the celebrated model of 'romantic friendship'.[67]

However, in creating their own myth, they also made themselves 'singular' and, in historian Martha Vicinus's phrase, 'their genteel eccentricity became a mark of their genius'.⁶⁸ This eccentricity included their dress. If we look at artistic representations and the reports of visitors to Plas Newydd, it would appear that, contrary to the newspaper reports, the Ladies did not adopt a masculine form of dress for one and a feminine for the other. Instead, written reports and a number of double portraits emphasised their striking physical similarity, and their dress suggested twinship, rather than dominant and submissive roles.⁶⁹ Their preferred style of jacket, the riding habit, was commonly found in elite women's wardrobes, especially in rural Ireland, although it was usually worn for riding and walking, rather than for everyday wear.⁷⁰ Later visitors did stress their male appearance. Mary Elizabeth Lucy of Charlecote in Warwickshire recalled a youthful visit to Llangollen and how 'these two ladies looked just like two old men'.⁷¹ However, far from being shocked by the women and their lifestyle, the gentry of the late Georgian period flocked to visit them.

Not everyone believed they were chaste, though. Anne Lister, when asked whether she thought the friendship of Misses Butler and Ponsonby was platonic, wrote about her doubt, knowing her own feelings for women: 'I feel the infirmity of our nature and hesitate to pronounce such attachments uncemented by something more tender still than friendship.'⁷² In her diary, Eleanor did describe more intimate moments. On 6 December 1785, she recounted:

> Rose at Eight after a tedious night Spent in coughing and with a most dreadful head ache. My dearest. My Kindest love did not sleep even for one moment the entire night but lay beside me watching and lamenting my illness and soothing by her tenderness the distressing pain of My Head.⁷³

While some scholars have suggested that these migraines may have been a code for (or a symptom of) erotic desire, it is impossible to tell.⁷⁴ As with the vast majority of couples from the period covered in this book, evidence of sexual intimacy was rare and fleeting; few letters survive that were as frank as those written by Maria Thynne, as there was a tradition for writers to ask for their more personal missives to be burnt.⁷⁵ What is clear from the surviving records of the lives of Eleanor and

Sarah, written by visitors, friends and the women themselves, was that they were devoted to one another. For example, Sarah described Eleanor's death in 1828 as 'the Sad Sad Event, which has annihilated as far as concerns this world the happiness, that for nearly Fifty One Years – the Almighty Giver of All Good, has Generously permitted me to enjoy'.[76] It was a partnership where they stood together to create their own space in the world, using the language of gender and class ideals to justify and celebrate their way of life.

Not all couples were as dedicated to each other as the Boscawens or the Ladies of Llangollen. This is not surprising, as the marriages of the elite have often been perceived as unloving, and adultery among the richest and most fashionable circles has been presented as common, with royalty thought to be particularly indulgent in affairs.[77] However, the degree of adultery may not have been significantly higher among the elite classes; their affairs have simply been recorded more, either in the scandalous press of the period or in their letters, which have survived in larger numbers than those of other social groups. The aristocracy should not be perceived as homologous; rather, a wide variety of emotions and beliefs shaped their activities. We can see this variety of emotions within the married life of Mary Talbot. Unlike Mary Elizabeth Lucy, Mrs Talbot did not express an early change of heart; in the first few weeks of their relationship, she found life with her husband, Thomas, difficult. In one letter sent to her sister in around February 1794 she explains the burdens, requirements and expectations of becoming the wife of a much older man. There was husbandly pressure to do what he wanted: when, with poor weather, they had been out little,

> he made me go out in the post chaise one day an airing, but it looked so pompous airing with four horses, besides as I was in perfect health there was no pretence for it and I could not bear it – I had rather wet my feet every day in the year.

She added: 'All my troubles and turmoils are, I am afraid, going to begin ... Adieu all snugness up in my own room; adieu all my dear cherished reverie. I must now always be present both body & mind, &, ... I am not very much used to that.'[78]

However, she seemed soon to find her place within the relationship. As her husband aged, she was able to take on more of a leadership role and, once a mother, became mistress of the house. The Rev. Sydney Smith reported, after a visit to Penrice in 1799, that he thought Mr Talbot 'fond of his wife and children to dotage. Lady Mary seems to be an amiable, valuable woman, who uses her influence over her husband to the best purposes.'[79] While the marriage may not have been as fulfilling emotionally for Mary as Fanny Boscawen's marriage to Edward seems to have been, she was able to make the union work, and to develop a home life where the children felt loved, even if she rarely felt the 'snugness' of her childhood room again.[80]

That motherhood was central to Mary Talbot's happiness was not unusual: in many relationships, it was the children that were important to making a country house a home. As it was expected that a wife would also be a mother, and domesticity was especially celebrated in this period, as historian Judith Lewis notes, 'quivers full of children were a part of the ostentatious display that characterized aristocratic life' in the late eighteenth and early nineteenth centuries.[81] Therefore, for a newly married woman, there was often a great sense of anticipation of news about a pregnancy. Although there was some concern that younger brides should not have children too soon if they were still considered 'delicate', the new bride would ideally provide a son and heir within the first two years of marriage. Some women provided good news for their families almost immediately: Mary Elizabeth Lucy gave birth to her first child less than a year after the wedding. She later recalled 'the joyful feeling knowing that I was a mother!'[82] When a pregnancy was not forthcoming, concerns could be expressed. Frances, ninth Viscountess Irwin, was reminded that she had a duty to stay strong so that she could provide an heir; and after the birth of two daughters, her sisters-in-law noted that she spent too much time away from her husband for a woman who did not yet have a son.[83]

Despite this interference, it is clear from her own letters that Frances enjoyed her pregnancies. She wrote to her close friend that: '[M]y invisible is I conjecture in good health, for I am so, and feel many a comfortable grump for the little mortal, which gives me great pleasure.'[84] This reflects how a healthy pregnancy could be a joyful experience for women and their families. If it heralded a new generation, the birth would be greatly anticipated and the mother-to-be could be given items to welcome the new baby into the dynasty. Isabella, third Viscountess Irwin, was particularly excited when Frances, her grandson's wife, fell pregnant in 1760, as she hoped that the long-awaited Irwin heir would be provided. She therefore took it upon herself to ensure that all the needs of the baby were fulfilled, according to the family's dynastic standards. Isabella's granddaughter wrote to the expectant Frances on her behalf:

> Lady Irwin desires me to tell you that the woman who makes the child bed linen knows well what is proper for you to have for yourself and what the Nurse you will have will expect, that she has bespoke everything that is necessary for you . . . They will be all sent together and are the prettiest playthings I ever saw, I hope if you approve of them you will continue the women for coats . . . My Grandmamma desires leave to present her Grandsomething with a Cradle which I am to bespoke.[85]

By sending these gifts, the dowager viscountess was ensuring that the new members of the dynasty were being cared for, and that familial traditions were being upheld. The family's network of staff and skilled workers were used by Isabella, and it was hoped that Frances would continue this patronage as mistress of Temple Newsam. As Frances had neither a significant 'mother figure' to guide her through her pregnancies nor the benefit of an aristocratic upbringing, Isabella was also acting in an advisory role.[86] Within the cultural world of the aristocracy, where continuation and tradition were central, the presenting of gifts was an important way of ensuring that women felt part of the family and supported in their pregnancies.

Although there were significant changes in the culture of childbirth in this period, with a shift from an all-female environment in the seventeenth century to a male-led medical event in the mid-Victorian era, that does not mean that the position of the mother was marginalised.[87] Elite mothers were able to use financial power and influence to gain access to a high level of specialist health care; the preservation of the life of the mother and child was important to elite families. Most elite women gave birth in London, as the capital offered the widest range of medical expertise, as well as providing sufficient dwelling space for relatives to stay nearby. By bringing together their family and their medical staff, they were trying to make childbirth as safe as they could. Many relied on family recommendations for staff. At the births of her first children in 1795, 1796 and 1798, Mary Talbot was looked after by Nanny Longford, the Somersetshire nurse who had nursed Mary's mother at Redlynch in 1790 during her last illness.[88]

However, things did not always go to plan. While the social norm was for male relatives, including the husband, to be excluded from the birthing room, in 1762 the doctor arrived too late for the birth of Lady Irwin's third child, and so the nurse had to fulfil the role of midwife, supported by Lord Irwin.[89] Pregnancy and childbirth held significant risks for women. Although during the Georgian period the rate of deaths in childbirth among elite women dropped significantly, the fear of death was still very real to women, especially following the high-profile demise of Princess Charlotte in 1817.[90] These fears tended to arouse religious feelings in women, and some wrote wills and farewell letters to their husbands.[91] Sometimes, these fears became reality. For example, Fanny Boscawen was seriously ill for several weeks following the birth of a stillborn daughter in 1754.[92] As with many pregnancies, careful preparations could be disrupted. Theresa Parker had planned to go to London to give birth to her second child in 1775. However, she caught a fever and the baby was born early at Saltram instead. On 20 October, she told her brother the full story. Her little girl was 'a very fine child not very large or small for her age, perfectly healthy, fair and quiet'. Theresa hoped she had got away with it: the fever seemed gone. Her husband had hardly coped:

> [I]t is impossible to describe Mr Parker's tenderness and affection to me throughout; indeed he alarmed himself much more than was necessary but had my fever lasted a few days longer he could not have stood it, as I believe he neither ate, drank, slept or could compose his spirits.[93]

Sadly, the fever soon returned and Theresa died the next month.

Although motherhood could bring great joy, it could cause great sadness, too.

The maternal duty did not just end with giving birth. As we have seen for the early modern period, motherhood was a role that many elite women fulfilled from their late teens until their death: as educators, carers and advisors, being a parent shaped their domestic world for most of their lives. This sense of maternal duty was keenly felt by many women. Fanny Boscawen assured her husband that the children 'shall be my sole care and study and that my chief purpose and the business of my life shall be to take care of them and to procure for them a sound mind in a healthful body'.[94] Although Edward was an absentee father for most of his married life, he was made aware of his children's progress in a stream of letters from Fanny. She described family life to him, and showed how he was playing a role in their activities, even when he was not there.

> I wish you could see us all supping together, for you just know I always regale with your fine tea before I go abroad. And with it enters two immense pieces of bread which, being sopped in very weak tea, are put into different plates for Ned and Fanny . . . After they are satisfied *c'est l'etiquette* to have a great game of romps, in the height of which I escape and gain my coach.[95]

Fanny was not unusual in this close relationship with her children; many mothers were directly involved in the lives of their offspring. While the reluctant aristocratic mother was a common theme in literature and art during the eighteenth century, the women in this study were actively involved in the care of their children.[96] Although the eighteenth-century radical writer Mary Wollstonecraft noted that 'the neglected wife is, in general, the best mother', the cases of Fanny Boscawen and Lady Irwin show that even the most besotted of wives could be affectionate mothers, too.[97] Lady Irwin wrote in 1767 that she could not 'bear to think of untwisting the two little tendrils which twine round my neck as well as my heart'.[98] This description of the tight hold that her children had on her affection reflects the very real devotion that many parents felt during this period.

Similarly, Theresa Parker's letters from 1772 to 1775 show that she was able to balance her enthusiasm for the redesign of Saltram with besotted motherhood. She wrote about her first child, Jack, enthusiastically to her brothers. In one letter to Lord Grantham from August 1774 she wrote:

> Here comes this little troublesome Boy who seeing the pen in my hand will make me draw a post chaise. You see some of his drawing or writing whichever you please to call it. It was with difficulty I prevented him scribbling all over the Sheet . . . I shall make him kiss the bottom of this letter perhaps you may distinguish the marks of his lips, it is the only way he can send you a kiss.[99]

That Jack was engaging with family epistolary duties at a young age seemed to especially delight Theresa. Some children were aware of the degree of affection they received, too. The happiness of the family life that Mary Talbot inspired at Penrice is best summarised in the words of her daughter Charlotte:

> This blessing and unmerited mercy I enjoyed with the generality of human beings born into this world, but the degree of it was more than common, and we have to thank God for a mother whose love and care was so unceasing, so enlightened, so individual, as I may say that each of her children felt beloved, appreciated, understood, warned and directed as though she were the sole object upon that mother's love was concentrated.[100]

While the dynastic role of the mother was important, it was the pleasures of motherhood – and especially the love that they felt for their children – that meant so many elite women were happy to perform the role.

With this affection came worry. By modern standards, there were high levels of infant mortality, even among elite families.[101] While such families were better able than most to provide a good diet and medical care for their children, that ability did not render the latter immune to illness. Smallpox was a particular concern; and while inoculation provided some peace of mind, parents and relatives were concerned when children were recovering from the effects of the procedure.[102] In order to ensure the health of their children, women took an active role in overseeing any advice and medication given to them if they fell ill. Fanny Boscawen was very conscientious about her children's health and about following doctors' orders. In 1755 this included taking an early-morning walk with her daughters. She noted that the doctor sent their youngest daughter 'every morning in the early dew that she might outgrow the difference there is between the two collar bones'.[103] Although elite parents were usually proactively concerned with the health of their children, this did not mean that they could always protect them from falling ill. While the Talbots were sufficiently wealthy that they could buy the best services from the Georgian medical market, two of their daughters died. The privilege of their wealth did not mean that they could have total success in avoiding parental grief.[104]

Mothers were not only concerned with the health and wellbeing of their children in relation to diseases, but also their long-term needs of care, education and discipline. There was plenty of advice regarding how to bring up children in the eighteenth century: from philosophical texts and medical treatises to children's literature, the care and management of infants were central concerns during this period.[105] There is evidence that many of the women in this survey read childcare manuals and guidance books for mothers. For example, just after the birth of her first daughter, Frances, Lady Irwin, ordered Sarah Pennington's *Unfortunate Mother's Advice to her Absent Daughters* (1761), a central part of the libraries of fashionable mothers in the sentimental age.[106] Some women delegated the care of their children, at least in part, to governesses, as they thought they could provide the moral and useful training that the increased focus on domesticity encouraged.[107]

Mary Talbot used Agnes Porter to educate her children. Agnes had fulfilled a mothering role after Mary's mother died.[108] This became a very close relationship: in the latter stages of her career, it was noted by Mary that Agnes received one hundred pounds a year 'and she always breakfasts, dines and sups with us and is our companion in the evening'.[109] When she retired in 1806, the Talbots gave Agnes a leaving present of 200 guineas.[110] As Agnes was so valued, Mary had high standards for her replacement. She wrote to a relative:

> I know you feel the great importance it is to have a proper governess to assist me in laying a good foundation of their youthful minds . . . I do not hesitate to request you to enquire far and near for a religious and well-educated woman . . . French and English grammatically, and the fundamental part of music, I think are very necessary accomplishments and to as many other acquirements as I can meet with in the same person I shall have no objection.[111]

When her plan to replace Agnes eventually failed, it caused Mary great consternation, although she was reminded by her sister that she was 'perfectly capable' of educating the children herself.[112] This reflects the fact that from the second half of the eighteenth century, didactic literature increasingly celebrated the role of the mother as educator, and it was an important way in which women could publicly use their intellectual skills for the good of their family.[113]

Academic education was not a mother's sole concern: she also needed to teach her children how to become members of the elite. Children's manners were very important, especially to those elite parents who were not titled, as the ability to perform the role of the diplomatic networker was crucial to those who wanted a successful political, military and/or professional career. Fanny Boscawen was keen to ensure that her husband knew she was doing a good job in this regard. She reported that she was pleased that two of their daughters were 'much improved both in persons, manners, speech, behaviour'.[114] She was very proud of their children, especially their eldest son, who she reported was taller and brighter than many of his peers.[115] During this period, it was not an uncommon concern for people to fear that sons may become 'too soft' if they spent too much time with their mothers – a particular worry for fathers who were frequently away from home.[116] Therefore, it is not surprising that Fanny was keen to tell Edward how their eldest son, Ned, was following in his father's footsteps; when at home from school, his holiday play was focused on flags, building castles and 'a battery of eight brass cannons mounted on wooden carriages'.[117] He played at being master of the house, too: when a colleague of the admiral's presented

Fanny with a black boy, clothed in the Boscawen livery 'most handsomely', Ned used him as his own page.[118] He was learning how to be like his father; and, like Edward, he was able to exploit the products of the empire for his own gain. Creating adults who would emulate the qualities of their parents was the ultimate aim of elite education, as it enabled the continuation of tradition. Therefore, with daughters and sons alike, mothers were central in training them to fulfil their elite duty.

As well as being a wife and mother, an elite woman also played a central role in running the household. In a continuation of ideas from the seventeenth century, Georgian didactic writings encouraged women to be active housewives, as a way of ensuring their virtue and the happiness of the family. It was still considered important for a wife to possess domestic qualities, even if, in practice, the amount of work she actually undertook was fairly limited. A successful union was often judged by whether it was a happy household. Thomas Robinson visited Saltram just a few months after his sister and John Parker had married. He commented: 'I do not recollect anywhere to have seen any gentleman live in better or more handsome style than our brother-in-law. The cheer is delicious, the table plentiful, the wines good and the servants attentive and numerous.'[119] However, while women were associated with being the mistress of the house, they needed to do this discreetly. Although domesticity was celebrated, elite values discouraged activities that could be described as work; the conspicuous consumption of leisure asserted the wealth and influence of the landed classes.[120] The fourth countess of Carlisle advised young women to 'Conceal, from the indifferent spectator, the secret springs which move, regulate and perfect the arrangement of your household.'[121] Elite women thus needed to be both visible and invisible mistresses.

Therefore, these 'secret springs' — the servants — were of central importance to the running of the country house. While some women were effective and active mistresses in their own right, as the household was often complicated in form, elite women could face problems in controlling all of their staff. In order to manage this, women would often use the senior staff to direct the other servants, and devolve to them the worries and problems of managing a large establishment. For Eleanor Butler and Sarah Ponsonby, this role fell to Mary Carryl. She was a maid from Ponsonby's Irish home, Woodstock House, who had been dismissed for wounding a fellow servant. By having her travel with them – and then stay with them – thanks to her 'masculine qualities' the Ladies had some protection in Llangollen, 'a village not remarkable for its sobriety'.[122] Mary was an effective gatekeeper for the many visitors, whose tips provided most of her income, and she was also a good cook; her salmon pie was especially commented on by guests.[123] It was not usual for housekeepers to cook: it was reflective of the small size of the Plas Newydd household that Carryl played such a central role in the kitchen. Admiral Boscawen suggested that the new housekeeper at Hatchlands would shy away from having to work in the kitchen and asked: 'Won't the hard service at first give her a disgust?'[124] Although he only heard about her through his wife's writing, he came to quite admire this housekeeper, and was sad when she left a few months later:

> I am very sorry your housekeeper thinks of leaving you. Your decayed gentlewomen seldom are good for anything, they want a place where there is nothing to be done. When I come home you will not much want a housekeeper, the fellow I have got is so handy and clever. But for what I know, some fly may sting him and he may leave me.[125]

Keeping good staff could be difficult.

While the housekeeper usually managed female members of staff, the Georgian elite mistress was often central to the hiring of new servants. In 1826, Sarah Ponsonby wrote a memorandum which set out the qualities she looked for in a Plas Newydd housemaid, earning a wage of six guineas a year:

> Perfect neatness in appearance and work – and simplicity of attire, and a good washer in the laborious part of brewing – a good sharpener of knives is most particularly requisite to our peace of mind – assisting the dairy maid in keeping the kitchen and all its utensils and furniture in perfect neatness – and making winter fires, in our library and eating parlour and at night in our bed-chamber, seems the heaviest parts of her requisite duty.

Above all, the Ladies sought a servant with 'good humoured willingness'.[126] This reflects the close proximity between the Ladies of Llangollen and their staff: the cottage was not big enough to avoid the servants. Therefore, for the house to feel like a home they needed to have good relations. In households, large and small, the relationship between servants and mistresses was one of interdependency, and the staff were significant social actors in the domestic life.[127] The elite family relied on servants to ensure the smooth running of the household, and dependable upper staff – whom the female head could leave in charge of the administration – were crucial in allowing her to pursue other activities, such as politics, leading building projects or educating her children. Therefore, there were concerns when things went wrong, and so staff could be easily fired. Thomas Talbot had to sack his butler at Penrice for drunkenness and for leaving things unpaid for in Swansea; and at Plas Newydd kitchen maids were fired quite regularly for impertinence, uncleanliness or for losing their virginity.[128] It is important to remember that the servants' actions would have reflected upon the elite woman's abilities as mistress of the house. In the mid-eighteenth century, for example, Frances, Viscountess Irwin, criticised the countess of Carlisle because her servants were badly behaved, and so she was considered to have a disordered household; the 'secret springs' that the countess later advised young elite women to hide were all too visible at her country house, Castle Howard.[129]

The social status of elite women, and the fact that their wealth enabled them to employ large numbers of staff, meant that it was not usually necessary for them to take on the labours of housework. However, increasingly the ideals of domesticity were considered to be signifiers of sensibility and femininity, and so it was important to perform the roles associated with the domestic woman. This included being the mistress of the household, an engaged mother and a loving wife. While these were ideals, many women took great joy from these activities; although some, such as Sarah Ponsonby and Eleanor Butler, had to shape their own narrative around these virtues, so that they could align with their distinctive way of life. Other women such as Mary Talbot were less happy at home, although she was both a caring mother and a keen gardener. Theresa Parker, Lady Irwin and Fanny Boscawen were able to combine their family lives with their roles in enhancing their houses and their elite networks, and they found great pleasure across all three spheres. These were all closely connected activities, and the family was central to the dynasty, as was the house and the connections that they built. However, the dynastic did not mean the loveless; it was often because of their affection for their families that the women were so keen to build the connections and properties that would enable their ongoing successes. This meant that country houses could be both centres of power and homes; and their mistresses were central to creating, connecting and caring for these properties and their families.

1 This portrait of Lady Alice Le Strange was one of a pair made by John E. Hoskins in 1617 of her and her husband, Sir Hamon.

2 Erected in c.1621, the Mildmay memorial monument depicts Sir Anthony and Lady Grace Mildmay lying together. For a woman who claimed, in her spiritual autobiography, to live a life of piety, it seems appropriate that she is now depicted perpetually in prayer.

3 The east wing of Apethorpe, Northamptonshire, was built in the 1620s for Sir Francis Fane, Grace Mildmay's son-in-law, on the request of James VI and I. Surviving masons' marks connect this property to master mason Thomas Thorpe, who also worked on Hunstanton Hall, Norfolk.

4 This portrait, attributed to Mytens, was reputedly painted when Maria Thynne was in the final stages of her pregnancy with her third son. Aged about thirty-four, she did not survive the birth in 1611.

5 Lady Brilliana Harley's defence of Brampton Bryan Castle was celebrated in the period immediately following her death in 1643, and has been the subject of numerous histories since.

6 The castle at Brampton Bryan was significantly damaged in the siege of 1643, and suffered further damage in 1644, when Prince Rupert reportedly commanded that the castle 'should be burnt and demolished'.

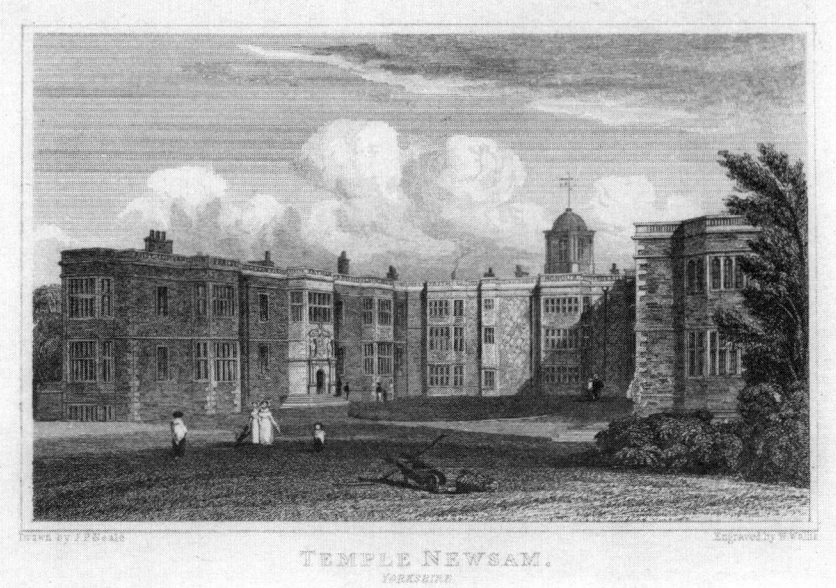

7 The south wing of Temple Newsam was rebuilt in the 1790s under the direction of Frances, Lady Irwin. This image dates from the period when her daughter, Isabella, Marchioness Hertford, was the owner of the property.

8 Frances brought a considerable fortune to Temple Newsam when she married Charles Ingram, later ninth Viscount Irwin, in 1758, roughly the date that this painting was completed.

9 The Robert Adam-designed ceiling in the drawing room of Hatchlands Park celebrated the naval successes of the property's owner, Admiral Boscawen, by including details such as Neptune flanked by pairs of Nereids.

10 The fine Georgian house at Saltram was shaped by two ladies of the house, Catherine Parker and her daughter-in-law, Theresa.

11 Sir Joshua Reynolds was a close friend of the Parker family, and wrote Theresa's obituary, which was published in the *Gentleman's Magazine*. This mezzotint was made following the exhibition of his portrait of Theresa at the Royal Academy in 1773.

12 Plas Newydd, home of the Ladies of Llangollen, is shown in this image with Castell Dinas Brân visible in the background. It was from that hilltop that Sarah Ponsonby and Eleanor Butler first admired the Vale of Llangollen when on a tour of North Wales in 1778.

13 This lithograph of a drawing of the Ladies of Llangollen shows them in their library, which they decorated in a neo-Gothic style.

14 This anonymous satire on the 1784 Westminster election campaign depicts Georgiana, fifth duchess of Devonshire, canvassing the electorate. The rumour that she kissed butchers in exchange for votes was so well circulated that it was alluded to in a pre-election meeting in Northamptonshire over a hundred years later.

15 Thomas Talbot commissioned the architect Anthony Keck to build a neoclassical house for him near Penrice Castle in the 1770s. It was at this property that he made his home with his wife Mary, and their children.

16 Although this image of Mary Elizabeth Lucy was based on one painted in 1850, when she was a widow who had lost three of her children, she is depicted as a young woman.

17 Charlecote was significantly restored and reshaped by George and Mary Elizabeth Lucy in the nineteenth century. This photograph was taken approximately eleven years after Mary Elizabeth Lucy's death.

18 This photograph shows Louisa, Lady Knightley with Helen, duchess of Albany at Fawsley Hall on 18 May 1905.

19 In the 1850s Pauline Trevelyan played a central role in reshaping the central hall of Wallington Hall. It features the work of numerous artists associated with the Pre-Raphaelite circle, including a sculpture by Thomas Woolner.

20 This is from the series of history paintings that William Bell Scott created for Wallington Hall. Pauline Trevelyan is included at the top right of the image; the child in her arms is her husband's niece.

21 This triple portrait by John Singer Sargent, of the Wyndham sisters (Lady Elcho, Mrs Adeane and Mrs Tennant), caused a sensation when it was displayed at the Royal Academy in 1900. On the wall behind them is a portrait by Watts of their mother, Madeline Wyndham.

22 A wedding gift to Hugo and Mary Elcho in 1884 from his father, Stanway House became the venue of many of the house parties of the Souls.

23 This photograph, taken in 1925 by Lady Ottoline Morrell, captures the long-standing and affectionate relationship between Arthur Balfour and Mary Elcho.

24 This photograph shows the homecoming to Kingston Lacy of Walter Ralph Bankes and Henrietta Jenny Fraser after their marriage in 1897.

25 This 1902 painting by Mary Gow shows Henrietta Bankes with her eldest daughter, Daphne. In contrast to this image, the memoirs of Daphne's sister, Viola, describe Henrietta as a distant mother.

26 The father of Frances Graham, later Horner, was a patron of Edward Coley Burne-Jones. Despite a significant age gap, Burne-Jones became very fond of Frances and he painted her on numerous occasions.

27 Formerly the main residence of the Horner family in Somerset, the house at Mells Park was gutted by fire in October 1917.

28 This memorial monument to Lieutenant Edward Horner was erected by his parents, Sir John (Jack) and Lady Frances Horner, in St Andrew's church, Mells.

29 After its purchase by Leeds Corporation in 1922, Temple Newsam was opened to visitors. This poster reflects the site's connection to the Knights Templar, and the ongoing fascination with medieval history among many members of the public.

Part Three

DEFERENCE, DESIGN AND DISTRESS, 1832–1918

The period from the start of the reign of Queen Victoria to the end of the First World War is one that has been subject to much scrutiny and revision. Although it was traditionally maligned as the age of serious, prudish, religious royalists, recent scholars have highlighted how it was an era of sexual freedom, of increased leisure activities, and of a rise in both atheism and republicanism.[1] However, some of the old epitaphs associated with the nineteenth century – especially the idea that it was an age of reform and innovation – do still hold true, with some important caveats. Within Britain, industrialisation, along with other factors, led to a growing population, increased urbanisation, and stronger and more visible class distinctions. Externally, the empire grew, which had an impact within the British Isles, as well as on international relations. It was a period peppered with warfare, which became increasingly global in scope. It was also a period of riots, rebellions and social discontent at home, although the major revolutions that were seen across continental Europe in the mid-nineteenth century did not fully develop within Britain. In short, it was an age of significant change.[2]

The elite classes were not immune to these changes. As in previous centuries, families with 'new money' from trade and industry began to move into the upper circles by buying land, building houses and demonstrating that they had sufficient pedigree to be seen as 'genteel'. However, the changing nature of the nation's finances meant that many of the emerging *nouveaux riches* were wealthier than those with 'old' money, and, in turn, numerous established families were drawn into commerce. This 'mutual assimilation' meant that both country life and London 'Society' welcomed more and more newcomers to the 'Upper Ten Thousand', although many of these continued to be perceived as outsiders by both the established families and cultural commentators.[3] Old power began to decline, too; while elite classes remained active within parliament, their influence slowly waned with the widening of the franchise, the introduction of the secret ballot and the Parliament Act of 1911, which significantly limited the power of the House of Lords.[4] The cultural world of elites was also subject to significant change, although many of the new artistic trends in the nineteenth century rediscovered, reframed or reimagined the 'old world'. The Gothic revival movement of the long nineteenth century celebrated medieval culture, and although Gothic novels quickly came to be associated with tales of wickedness, there was a strong association made between the arts of the Middle Ages – especially the architecture – and both Englishness and virtue.[5] The fast pace of change in the nineteenth century meant that some patrons wanted to cling to older certainties, which the medieval world provided; and so Gothic and Tudor revival architecture became a favoured style of many country-house designers in this period. Alongside this there was a growth in novels and art that used British history as a source, with many of the images and narratives drawing on the medieval and Tudor periods for inspiration.[6] The virtues of the medieval world were also explored in the art and literature of the Pre-Raphaelite Brotherhood, a group formed in 1848, which sought to explore and represent contemporary realities through art.[7] One way in which they – and other artists who became aligned to the group – tried to do this was through representations of classical and medieval worlds. In combining the old and the new, they moved away from the conservatism associated with the Gothic revival and instead used the past to drive their avant-garde projects.[8] This, too, can be seen in country houses, especially those built after 1870, when the Arts and Crafts movement and vernacular buildings increasingly influenced new architecture. However, as historian Adrian Tinniswood notes, the 'country house scene was eclectic' in the late Victorian age, with buildings influenced by Georgian, Italianate and French tastes all being designed.[9] As those living within houses became more diverse, so too did their taste, style and ideas.

The diverse, and sometimes contradictory, nature of nineteenth-century society and culture can also be seen in the gender ideals of the age. This period has been especially associated with the idea of the separate spheres, and the ideal of domesticity remained influential in mid-Victorian Britain. Rev. Charles Kingsley declared in 1855 that a woman's 'first duties [were] to her own family, her own servants'; and this was a view that could be seen in many didactic and fictional texts from the period.[10] However, these ideals were not confined to women. They were also used to critique the actions of men, and the importance of appropriate behaviour from husbands and fathers became the subject of public and legal debate.[11] Similarly, the public sphere was more complex than the separate spheres model suggests. While the 1832 'Great' Reform Act removed the vote from women, they were not consistently denied access to political spaces and conversations, and by the latter part of the century could hold local political office.[12] Women were also active in many other public activities, such as paid and charitable work, writing and medicine. However, they were not usually doing so on equal terms with men, and the increasing professionalisation of society often meant that formal positions were not open to women. For example, while Angelica Kauffman was one of two women who were founding members of the Royal Academy of Arts in 1768, the next female members were not elected until the 1920s.[13] There were significant legal gains for women, especially in relation to property rights and divorce; but it was not a period of gender equality, as the emergence of feminist movements throughout the century reflects.[14] While the idea of separate spheres may suggest a rigid degree of enclosure and liberation along gendered lines that did not exist in practice for most people, there were distinct gender ideals that shaped familial and public life.

How much did these contradictory forces shape the lives of elite women? This part examines the experiences of a variety of women who played active roles in both public and private life because, as we have already seen, these were expected activities for the mistresses of country houses. We continue with the story of the life of Mary Elizabeth Lucy and her role as mistress of Charlecote from 1823 to 1889. Mary Elizabeth worked with her husband to restore the house, as did Pauline, Lady Trevelyan (1816–1866), who had a significant impact on the interior design of her house at Wallington, Northumbria. The daughter of Rev. Dr George Bitton Jermyn, Pauline married Walter Trevelyan in 1835. Theirs was a union shaped around a shared interest in science, travel and art, especially the work of the Pre-Raphaelites.[15]

Another supporter of the work of the Pre-Raphaelites was Frances, Lady Horner (1854–1940), the daughter of William Graham, one of Edward Burne-Jones' main patrons. In 1883, Frances married John (Jack) Horner, whose family had been resident in Mells, Somerset, since the dissolution of the monasteries. In contrast, Frances was not from a traditional landed elite background; but her marriage and her friendships with leading social and political elites, many of whom feature in her autobiography, meant that she became part of the fashionable social world in the late Victorian and early Edwardian periods.[16] According to Ottoline Morrell, Frances was a woman who could 'manage society, friends, a family, garden and household with ease and success'.[17] This was especially important as the Horners were part of the informal aristocratic group known as the Souls. This group of friends included politicians, artists, writers and aristocrats, who shared artistic tastes and, often, lovers.[18]

Another member of this group was Lady Mary Elcho (1862–1937), later eleventh countess of Wemyss. The daughter of Percy and Madeline Wyndham, her marriage to Hugo Charteris, Lord Elcho, in 1883 was not a successful union, and they both had affairs. Her letters to Arthur Balfour, prime minister between 1902 and 1905, reveal their intimate relationship, as well as her love of her role as mistress of Stanway, the Elchos' country house in Gloucestershire.[19] Another unhappy marriage can be found at Kingston Lacy, Dorset, at the start of the twentieth century. Henrietta Fraser (1867–1953) married Walter Bankes in 1897. While their short marriage was generally discordant, she played the role of 'lady bountiful' very effectively – both during her marriage and as a widow, when she continued to be the mistress of the estate until her son came of age.[20] Another effective 'lady bountiful' was Louisa, Lady Knightley (1842–1913). Her childhood of royal duty (she was the daughter of a member of the royal household, Major-General Sir Edward Bowater) prepared her for a life of service. She not only served the royal family, but after her marriage to Sir Rainald Knightley in 1869 she became involved in politics and was an active member of many local, national and international charitable movements. She charted her activities in detailed journals – a great resource for scholars wanting to explore the continuities of feudal ideals in late Victorian England, especially at her marital home of Fawsley, Northamptonshire.[21]

All these women faced challenges to their ability to be successful mistresses. Economic changes meant that some had fewer resources than they needed to meet their ambitions for their houses and families. Some faced significant personal sorrow, either in the form of their own ill health or that of their loved ones. The death of children, whether from illness or as a result of war, shaped the emotional world of many women, and three of the women whose lives are explored here published lengthy dedications to their children. However, in spite of these difficulties and (in some cases) a less than happy domestic life, they all showed a real dedication to shaping their homes and their local communities, and to being the mistress of their country house.

CHAPTER 7

Beyond the Country House

Although country houses were supposed to be, in theory, places of retreat, in practice they were not islands. They were closely connected to local, national and international communities and economies. Landowners had a sense of responsibility to their tenants, even if it was only driven by a selfish desire to ensure that their land was as economically profitable as possible – especially during the nineteenth century, when the costs of running an estate took up an ever greater proportion of their rental income.[1] While there were absentee landlords, many took an active interest in the lives and living conditions of those who inhabited the communities neighbouring their country houses. A significant number of aristocrats were involved in national politics during the reign of Victoria, both as representatives in parliament and as members of the royal court, and some played an important role in national charitable movements. The seventh earl of Shaftesbury, for example, was active in a wide range of political and charitable activities, including the reform of housing, education and working conditions; his philanthropic works are commemorated by the Shaftesbury Memorial Fountain in London's Piccadilly Circus, popularly known as 'Eros'.[2] Elites also played an increasingly important role internationally. As the British empire grew in the nineteenth century, so too did the opportunities for aristocrats to take up political roles overseas, as well as to travel both along and beyond the traditional route of the Grand Tour.

These wider concerns were not left to the male head of the dynasty, or to younger sons who needed suitable employment. Women – as wives, daughters and sisters – were also active in the life of country houses outside the park walls. In many ways this reflected their dual duties: to their families and to their class. This meant that they had responsibilities not only as wives and daughters, but also as members of the governing classes.[3] Although there was a growing discourse during the nineteenth century that women should be excluded from public life, historians have found that many of them were able to challenge these ideas.[4] Elite women knew that wealth and class made the real difference in terms of access to public life, and so birth overrode gender, meaning that they were more freely able to enter the public sphere than their middling-sort counterparts, both within the countryside and in urban areas.[5] This chapter considers how women were mistresses of more than just their country houses. Many had an impact on their local communities, both through the improvement of the estates and as hostesses for community and charitable events. It then considers their political roles, both in the local constituencies and on the national stage, focusing especially on their engagement with political groups and the movement for female suffrage. The second part of the chapter considers the experiences – political and philanthropic – of aristocrats abroad, whether they were visiting for pleasure or in the service of the empire. Although traditionally seen as quintessentially British, country houses and their families were shaped by global ideas, goods and wealth.[6] These wider worlds – both the international stage and the communities just beyond the park walls – were very much part of elite life, and mistresses' sense of duty did not just remain 'at home', as there were opportunities and responsibilities beyond the Victorian country house.

Among the elite classes there was a strong sense that, in return for the privileges and power that they enjoyed, they had a degree of responsibility to 'rule, guide and help' their social inferiors.[7] This was nothing new, although during the age of political and economic revolutions in the late eighteenth and early nineteenth centuries paternalism came under a new level of scrutiny from those who wished to either critique or defend the aristocratic order.[8] One of the main responsibilities of a member of the elite was to the tenants who lived on the country-house estate. While traditionally estate management was seen as a wholly masculine activity, as we have already seen, women could be involved in the management of the properties and businesses that the family owned.[9] Elites often followed the model of landownership as stewardship, where they managed the land for future generations; and so, while they may have had ideals that were embedded in the past, most landowners had a strong sense of duty to preserve their estates, and their associated privileges, for the future.[10]

This stewardship was something that young elite women were aware could become part of their adult responsibilities. In a text that recalled her childhood in Suffolk, Louisa Bowater, later Lady Knightley, noted that in her youth she

> learnt to live the happiest life in the world, that of an English country gentlewoman, an excellent preparation for my future life in Northamptonshire. 'I think my beau-ideal,' I exclaimed . . . 'is to live in the country and manage my estate to perfection.'[11]

Therefore, following her marriage to Sir Rainald Knightley in 1869 it is no surprise that she was keen to improve the estate at Fawsley, her new Northamptonshire home. Louisa quickly realised how much work was needed to bring the estate cottages at Fawsley up to scratch. It was not unusual for the improvement of estate cottages to be led by the mistress of the household, and some were actively involved in the design of the buildings.[12] Louisa was excited by the project, reporting in her diary: 'imagine how much I felt in my element!'[13] However, she knew that cost would be a problem, and so was grateful when her mother offered to send her a manual on housing the poor. She wrote back, saying that she was always looking for hints, but her husband added a postscript to his wife's letter, half in jest, begging her not to bring the book on her next visit and complaining that 'Louisa's bother about Ames's cottage has cost me thirty pounds already. She and her cottage improvements are the plague of my life.'[14] However, the newly married couple soon learnt to understand each other's roles, and Louisa, in that spirit of *noblesse oblige* that she learnt as a teenager, began to undertake the obligations that came with upper-class privilege.

Similarly, in Dorset, Henrietta Bankes took a proactive role in improving the estate at Kingston Lacy. Henrietta married Walter Bankes in 1897 and quickly took up her role as lady of the manor. This became a long-term responsibility that she often fulfilled independently. Her husband did not share his wife's deep sense of duty, and when her son inherited Kingston Lacy he was only a toddler, so she continued to manage the site during his minority. Henrietta's daughter later reflected that 'building never stopped in the Bankes' villages' during her mother's long reign as mistress of Kingston.[15] This type of work often had multiple aims. While it may have been motivated by a desire to improve the inhabitants' living conditions, there was also a need to retain villagers, so that they could work on the landlord's estates; this was a period when there was growing migration to either urban areas or, in some parts of Britain, overseas. There was also a desire to create a more aesthetically pleasing estate, and there are many examples of estates being rebuilt so that they fulfilled new ideals of domestic architecture.[16] In 1899, Henrietta inaugurated the Kingston Lacy Cottage Garden competition to encourage estate workers to improve the cultivation and management of their gardens. It appears that Henrietta held the same high standards for her tenants' gardens as she did for those in her own home.[17] This may have been an innocuous desire to improve the living conditions for all on the estate, but, as historian John Archer has argued in relation to allotments, it may also have been a way to control the poorer tenants and reassert the ties of deference.[18]

As well as their formal role as landlords, some elites took a more charitable interest in their tenants and other inhabitants of the local communities. Many men and women focused on social and educational reform in the context of late-Victorian retrenchment and idealism.[19] For example, in 1870 Louisa Knightley installed a new schoolmistress at Badby and trained the parish choir; throughout her married life she injected energy and enthusiasm into the local social work, which she regarded as the essence of her role as mistress of Fawsley. Elite women's charitable works were often criticised; a common trope among those who questioned the power of the aristocracy was the stereotype of an elite woman as a social butterfly, who played the role of the charitable mistress of the estate for nothing more than mere diversion. However, many were serious about this role, and there was an expectation amongst the upper classes that women would act in a maternal capacity towards those who were dependent on the elite family for their income.[20] Some did this through supporting those who worked on the estates, whether as farm labourers or in local artisan trades. Lady Pauline Trevelyan, for example, championed the lace workers on the Trevelyans' Somerset estate, and she was one of many who helped to promote the local Honiton lace industry during the nineteenth century.[21]

Other support may have come in the form of personal visits to the households of the poor, finding employment for those in need and providing families with gifts. This active work had been part of elite women's expected duties since the medieval period, and during the nineteenth century it was encouraged by conduct writers. For example, *The English Matron* (1846) argued that nothing improves more 'the habits of the poor than superintendence'. The author added that it was the duty of 'the wife of a great landed proprietor' to establish 'a neighbourly and kindly feeling among the tenantry who are within her reach'.[22] This work was clearly important to Louisa Knightley, and she reflected on these duties in her diary in April 1873: 'May God bless and prosper all the works we have started, especially the systematic district visiting which has brought me in touch with all classes of people ... and gives me some real insight into the lives of Rainald's cottagers.'[23] While the distance between the country houses and the estate cottages may have been modest in terms of miles, in terms of life experience it was often very great indeed. Therefore, through these personal visits, women like Louisa could try to understand the needs of those living on the estates, and thus direct their philanthropic efforts accordingly.[24]

A common feature of country-house philanthropy was treating. In 1903, the Bankeses invited a hundred guests from the almshouses in Wimborne and the Union workhouse to enjoy tea and games on Kingston Lacy's lawn.[25] In many elite households, Christmas was a particular focus for charity. While the 'open house' hospitality of the medieval and Tudor period had long gone, a carefully managed form of philanthropy that did not intrude upon the family's private celebrations can be found in a number of country houses during the nineteenth century.[26] This can be seen in the reports in the *Western Gazette* about the Christmas season at Kingston Lacy in 1902, when Walter and Henrietta not only entertained their employees and their families, but also the inhabitants of the local almshouses and hospital.[27] Likewise at Fawsley, tenants of the Knightley villages were treated with 'bundles of calico, flannel and blankets' in 1869.[28] Julia Cartwright, who edited Louisa's journals in 1916, remarked on the ingrained feudalism of this district of Northamptonshire, noting that

> women and girls dropped low curtsies, men and boys touched their caps and pulled their forelocks at the sight of any of the quality ... doles ... were distributed in the great hall every Christmas ... But of the real existence of the poorer neighbours and dependants, of their habits and thoughts and ways of living, the inmates of the big house knew nothing.[29]

As the philanthropic activities of the household were designed to connect the family with the local community, they were usually shaped by the interests of the landlords, rather than the needs of the tenants. This type of charitable work enabled them to engage in an imagined re-creation of chivalric benevolence that both reaffirmed their status and justified the old order in a new and changing world. However, it did not mean that they necessarily understood the lives and needs of their tenants.

This is not to say that they ignored the requirements of the people on their estate. Tenants were seen to be part of the dynastic concerns of the country-house family, as well as crucial to its economic survival. It was a relationship shaped by duty and deference, reflected by the presumption that tenants would play an active role in the celebration of family events; by providing opportunities to engage with these events, social cohesion would be maintained.[30] As we saw in Chapter 6, the estate often celebrated the marriage of the head of the household. This was expected when the elite family's adult children got married, too. The description by Mary Elizabeth Lucy of her daughter's wedding in July 1847 shows how the local community was fully involved, offering gifts to the new couple, playing music alongside the road for the wedding party and decorating the church. Tenants were invited to a celebratory breakfast, and every cottager was treated to 'beef, plum pudding and good ale'.[31]

This type of celebratory activity was also seen in other events that included tenants during the nineteenth century. At Kingston Lacy, there were community celebrations following the birth of Henry John Ralph, the longed-for Bankes heir, in July 1902.[32] The *Western Gazette* reported the rejoicing at Corfe Castle:

> [T]he Custodian of the castle had flags flying and bunting displayed at the gateway . . . Cannon was fired at intervals while the bells rang merrily . . . That the young heir may grow up to be healthy, a pride to his parents and a blessing to his tenants and a God-fearing man, is the heartfelt wish of all in Corfe Castle.[33]

The birth of the first son had a long tradition of being especially celebrated by the family, due to the ongoing importance of primogeniture; but it is interesting to see how these events were marked by the wider community. In 1820, the christening of Rainald Knightley, who later married Louisa, was marked with a dinner for over 200 guests, most of whom were tenants, followed by dancing. The local vicar noted in a letter to his wife that 'the little boy was carried up and down . . . for the Tenants to see, and afterwards given to Papa and Mama, and then carried about again'.[34] The showing of the baby to the local community was an important step in starting the face-to-face contact that was vital to gaining and maintaining deference in rural communities in the nineteenth century.[35]

When elite young men came of age, there were also celebrations. These helped to cement the place of the eldest son as the heir, and thus ensure that the continuity of elite power was publicly marked.[36] The festivities for Ego Charteris, eldest son of Lord and Lady Elcho, in December 1905 included a party for 200 estate labourers and then, a few days later, one for the children, schoolmistress and mothers, featuring fireworks and meat pies.[37] These celebrations were shaped by tradition and had an emphasis on 'localism', which encouraged a degree of loyalty, but involved sufficient rituals that meant that the difference and distinction between the tenants and the landowners was emphasised.[38] The events worked as a way to share with the wider audience the performance of elite family life, and to embed ideals about deference that maintained the rural social order.

This sense of deference was especially notable following the death of a landowner.[39] Funerals were also usually major estate events, and the associated expenditure and display reflected an obligation to the deceased, but also the continuity of the dynasty.[40] They could therefore be lavish affairs. A description of the funeral of the fifth duchess of Rutland in 1825 sets out how 160 of the Rutlands' principal tenants led the procession, and notes that servants filled four of the seven coaches that followed the hearse.[41] While very large funerals became less common in the later nineteenth century, there was still an expectation that it would be a family and estate affair. In 1868, nearly 2,000 people filed past Lord Cardigan's coffin, for example.[42] Therefore, there was some ill ease in the Kingston Lacy household when it was discovered that Walter Bankes, husband of Henrietta, had a codicil to his will which directed that he should be cremated at Woking Crematorium, with a funeral service held simultaneously at Studland, in Dorset, and that his ashes were to be placed in the family vault at Wimborne Minster.[43] In the early twentieth century, cremation was unusual; the first legal cremation in England of the modern period had only taken place in 1885, and there were only 105 cremations in London in the first five years following the Cremation Act of 1902.[44] In making this request in 1903, Walter Bankes was rejecting the tradition for members of prestigious county families to be buried with pomp alongside their ancestors, and his choice reflected a wider shift away from the elaborate funerals of the high-Victorian period.[45]

As his widow, Henrietta followed her husband's instructions upon his death in November 1904. However, she refused to be deprived of the formality and grandeur of his public funeral, and so designed an event to enable the celebration of his life by the regional community. There was a procession from Kingston Lacy to the Minster; tenants from across his estates, Wimborne inhabitants, representatives of the county families, police officers and even coastguards from Studland attended this impressive event.[46] This encouraged a sense of continuity at a time of change, as tradition can be a real comfort in difficult circumstances. As Walter's uncle reflected in his diary: 'I think if people only realised how distasteful cremation is to the sorrowing relations, they would never leave in their wills the wish to be cremated ... [Henrietta] was horrified at the idea but we dared not set aside poor Walter's instruction.'[47] This example reflects how funerals were important for the living (as well as for the dead), and the fact that in her desire to assert the status of the Bankes family on behalf of her infant son, Henrietta was torn between her needs, her dynastic ambitions for her son and the final requests of her deceased husband. By combining her husband's private wishes with a public spectacle involving the local community, Henrietta was able to find a solution that balanced these different demands.

It was not just servants and tenants who were part of the social world of the country house. It was also important to have gatherings where genteel neighbours could be invited. The size and scale of weddings among elites varied greatly during the nineteenth century, with some wanting just smaller community affairs, while others enjoyed bigger celebrations that included a significant number of elite guests.[48] The wedding celebrations of Walter and Henrietta Bankes in 1897 are an excellent example of the latter. It was seen by the popular press as one of the 'fashionable' weddings of the summer, and the *Lady's Realm* magazine noted that Miss Fraser's 'was one of the white weddings which have been so much in vogue lately'. There were a considerable number of guests, with approximately 400 names listed in the various reports of the event, including Prince and Princess Henry of Pless, members of senior aristocratic families and representatives from nearly all of the Dorset titled families. As both the Bankes and the Fraser families were untitled, their ability to attract such a guest list reflects the more fluid nature of elite society in the late nineteenth century, as well as how an impressive event could attract impressive guests. However, as not all the local gentry were able to attend this London wedding, it was then followed up with a garden party at Dorset, after a traditional welcome from the tenants.[49] The *Sunday Times* reported on the event, noting that the party was 'we suppose to introduce Mrs Bankes to the county on her recent marriage'.[50] Forming connections to the local gentry was an important part of the networking of the elite woman, because being an established leader of the community – whether it was with tenants, neighbours or peers – was fundamental to being a successful mistress of the estate.

This networking could also sometimes include being the hostess for royal parties. This was another long-standing tradition, as one of the original functions of a country house was to provide accommodation and entertainment for royal travellers.[51] Although this declined in practice during the eighteenth century, royal visits continued, and even expanded, in the Victorian period, in part thanks to improved transport networks. By the late nineteenth century, the prince and princess of Wales were regular visitors at country-house parties, and these could sometimes be large affairs. For example, when they attended a week-long shooting party at Blenheim in the 1890s, there were over a hundred people in the house, thirty of whom were guests, and Consuelo, duchess of Marlborough, found it hard work to navigate the expectations of the royal guests regarding dress, service and conversation.[52]

The widowed Henrietta Bankes oversaw a number of royal visits to Kingston Lacy, including one by Edward VII in 1905 and another by the kaiser in 1907, both of whom came to see the art collection at the house.[53] These were major events for the Bankes family, and one of the daughters recalled that when the kaiser visited, 'we were all to have new clothes for the occasion and Daphne [her sister] and I were given huge white hats resplendent with curling white ostrich plumes'.[54] Louisa Knightley also hosted royal visits, but they were more informal in nature. From her youth, she had connections to the royal court, as her father, Major-General Sir Edward Bowater, had been an equerry to William IV; Queen Victoria arranged for the Bowater family to live in a cottage in Richmond Park.[55] In 1861, the Bowater family was asked by Prince Albert to escort his eight-year-old son, Prince Leopold, to Cannes for the winter, as it was believed that the warmer climate would be good for Leopold's health. During this trip Louisa's father died, and just a few hours after this loss they received news of the death of Prince Albert.[56] A bereaved Louisa was seen to have played a crucial role in supporting the young prince in his distress, and subsequently she was regularly invited to events at Buckingham Palace and other royal residences.[57] Although she was prevented from being a formal member of the royal household, as her father was not a member of the peerage, they found a place for her as an 'extra-lady-in-waiting' to Leopold's wife, Helen. Throughout her married life she remained in contact with the royal court; she and her husband were invited to many formal and informal royal family occasions, and two of the princesses supported the philanthropic work that Louisa undertook during her widowhood. Members of the royal household also visited her in Northamptonshire, and Louisa's last two visitors at Fawsley, in the weeks before her death, were members of the royal family.[58] These connections reflect how, although she was from a more modest background than some of the other elite women in this book, Louisa Knightley was able to have significant influence beyond Fawsley.

This influence was not just because of her royal connections. As we saw in Chapter 5, elite women could be active in a range of political roles; and Louisa Knightley was involved in many of the activities and societies associated with the Victorian political woman. While there were numerous changes to the political landscape in the nineteenth century, there were also some continuities in the position of elite families in Westminster politics. Although the Reform Act of 1832 did remove many of the pocket and nomination boroughs that were directly under the control of the landowners, it did not curtail the influence of elites within elections, where it was perceived to be 'legitimate and beneficial'.[59] This meant that elite engagement in campaigning continued; and while there was a growing 'masculinisation' of politics, women could still be active participants, canvassing for votes for their preferred candidates, hosting influential parties and using philanthropy as a way of encouraging the electorate to turn out and vote for their preferred cause.[60] Some women had considerable power; for example, in the mid-nineteenth century any Conservative wishing to stand for any of the county or borough seats in Durham sought the approval of Frances, third marchioness of Londonderry.[61] The political hostess remained an important figure into the early twentieth century. Writing in 1931, the countess of Warwick reminisced:

> They provided, in town or country, a rendezvous where men of all shades of opinion . . . might meet to discuss the affairs of the session

and the day . . . To be on their list for entertainment of any sort was to have a certain cachet. They exercised their power largely through their pull over their own sex. A man might start his political career with every intention of being independent . . . But if he proved too difficult, there were many ways of bringing him to heel, and the most effective was by cutting him off from the social centre! This might not matter to him, but it mattered terribly to his wife and daughters, who could be counted upon to bring domestic pressure to bear.

Hence the political hostess owed much of her influence to her hold on the wives of politicians, and the rest of it to her natural talents and capacity for diplomacy.[62]

High society continued to play a crucial role in shaping political networks through the late Victorian age, and wives of political figures were still expected to host parties, both in the London house and in the country house. Although they lost some of their influence following the return of the two-party model after 1868, when there was a shift away from political patronage being managed through social politics, they did not disappear completely; as in the eighteenth century, women continued to play the important role of 'confidante'.[63] However, while this role was often fulfilled by a spouse, the women who had influence with political men were not necessarily their wives. William Gladstone's wife disliked the hostess role, but his daughter was an effective political operator.[64] Other political men relied on friends, especially if they were unmarried: Frances Horner hosted dinners on behalf of Herbert Asquith in the early stages of his political career, before he married Frances's friend Margot.[65] Similarly, Arthur Balfour was able to climb to the position of prime minister in 1902 with the support of his friendship group, the Souls. This group of (largely) well-born friends consisted mainly of Conservatives, and included the Curzons, Frances Horner and, most notably, Mary, Lady Elcho.[66] Historian Nancy Ellenberger argues that the psychological support that Mary Elcho provided to Balfour was important in enabling him to reshape his reputation, and that his relationship with the famously beautiful Mary helped 'Arthur to confound the marginal status associated with a childless, celibate and potentially effeminate male'.[67] It was also beneficial to Mary: with Balfour's ear, she had access to the guest lists and to the seating plans of celebrated individuals at his dinner parties. As the confidante of the most powerful man in the country, her public role and reputation soared. Mary was invited to great houses of England that she had not visited for years. She wrote after a visit to Chatsworth in 1904: 'I appear to be having one of those odd and apparently causeless bouts of appreciation which some people have at intervals.' She added 'I do think that the discovery that I am a *well-informed* woman must greatly add to my assets'; it was because of her access to Balfour that others wanted Lady Elcho's company.[68]

While not as close to the top tables of power as Lady Elcho, Louisa Knightley also played the role of a political advisor. She was really a reformer at heart, and so Louisa was only won over to supporting the Conservative cause on a gradual basis, after her marriage. Rainald was MP for South Northamptonshire between 1852 and 1892, and while he was, in his own words, a 'staunch and consistent Conservative', he also prided himself on his independence, and was widely recognised as a leading backbencher.[69] Keeping his seat in the 1885 election was a challenge, though; he faced the introduction of the secret ballot, a widened electorate and new parliamentary boundaries. It was also an election that was increasingly shaped by national political issues, rather than local concerns.[70] Therefore, it was going to be an election where an effective campaign was important. However, as it was also the first contested election in his constituency since 1868, Rainald was lacking experience in this area, and the local radical newspaper, the *Northamptonshire Guardian*, declared: 'To the great bulk of his constituency his personality has been an enigma.'[71] Rainald therefore knew that he could not simply rely on the loyalty of his tenants to carry him to victory. He needed a fresh approach, and it was his wife who provided this. Although Louisa found canvassing 'a new and strange undertaking' at first, she campaigned energetically for him.[72] She personally canvassed all the villages in the region, engaging in what she called 'perpetual politics'.[73] For the market towns she took a different approach: she founded the Daventry Ladies' Committee to gain support from the wives of tradesmen for the Knightley cause, in the hope they would persuade others to vote Conservative.[74]

However, while she did have some successes, in other places she was aware that her husband's message was less well received; after one day's canvassing she noted in her diary that 'a good many say they should not vote at all and I hope they won't'.[75] While she had been involved in charitable work on their estate, she was shocked by the living conditions that her campaigning brought to her notice. After a trip to Towcester, she noted in her diary that she had spoken to 'some very radical shoe-makers in some horrid little Courts ... I should be a radical myself if I lived in such holes.'[76] Her activities attracted some censure: at a meeting on 19 October 1885, one of the members of the audience criticised Lady Knightley's electioneering and drew parallels between her work and that of the fifth duchess of Devonshire in the 1784 Westminster election. He asked Sir Rainald: 'How many butchers had Lady Knightley kissed, or how many does she intend to kiss?' This led to great uproar, and when some kind of order was restored, Sir Rainald reportedly spoke to his adversary directly, saying 'No man in Northamptonshire, until this evening, has been such a gross blackguard as to insult my wife.'[77] Lady Knightley, who was not present, remarked in her diary that this event would do the radical movement no favours. She was right: Conservative sympathisers reacted by turning out in significant numbers at subsequent meetings and reminded voters about this dreadful behaviour.[78] She grew in confidence, and so was disappointed when he only won the seat by a small margin. However, other observers were surprised that he had secured victory; one leading political hostess later told Louisa that 'Rainald was thought to be among the doomed ones' and others argued that he 'owed his seat' to Louisa's 'energy and ability'.[79] In South Northamptonshire, as with other county seats, the influence of the mistress of the estate was notable and was one of the many factors that limited the electoral successes of the Liberal party in the English counties in the late nineteenth century.[80]

Although Louisa Knightley was following the traditions of eighteenth-century women in her electioneering, she was also part of a new movement. During the mid-nineteenth century there had been a growing ill ease regarding 'lady politicians' among both the aristocratic classes and wider society. Some women who supported members of their family in elections were apologetic for their role as canvassers and explained that they were acting out of domestic duty, rather than desire for political influence. However, by the 1870s and 1880s there was a resurgence of women in political spheres.[81] There was a growing recognition that women could play an important role in supporting the political parties on a national level; this took those women beyond their role in just supporting family members.

Both the Liberals and the Conservatives created groups in the 1880s to include men and women from across the social classes in the work of the political parties. However, members of the elite, including women, soon took the leading role in these organisations. Founded in 1883, two years before the Women's Liberal Federation, the Conservatives' Primrose League was partly a response to the expansion of the franchise and was partly formed due to the passing of the Corrupt Practices Act of 1883, which meant that those seeking a vote had to employ different electioneering methods than had previously been used.[82] This led to a growth in the use of volunteers for canvassing; and from 1884, after they were allowed to join the League on the same terms as men, a growing number of women were involved. While women were excluded from joining the Conservative party, men and women, as 'knights' and 'dames', could work together in 'habitations', which were based within electoral divisions and so were well placed to respond to the demands of a candidate when an election was called.[83] Louisa Knightley, who was enrolled as a dame in May 1885, was sceptical at first, but she reflected: 'It sounds rubbish – but the objects . . . are excellent – and I can quite believe that the paraphernalia helps to keep Conservatives together.'[84] Louisa found the habitations very useful, and they played a central role in the successful election campaign for her husband in the South Northamptonshire constituency. She was behind the foundation of the Daventry (Knightley) Habitation in 1885, and in 1887 she was elected its dame president. Lady Knightley reflected on her political life, noting: '[T]he semi-public life I lead is good – and right – and womanly, and yet it seems as tho' I were called to it – both by the position and the powers of speaking and organizing God has given me and by Rainald's liking me to do it.'[85]

In addition to the local groups, there was a national Grand Council, with an associated Ladies' Grand Council that was largely a subservient group, and which, unlike its Liberal counterpart, did not develop a programme of its own. Lady Jersey remarked in 1890 that we 'ladies of the Primrose League are not in the least desirous of trenching on any department which does not belong to us; we don't wish to govern the country'.[86] It appears that the meetings of this group were, according to Louisa Knightley, ill-managed affairs; however, the habitations were useful to many candidates and the Primrose League was a success. Lady Randolph Churchill, whose husband played a central role in the formation of the League, later remarked that, in spite of the medieval flummery, it played a central role in the success of the Conservatives at the end of the century.[87]

These political groups offered fertile ground for discussions on one of the major debates of the Edwardian age: the expansion of the suffrage to include some women.[88] This was a political conversation too far for some elite women. Prominent political hostess and Primrose League member Lady Jersey was an active campaigner against female suffrage, and she chaired the anti-suffragists' executive committee in 1910.[89] Many, though, were agnostic on the issue, neither supporting the cause nor the anti-suffrage movement. As historian Pat Jalland notes: 'Many assumed that they already possessed more important indirect political influence than the vote could give them. They enjoyed the protection of class, wealth and privilege, which could be more powerful than consciousness of gender.'[90] Some elite women recognised this privilege. Edith, Lady Castlereagh wrote a letter to *The Times* in 1912 strongly advocating for working women to have the vote and noting: 'It is not "for the noblest women in England" as such, that the vote is really desired, except for the recognition of the principle, but it is chiefly wanted for her poorer sister.'[91]

Louisa Knightley was a firm advocate of women's suffrage and tried to challenge objections to it in a speech in Northampton in 1893. She said that 'people talk a great deal about it being unwomanly', but she believed there could be 'nothing in the slightest degree unwomanly ... in a drive or a walk to the polling booth once in four or five or six years'.[92] It was reported in the newspaper *Votes for Women* in 1908 that Louisa had been named as the first president of the Conservative and Unionist Women's Franchise Association. It noted that the 'new

Association intends to employ only educative and constitutional methods, and to try to convince, not to coerce'.[93] This reflects how, while there were many members of elite society who supported female suffrage, they mainly preferred the use of more subtle methods than those employed by the militant suffragettes.[94] Instead, they favoured the use of soft power, which, as elite women who had access to politicians, they had the privilege to enjoy.

This is not to say that women in general did not have some political influence in this period. Although they did not have the right to vote in parliamentary elections after 1832, they could get involved as both electors and candidates in local politics, and the role of women in politics became increasingly formalised from the 1880s onward. Many roles in local government were seen to be especially suited to women, as they could be regarded as an extension of female domestic skills beyond the private sphere. So, from the 1870s, women were gaining elected positions – at first on school boards and later on poor law boards, parish councils (from 1894) and borough and county councils (from 1907).[95] This included women from across the social sphere; however, because of their experience of working in local communities, many were from genteel backgrounds. It is therefore not surprising that Louisa Knightley should have become active in political affairs: she was the chair of the parish council of Badby, was co-opted onto Northamptonshire education committee in 1902, and served on its higher education committee from 1903 to 1913.[96] Others took the next step, and titled ladies were among the first women to take their seats in parliament following the passing of the Sex Disqualification (Removal) Act 1919.[97] The nineteenth century saw the formal exclusion of women from the election of MPs and a growing discomfort at their political activities, but then saw a remodelling of their involvement in political works – first as part of their domestic sphere, and then as something they could engage in as political actors in their own right. While for much of the century elite women may not have had the same degree of political power as was enjoyed by their eighteenth-century counterparts, increasingly they gained influence not just as representatives of aristocratic families, but as individuals.

However, formal political roles were not the only way in which elite women could become involved in national issues. Their charitable and philanthropic work could help them have an impact locally, nationally and internationally. While in the early nineteenth century moving beyond local feudal duties was unusual among elites, there was a growing number of upper-class women active in philanthropic work in urban centres or for national causes – whether it involved running charitable bazaars or more hands-on work, such as that undertaken by women such as Lady Henry Somerset, Lucy Cavendish and Caroline Talbot.[98] Increasingly, women became aware of how philanthropic work could give them status and influence distinct from the political world, where their position was often questioned and their activities were shaped by the demands of men.[99] They could frequently act in a leadership role within such philanthropic organisations, and many elite women were actively involved in committees, including Louisa Knightley. Before she took up her roles in local politics, she felt that she needed a project of her own into which she could inject her idealism and drive, as improving the Fawsley cottages and running her husband's election campaigns did not seem enough. She wanted to be a force for social and moral improvement, and the Girls' Friendly Society was just what she was looking for. Founded in 1874, the GFS aimed at protecting young girls' modesty by providing them with a religious education and training in domestic service, as well as a mentor in the form of an upper-class Anglican woman.[100] Louisa was inspired, and noted in her journal for 26 February 1876: 'I really think it is the thing which I have so long wanted.'[101] This was a charity that was as concerned about the morality of young women as it was about improving their opportunities; and when the local GFS held a picnic at Fawsley in June 1876, the address to the assembled members was on 'Purity'.[102] Louisa's leadership skills were quickly recognised, and she oversaw the organisation's Peterborough diocesan council for more than twenty-five years, only resigning in 1904. This was not her only charitable work: she was also active in the Working Ladies' Guild, which was established in 1876; she was one of the original committee members. As a widow, alongside her work in local politics she became active in the National Union of Women Workers, an organisation that drew its members from across the political spectrum, becoming its vice president in 1906. She was also involved in a group that was set up to prevent the exploitation of industrial workers, especially women, and was a regional president of the Society for Promoting the Return of Women as Poor Law Guardians. It is clear that she was a woman who liked to be involved, and a friend remembered that 'she often said laughingly that her vocation in life was to sit on committees'.[103] Lady Knightley was actively involved in these groups and had a significant impact on the work they did; she understood the possibilities for middle- and upper-class women to lead others to achieve a common social end, and she took those opportunities seriously.

The shared sense of responsibility that Louisa Knightley had was felt more widely during the First World War, when communities began to respond to the national crisis. There was a massive increase in charitable voluntary action, with nearly 18,000 new charities founded between 1914 and 1918. Pre-existing charities and groups – such as the Red Cross – also launched into action, and elite women were involved in organisations old and new.[104] One of the new groups was the War Refugees Committee, which encouraged people to house Belgians who had fled their homeland. The mistresses of country houses were in an ideal position to support this initiative. For example, Frances Horner housed the family of an Antwerp banker in the former home of the curate of Mells. Frances later recalled that, as the house had no indoor sanitation, 'I often think how uncomfortable they must have been, as the house they lived in was primitive in its equipment.'[105] Part of the reason for her embarrassment was that after the war, one of the Horner daughters was invited to stay at the Belgian family's home, and enjoyed a grand style of living in one of their several chateaux.[106]

Other elite women ran hospitals based at their country houses; over 250 of them were offered as convalescent homes during the Great War. The wife and daughter of the earl of Harewood both helped in the running of a convalescent home at Harewood House, Yorkshire; and Almina, countess of Carnarvon, ran a hospital first from Highclere Castle and later from a property in central London.[107] As providing medical care to those in need was a traditional duty of the mistress of the house, others were keen to follow these women's lead. However, although Mary Elcho wanted to do the same at Stanway, her husband discouraged her. Lady Elcho, now the countess of Wemyss, had to find other ways to be involved, such as offering her services to the hospital in nearby

Winchcombe, along with her daughter Cynthia.[108] She also played an important role in creating the first settlement of the Scottish Veterans' Garden City at Longniddry, part of her husband's Scottish estate. This organisation provided housing for disabled veterans, and Mary helped organise fundraising bazaars, one of which raised over £3,000.[109] She also co-founded the North Cotswold group of Women's Institutes after the war, thus providing important support to women in the difficult years immediately following the end of the conflict. At Mells, Frances Horner also supported the local Women's Institute; she reflected how, during the war, the Institute had provided opportunities for women of different ages to all work together, and how it meant that older women felt like they could contribute positively to their communities. She added that after the war 'I think the Women's Institute movement has come to meet this need for us, and that is why it has gone ahead with such grand strides and is becoming a force in English life.'[110]

These experiences during the First World War show how women's local and national charitable work could also sometimes have an international element. In the nineteenth century there were many connections between the local and the global. The so-called 'civilising mission' of the British empire attracted some elite women to get actively involved. There had long been a tradition of giving to charities that supported missionary work, and women often hosted events. The Society for the Propagation of the Gospel in Foreign Parts, for example, held an event in the grounds of Kingston Lacy, which focused especially on supporting clergymen working in Canada.[111] In the mid-nineteenth century many elite women, encouraged by Harriet, second duchess of Sutherland, were involved in calling for an end to slavery in the United States.[112] Other women became actively involved in the imperial philanthropic movement of the late Victorian and Edwardian periods.[113] Unsurprisingly, this included Louisa Knightley, whose charitable work moved from the local to the national and the international, following the pattern of some of the charitable organisations she was involved in, especially the GFS. That organisation became increasingly interested in women's emigration, and Louisa played a key role in this work. In 1901, she wrote an article entitled 'The Empire and the GFS' for *Girl's Quarterly*, where she argued:

If the British race is to further the Kingdom of God throughout the vast dominions over which our beloved Queen bears sway, it must be by having a high standard themselves, and living up to it. And who, but the women of that race, are to raise the standard?[114]

Louisa was an active member of various emigration and colonisation organisations, and in 1903 she became the first president of the South African Colonisation Society and edited its official publication, *Imperial Colonist*.[115] In August 1905, Louisa travelled to address the annual conference of the British Association in Cape Town on 'The Terms and Conditions of Domestic Service in England and South Africa'. She then undertook a demanding tour of the region, taking in some of the Boer War battle sites, a war cemetery at Pretoria and the Victoria Falls. This 'journey of a lifetime' by the sixty-three-year-old Louisa was, as she declared in the *Daventry Express* when she came home, 'a truly wonderful experience' – although in her diary, she anxiously reflected on the realities of empire, especially in regard to race relations.[116] As she found when undertaking visits in Northamptonshire, both as mistress of the manor and as a canvasser for her husband, seeing the realities of the lives that she was attempting to 'improve' could make her feel that her actions were inadequate. The gap between charitable endeavour and lived experience was sometimes very great indeed.

It was not just through philanthropic works that the elites were involved with the wider world. Some members of the British elite had empire childhoods: Henrietta Bankes, the daughter of a merchant in the spice trade, was born in Sourabaya, Java in 1867; her father had met her Dutch mother there on his travels.[117] Global trade was an important facet of the income of many of the nouveau riche families who became part of elite society in the nineteenth century. Frances Horner's father and grandfather ran a company that imported goods from India and Portugal; and as a younger man, her father William Graham had spent time in Bombay and Lisbon.[118] Others worked in the empire. Some aristocratic men were reluctant to take up jobs abroad, as they felt they had more attractive propositions than 'imperial exile'.[119] They could also be risky roles: one of the brothers of Lord Hugo Elcho died from a fever on his way home from the African Gold Coast in 1873.[120] These risks meant that, for much of the nineteenth century, imperial opportunities were usually only taken up by younger children in gentry families, who recognised that they might be able to live a genteel lifestyle overseas on a more modest income than would be required in Britain.[121] These included roles in India, such as in the East India Company or the military.[122] For example, Mary Elizabeth Lucy's daughter, Carry, married Captain Pawlett Lane, whose regiment was involved in responding to the Indian uprisings of the 1850s. He remained a member of the military and in 1860 they left for India, leaving their infant son at Charlecote. While in India, Carry suffered several serious illnesses and had a stillborn child.[123] She also faced the challenges of managing a household at Murree, a Punjabi hill station; she was relatively young and was without her network of relatives and friends to guide her in how to manage servants – who, to her, were quite different from those she had encountered in Warwickshire. She wrote to her mother:

> Since I have been here I have been almost helpless from weakness. You know, dearest Mamma, in general I do not want much waiting upon, but I am glad to say I have an Ayah who is always at my 'beck and call' and never keeps me waiting a moment . . .
>
> I am obliged to be very strict with all our Indian servants, they require so much looking after or one's household would never be kept in nice order. Pawlett gives me great credit for my management. I keep the accounts, pay the servants' wages, and he manages the stable department. We have a very good cook and we have two cows and I see to the milking and churn the butter in bottles. I attend to my garden and poultry.[124]

It would seem that the Pawlett Lanes created their own version of English pastoralism in Punjab, and Carry was keen to be seen to be performing the ideals of the country-house mistress, even though she was many miles from home.

They did not just take the country-house way of life to the empire, but also took elements of the empire back to the country house. This was not just through letters like the one above, but also through objects: during the nineteenth century, empire goods were a central feature of elite consumption patterns.[125] Pawlett Lane bought his wife a 'beetle wing' dress while they were in India; although these were made in Europe, including by the House of Worth, this form of decoration can be traced to Mughul India.[126] This dress was remarked on for its beauty when she wore it in England, reflecting how it was able to be both exotic and acceptable.[127] He also brought items back for the Lucys. On his first visit home after the marriage, Pawlett Lane, now a major, brought back as a gift for his mother-in-law five pearls that were part of the 'loot taken at Lucknow', which Mary Elizabeth had set into a ring. From this 'loot' Pawlett Lane also gave his brother-in-law an eighteenth-century dress sword that had belonged to the king of Lucknow, which was placed on show in Charlecote.[128] Items seized from Lucknow in 1857 also became part of the collections at Wallington in the late nineteenth century, after it was inherited by Charles Edward Trevelyan, who worked as a senior Indian civil servant.[129] The wider world was a key provider of *objets d'art* and the raw materials for luxury goods that adorned many elite homes in the Victorian period – as well as, in some cases, the plentiful funds to build new properties.[130]

For politically active families, empire and its complexities were also part of their world in the late nineteenth century. Mary Elcho, Frances Horner and their friends in the Souls had a number of direct connections to global politics. Collectively, they not only believed in the imperial cause, but a number of the male members of the group held positions directly involved with its work, such as colonial secretary, secretary of state for India and secretary for Ireland.[131] In particular, Arthur Balfour had to directly tackle the changing nature of the empire during his time as prime minister and, later, as foreign secretary, especially the status of British dominions and Britain's interests in the Middle East.[132] Mary's son Ego went to Washington in 1908 as an honorary attaché to the British ambassador to the United States; in his letters home he shared with his mother confidential details of forthcoming treaties, showing again how family links meant that women could be part of political circles.[133] Some of the female members of the Souls were also directly active in global politics. Many of them were part of the Victoria League, one of the numerous patriotic and imperial organisations active in the early twentieth century.[134]

Leading Souls member George Nathaniel Curzon was viceroy of India (1899–1905) and, as was the case with most diplomatic spouses, his wife Mary was more than a mere 'decorative appendage' as the vicereine. She knew that it was important to be a success – not just for her husband, but also for the 'greater good of the Raj'; in August 1898, *The Sketch* reported that, as vicereine, she was 'the most important woman socially in a country of two hundred and ninety million people'. As well as being an effective hostess – despite (insensitively) describing the 'constant entertaining' as 'slavery' – she was also an effective politician.[135] Being in India meant that George Curzon was sometimes forgotten in the political circles of London, and so when his wife returned to Britain without him, she played the role of his emissary, in presenting to the royal court and members of the Palace of Westminster the work of her husband. She was well informed about Indian and imperial politics and was shocked at the level of ignorance among the British political elite. She also sent advice to her husband about people he should write to if they had ideas or concerns that needed correcting or if they could be used to his advantage. This meant she could advise him on the next steps of his political career; many of his circle saw him as the next foreign secretary or even a future prime minister. Mary Curzon was described by another elite woman as 'the most helpful wife a public man ever had, and a most wonderful ambassador'; after her early death in 1906, her husband withdrew from public life for nearly a decade, reflecting how important she had been to him politically and personally.[136]

It was not just those who were actively involved in diplomatic activities or charitable works who travelled overseas: there was a long tradition of this among the elite classes. The Grand Tour of the eighteenth century had its roots in the travel writing of men like Richard Lassels, whose *The Voyage of Italy* (1670) set out the ideals for a 'grand tour' of France and the 'giro of Italy' that could benefit young men socially, intellectually, ethically and politically. In the course of the eighteenth century, more places were added to the itinerary, including Prussia and the Alps; and especially after the Napoleonic wars growing numbers of men and women of all ages travelled to Europe. Although those who were going on these trips were more diverse than the traditional ideal suggested, many of them were keen to benefit from the 'improving' qualities of travel that shape the original discourse.[137] It was this idea that encouraged the Lucy family of Charlecote to take a continental tour in 1841. This was no small undertaking, as the party was made up of a tutor, a courier, a nurse maid, the footman and six children; although one of these, Edmund, was still a babe in arms, George decided the trip would be educational for the whole family.[138] Mary Elizabeth Lucy's journal of the trip shows how difficult travel could be with a young family: on one occasion they were fourteen hours at sea on a steam packet just to get to Boulogne. But the greatest calamity occurred following a perilous journey in deep snow over the Mont-Cenis pass, when Mary Elizabeth's baby died in her arms. She was deeply distressed by this death and the 'wretched' night, when she held the body for '*eleven* long hours', as they continued their journey to Turin.[139] They could not go back to Charlecote, since it was occupied in their absence by paying tenants; and so they arranged, with the help of the British ambassador, to send the child's body back home without them, so that he could be buried with his brother, who had died before the family embarked on their travels.[140]

The grieving family eventually made it to Rome. But initially they were rather discomfited: although one of the main drivers behind the trip had been to view the city's celebrated art, an embarrassed Mary Lucy found herself hurrying her daughters 'past statues of naked gods that their native innocence might not be impaired'.[141] However, they soon settled into life in Rome. They delighted in the treasures of the Vatican, enjoyed visiting the studios of artists and became so well established that they were regular guests of Prince Torlonia and were formally presented to the pope.[142] However, they faced further difficulties on their return journey: Mary Elizabeth was pregnant, and while she was keen to reach Paris for her confinement, they did not get there in time, as she was taken ill at Nancy, where her sixth son was born on 24 August 1842. As both she and the baby were unwell, they spent five weeks at the hotel in Nancy, before heading to Paris for further recuperation. Therefore, the family did not arrive back at Charlecote until May 1843. With a death and a birth on a single trip to Europe, Mary Elizabeth had really experienced the complexities of travel in full.[143]

The travel experience of the Lucys was one where their domestic life, and all its difficulties, went with them. But for others, travel provided opportunities for people to become – temporarily – someone else, and to experience culture and life differently from how they were able to at home. Many English homosexual men travelled overseas to avoid prosecution, and some were forced into exile. In the late eighteenth century, William Beckford of Fonthill used European travel as a way of avoiding scandalous rumours regarding his sexuality; and William Bankes, who owned Kingston Lacy, was exiled to Europe following his arrest for 'attempting to commit an unnatural offence' in June 1833.[144]

It could also be used as a way of escaping domestic issues at home. Mary Elcho's visit to Egypt was, in many ways, prompted by her husband's public affair with the duchess of Leinster. She was invited there by Wilfrid Scawen Blunt, who, as an anti-imperialist, held views that were different from those promoted by most members of her social circle.[145] As they were cousins, Wilfrid knew Mary well; he had spent some of his childhood holidays with her and the wider Wyndham family, and she had been one of the bridesmaids at his wedding in 1869. In 1893, Lady Elcho told Blunt how much she admired his life in Egypt and confessed her desire to take her children there; the Blunts had founded the Crabbet Arabian Stud, and he had bought an estate near Cairo, spoke Arabic and wore Arab dress. A known womaniser who had recently had an affair with Mary's mother, Madeline Wyndham, Blunt seems to have been keen to get Mary to Egypt; El Keysheh, a new pink house that Blunt built at Sheykh Obeyd, was designed in anticipation of her visit.[146] He achieved his aim, and in 1895 she went, taking three of her children, a governess and a maid with her.

Blunt's account of the affair is interesting, as it is clear how, at least in his eyes, she became transformed during her time with him. He left her Arab clothes to wear, and when he saw her dressed in them, he claimed, in his diary, that he burst into his song of Solomon: 'She is the ideal for which I have all my life been waiting . . . an oriental woman whose life it is to be kissed and kiss.'[147] Wilfrid was clearly in love with her. He wrote of how he 'was happy before she came but this is more than seventh heaven', and recorded that after ten days 'my extremest hopes were fulfilled'.[148] In the next days, Mary, his 'fairy queen', wandered through the gardens with him; she listened to his poetry and to the Arab boy playing on his rebab. During one of their expeditions, they camped each night in a different wadi, Wilfrid under his carpet-shelter, a little apart from the main camp, where Mary came to him. He wrote: 'I think the Arabs with us knew that we were lovers – indeed they must have known it, for there were Mary's naked tell-tale footsteps each morning in the sand . . . Mary is now my true Bedouin wife.'[149]

Wilfrid and Mary were shaken out of this orientalist fantasy when her husband, who had been with his dying mistress in France, came to Egypt to see his wife and children, as he was concerned that they may have become the subject of public gossip.[150] The difference between Wilfrid (who was committed to the Egyptian way of life) and Hugo (who was not, and who went fishing 'after the fashion of English men') led to conflict between the two men. Wilfrid noted:

> When I came out this morning before sunrise to the tent, I found his Christian hat in it where he had left it yesterday, and it moved me to anger. I feel that she has brought a stranger into my tent, she who was my Bedouin wife, and that when I get her once more into the desert, I shall cut off her head.[151]

The fantasy seems to have died completely when the Elcho family and Blunt visited the Cairo museum dressed in European clothes.[152] However, the fact that Mary was pregnant meant that it could not just be a holiday affair that was simple to forget. As with many others, Lady Elcho's activities beyond the country house had an impact when she returned home.

While early modern didactic writers advised women that they should 'keep house', by the end of the nineteenth century this advice was largely being ignored, and some elite women had a considerable impact beyond their domestic sphere. They could be mistresses of their estate, not just in an extension of their household management roles, but in charitable and political activities that shaped the lives of their tenants, too. These activities were, in some cases, on a national scale, and women like Louisa Knightley were active participants both in organised philanthropy and in shaping discussions about the status of women in domestic, economic and political roles. They were also engaged with the wider world, sometimes taking their whole family with them (as we saw with Mary Elizabeth Lucy) or encouraging other people to settle overseas. The wider world also came to them and their country houses, in the form of tenants and guests, such as those who attended the Bankeses' elaborate wedding celebrations, or the lasting problems of holiday romances, as we will see with the study of the Elchos' marriage in Chapter 9. These connections with the wider world also had an impact on the views that people held, whether on politics, the rights of certain groups, or art and literature. This meant that elite women could be the mistresses of ideas and culture, as we will see in the next chapter.

CHAPTER 8

The Artistic House

> It was interesting for me, coming up to town and plunging into all the best that London had to give – art, politics and society – and then going back to Mells, was like taking a deep bath into the country, remote, old-world, feudal, with all the charm that lack of wealth can give a place, and all the beauty of the west in its woods and meadows.
>
> Frances Horner, *Time Remembered* (1933)[1]

Frances Horner's comments reflect the idea of the country house as a place of retreat – somewhere to return to from the politics and noise of the city. As we have seen, elite women did spend a great deal of time not 'at home', but in charitable work, forming connections, electioneering and travelling. The idea of returning home – a place of comfort which could provide the relaxation of a 'deep bath in the country' – must have been appealing, especially as an alternative to the increasingly industrial Victorian London. However, the idea that a country house was a place without art, politics and society is misleading. It could also be the centre of election campaigns, as Fawsley was for the Knightleys; or the location for large parties. Crucially, country houses were also places where the artistic movements of the nineteenth century could find a space to be discovered, displayed and debated.

Women played an important role in these debates. They were often well informed about art and culture through their formal and informal education; and some, such as Frances Horner, were at the heart of fashionable artistic circles. They could use their ideas and knowledge to reshape their homes, and in this chapter we draw on the examples of the Lucys at Charlecote and the Trevelyans at Wallington to see how couples could work co-operatively in reshaping their houses. While some families were drawn to older objects, others were engaged with new art; because of the ways in which history was being used as a tool for legitimisation or for reaching a 'truth', some elites were especially attracted to these ideas and cultural outputs. This meant that some women became patrons of the work of artists, such as the Pre-Raphaelites, and the influence of this group – and of John Ruskin – on Wallington is also examined. The chapter looks, too, at the group known as the Souls and shows how they were connected to artistic worlds; it highlights how these networks not only helped to make the Souls' homes artistic in a material form, but also how arts and culture shaped the parties that were hosted by women such as Frances Horner and Mary Elcho. Overall, this chapter shows that while the country house could be a place that was quite distinct from an urban home, it was not necessarily remote. Indeed, it could be closely connected to the artistic works and cultures of the Victorian period, and women could be both mistress of the house and of the arts.

The importance of understanding art and culture to being a successful member of the elite classes is reflected in the formal and informal education of young women. Many were educated at home – at first alongside their brothers, and then separately, often by a governess. For example, Percy and Madeline Wyndham adopted a traditional governess regime for Mary, their eldest daughter (later Lady Elcho).[2] While some governesses worked their charges hard, more liberal parents may have requested a more benign approach. As an adult, Frances Horner reflected:

> I was brought up in the rather limited way, as regards education and liberty, that distinguished the early Victorian era, yet we were considered advanced for the time. We had governesses at home . . . and a great deal was done for our pleasure and well-being . . . money was not much considered . . . the discipline such as it was, was very loving, and more concerned with the spirit than the mind or body.[3]

It was not necessarily a sign of emotional or academic neglect to educate daughters at home, and in some cases a great deal of money might be invested in their education. This could involve hiring an army of specialist tutors: dancing, drawing and music masters might be employed, along with language specialists, in order to complement the governess's skills. For the young Frances, this included mathematics and Latin tutors, paid for by her father: he was keen to indulge his children's wishes, and the intellectually curious Frances wanted a more classical education than that offered by her German governess. However, even with more liberally minded parents, a girl's education was often shaped around preparing her for life as a wife, mother and chatelaine.[4]

This could include developing an understanding of the arts, which was usually through informal learning, as an elite girl's education was not limited to the schoolroom. It could take the form of sociable reading, educational visits and even some leisure activities, many of which were central to developing the children's interest in culture. Madeline Wyndham often took her children into the Lake District to draw and to paint, and she was a talented decorative artist in her own right.[5] She read Arthurian tales aloud to them and had miniature suits of armour made for the boys, thus introducing them to the medievalism that was such an important feature of the aesthetics of the mid- and late nineteenth century.[6] The Wyndhams were closely connected to these artistic worlds. Madeline took the lead when it came to buying contemporary art from painters like James McNeill Whistler; and as a couple the Wyndhams commissioned George Aitchison, the decorator of choice for avant-garde patrons, to redecorate their London town house. The Wyndhams were also close friends with Lord Frederic Leighton; meanwhile young Mary came to know the Burne-Jones family very well and spent a great deal of time with the artist's children when growing up.[7]

Similarly, Frances Horner's father was a patron of modern painting and, when the family moved to London, he regularly took her to artists' studios. Dante Gabriel Rossetti much impressed her, as did the married Sir Edward Burne-Jones, twenty years her senior. He in turn was fascinated by her Pre-Raphaelite looks and thought her an ideal model for him. For a while she became his muse and she appeared in a number of his paintings, including *The Golden Stairs* (1880).[8] She greatly admired him, and later reflected that when Burne-Jones became her friend he 'poured into my lucky lap the treasures of one of the most wonderful minds that ever was created'.[9] There was clearly an emotional connection, too: he was devastated when Frances got engaged, and she burnt all his letters to her on the eve of her wedding. She was also a gifted artist in her own right, and Frances's embroidery was exhibited at the fourth Arts and Crafts exhibition at the New Gallery, London, in 1893.[10] Women did not just admire art; they could inspire and create it, too.

It is therefore no surprise that when these young women became brides they were often interested in the form, shape and condition of the country houses that they moved into. These buildings combined their interests in domesticity, dynastic duty and aesthetics, which had been at the heart of their education, and so many of them had clear ideas about their ideal home. Following their marriage in 1835, Pauline and Walter Trevelyan had difficulty in finding a home of their own. Walter's father was still alive, but was estranged from his wife, meaning that they lived in separate properties for much of the year. Thus the choice of family properties for the new couple to live in was limited, and they had to live with relatives. Pauline found life with the Trevelyans difficult; although her mother was from a genteel background, her father, a vicar in east Cambridgeshire, was not wealthy, and so some of her new in-laws regarded her as a bit of an interloper. Despite this, when Walter's father offered them a house near him in Devon, they turned it down as it did not suit their aesthetic ideals, being a 'placid ugly brick house'. Although it enjoyed views out to the sea, the sea was deemed to be 'not worth looking at'.[11] Instead, they went to live in Edinburgh, playing a part in the intellectual circles of the urban elite, as well as spending a great deal of time travelling. In 1850, following the death of Walter's father, they were able to move into a Trevelyan country house at Wallington, Northumbria. It was this property that they turned into their ideal home.

Other women found that the country houses of their husband did not suit their own tastes. When the newly married Frances Horner first went to her husband's home, Mells Park, in 1883, she found a house that was a home not only to Jack, but also to his mother and his sisters.

It was also a property – and a family – that was stuck in a different age, and a great many of the rooms in the fine Georgian house were unfurnished.[12] The Horners lived primarily in the library, morning room and drawing room, but in the rest of the house there were very few curtains or carpets. Instead, Frances recalled how the house was stuffed full of things: 'immense collections of minerals in all the drawers, stuffed birds and stuffed animals on all the tables and shelves; collections of seaweed, bird's eggs and dried fish filled every corner'. Frances found this 'all very surprising', especially the fact that there were no pictures except family portraits; her distressed father kept saying he must send her some more up-to-date works of art.[13] At Mells, Jack's sister had 'kept house' for him, and she, like the rest of the family, was much more interested in the scientific than the artistic. As this was very different from the surroundings in which she had grown up, it took Frances some time to realise that she was moving into a much-loved family home. However, it needed updating. Later, when her widowed mother moved into Mells Park, it meant that some of her father's art, and finances, came with her. This enabled Frances to slowly turn the cold house, full of Victoriana, into an informal and modern house, using the model that the Wyndhams had employed at Clouds.[14]

As Clouds was regarded as one of the ideal country houses of the late Victorian period, Mary Wyndham, when she became Lady Elcho, had high expectations of her marital home. The main seat of the earl of Wemyss, her father-in-law, was at Gosford, outside Edinburgh. When she first saw it in 1883, during development works when large new wings were being added, Mary hated it. She came to describe Gosford as 'a large and gilded, dead and empty cage'; this was kinder than the description given by the architect Sir Edwin Lutyens, who likened it to a rendition of 'God Save the King', sung flat.[15] Gosford represented everything Mary did not want her married life to be. She was therefore relieved to find that her new husband's family had more than one country house, and that Stanway, Gloucestershire, was quite different. Built of golden Cotswold stone in the sixteenth and seventeenth centuries, Stanway's romantic charm captured Mary Elcho straight away; she fell in love with her husband's home in a way that she was never quite able to do with the man himself.[16] 'A sort of heavenly feeling comes over one and laps one about', she wrote, after their first visit to the property in July 1884.[17] She was therefore delighted when the house was given to the couple as a wedding present by the earl of Wemyss, even though its interior had been much neglected. That meant, however, that it had escaped, in the words of a family friend, 'Victorian uglification'.[18] Mary later reflected that 'Stanway probably suffered less through neglect than it would have, had it been continuously lived in during that dangerous period when old-fashioned things were despised and swept away.' The Elchos rearranged the internal layout of the house, and swapped the servants' hall for a dining room, and the dining room for a library, which became her husband Hugo's favoured space, as it was 'a cosy comfortable room with easy chairs'.[19] This emphasis on comfort was an important feature of the country house in the Victorian age, and the desire to make a house a warm and welcoming place shaped many of the improvements to the properties during this period.

It is important to remember that both the husband and the wife may have had concerns about their home; we should not think that bachelors were happy to live in uncomfortable houses and that they needed wives to improve them. As we saw in the eighteenth century, some men updated their houses in advance of getting married. Rainald Knightley thought he could not get married because of the state of Fawsley Hall: he believed 'if he took his wife to live there it would certainly break her heart'.[20] So, in 1866 he engaged the architect Anthony Salvin to start a large-scale rebuilding project. At a cost of over £13,000, Salvin provided a new range of ground-floor public rooms, as well as bedrooms and attic servants' quarters, remodelling the north range and great hall in the Tudor revival style.[21] It was to this house that he brought his new bride, Louisa, in 1869.

However, for others, getting married provided both the motivation and the income to enable much-needed repairs to take place. George Lucy had been planning the restoration of Charlecote for some time, but much of the work really only took place after he married Mary Elizabeth. At first, she was entranced by Charlecote; it was a fine Tudor property, and as she had grown up in a castle, it reflected her love of older buildings. She commented that the writer Washington Irving, who visited in 1820, had been correct in noting that the 'old hall did indeed look ... "as it might have done in Shakespeare's time".[22] However, she found the house very cold and, on her return following her sister's wedding, she realised just how shabby Charlecote was and how modern her sister's new home, Compton Verney, looked in comparison. The Tudor brickwork at Charlecote had been damaged in places by a stucco wash applied in the eighteenth century, and there was an urgent need for better plumbing, as the whole household was reliant on two earth closets that were situated in the turrets at either end of the property. As the house was in poor repair, it seemed an ideal time not only to rescue it, but actually to reshape it to fulfil the neo-Gothic ideals of the period. One of the leading proponents of medievalism, Walter Scott, had visited Charlecote and described it as 'the abode of ease and opulence'; he seems to have encouraged George to think that he could turn Charlecote into a property on a par with Scott's celebrated home, Abbotsford.[23] The Lucys wanted to adapt the property so that it would be suitable for modern life, but they also wished to keep intact the spirit of the older building. This led them to add a new kitchen, servants' hall, library and dining room, while the hall was updated, enabling them to mix the old with the new. However, it was not an easy project. The Lucys moved out to one of the cottages, sending their children to their grandparents at Bodelwyddan, and they seem to have taken a direct role in overseeing the subcontractors who fulfilled different elements of the project. Even when the work was completed, the updates were not wholly successful: the winter of 1844–1845 was a dreadful one, and despite the fires in every room, the newly built wing was never really warm.[24] However, the house was modernised and improved, and by working together on forming their house and home, Mary Elizabeth and her husband became a close and loving couple.

Alongside updating the main structure of the house, there was often a need to improve the gardens and parkland. When a house was uninhabited or not managed closely for an extended period of time, the gardens were often the first thing to fall into decline. When she first arrived at Charlecote, Mary Elizabeth found nettles growing waist high in the wilderness that Capability Brown had planted with Scots pine in the previous century. She disliked the large beds with shrubs and 'old fashioned' flowers, so 'caused my husband to let me root them all up'.[25]

Within five years, by the time their third child was born, the undergrowth was gone and the flowers whose planting she had supervised now carpeted the ground. It did not all go to plan, as she was frustrated that she was not able to grow lilies, despite her husband's best efforts: he brought back pulverised seashells from his constituency in Cornwall to try and encourage them. It is clear that Mary Elizabeth Lucy knew what she wanted, and had managed her own little garden as a child, but nature does not always heed a gardener's desires.[26] She was not unusual in her enthusiasm; as we have already seen, some women were actively involved in garden design during the eighteenth century, and it remained a space where they were able to take an active role in shaping the estate. While professional horticulture continued to be dominated by men, there were growing numbers of women who were writing about gardening; Jane Loudon, for example, published *Instructions in Gardening for Ladies* (1840) and *The Lady's Country Companion or How to Enjoy a Country Life Rationally* (1845). Some female garden designers, such as Gertrude Jekyll, became very influential; a relation of Frances Horner, she worked closely with architects such as Edwin Lutyens and provided detailed planting schemes for new country houses at the turn of the twentieth century.[27] Elite women were also happy to take on the challenge of improving their gardens. At Wallington, Pauline Trevelyan embellished the walled flower garden with a series of seventeenth-century Dutch lead figures, although her husband later had some melted down, as he deemed them to be indecent.[28] She seems to have enjoyed some hands-on gardening, too; when the artist William Bell Scott first visited Wallington he was greeted by 'a little woman as light as a feather and as quick as a kitten, habited for gardening in a broad straw hat and gauntlet gloves, with a basket on her arm, visibly the mistress of the place'.[29]

Others were a bit less enthusiastic about gardening. Frances noted in her memoir that the house at Mells Park

> stood high and on rock. Indeed, it was on a spur of Mendip, and so it was not easy to make a garden; but the natural beauty and the way in which the ground had been laid out, almost compensated one. It was a true illustration of the saying, that the English landowners of

the eighteenth century ruined themselves by making lakes, and their descendants ruined themselves by trying to clear them from weeds.[30]

As well as having to deal with a difficult landscape, the Horners also only had a modest income, and so they concentrated on developing the arboreal collection. For Jack, the focus was on conifers: like his father, he valued them as specimen plants. However, Frances favoured deciduous trees, and so they compromised, and she was able to preserve the beech avenue and plant a great number of thorns, whose blossom she especially enjoyed.[31] After they moved to the smaller Mells Manor following the death of Frances's mother in 1900, the gardens became a central location of their day-to-day life and their entertaining. Guests like Ottoline Morrell remembered how the house had a 'lovely medieval garden', and Frances recalled how they enjoyed a 'constant garden life' in the summers in the Manor, although she was quick to credit the beauty of the gardens to a friend, who lent her good taste and knowledge to their design.[32]

Other women focused their time in the garden on enjoyment, overseeing work rather than getting physically involved in making changes to the outdoor spaces. The gardens at Kingston Lacy had been well managed throughout the latter part of the nineteenth century, and so when Henrietta Bankes first arrived at the property, she did not need to make substantial changes. However, over time, she added some summer houses so that she could sit and enjoy the gardens. She did show herself to be the mistress of the gardens on a few occasions, most notably when she curtailed her head gardener's love of chrysanthemums by insisting that they had *only* 200 pots of the flower.[33] For her the gardens were part of the prestige of the house, and a place where they could welcome guests as diverse as Edward VII and members of the Wimborne District Gardeners' Association. Although she did little of the work directly, the reputation of the gardens at Kingston Lacy was probably the reason why she was regularly invited to open a number of the local horticultural society's annual shows; the servants' work was seen as the labour of the mistress of the house.[34]

While there was an emphasis on updating the house and gardens, there was still a desire to preserve the historical elements of a property, as it was one of the things that legitimised the family dynasty. There was a real interest in the 'old' in the Victorian age, especially in relation to the interiors. As with previous generations, there was a desire to collect old masters to adorn the walls of the houses: the Lucys' 'grand tour' was, in part, motivated by George's desire to collect art, so that he could gaze, as his forebears had done, on pictures from Florence and Rome.[35] Given his straitened financial circumstances, George had to think of cost-effective ways to purchase the type of goods he wanted for Charlecote. One way was to purchase items second hand, including from the sale of goods from William Beckford's Fonthill Abbey in 1823: George bought over 1,500 lots of furniture and *objets d'art*, and while he spent over £3,000, all items (bar three) cost him less than £100 each.[36] Because Charlecote had such close connections to the Tudor period – especially through the tale that William Shakespeare had reputedly been caught poaching in the grounds – the items from Fonthill, a neo-Gothic masterpiece, reflected the Lucys' taste.[37] While he made some excellent purchases at the auction, this was not always the case. George bought items that the dealer claimed had been given to Elizabeth I and had been housed in nearby Kenilworth Castle, whereas in reality they had been made in India between 1690 and 1710. These included some chairs, which needed new embroidery that Mary Elizabeth Lucy provided. Because Elizabeth I had briefly visited Charlecote in 1572, this needlework included the addition of the monogram ER to the design, thus emphasising the erroneous connection of the objects to the monarchy.[38]

While some historic items were bought, others were rescued and restored; the Lucys used the language of 're-edifying' Charlecote to reflect their desire to make it a comfortable family home, but one that was still decorated in appropriately historical fashion.[39] Likewise, although Mary Elizabeth oversaw the rebuilding of Charlecote church, she ensured that family monuments were wrapped up securely when the old church was pulled down.[40] Mary Elizabeth, despite having married into the family, understood and tended faithfully to the Lucy family's heritage, and she wrote a history of the family as a gift for her son in 1862.[41] Similarly, when she was widowed she resisted family pressure to leave the house: 'No I will not let or leave Charlecote even if I have to live upon a crust,' she declared, 'nor shall any of the paintings or furniture be sold.'[42] She continued to update the house in her widowhood, refurbishing the drawing room in the 1850s in a style that followed the work that she and her husband had undertaken together in previous decades.[43] She recognised that the house and its objects were carriers of the family's memories and their dynastic status, and keeping them together brought her comfort in her grief. It also helped to make the house a home; as American novelist Nathaniel Hawthorne noted, following a visit to Charlecote in the 1850s:

> All about the house, and the park, however, there is a perfection of comfort and domestic taste, and an amplitude of convenience, which must have taken ages, and the thoughts of successive generations, intent upon adding all possible household charm to the house which they loved, to produce. It is only so that real homes can be produced; one man's life is not enough for it.[44]

This interest in the past also shaped the work that the Trevelyans undertook at Wallington in the 1850s. In the early years of their marriage, the Trevelyans established themselves in the literary and intellectual circles of Edinburgh, and it was at this time that Pauline developed the networks that led her later to become a patron of Pre-Raphaelite artists. She first met John Ruskin in 1843 and they became close friends. She much admired his first book, *Modern Painters I* (1843), and her enthusiasm for it might explain his boast that 'the happiness of her own life was certainly increased by my books and by me'.[45] They wrote regularly to one another, and in their letters they often discussed art and architecture. We can see their shared taste in their respective travels overseas: the Trevelyans sought out the Gothic as well as the classical, just as Ruskin had done when he visited Venice. For example, it is notable how Pauline preferred the Gothic beauty of St Mark's basilica in Venice to the Palladianism of Santa Maria della Salute.[46] Ruskin's influence can be seen in the redesigned central hall at Wallington that the Trevelyans oversaw in the 1850s. This was a central courtyard that they roofed over to create a combined living and exhibition space. In it, one of the roundels is a bust of Pauline, with the text 'Pauline Lady

Trevelyan 1816–1866. She enclosed & decorated this hall on the advice of John Ruskin.'[47] Pauline and Walter did not slavishly follow that advice, though: as Lucy West argues convincingly, the Trevelyans had their own sense of taste; and while Ruskin's ideas were influential in shaping that taste, they led the project.[48] Concepts from the Gothic revival, from the work of the Pre-Raphaelites and from Italian design all came together to shape their ideas for the hall. They hired the Newcastle architect John Dobson, known for his neoclassical work, and they planned that the hall would be turned into a salon with arcades, pillars and a gallery. Pauline always envisaged that the pillars, spandrels and upper spandrels would be painted, featuring bulrushes, foxgloves, oaks and elms, following the focus on the natural that was a feature of designs created by Pre-Raphaelite artists.[49] The Trevelyans wanted to turn the hall into a showpiece of Pre-Raphaelite art and design, featuring eight large canvases that charted the history of Northumberland. To this end, Pauline made contact with the artist William Bell Scott, a close friend and confidant of Dante Gabriel Rossetti; Bell Scott had been appointed head of the Government School of Design in Newcastle in 1842.[50] In 1852 she had published comments on a couple of his paintings in a review she wrote for *The Scotsman*. She found 'a certain fire and poetic feeling . . . in spite of the mistaken system on which they are painted. The want of models and close study is glaringly apparent.'[51] Despite her own concerns about his abilities, which were shared by Ruskin and Rossetti, Pauline invited Bell Scott to Wallington.[52]

From Pauline's diary it seems clear that she took to Bell Scott at once, and she invited him for a return visit to discuss her great scheme for the decoration of the central hall. Together they developed plans, which Bell Scott sent to Ruskin, who in turn sent his brief endorsement of the scheme on to Pauline.[53] William Bell Scott painted the canvases at his studio in Newcastle; they were then exhibited at the rooms of Newcastle's Literary and Philosophical Society and the French Gallery on Pall Mall, London, prior to being hung at Wallington. This meant that they had a wider audience before they became part of a private collection, thus reflecting the Trevelyans' commitment to the public benefits of culture – a key feature of Ruskin's civic-minded principles of Gothic art.[54] The canvases told the stories of individuals such as Bede and Grace Darling, as well as general stories of Northumbrian history, from the building of Hadrian's Wall through to a depiction of modern Tyneside's industry. Although Bell Scott worked on these away from the house, Pauline's diary entries show that during the period from 1853 to 1861 she was focused on this great scheme of painting.[55] It was also an effort that was shaped around collaboration; paying heed to Pauline's earlier criticism of his work, and reflecting the Pre-Raphaelite commitment to drawing from life, Bell Scott used the Trevelyans' family, neighbours and staff as models. The hermit Cuthbert was based on a local clergyman; Walter Trevelyan appeared in *Bernard Gilpin* (1859); and in the *Descent of the Danes* (1858), Pauline herself appeared as a model, one of a group of terrified Britons in flight; at her feet is her dog Peter and the child in her arms is Walter's niece.[56] Similarly, the work in the hall was a shared endeavour. In the summer of 1856 Pauline and Bell Scott worked together painting flowers on the spandrels. They invited other artists from her Pre-Raphaelite network to paint pillars when they came to stay. This sense of a shared endeavour meant that the interior of Wallington was the result of 'healthy and ennobling labour', and so was in line with Ruskin's arguments against mass production and the 'dehumanisation' of the worker.[57] Therefore, it is of note that although Ruskin did work on the space, according to family tradition, he lost his patience when there was some confusion over whether he was painting corn-cockles or cornflowers, and refused to finish his work.[58] This was not the only moment of disharmony; Walter was never as enthusiastic about Bell Scott as Pauline was, either as a person or as an artist. Her biographer, John Batchelor, notes that 'courteous disagreement about Bell Scott's work characterised much that Pauline and Walter said to him and to each other over the years'. For example, Walter did not like Bell Scott's conceit of masks in the lower tier of the spandrels and instead persuaded him to paint medallion portraits of famous Northumbrians, from Hadrian through to George Stephenson. The central hall attracted plenty of opinions, but according to Batchelor it was a place where 'Pauline tended to get her own way'.[59]

Although the Trevelyans and Bell Scott did not always agree, it was important to them that they should support the north-east's proud record of artistic achievement. Dobson and Bell Scott were both local men; the Trevelyans employed local craftsmen; and they included illustrations of native plant and animal life in their decorative scheme. In displaying the region's history and the endeavours of local people in the series of paintings, Pauline Trevelyan was demonstrating her love of the region, and her strong sense of duty to her home. Although relatively new to the county, she recognised her paternalistic duty and used the arts and crafts of Northumberland to celebrate its history. However, the Trevelyans' artistic patronage was not just confined to the north-east of England. They were major patrons of the Oxford Museum (today the home of the Oxford University Museum of Natural History). Not only did they make monetary donations, but Walter also sent specimens to be included in the collection and Pauline designed a capital for one of the columns.[60] Ruskin was also involved in this project, and he encouraged Pre-Raphaelite artists to submit designs for the interior.[61] It was from this connection that Pauline identified artists to work on Wallington, which was being developed at the same time as the museum; she also commissioned one of the architects to design her a house at Seaton, Devon, another part of the Trevelyan estate.[62]

One artist the Trevelyans identified through their connections to Oxford was Thomas Woolner, another member of the Pre-Raphaelite network. They commissioned him to create a sculpture of a young mother teaching her son to pray. Pauline's title for this sculpture, *Civilisation*, reflects the idea of humankind's progress – a theme reflected in a great deal of the art that was housed in the hall.[63] As the artist noted, he chose a mother rather than a father, as 'the position of women in society always marks the degree to which the civilisation of the nation has reached'.[64] It was also fitting that a space whose design had been so driven by a woman had an idealised female at the heart of it. Unfortunately, Pauline did not live to see it completed; her health had been very poor for many years, and she died in 1866. Woolner wrote to Sir Walter about his sadness that 'the lady I most wanted to admire it cannot now give the high honour of her applause; and my proudest hope is that it may henceforth be pleasantly associated in your mind with her most precious memory'.[65] Wallington was very much her place, and the central hall her design.

Therefore, it is fitting that at Wallington Pauline encouraged the work of a number of female artists, just at the point where the role of women in art was the subject of national debate. Pauline had been involved in fundraising for the Female School of Art (founded in 1842), and encouraged a number of women, including Emilia Francis Strong, later Lady Dilke, to contribute to the decorative scheme at Wallington.[66] As the editor of her letters, who was also the Trevelyans' librarian, later reflected,

> She was singularly unselfish, and earnestly desired to be a power for good to all with whom she might be associated. Her quick discernment enabled her easily to discover latent power in her friends, and she knew well how to give it direction, and cause it to bear fruit.[67]

Pauline celebrated the work of female writers, too, such as Elizabeth Barrett Browning. However, although she was friendly with Christina Rossetti, she did not seem that interested in her poetry; apparently it did not stand comparison with the work of Algernon Swinburne, whom she greatly encouraged in his poetical endeavours.[68] She was also interested in supporting artists to develop their skill as photographers. Her husband was a childhood friend of Henry Fox Talbot, and she was given her first camera in 1845.[69] Pauline Trevelyan was not a traditional country-house mistress: one guest thought the house uncomfortable and concluded that she was little concerned with household management. Instead, she was more interested in the guests, their ideas, and in helping them to develop their skills and networks so that they could succeed.[70] In doing so, she was able to create a genuinely artistic house through the work that was collectively produced in and for Wallington.

The example of Wallington shows how important friendship circles were in shaping patronage networks. Another band of friends known for their connections to the arts were the Souls. As a group they were known for their shared love of literature and art; and while they were often perceived as being too absorbed with one another and their emotions, the nature of their friendships embodied the ideals of late nineteenth-century aestheticism.[71] They had many artists in their friendship network. As a young woman, Frances Horner had acted as hostess when artists visited her father at home (since her mother was not very interested), and she was the one who arranged the loans of the family's art to various museums and galleries. Even after her marriage, she was very close to Burne-Jones, and it was primarily through this connection that Frances was invited to Souls events.[72] Therefore, it was fitting that when Laura Lyttelton, one of the Souls, died in childbirth in April 1886, it was to Burne-Jones that they turned in order to commemorate their much-loved friend. Frances Horner commissioned a memorial to be placed in St Andrew's church in Mells; Burne-Jones made a second version, which he kept at his home; and he sent a sketch of the monument to Mary Elcho, whom he had also known since she was a child.[73] Even those members of the Souls who did not have familial or personal links to the Pre-Raphaelites became patrons. For example, Arthur Balfour commissioned Burne-Jones to produce a series of pictures for his drawing room at 4 Carlton Gardens. This work was never finished, though, and Balfour had to content himself with Burne-Jones' studies for the Briar Rose series, which hung in 10 Downing Street during Balfour's time as prime minister.[74]

Beyond the Pre-Raphaelite network, other artists were part of the circle of the Souls. Portrait painter John Singer Sargent stayed at Mells Park in 1896. Frances Horner told Burne-Jones: 'I liked Mr Sargent, he was very nice & not the least like an American & he wasn't very like an artist either!'[75] Sargent agreed to paint her children – news that upset Burne-Jones: he thought Frances's daughter Cicely 'was made to fulfil a dream of mine'.[76] Horner may have been introduced to Sargent through Mary Elcho, who first got to know the artist when he spent some time at Broadway, a village in the Cotswolds, near Stanway. Mary visited him in 1886 when he moved to London, and so when her father paid Sargent £2,000 in 1898 to paint Mary and her two sisters, she and the artist had a well-established connection.[77] The *Wyndham Sisters* portrait was completed the following year; and when it was shown at the Royal Academy in 1900, the prince of Wales renamed it the *Three Graces*.[78] The painting was a success with the critics, too. *The Times* newspaper enthused 'this is the greatest picture which has appeared for many years on the walls of the Royal Academy'.[79] This gave Sargent access to the network of the Souls, many of whom became important patrons, while some became friends; Lady Elcho's brother-in-law, Evan Charteris, was Sargent's biographer.[80]

Similarly, it was through his connections to the Souls that the architect Sir Edwin Lutyens made many of his contacts that led to important commissions. He had helped the Horners with improving their London house in 1895, and with alterations to Mells Manor in 1902, after the Horners moved there from Mells Park to save money.[81] Frances Horner was a great admirer of his work; but aware that she could not afford to hire him for very big jobs, she helped him find commissions. These included the Royal Pavilion for the Paris Exposition (1900) and, over thirty years later, the job of redesigning Campion Hall, Oxford.[82] He also received commissions from a number of the members of the Souls, including Gerald Balfour and Alfred Lyttelton; and George Nathaniel Curzon was on the committee that employed Lutyens to design the Cenotaph, Whitehall, for Armistice Day in 1919.[83]

This shows how the Souls had considerable social influence in relation to their championing of the arts, leading the countess of Warwick to admit that 'they sent us all back to reading more than we otherwise should have done'.[84] The Souls were not only well read, but were also immortalised in some texts: Arthur Balfour was said to have inspired the character of Evesham in H.G. Wells' *The New Machiavelli* (1911) and Stanway may have provided inspiration for one of the houses in Edith Wharton's novel *The Buccaneers* (1938).[85] The Souls did not just inspire authors from afar; they were part of their circle: both Wharton and H.G. Wells were regular guests at Stanway. However, the Souls was not just a network that inspired and supported artists and writers; increasingly, they lived those ideals as well. Some of the main Souls, like Wilfrid Blunt and Margot Asquith, were writers of fiction, while others, like Mary Elcho and Frances Horner, wrote their own memoirs.[86] Frances Horner was a gifted artist, an effective patron and, as her friend Margot Tennant commented, 'a leader in what was called the high-art, William Morris School and one of the few girls who ever had a salon in London'.[87] The Souls were confident in setting their own taste, dressing differently and engaging with the ideas and culture of elite society.

This was most clear in the parties that they held. Weekend gatherings were an important way in which they interacted. Of course, country-house weekends were not confined to the Souls, and they became a central part of elite society in the Edwardian age. They often had a functionalist purpose, enabling the networks of power to be maintained, whether they were for forming political, social or marital alliances.[88] However, those that were run by hostesses who were part of the Souls seem to have been more relaxed and personal than many other gatherings in the late nineteenth century. Frances Horner reflected on how the atmosphere of the Souls was liberating. She noted that the preference for mixed company, and the demeanour appropriate to it, broke down traditional male reserve about topics of conversation.[89] This helped to avoid the 'vapidity' that was common in other parties, and instead their conversations ranged from literature and art to politics and science.[90] Frances was a spirited conversationalist, not afraid to hold bold positions; following a party at Wilton House, the home of the Pembrokes, Betty Balfour described a discussion she had led on which of the traditional virtues should be eliminated:

> Truth was done for, as a virtue which no moral being attempted to practise. Hope was declared a tiresome, weak-minded thing. Faith followed as a gift you either possessed without effort or were wrong to cultivate. Charity was left grudgingly. Mrs Horner wanted to do away with Justice but, Lord Pembroke clung to it.[91]

Other hostesses also encouraged inclusive conversations and pursuits. Mary Elcho liked to create a group *esprit* among her guests by encouraging activities that were less hierarchical and male-dominated than those that were commonly a feature of parties in the mid-Victorian age.[92] This was at the heart of her first party for 'the Gang' at Stanway in the winter of 1884. Laura Tennant wrote about the visit, noting that 'it's such fun here . . . we talk to the top of our bent . . . we play games and the piano – we none of us open a book or write a letter – we scribble and scrawl and invent words and reasonless rhymes'.[93] What was distinctive about this event was that it was dominated by young adults who enjoyed mixing with no household rules, and so the conversation was freer.[94] This became a feature of many of the gatherings of these friends, and it was what came to define them as a group. According to Mary Elcho, it was at one of these parties that the group got its nickname. Lord Charles Beresford, a Royal Navy commander, was reported to have said during one of the Elcho parties 'Oh, I can't talk to you people, you are all Soul.'[95]

This combination of conversation and freedom was usually cultivated by the mistress of the house. While she may have first been invited into the Souls' circles because of her connections to Burne-Jones, Frances Horner was soon seen as much more than just a muse.[96] Visiting Mells in 1892, Emily Lytton found Frances 'a perfect hostess, so kind, so natural, so amusing and altogether delightful', while the children were 'very precocious and already play intellectual games'.[97] However, organising a relaxed party could mean a great deal of work. Lady Cynthia Asquith, daughter of Lady Elcho, set out the challenges of being a perpetual hostess:

> [I]t is a fallacy to suppose that any woman who ran a large and hospitable country house ever had a *light* job. The simplicity of pre-war domestic life has been greatly exaggerated. True, the well-to-do hostess did not need to do any actual housework herself, for servants were easy to find . . . But being human, however efficient and obliging, they always tended to quarrel with one another, so that domestic politics were often inflamed and very preoccupying.
>
> And what a vast amount of organisation keeping 'open house' involved! . . . The plan of the bedrooms would be pored over until some way of packing fourteen guests into ten square rooms was devised.[98]

Stanway was ill designed for so many guests, and Mary often fretted about being a hostess. This led to her being regularly teased by her children for her 'furniture manias', when the servants trundled pieces to and fro about the house under her direction.[99] She joked about this to Arthur Balfour: 'When a man's tired he rests, when Mary Elcho or a woman's tired she moves furniture.'[100] However, she was very capable of creating the ideal aesthetic space. She enjoyed lively conversations; her broad knowledge and her ability to be impartial meant that she was gifted in encouraging the spark of a topic that could turn into a full debate among friends. She was welcoming of all, which led to some criticising her for taking her 'unsnobbishness' too far.[101] She was also excellent at hosting and devising games; her daughter remembered how H.G. Wells 'revelled with boyish glee in any kind of game indoors or out-of-doors, skilled or unskilled and games always played a very large part in Stanway life'.[102] Later, Mary Elcho reflected that her sitting room had been.

> the scene of all sorts of amusing talks and readings aloud with innumerable friends, who cheerfully ignored the icy blasts that pierced the leaded panes; there they have sat laughing round the fire, warming themselves too with argument and wit ... My sitting-room is so steeped in memories that it is almost impossible to sit in it alone.[103]

Although her friends were known for their wit, they were, in her words,

> not poseurs, they were real and very much alive, keen and strenuous in work and play, 'not idle singers of an empty day', just a group of intimate friends who lived and loved long ago.[104]

What Mary created at Stanway, as Pauline Trevelyan did at Wallington, was a place where ideas could be shared. Although at Stanway the arts were more literary and performative than at Wallington, it was every bit as much an artistic house. Beatrice Webb thought that Mary Elcho acted as an effective bridge between aristocrats and the bourgeoisie, and between artists and bureaucrats.[105] She did find it all-consuming. Mary's daughter later reflected that 'Mamma never seemed to have her own house to herself, or to be able to enjoy the immediate present.'[106] However, what she created at Stanway was something that she was proud of. She told Arthur Balfour on 12 September 1912 that

> Stanway seems to be a wonderful centre of Love and Vitality (Life) Radiance and Harmony and I begin to see dimly that I *have* done something, or to speak more humbly and truly but lengthily, something has been done through me for to have built up this home life *is* something, and to have the radiating centre from which people can draw something and pass it on is like having founded a watering place![107]

Entertaining was so important to her that she was still hosting parties at Stanway a week before she died, at the age of seventy-four.[108]

What the examples of Charlecote, Mells, Stanway and Wallington illustrate is how country houses could be places that embodied the artistic and cultural movements of the nineteenth century. Whether these ideas had an impact on the design of the house, the art that they held or the people that they hosted, country houses were places where artistic ideas were discussed and realised. This sometimes involved a return to the old, as seen by the Lucys' love of antiques – even if the pieces were not always as old as the couple had been promised. On other occasions, it reflected the desire to celebrate progress, as we see in Thomas Woolner's *Civilisation*, made for Pauline Trevelyan's celebrated central hall at Wallington. They were also places where ideas were discussed and played with, overseen by hostesses like Frances Horner and Lady Elcho. However, these parties were not always fun for everyone, and they could lead to the houses shifting from being joyful to unhappy homes. The artistic and the passionate sometimes came together, as we have already seen with Wilfrid Scawen Blunt's poetic and performative pursuit of Mary Elcho. This conflict, along with other domestic problems, meant that sometimes the country house was not a place of art, but rather of war.

CHAPTER 9

The Family at War

In a poem entitled 'Wedded Love', dated 29 January 1836, Pauline Trevelyan compared the condition of a bride with that of the poet or philosopher, and she argued that the married person is the happier:

> But how should one, supremely blest
> In all the joys of faithful love,
> Delight to turn in thought away
> From bliss that mounts all thought above?

> Love sways not a divided heart,
> The jealous muse will reign alone;
> Though hers may be the loftier part,
> Be his and mine the happier one.[1]

This happiness was something that she and Walter enjoyed; and similarly, despite the earlier difficulties in their union, the Lucys of Charlecote became a close and affectionate couple. The Knightleys of Fawsley were also an effective team who cared for each other deeply. On the death of Rainald in 1895, Louisa Knightley wrote in her diary: 'The saddest day of my life: my darling, precious treasure is gone, and though to him it is all gain, to me it is irreparable loss; and from being the happiest of wives I am a widow.'[2] However, these happy marriages were not always peaceful, and they all faced some difficulties. While he was generally tolerant of Louisa's political activities, especially when it benefited him, Rainald could be a little dismissive of her work. He prevented her from becoming the national president of the Girls' Friendly Society, which he liked to call the 'Great Fuss Society'.[3] For their part, the Lucys' family life was marked by sadness following the death of two of their sons, whose short lives and deaths Mary Elizabeth commemorated in published accounts.[4] Pauline Trevelyan suffered from ill health for many years, causing her husband much anxiety, which limited their ability to travel as much as they would have liked.[5] However, these couples generally worked as units, bound together by affection, rather than just a sense of duty.

For others, familial relations were much more difficult. The country house was not always a happy place; and for some, disputes shaped domestic life. There were unhappy marriages, particularly those in the Bankes and the Charteris families; and relationships between parents and children were not always peaceful. As well as domestic conflict, wars also had a direct impact on the lives of those resident in and around country houses. As we saw in Chapter 7, family members were directly involved in colonial warfare, and the Boer Wars mobilised women like Louisa Knightley into philanthropic action. The First World War also had a significant impact on both country-house families and their wider estates. This conflict had a lasting legacy; the Horners' village of Mells became the location of numerous individual and collective memorials after the war, and so the history of the village and the conflict have become tightly interwoven.[6] This all had an impact on the degree to which a woman felt able to be mistress of a country house – especially if her husband had a mistress of his own. While some country houses fulfilled the ideal of a stately *home*, others were places of conflict.

One of the main causes of an unhappy family life was the ill-suitedness of the master and mistress of the house to one another. Throughout the period covered in this book, parental involvement in the selection of a suitable spouse was not unusual. This sometimes led to a happy union, as we have seen with the Lucys; but in other cases the subsequent marital relations were fraught. During the nineteenth century, parental matchmaking became more complex as, due to the rise of 'new wealth', marriages between members of 'noble' and 'common' families occurred more frequently.[7] There was also an increasing international element, and in the later part of the century there were growing numbers of transatlantic marriages, where wealthy Americans married less wealthy but titled Brits.[8] In short, there was a growing pool of people for matchmaking parents to draw on. But while those who had money and those who had social prestige were not always aligned, marriages that may have been formed for financial reasons were not necessarily unhappy. For example, while the fifth earl of Carnarvon's 1895 marriage to the extremely wealthy Almina Wombwell helped to pay off his debts and, later, fund his archaeological endeavours, it was a union shaped by affection.[9]

Instead, unhappy marriages were often a result of the couple having a mismatched degree of affection for one another and/or incompatible personality types. We see this in the engagement and marriage of Mary Wyndham and Hugo Charteris, Lord Elcho. They grew up in the same circles and first met in 1880 at a house party at Wilton. It was clear that Mary's mother was keen on this union, and in February 1881 Madeline Wyndham brought Hugo and her eldest daughter together by inviting him to the family home, Clouds. At first Madeline's plans were thwarted by Hugo's posting abroad, but they were revived in the spring of 1883. Her plan that year, Mary discovered, was for her to 'go in' for Hugo, and Madeline hoped there would be a wedding that summer.[10] Mary already knew about Hugo's unsociability, his love of gambling and his reputation for philandering; he also had a morose streak and biographer Nicola Beauman suggests that his moodiness 'was caused by boredom so acute it was almost an illness'.[11] Despite this, Mary finally submitted to her mother's insistence that she should marry Hugo, and a proposal was formally accepted in July.[12]

While this union between the Charteris and Wyndham families was a good match, there were concerns early on about whether it was going to be a happy marriage.[13] Mary tried to believe in her mother's intentions for her, but she suffered some sleepless nights; however, in her letters she tried to reassure Hugo (and herself) that she was 'completely happy' with 'darling Hoggolindo . . . angel-Hoggie'.[14] But it was barely a fortnight before Hugo was back gambling: a flutter on the stock exchange, Mary was informed, had cost him £700. This behaviour seems to have made Mary uneasy and was probably the catalyst for her writing a stilted letter to Hugo:

> Dear Lord Elcho: I have hour by hour become more forcibly painfully and unmistakably convinced that when I accepted you a fortnight ago I did *not* rightly understand my own mind. I feel so perfectly certain that I do *not* love and *respect* you as I feel I should that I feel it my duty, my positive and absolute duty, to break off our proposed marriage.[15]

She then added, in her more usual style:

> I hope you will not mind much! Th' yr pride may be shocked first – I feel assured that you will so feel it to be all for the best for both of us & I trust you will think of me kindly as your true friend.[16]

It seems that this letter was swept aside; too many people knew about the engagement, and so ending it would cause a scandal. So, the marriage went ahead in August. Hugo sent Mary a reassuring letter the day before, hoping that 'God [will] give you strength to go through it all – and make me a good Hogs worthy of the little angel Mogs.'[17] She did go through with it, although, based on the rather functional entry in her diary, it was with relatively little emotion. Throughout her life Mary had a strong desire to please her mother, later writing to her: 'I would rather kill myself than make you miserable and disappointed in me. I hope you never will be.'[18] Like many other women of her class, Mary knew her duty and did what was expected of her.[19]

Once wed, young brides had to negotiate the realities of married life. The testing ground for this was the honeymoon. This was increasingly used as a period of travel, rather than a time when the bride was introduced to her new family, home and tenants. As Frances was keen to put off living with her in-laws for as long as possible, the Horners had a lengthy honeymoon in 1883, first in Surrey and then in Italy; and so, when they formally returned to the family seat at Mells, six months after the wedding, Frances was visibly pregnant.[20] In both fictional and non-fictional descriptions in the Victorian period, the honeymoon was often understood to be a period of transition, and so could be a time of both anxiety and joy.[21] For the Elchos, at first their marriage seemed happy: Mary wrote joyfully about their relationship and about how they had got drunk on champagne during their honeymoon. However, although there are hints that the new couple enjoyed intimacy at first, as the early letters between Mary and Hugo make reference to 'lonely little cots' when they spent time apart, there were warning signs that all was not well. Hugo spent the honeymoon either stalking in the Scottish Highlands (an episode on which Mary later looked back with sadness) or sorting out their finances.[22] This was all far away from the ideal of the two individuals 'transforming' into a couple during a honeymoon; Hugo was very much conforming to old patterns.

Part of these old patterns included his flirtations with other women. Infidelity was not unusual in elite circles in the late Victorian and Edwardian ages. Although it was nothing new – there is evidence of marital infidelity throughout the time period covered by this book – the nature of elite life in this era meant that there was an increase in opportunities for affairs among social equals. Angela Lambert, a biographer of the Souls, notes that the 'country house weekend must have throbbed with illicit sexuality', as these parties often provided opportunities for extramarital relationships to be pursued.[23] While for some women, like Frances Horner, these appear to have remained just flirtations (even when some suitors were quite determined), for other couples they developed into more meaningful partnerships.[24] In the first few years of their marriage, between 1884 and 1889, Mary Elcho was almost constantly pregnant, although her mother complained that Mary and Hugo seemed '*never* to be together'.[25] In 1889, after Mary was warned of the danger to her long-term health if she carried another child to term, the Elchos chose abstinence, the most secure form of birth control. However, Hugo's reputation for womanising raised some concern that the couple's celibacy would encourage him to satisfy his sexual needs elsewhere.[26] There are suggestions that there were a few brief affairs in this period, and in 1890 Hugo began an intimate relationship with the celebrated beauty Hermione, duchess of Leinster, who was estranged from her husband. That year he was regularly to be found at her home, Carton in County Kildare. The relationship probably also led to the birth of a son who, following the death of his two (legitimate) older brothers, later became the seventh duke of Leinster.[27] After Hermione's death, there was then a sequence of mistresses, including the divorcee Lady Angela Forbes. This became a long-term pairing, and so Mary formed a working relationship with her. For example, when Angela's eldest daughter needed a place in a school, Mary helped to get her enrolled at the Malvern boarding school that the Elchos' youngest children were also attending.[28] Along with the house parties, a busy social life and the children, Hugo's affairs became just another problem for Mary to manage.

Among the elite women whose lives have been explored in this book, there were different responses to having an unhappy home life. One approach was to quietly bear it, which is what Henrietta Bankes of Kingston Lacy seems to have done. Although they had a glorious wedding celebration, the Bankeses' marriage quickly grew stale. Henrietta's daughter later reflected that when she 'first met my father she had been overwhelmed by his elegant charm . . . once her fate was decided forever she discovered he was perhaps not quite as exciting as she had thought'. Walter Bankes fell back on his 'hunting, shooting, fishing and racing, drinking a bottle of port a day, not bothering to talk very much to anyone, except his gamekeeper and, perhaps, his secret mistress'.[29]

Walter and his mistress, Elizabeth Marshall, were rumoured to have already had two illegitimate sons before his marriage to Henrietta; and when Henrietta pleaded with him to end this extramarital relationship, his taciturnity deepened. Coming downstairs one morning Henrietta found a terse note: 'Have gone to New York.'[30] The fact that he would make such a lengthy trip without discussing it with her first reflects the lack of communication between the couple. Although silence from a wife was an idealised expectation in some early modern conduct books, by the start of the twentieth century it was not seen as a positive sign. The Bankeses' very separate lives were reflected in his will; not only was Henrietta distressed by his unexpected request to be cremated, but he also left £40,000 and the freehold of both Knoll House and Combe House at Studland to Elizabeth Marshall. Disposing of the holiday properties that had been at the heart of their family life was marital breakdown writ large. But, although it may have brought her little comfort, Henrietta did, in a sense, have the last laugh: not only did she later buy back the Studland holiday homes, but also she had the prestige associated with being the figurehead of the Kingston Lacy estate for many years, as both wife and widow.[31] Elizabeth Marshall may have been Walter Bankes' mistress, but she was never the mistress of the manor.

Other unhappy wives responded by finding emotional comfort elsewhere. This might be provided by their natal family, as we saw in the case of Anne Dormer in the 1680s. Others might form new relationships. This could be tricky: socially and legally, female adultery was more problematic than male adultery. Before 1923, although a wife had to demonstrate additional aggravating factors, such as cruelty, alongside adultery in order to gain a divorce, a husband could divorce his wife on the grounds of adultery alone.[32] Emotional comfort could take many forms, and some women – like Minnie Benson, wife of the archbishop of Canterbury – found this in relationships with other women.[33] Mary Elcho also found emotional comfort outside her marriage. Her brief affair with her cousin Wilfrid Blunt, described in Chapter 7, took place as her husband was at the bedside of his dying mistress, the duchess of Leinster. When she returned to England in April 1896, it soon became clear that she was going to have to confess the affair to her husband, due to the 'beautiful secret' of her fifth pregnancy, as the baby was Wilfrid's child. Keeping this fact secret from the wider world was simply a matter of Hugo remaining mute and shielding Mary; but she needed her husband to be onboard. When Hugo heard about the pregnancy, he was reported to have fallen silent for three days: part of his anger was that people would think he was having sex with his wife when his mistress was dying.[34] His wrath was then directed at Wilfrid, to whom he wrote with the furious accusation that he had 'wrecked the life and destroyed the happiness of a woman whom a spark of chivalry would have made you protect'.[35] Although Hugo forbade Mary from having any contact with her lover, a month later she wrote to Wilfrid. In this letter she reflected on her gratitude to Hugo 'for not making my life unbearable' about her infidelity.[36] Mary does not seem to have regretted what happened; many years later, in 1921, she wrote to Wilfrid about how 'the stars of Egypt are an undying memory – and footprints in the sand!'[37]

Wilfrid, though, was not Mary's main *grande passion*: for much of her adult life she loved Arthur Balfour. Mary and Arthur had met at Leighton House in 1879, before she was engaged to Hugo. Arthur was then 'glamorous but unobtainable', as the editors of their letters put it.[38] Lord Salisbury's favourite nephew, Arthur had inherited the Whittingehame estate in Scotland in 1869, and in 1872 he bought 4 Carlton Gardens, locating him at the heart of London society. Arthur was near-sighted and not at all athletic; to some of his university contemporaries he was known as 'Pretty Fanny', and he was mocked for his habit of collecting blue china. In spite of this, Max Egremont writes that he was 'feted for his good looks and charm of manner, guaranteed a welcome by his connections and position'.[39] The charm was legendary: 'he has but to smile and men and women fall prone at his feet', declared a female friend who was besotted with him for many years.[40] Mary, too, fell for his charm; it was 1880 when she first went to his country house, and this was the start of a long-lasting friendship.

The nature of this friendship was the topic of much debate at the time – and has continued to be. H.G. Wells thought Balfour had 'no hot passions, but only interests and fine affections'; and his biographer Ruddock Mackay thought that he 'evidently experienced no urgent sexual desire'.[41] However, in the early stages of their relationship, Arthur was Mary's favoured suitor and it was just 'accidents' that kept them apart: Arthur did not visit Mary on one occasion, and this absence gave Hugo Elcho the opportunity to win her hand.[42] But their friendship was recognised by their close friends. One described Arthur as 'devoted' to Mary, and Wilfrid Blunt knew that Arthur had a 'passion for Mary' and she a 'tenderness for him'. However, Wilfrid was not sure about the exact nature of their relationship, and reflected that 'perhaps it is better not to be too wise and as all the house accepts the position as the most natural in the world there let us leave it!'[43] While Mary told Wilfrid her relationship with Arthur was 'a little more than friendship, a little less than love', it is clear from the letters between Mary and Arthur that there was more than platonic affection to their relationship.[44]

In 1928, Mary imagined how people would talk about her and Arthur: 'How pathetic to see Arthur and Mary Wemyss [her title after 1914]. How sad is the end of life . . . How sad to outlive romance. I believe they were lovers once, though nobody knows the truth about these things!'[45] In a final letter preserved at Stanway from 7 March 1929, Mary wrote: 'I wish you once and for all to know that . . . you have been a WONDERFUL FRIEND, some people might say a l.v.r but that might be excessive!' She went on:

> Re the Memoirs, Ettie [Desborough] tells me you have got to '86 – still a long row to hoe! – as I was writing to you of our changing gear through the ages I jotted down a few dates and our respective ages. 1880, my first visit to Strathconan, me 17 you 31. 86! Laura [Tennant]'s death, my son Guy's birth, me 24 you 38, early 1887, you became Chief Secretary for Ireland and shortly before that, in the same year, a small very private and personal incident (gear changing!) took place in yr downstairs room 4 C.G. – me 25, you 39 – but you won't describe this incident in yr Memoirs important tho' it was.[46]

This 'incident' of 1887 is of note, as that was the year that he wrote to his sister-in-law, Lady Frances Balfour; he instructed her that, in the event of his death, she should 'cut open with your penknife the accompanying pouch and read the scrawl inside, it relates to a matter with which only you can deal'.[47] It was not until 1930 that Frances and Mary cut open the bag together and found a note to Frances and a diamond brooch.[48] The message was as follows:

> I want you to give [Mary] as from yourself this little brooch which you will find herewith: and to tell her that, at the end, if I was able to think at all, I thought of her. If I was the means of introducing any unhappiness into her life I hope God will forgive me. I know she will. I think I have made arrangements by which all letters will be burnt which ought to be.[49]

These letters suggest that there was something more intimate to their relationship than his just being a 'wonderful friend'. In particular, the plans to burn letters is of note, as this act of destruction was one that was commonly undertaken by those involved in illicit love affairs, or those wishing to hide from public gaze inappropriate emotions.[50] However, the decision, by both parties, to destroy some letters means that the nature of their feelings are difficult to fully understand. Because of the impact that a public discovery of an adulterous relationship would have had on the reputations of both Mary Elcho and Arthur Balfour, it is not surprising that it is hard to find solid evidence of their intimacy. However, there are hints.

Some of these hints come from the suspicions of their friends, family and especially Hugo, who clearly understood that there was a relationship, but did not quite know what form it took. When he found out about Mary's affair with Wilfrid Blunt, he reportedly exclaimed 'If it had been Arthur I could have understood it, but I cannot understand it now.'[51] Mary also told Arthur, in August 1890, that Hugo had taken the chance before a dinner at her sister's house to tell her 'that he thought you were fond of me . . . and asked me to tell him whether you ever told me so and exactly what you said'. She added that Hugo's questions about Arthur 'screw up my entrails! and make me feel quite quivering'.[52] Intriguingly, half of this letter is torn away; what did Arthur, Mary or later archivists want to hide? Hugo was not alone in his suspicions. Mary's mother was excessively worried about her daughter's marriage, even in the mid-1880s; and her mother-in-law, Annie, tenth countess of Wemyss, recruited Laura Tennant to shadow Mary wherever she went when Arthur was on the horizon.[53] Friends also noticed the relationship: Frances Horner reported to a fellow Soul that a mutual friend had asked her '[A]re you a cynic? . . . What do you think of Marriage? I wanted to ask you – are you happy about Mary Elcho and Arthur Balfour?'[54]

Were her husband, family and friends right to be suspicious? And why did Hugo's suspicions make Mary so anxious? Generally, the Souls were famed for their discretion regarding extramarital affairs, so we have to wonder what made the couple subject to gossip. There are some clear indicators that there was some sort of desire. Arthur joined the Elchos on a walking trip in 1886, and in her sketch book Mary drew a heart with wings and Arthur's name, and depictions of secluded woodland walks with 'how I wish I could, but you know it would be impossible' written backwards in tiny writing.[55] In some of her letters from this period she alluded to hiding things from the view of servants – and the public more widely – and also mentioned how she thought that the East Room at Stanway was 'the right paradise for both of us'.[56]

There are also some indications of some physical intimacy between Mary and Arthur. Along with the mention of the 'gear changing' incident, a letter sent from Gosford (the Wemysses' Scottish house) on 1 February 1906 provides some suggestion of both historical and continuing physical connections. The importance of this letter is emphasised by two key annotations. At the top, Mary wrote 'Burn'; and in the postscript she added: 'I must settle to pay my first visit one day week of 12th if possible and be received by you alone and step over the threshold and I shall remember a certain day exactly 20 years ago. f-rst k-ss.'[57] It is unclear whether she meant 1886, or the 'gear changing' incident of 1887; but we know that she had invited him to dinner on 2 February 1886.[58] The content of the letter suggests that there had been some degree of intimacy during his visit to Gosford: 'I hope my prolonged caressing has not bothered you, I shall hope soon to reduce [sic] you and anyhow I shall hope to see you soon – Clarissa.'[59] This was one of a series of letters where she adopted the character of Clarissa, the titular heroine of Richardson's 1748 novel, who was deceived, kidnapped and raped by the character Lovelace. Interestingly, she casts Arthur as Lovelace in one letter; when his party suffered a significant defeat in the general election of January 1906, she wrote 'poor Lovelace is at this moment pretty well played out – after four meetings a day and a severe *beating* which he certainly deserved – not on account of his public life but of his infamous private conduct. When I return . . . Lovelace will have come rested I hope.'[60] On the basis of this letter alone, it is not clear what she is suggesting, but it does indicate that, in Mary's own phrase, their relationship was 'a little more than friendship'.

However, was it really 'a little less than love'? There are a number of gaps in the Balfour/Elcho archive, but what does remain suggests that there was some physical affection. While Mary's daughter Cynthia may have been mistaken in believing that Arthur was her father, one of Balfour's biographers suggests of the 'gear changing' incident of 1887 that 'it does not overtax the historical imagination to wonder if he and Mary might have become lovers on at least this occasion'.[61] There was also the 'first kiss', and in 1887 Balfour wrote to her to tell her that

> I'm going to make some new arrangements for next week while you are here – '*I* am to do and *say* what I like and you are to do exactly what *I* like!' Those are some of the rules, more can be made (by me) as we go along! Of course you may have a 'systeme' [sic] but it must agree in the spirit and the letter with mine![62]

This was a bold way for a man to write to a woman who was not his wife. While it could be interpreted innocently, a surviving letter from two months later admits that he had burnt one of her previous letters – which suggests that there were some elements of their relationship that they wanted to remain private.[63] According to historians Ridley and Percy, the physical side of Mary and Arthur's relationship was stronger in the period 1903–1905, when he was prime minister, and may have involved role swapping and possibly some flagellation.[64] The hints of this can be seen, for example, in a letter from 1904. In it, Mary noted how sad they both were at her parting and wished they could have had more time together:

> I think it was quite clever of me to fit in everything so well and manage to get to you – you see I felt it my duty to put you in your place (on your knees at my feet) and that I flatter myself I have thoroughly done . . . Sunday was a little disappointing . . . I should have liked to have had some fun with you in the morning. I was in great spirits and full of mischief . . . two hours is what I like: one for boring things and one for putting you in your place.

After a lot of other news and general chat, she finished with: 'Bless you. M.E. [Mary Elcho] I hope you are all right? Destroy.'[65] Thankfully for the historian, he failed to do so. Similarly, in other letters Mary wrote that she longed 'to be there always to keep you in yr place'; that 'not having to keep you in order made a great blank in my life'; and that when listening to a concert 'I felt a mass of impertinence and just longed to smack your "bottie" '.[66]

Their St Valentine's Day letters also suggest a degree of intimacy. Mary made allusions to Shakespeare's *Romeo and Juliet* in her letter of 14 February 1905, while in 1906 she wrote 'I think my first visit to you ought to be February 14th . . . I shall be so glad to see you.'[67] In 1907, her letter was bolder. She drew three objects on the letter and wrote: 'The Valentine objects are somewhat obscure – to the left is a birch rod, to the right a brush and a tin bottle of squirting grease (smells of peppermint!).'[68] We do, though, have to read these letters with a degree of caution. During the nineteenth century, while it was mainly associated with expressing love and affection, 14 February was also a day when a whole series of emotions could be shared. Comic and satirical St Valentine's cards were also a particular feature of the mid-Victorian period, and while they had declined in popularity by the age of the Edwardians, it was still a day associated with playfulness.[69]

Possibly the most intriguing of all Mary Elcho's letters to Arthur is one she wrote from Paris in June 1905:

> I saw a representation of a young ladies' school at the theatre Thursday night – it reminded me, not that it in any way resembled it, of our school – the one I have aptly and rather wittily named 'the finishing school' – certainly, in many respects you gave that poor young girl a 'liberal education' and left no regions of her little body! unexplored, after that night there will have been few surprises left for her.[70]

Quite when 'that night' was remains unclear; like a great deal of the evidence of their relationship, it has been lost to the historian.

When writing about the Elcho/Balfour relationship, some historians have suggested that it was very much shaped by Arthur's needs – especially his desire for psychological intimacy – and that it was focused on helping him in his political career.[71] They have echoed the ideas of Mary's friend Edward Marsh, who recalled how Balfour found in Lady Elcho 'a tower of strength and a haven of rest'.[72] However, the relationship was important to Mary, too; after seeing a doctor who gave her a 'long psychological lecture' in 1895, she reflected that she had 'got into the habit of living externally and cannot find my own soul!'[73] Arthur was one of the few people she could be honest with; and so, as one of his biographers argues, Mary and Arthur's relationship 'evolved from friendship to intimacy and finally to interdependency' over five decades.[74]

However, Mary claimed that the idea that Arthur had been her lover was 'excessive'.[75] It may be that she did not think her relationship with Arthur was adulterous. This might reflect the nature of their intimacy; it is not impossible that a woman who had been warned about the dangers of further pregnancies and who had already had a child by another lover may have avoided some sexual activities. Therefore, following the ideal of Victorian chivalric literature, they may never have consummated their relationship in the traditional sense, and so she may not have perceived their intimate interactions as the acts of 'lovers'.[76] Whatever the nature of their relationship, they remained close friends into the 1920s, and he stayed with her at Stanway following his mild stroke in 1928.[77]

Hugo, who succeeded his father as the eleventh earl of Wemyss in 1914, did not live permanently at Stanway at this point. For twenty-three years, until they both died in 1937, Mary and Hugo mainly lived apart – he with his mistress Angela Forbes at Gosford; she with a brood of children and grandchildren, as well as many visiting friends, at Stanway. They were not completely estranged: Hugo frequently came to Stanway, and Mary usually went north to Gosford in the summer. Both of them also spent time in London, where they shared a house. Like most women of her generation, divorce was not an option: among those born in the 1850s and 1860s, less than one marriage in thirty ended in divorce.[78] When one's husband or lover had a leading national role, such as prime minister, it was even more unlikely. Instead, these women found other ways to cope. For Mary Elcho, that was through an external show of continuity in terms of marital relations, while seeking affection and solace elsewhere.

Conflict within a family was not just between a husband and wife; it could involve the wider family, too. The extent to which unhappy marriages also shaped the experiences of the children was variable. The Elchos' daughter Cynthia later looked back on her childhood with affection. While she could find her mother's fondness for hosting parties for the Souls frustrating, she knew she was loved.[79] Writing of Mary, she noted that, as a mother, perhaps her greatest merit was combining with the maximum of fondness the minimum of possessiveness. Her unintrusive love for her sons and daughters never put fetters on them. She was indeed so unexacting that though her ceaseless concern for her children was touchingly evident, she did not even expect – far less demand – their confidences.[80]

Although she was a loving parent, Mary was not always with her children. Physically and emotionally scarred by her repeated pregnancies, she took to spa trips after each season to repair her exhausted body. In the early 1890s, leaving her four children became a way of life for her. She spent almost six months of both 1890 and 1891 away at house parties, on trips to improve her health or in London, apart from her little ones, who sometimes stayed with their grandparents at Clouds.[81] Yet she was a caring mother; she later wrote *A Family Record* (1932) for her children and grandchildren, as a way of capturing her children's lives for posterity.[82]

Viola Bankes' record of her childhood was less positive than Cynthia's. Viola was aware that, as she was a daughter and not a son, she was a disappointment to her parents from the start; she felt that both of her parents paid her and her sister little attention during her time at Kingston Lacy. Unlike the parties at Stanway, Henrietta's entertaining took place in a private world that left out her children, who were of little interest to 'Mama's entourage of ambassadors, artists or society beauties'. Viola reflected that 'we might be put on show for a few minutes, then we were whisked away again, before the visitors could become bored with us'.[83] They were so excluded from their parents' lives that they were not aware of their father's final illness in 1904. Viola recalled that

> in a house so massive as Kingston Lacy, particularly when we children used only the back stairs and were never allowed to use the marble staircase [that led to Walter's bedroom], it was easy to keep the presence of an invalid secret.[84]

Walter had told his children that he was going to India to collect shells; as young children, they did not realise that this was their distant father's clumsy attempt to say goodbye. They continued to believe he was on his travels until one day, in about 1909, Viola asked the governess a direct question about when Daddy would be coming home. She was told: 'Don't be silly. How can you talk like that when you know that your father is dead?'[85] While in many households the idea of the distant Victorian father was a myth, in some other country houses, it was very much a lived reality.[86]

As the widowed chatelaine of Kingston Lacy, Henrietta made some attempt to be a good mother of sorts:

> As we grew older she saw us every day after tea and allowed us to sit quietly playing 'beggar my neighbour' so long as we did not talk while she was writing . . . It never occurred to me to wonder whether she was happy. She would have thought it extremely vulgar to show any emotion.[87]

Despite her attempts, Viola and Henrietta never had a close relationship, and while Henrietta did her best to launch her daughters into society, they both spurned her efforts. Viola's engagement to an Australian doctor 'set the seal' on their estrangement: she only found out about her mother's death (in 1953) thirteen days after the funeral. While Henrietta Bankes was respected by servants, estate workers and villagers, she was a distant mother.[88]

Even in families where the couple were more happily married, there could be difficult relationships with their children. As a teenager and young man, Frances Horner's son Edward caused a great deal of concern to his parents, who were also facing financial worries at the same time. Jack received a stipend of £1,200 a year as Commissioner of Woods and Forests from 1895, but they relied on this as they had relatively little money from the estate. The income from rent was less than they spent on maintaining their tenants' properties, and so they had to let their main country house of Mells Park and move to the more modest manor house in the village in order to cut costs.[89] This meant that they were frustrated when Edward did not seem to make the most of his time at school. Frances wrote to him:

> I want you to turn your mind to the serious part of your life at Eton . . . You know it is . . . a big expense, but neither your father nor I shall ever weigh that as long as you are doing your best to take advantage of it in every way and get all the good and happiness you can out of it.[90]

Her letters show that she had become concerned about him and his general unhappiness. She reminded him:

> You see, you aren't at Eton just only to enjoy yourself, you are there to get equipped for life intellectually, morally, physically, and if you can once get that into your head it will make you vastly independent of all the little ups and downs of life.[91]

However, these letters did not help, and Edward confided to a friend that such diatribes made him 'inclined to commit suicide'.[92] After Eton came Oxford, but Edward's unhappiness and his difficult relationship with his parents continued, as they were frustrated with him for running up bills: his mother told him that she and his father were 'sick with disappointment'.[93] A good-looking young man, described by one commentator as having the 'dazzling beauty of a Greek athlete', he enjoyed socialising much more than studying, and on one occasion got arrested for drunk and disorderly behaviour. When it emerged that Edward had been awarded a third-class degree, Frances took it badly. She had hoped that Edward would become the leader of the 'Coterie', the gilded generation made up of the children of the Souls.[94] Edward was the subject of the Horners' political ambitions, as their other son, Mark, had died of scarlet fever in 1908.[95] This death brought real sorrow to the family; on the first anniversary of his death Frances wrote: 'I do not think there has been one day since this time last year that I have not felt unhappy.'[96]

While her relationship with her surviving son was strained, Frances knew his importance to the future of the family, and so continued to provide a space for him and his friends in her homes.[97] Edward, though, was not always grateful; his friend Patrick Shaw Stewart wrote to Diana Manners in November 1913 about a dinner Edward had hosted at the Horners' London house:

> The dignified silence of Sir John, the somewhat resentful radiance of Lady Horner and the unplumbed despair of Edward as he contemplated his really very happy guests. I believe he would like his parents to have porridge in their rooms on the occasions when he may entertain there, on the ground[s] that there is no room in the house large enough for them to look merely incidental in. Everyone who has ever known parents knows the feeling, but few give way to it so mournfully as Edward.[98]

It seems that his friends' affection for his parents was not always shared by the twenty-two-year-old Edward who, despite embarking on a legal career, was still engaging in a youthful rebellion against his parents and their world view.

This type of interfamilial conflict was soon dwarfed by a much bigger war. The start of the First World War meant that country houses and their inhabitants faced new challenges. There was a distinct form of patriotic duty among wealthier families, and many already had existing connections to the armed forces.[99] In addition, there had been, in a popular phrase of the period, an outbreak of 'pageantitis' in the period before the First World War, which had shaped children's play, the scouting movement and the discourse associated with soldiers in colonial conflicts that positively connected their deeds with those of crusaders. This all meant that members of the elite were well aware of the ideals of medieval chivalry and the associated values of honour, duty and courage that were expected of men and women of their class.[100] While there are some known examples of aristocratic mothers trying to use their connections to protect their children from the arena of war, many of the sons of the elite were quick to volunteer.[101] This was true of the children of the Souls; while they had called themselves the 'Corrupt Coterie', they had a keen sense of patriotic and imperialist duty, which meant that some saw the Great War as the road to salvation. This included Edward Horner, who, bored by his job and in debt, was keen to see action.[102]

After war was declared, the 'brilliant, restless and dissatisfied' Edward wrote: '[G]etting out's the point, beside which nothing else matters.'[103] He held a subaltern's commission in the North Somerset Yeomanry;

but frustrated that he could not see action immediately, he used his friends and his mother to make the contacts so he could do his duty. By January 1915 he was on his way to France. He soon found life on the front line 'devilish [sic] uncomfortable', and told his mother in March 1915 'I shall honestly be able to say I have roughed it by the end of this week.'[104] He had a way out; a friend of the Souls, Field Marshal Sir John French, had told Edward that he 'wanted to send me home with a message to avoid the trenches'. Edward declined, telling his friend Diana Manners, 'but I couldn't do it could I'.[105] When Edward was hit by a shrapnel bullet in 1915 which injured him so badly that he had to have a kidney removed, Sir John French made sure that his family was well informed. As Frances was determined to get to see her son in person, she and her family used their network of friends so that they could travel to Boulogne with a leading surgeon; good connections could have a significant impact on an individual's war experiences.[106]

Edward found recuperation difficult, especially after he was told flatly that, lacking a kidney, he could not be passed for active service. However, in 1916 he was sent to Egypt and found himself having to train Australian recruits in the first principles of musketry, before being appointed as an aide-de-camp with the Anzac units. He was desperate to be back in active service and was delighted to be returned to France in spring 1917. He wrote to a friend 'I am looking forward to the Front again ... as better than this life'; but by the autumn he wanted to return home.[107] Frances Horner sent Edward food parcels, which he thanked her for. He wrote wistfully: 'This is Sunday afternoon, very peaceful in our pretty farm but I think longingly of the Mells Sunday luncheon with its divine food and merry atmosphere and love surrounding me.'[108] After being at war with his parents when he was growing up, a more reflective Edward appears to have recognised how they did care deeply for him. On the second day of what became known as the Battle of Cambrai, Edward's cavalry squadron was sent to Noyelles, where he was to try to stop German troops from coming into the village. He was shot and died that night, 21 November 1917.[109]

Edward Horner was not the only 'son of the Souls' who died; for this group the period between 1915 and 1917 was especially devastating, with eight of the leading members of the Coterie dying.[110] One of the first was Hugo and Mary Elcho's son, Yvo Charteris, who died in October 1915. He was still at Eton when the war broke out, but he insisted on leaving early to take up a commission in spring 1915. It took some time for him to be given the details of where he was going to be deployed. Mary Elcho recalled that when she found out that he was going to be drafted, she was so shocked that she 'acted like an automaton'.[111] It then all happened quickly: on 4 September 1915 he received his warning telegram, and on 7 September he was advised that he would leave in four days, so he went to Gosford to say goodbye to his family. On this visit he went for a walk with his sister in the woods. She recalled, in her mother's account of her children's lives, that 'we walked with arms around each other . . . He said to me with his little tender whimsical smile, "you know I may not come back".'[112] He was right. Yvo died as a platoon commander in October 1915; he had not even been in France for two months.[113] His death was soon followed by that of his elder brother, Ego Charteris. He had signed up early in the war and left for Egypt in April 1915. There he was joined by his wife and his sister, who worked with a Voluntary Aid Detachment (VAD) in Alexandria. At first, he had a much more genteel war experience than his younger brother; he and his family were able to enjoy a colonial lifestyle, with servants and cooks. While his regiment was sent to Gallipoli (which he described as 'the last word in hell'), he remained in Egypt, and wrote to his mother that he did not expect to hear a shot fired in anger. He was wrong. His regiment saw action at Katia, east of the Suez Canal, and his family eventually received news, after a number of weeks of waiting, that he had been killed in April 1916.[114]

Both Mary Elcho and Frances Horner mourned the death of their sons greatly. Mary wrote to Arthur after the death of both her sons, and the loss of a number of their friends' boys, too. She said: 'I'm very glad that this generation had a happy time, they had so short a time and it was not wasted – they were "heroes" and they had a glorious youth.'[115] These deaths connected the women of the Souls; Frances Horner wrote to Mary Elcho the month following Edward's death, noting:

> we know each other's lives and what it has all been. I don't feel unhappy about Edward as we had such a heavenly fortnight with

him and he seems hardly to have let go his hand. He went off radiant and I seem to hear nothing but love and praise round his name.[116]

In many ways it was Mary's daughter, Cynthia, who expressed the feelings of loss most clearly. Following the death of a friend in 1915, she wrote in her diary: 'Oh why was I born for this time? Before one is thirty to know more dead than living people? Stanway, Clouds, Gosford – all the settings of one's life – given up to ghosts.'[117] A couple of years later, on the news of Edward's death, she reflected that he

> seems almost the last link with my youth . . . Soon there will be nobody left with whom one can even talk of the beloved figures of one's youth. I felt stupefied with the thought of this new load of misery crushing down on the already broken – but so curiously dried up and sterilised myself.[118]

The reason for feeling 'broken' by 1917 was not just the ongoing sadness and distress caused by the loss of loved ones. The war also had a significant impact on life on the Home Front. The outbreak of the Great War coincided with a time of upheaval for the Elchos. Hugo became earl of Wemyss in 1914, following his father's death, and he was keen to let Stanway, in order to economise; the legacy of declining agricultural income, combined with an increased tax burden, meant that many major landowners found the 1910s financially difficult.[119] Once the news of the war broke, while the decision to move the whole family to Gosford was put on hold, in a fit of prudent patriotism Hugo threatened to sack any servant who did not enlist. This was thought to be a step too far by many, especially his wife. She wrote to Arthur Balfour in August 1914 to tell him that she had 'strong feeling against' this approach '(quite apart from the fact the policy was thrust upon me) . . . I have no chauffeur, no stableman, no odd man to carry the coals . . . Here someone must stay and do the work and they are like trees rooted to the soil.'[120] In her diary Mary wrote 'I felt a very strong urgent impulse to ask Hugo to let me remit dismissal notices in order that those who go feel they go freely.'[121] Hugo seems to have been persuaded not to force people to sign up, and Mary's gentler approach appears to have been successful: at least a dozen Stanway employees joined the armed forces.[122] In the end, Hugo managed to raise some income by letting out Amisfield, another of the family's Scottish properties, so that it could provide accommodation for the First Regiment of the Lothians and Border Horse.[123] In giving up one of his properties and some of his staff to the forces, Hugo would have been seen as having done his patriotic duty; the Parliamentary Recruiting Committee, for example, wanted to encourage employers to ensure that their butlers served the nation, rather than their masters and mistresses.[124] This meant that soon many members of the household and estate workers were away fighting, causing great disruption to rural life.[125] Therefore, it is notable that when the Horners suffered a devastating fire in 1917 that destroyed Mells Park, Frances reported that while she felt 'quite bewildered', it was also the case that 'I don't feel as if I cared.'[126] Even before the death of her son (Edward died the following month), Frances seems to have been well aware that this fire was not the great crisis of the age.

While at the start of the war there were some aristocrats who bewailed the lack of chauffeurs, by its end many mistresses of the estate, including both Mary Elcho and Frances Horner, were conscious that the whole community had been impacted by the Great War. This was reflected in their philanthropic work during the conflict and then in their post-war memorial activities. Mary Elcho chaired a committee of parishioners, and it was on their behalf that she commissioned a monument to the 'Men of Stanway'. Using her connections to leading artists, she was able to employ Alexander Fisher to create the sculpture of St George and the Dragon, and Eric Gill for the lettering; their neighbour, architect Sir Philip Sidney Stott, produced the stone plinth and column.[127] Similarly, renowned artists were brought to the village of Mells. Frances Horner worked with Edwin Lutyens to create a monument to her son; she commissioned the equine artist Sir Alfred Munnings to create a statue of Edward on horseback, while Lutyens provided the memorial tablet in August 1919.[128] Although the Horners had been significantly impacted directly, having lost both a son and a son-in-law, the family was aware that the wider village had losses, too. Therefore, they arranged for Lutyens to explore the village with Katharine Asquith, the Horners' widowed daughter, to find a perfect site for the war memorial at its centre. Sir Edwin described in a letter to his wife how they had managed to present their plans for the memorial 'with a little tact and patience' to the villagers, who carried the proposal 'with acclamation'.[129] The final memorial is a column topped with the figure of St George slaying a dragon – a copy of a statue in the chapel of Henry VII in Westminster Abbey.[130] The choice of imagery for these memorials reflects the ways in which chivalry, medieval myths and an idealised version of the crusades provided inspiration for commemorating the Great War, and helped support mourners to feel that the dead had claimed their place in history.[131] However, this was a medievalism fit for the modern world, and the designs were less ornate than those associated with early nineteenth-century Gothic revival art. They therefore fulfilled the ideal of simplicity in their design, which was associated by contemporaneous commentators with sincerity and respect for the dead.[132]

This sincerity and respect can be seen in other memorials. There was a real concern that individual stories might be forgotten in an ever-changing world, and so chronicling people's histories – either through listing their names on memorials or by writing their histories – became important.[133] Across the network of the Souls, a number of women produced written memorials to their children, following a pattern similar to that employed by Mary Elizabeth Lucy in the 1840s. During the conflict, public expressions of grief were discouraged, for fear that they might undermine the morale of soldiers on leave; and so writing provided an alternative form of expression for emotions.[134] While some of these – such as Pamela Tennant's piece *Edward Wyndham Tennant* (1919) – were produced quite quickly, Mary Elcho found it more difficult. When, in 1917, she started to write the book that she would later call *A Family Record*, she found the process of collecting her sons' letters hard. In looking at them, she reflected: 'I see the glorious crowns of life nipped off and life's hopes and aspirations – and incidentally one's own heart! – lie bleeding in the dust.'[135] Mary was terrified that she might not do justice to Ego and Yvo – or, perhaps worse, expose them to some criticism. She told her close friend Ettie Desborough in October 1931, with the book at last in the press, that it was written in 'heart's blood'.[136] The book starts with her first arrival at Stanway, and so it really was a *family* record. Mary wanted to get away from the notion that the death of her sons in battle meant that anything else 'would have been unworthy of their beginning'.[137] Their glorious deaths, she believed, were not simply an assumption that should be written into their lives. Instead, she wanted to produce a volume that told their whole stories, as much-loved members of their family and of wider elite society. For Yvo and Ego, war was just a tiny part of their story, and she wanted to celebrate their lives away from the conflict, too.

The Victorian and Edwardian country house could be a happy place. It could be a location where couples worked together to redesign the interior; a space to bring together friends and artists; or a place where family events were celebrated with the wider community. However, it was not always a place of love and comfort. For some children, the house was a place where they knew they had to behave, in order to maintain domestic peace. For some wives, the domestic interior was where they had to avoid seeing their diffident husband flirting with other women or just ignoring them completely. While some women, like Mary Elcho, were able to find comfort in other relationships, others, like Henrietta Bankes, appear to have had to quietly endure their husbands' behaviour.

The death of children, whether through illness or conflict, also brought great sadness. The houses and the associated villages became places of remembrance. In many ways this is fitting: country houses were always places of memory. They were, and are, places where the dynastic memory of the family was made tangible and celebrated. This is why so many families wanted to make their mark on the property, by reshaping the interiors, as we saw at Wallington and Charlecote. However, for others they became places to preserve and cherish. While there may have been sorrow experienced in some of these properties, they were still places with which most mistresses developed a close emotional bond. They were places that they wished to protect. This is reflected in what Mary Elcho wrote about her beloved Stanway in her *A Family Record*:

> Have houses souls, or do we only invest them with our own imaginings? Stanway, people say, has an atmosphere of its own. Those who doubt should gaze at Stanway in the moonlight when its shining

traceries and deep black shadows are almost frightening in their stern beauty. They should see it again, smiling in the sunlight, when children are there and like a golden hive it is humming with life and fragrant like honey. Its mellow walls are steeped in the joys and sorrows of many generations who have lived and loved within them. And then, when shadows lengthen and shouts of laughter cease, they see another Stanway.

Moonlight's glittering armour, sunlight's golden robes have vanished, Stanway in the twilight wears a soft grey mantle, and the atmosphere is one of gentleness and peace. Does Stanway care as we care? It tells no secrets, but welcomes us impartially through its ever open door.

Stanway, House of Memories, Farewell![138]

Conclusion: Defending the Country House

Ettie, Lady Desborough, one of the Souls who had lost sons during the First World War, spent the morning of 11 November 1918 in a military nursing home with her daughter, who was working there. That evening she wrote to her friend, Mary Elcho: 'All day the thought of you has burnt in my innermost heart. Victory, and you and I look in vain for our Victors.'[1]

Although they were aware of the successes of the many, the end of the First World War was not necessarily a time of great celebration for the mistresses of country houses. Many of their families had suffered notable losses during the conflict. C.F.G. Masterman wrote in *England after War* (1922) that the 'flower of the British aristocracy' was killed at Ypres, and that across the war the 'British aristocracy perished, as they perished in the Wars of the Roses . . . in courage and high effort, and an epic of heroic sacrifice, which will be remembered so long as England endures'.[2] Masterman made these claims based on his lived experience, but later demographic research has supported his and other contemporaneous writers' argument that, for the elite classes, there was a 'lost generation'.[3] Some families felt this acutely, as their male heirs had died. Occasionally, this meant that the property passed down the female line. For example, when Jack Horner died in 1927, the estate of Mells was left in trust to his wife Frances, and it was then inherited by their daughters, with Katharine retaining the manor house and the village of Mells.[4] While the losses were significant (about a fifth of those peers and sons of peers who signed up lost their lives in the Great War), it is important to remember that the vast majority of the elite came home alive, and very few titles became extinct because of the conflict.[5]

This did not mean that everything was straightforward. The financial problems that beset the elite classes before 1914 had not gone away. Income from land, the mainstay of aristocratic wealth in earlier centuries, had fallen significantly in the late nineteenth century. Falling rents, alongside an agricultural depression, meant that, to quote Randolph Churchill, 'the bloom had altogether rubbed off the peach' of land as an investment.[6] This led to some houses that had remained in family hands for many years being transferred to the care of the newly monied. Apethorpe, which was owned by descendants of Grace Mildmay's daughter, was sold in 1904 to a member of the Brassey family, which had made its fortune as a railway contractor.[7] Sometimes, while they could keep their main house, other properties were sold; for example, although they were able to retain Fawsley, Louisa and Rainald Knightley sold their London house in 1890.[8] It was not just about a decline in rental income; during the early twentieth century the elite classes also faced high levels of taxation. 'Estate duty', introduced in 1894, caused particular concern; this was a 'death duty' that taxed estates at the principal value of the land, replacing the previous probate tax system, which had levied tax on the rental income – usually a far lower sum.[9] For the Elchos, following his inheritance of the estates of the earl of Wemyss, Hugo was left with a significant death duties bill. In 1915 his daughter noted in her diary that there was '£28,000 to be paid for eight years'; at this point the family's annual rental income was £55,000.[10] There were additional taxes, too, and in some cases the tax burden on rental income increased from 9 per cent to 30 per cent between 1914 and 1919. The difficulty was exacerbated by rising interest rates and a dramatic increase in the cost of repairs and maintenance. It is therefore not surprising that there was a significant sale of land by major landowners in the period immediately after the war. It has been estimated that between six and eight million acres were sold in England and Wales between 1918 and 1921, and the sale of land continued over the following decades.[11] Some of these purchasers were local authorities. For example, Temple Newsam, the former home of Frances, ninth Viscountess Irwin, was sold in 1922 to Leeds Corporation; the property was preserved and opened to the public the following year. Similarly, Plas Newydd was bought by the local council in the 1930s, and it continues to attract visitors, as it did when the Ladies of Llangollen were resident.[12]

Not all country houses were saved. Masterman, noting the high number of country houses for sale in the early 1920s, argued of the elite families that 'their property perished in battle, no less than their children'.[13] The political influence of the great landowners in the early twentieth century was one of the main reasons why inhabited country houses were not included in early conservation legislation: there was a sense that if an Englishman's house was his castle, he should be able to do with it what he wished, including demolishing it. Some chose to do just that: about 5 per cent of the national stock of country houses was demolished in the interwar period.[14] One of these was Amisfield, one of the Elcho family's Scottish properties, which was destroyed in 1923 after the War Office moved out and no new tenant could be found.[15]

While women like Louisa Knightley had been keen to encourage the recording of the histories of country houses and their families, there was a general lack of enthusiasm for preserving elite domestic architecture. The small number of people who wanted to protect stately homes were mainly interested in caring for those built prior to 1700. Among the elites themselves, many of the younger generations found the country way of life boring, and there was a desire to diversify investments, so that not all their money was just in land. This was especially appealing after the dramatic fall in farm prices and associated rental income after 1929.[16] If they were not going to disappear, country houses needed to be defended.

Some mistresses played an active role in this defence. In order to keep the Kingston Lacy estate solvent for her (not yet adult) son, Henrietta Bankes arranged the sale of some land and property, raising over £57,000 in 1919.[17] Others were involved in the letting of the property. Despite Mary Elcho's protests, her husband Hugo was keen to sell or let out Stanway in 1914; and while the outbreak of war had curtailed that plan, Stanway was first let on a short lease in 1919.[18] In 1921, Mary was saved from permanent banishment from her home by

CONCLUSION: DEFENDING THE COUNTRY HOUSE

the playwright and novelist James Barrie. He had employed Cynthia Asquith, the Elchos' daughter, as a secretary, and he took on the house each summer until 1932, with Cynthia acting as its mistress. As Barrie paid 200 guineas for the privilege of playing lord of the manor for six weeks, Mary Elcho was able to live in Stanway for the rest of the year; it remained her home until her death in 1937.[19]

Similarly, the next generation of women were central to giving the Horners' property in Mells a new lease of life. After Mells Park burnt down in 1917, Frances Horner hoped that the property could be rebuilt, although she knew that she and her husband would probably not be able to afford to do so. She was therefore delighted when it was bought by the banker Reginald McKenna in 1922, who had married Frances's niece in 1908. The McKennas rebuilt the property using the Horners' family friend Edwin Lutyens as an architect, and Mrs McKenna's paternal aunt, Gertrude Jekyll, as a garden designer.[20] This rebuilding is a reminder that it was also not complete doom and gloom for the country house. New properties were still being built in this period, including two of the largest country houses that Lutyens designed: Gledstone Hall, Yorkshire and Middleton Park, Oxfordshire. They were still favoured as places to host weekend parties, and field sports remained hugely popular; and so the associated country house continued to be a *beau idéal* among many of the wealthier classes.[21]

Other elements of the old way of life remained: Henrietta Bankes hosted a garden party in 1923 to mark the coming of age of her son, Ralph, the owner of Kingston Lacy. In a return to pre-war traditions, one of the eldest tenants presented the young man with a gift on behalf of the tenant community. In total, 1,600 people were invited, including large numbers of tenants. However, this was Henrietta's last great hurrah as mistress, and nothing similar was seen on the Bankeses' estate again.[22] The old ways were changing; shortly after Mary Elcho's death, she was described by her friend Edward Marsh as 'one of the last enchantments of the old world'.[23] Victorian and Edwardian mistresses began to feel like the ghosts of a bygone age.

In many ways, the Second World War posed a greater threat to country houses than the First World War, as many properties were forcibly requisitioned. Although some houses acted as hospitals – including one for the

American forces that was built on part of the Bankes family estate in Dorset – it soon became clear that the nature of warfare had changed, and there was not as great a requirement for convalescent hospitals as there had been in the Great War.[24] Instead, the houses were used for many other purposes, such as housing evacuees, protecting museum collections that had been moved out of London, or becoming bases for the armed forces. At Longleat, which is still home to the Thynne family, the house became the new home of the Royal School for Daughters of Officers of the Army during the war, as the school's own buildings were requisitioned by the admiralty. In the park was an American military hospital, where the marquess of Bath's daughter-in-law worked in administrative roles. Other families left their homes. Hilary Bankes, daughter-in-law of Henrietta, spent the war in a series of rented properties, so that she and her children could be near her husband, who was serving in the navy.[25] Once war was over, the continuation of rationing, combined with limited access to building materials, meant that those houses that had suffered war damage or significant wear and tear during requisition could not be repaired to a high standard. In addition, post-war taxation was high; for example, the duke of Northumberland paid 70 per cent of his £130,000 rent roll in income tax and surtax in 1949. After essential costs, this left him with £2,600 a year – inadequate to run even one of his two country houses.[26] The mistresses of country houses faced a real challenge.

It is thought that between 600 and 1,000 country houses were demolished in the years immediately after the Second World War.[27] While most of the houses that feature in this book survived, some only just navigated the difficult post-war period. Hunstanton Hall, the home of the Le Stranges, was largely destroyed by fire in 1853. While the property was restored at the end of the Victorian period, following another fire in 1951 part of the house was divided into apartments and sold.[28] Fawsley Hall was largely empty following Louisa Knightley's death in 1913, barring two periods of requisition by the armed forces in the two world wars. It was used as a timber mill in the 1960s and then established as a hotel the following decade.[29] Penrice Castle remained in the ownership of the Talbot family until the early twentieth century, when it was inherited by Lady Blythswood. Some of the estate was sold to cover death duties, and parts of the house were demolished as they were in poor condition.[30]

Other houses were saved thanks to the growing preservation movement, in part encouraged by architectural scholars, such as Nikolaus Pevsner, who championed the architecture of the country house.[31] However, few thought that every last country house should be saved and be privately owned; there was a growing belief that if the family could not maintain the house, it should be sold for alternative uses, or donated to the National Trust. It was at this point that the National Trust began to change from being an organisation that was primarily concerned with the preservation of the countryside to one that became closely associated with the country house. In 1934 the Trust had only two country houses among its properties; but a change in the law meant that the charity was able, among other things, to earn income from its properties, and to allow the donors of estates to live on in the houses as tenants. This meant that donating a property to the Trust became more attractive to both parties, and by the end of 1945 it had twenty-three country houses in total.[32] These included Hatchlands (which Fanny Boscawen had sold in 1770), which was donated to the Trust in 1945. Another was Wallington; this had stayed in the Trevelyan family after it was inherited by the cousin of Walter Trevelyan, as he and Pauline had no children of their own. It was later inherited by Sir Charles Trevelyan, a serving Labour MP, who set about restoring the property and applying socialist principles to the work he and his wife did at the estate. As he wanted the house and its land to be available to the wider community, he decided to donate it to the National Trust. Other properties followed soon thereafter, including Charlecote, although the negotiations over this property were complex. This was in part because the secretary to the National Trust's Country Houses (later Historic Buildings) Committee, James Lees-Milne, was concerned with the building's merits. He disliked what he called the 'Victorian fakery' of the property; one wonders how Mary Elizabeth Lucy would have responded to this description of her and her husband's work at the house.[33]

Not all properties that survived went to the National Trust. Most houses remained in private hands, and some opened their doors to paying visitors. Over a hundred English country houses were open to the public in 1951, the year of the Festival of Britain; and by 1961 the figure had risen to over 300, a third of them privately owned.[34] They included Longleat, which (possibly erroneously) claimed to be the first house open to the public on a commercial basis. In 1949, its first year fully open, it had 134,000 paying visitors.[35]

However, not everywhere was as successful as Longleat, and there was still concern about houses being destroyed. From the 1960s, a combination of inflation and increased taxation meant that the upkeep of numerous landed estates became unaffordable for their owners. Following a 1974 exhibition at the Victoria and Albert Museum entitled 'The Destruction of the Country House' – which greeted visitors with a list of the significant houses that had been erased from the landscape over the previous hundred years – a clamour arose among the public for changes to government policy, in order to support the owners of such properties.[36] This led to another flurry of properties going to the Trust. These included Kingston Lacy, which was in really poor condition when the National Trust took it over in 1981: the dry rot was so serious that it was possible to look down into one of the ground-floor rooms from an upper-floor bedroom.[37] Other houses remained primarily private homes. Rousham House, which was significantly remodelled by William Kent in the eighteenth century, remains the property of the Cottrell-Dormer family. While the castle at Brampton Bryan was largely destroyed the year after Brilliana Harley's death, following a second siege, the mansion that was later built next door by her son is still inhabited by her descendants. Similarly, although she did not have to protect her house from combatants, as Brilliana had done, Mary Elcho would probably be pleased to know that her efforts to keep Stanway in the Charteris family were successful.[38]

Although changes to fiscal regulations and socio-economic conditions meant that many country houses began to be profitable businesses again, running these organisations takes a great deal of work.[39] Women are still actively involved, and there has been a significant degree of continuity in the role of being mistress of a country house. While the language used has clearly changed, many of the roles and responsibilities that women running country houses today face have a direct connection to the activities that women have engaged in over the last 450 years. This is, in part, because those ideas about what makes a mistress that are to be found in the writings of William Gouge in *Of Domesticall Duties* (1622) and Samuel Johnson in his dictionary retain considerable relevance. Throughout the period 1580–1920, managing the staff both within and associated with the country house was an important duty. In some households the relationship with staff could be quite fractious; in others it was central to the inhabitants' happiness and success, as we saw with the Ladies of Llangollen in Plas Newydd. The model of women playing a role in 'decking the house' continued, too. This included playing an active part in wholesale changes to the property (as Pauline Trevelyan and Theresa Parker did) and ensuring that the house remained in good order (as was the case with the interior decoration work undertaken by Mary Elizabeth Lucy). Whereas in the past this may have included complete rebuilding (as we saw at Hatchlands), today there is more of an emphasis on conservation and preservation. However, the idea of 'decking' has not really disappeared. For example, the mistress of Eastnor Castle, Herefordshire, Imogen Hervey-Bathurst, has recently launched a new line of wallpapers and fabrics inspired by the house's interiors.[40] Similarly, the emphasis on motherhood and the importance of women preparing their children for their duties as members of the elite can be seen across the years – whether it was Grace Mildmay writing her spiritual autobiography for her daughter and granddaughter, or Mary Talbot ensuring that her children had the best possible governesses. More recently, some elite women have continued this commitment to protecting their children's dynastic heritage: Elizabeth Dent-Brocklehurst ignored her lawyer's advice to sell the heavily indebted Sudeley Castle, Gloucester, after the death of her husband in 1972, and instead worked to make the house an attractive tourist proposition, so that their children could retain, in her words, 'their home and birthright'.[41]

In some regards the continuities are surprising. While the legislation regarding primogeniture has changed for members of the royal family, there are fewer than ninety peerages that can be inherited by a woman.[42] Modern families do not have to use this model when passing on their estates, and many families have split them across their children.

However, the fact that male inheritance remains part of the modern legal framework shows how the old world still shapes the new.

The duty of a mistress to 'provision' her home has altered significantly in the last 450 years. However, as with most of the other changes to the role of mistress, this has been driven more by socio-economic change rather than by shifting gender ideals. Changing consumption patterns meant a shift away from the lady of the house directly overseeing the food made within the kitchen or producing medicines, as Grace Mildmay did. However, from the sixteenth century through to the twenty-first century we can see the active involvement of the country-house mistress in providing for the household in a variety of ways. Previously, this might have included estate management – as we saw in Maria Thynne's feisty letters to her husband. Today, it could involve the mistress of the house working for an outside organisation or leading income-generating activities within the modern country-house business – designing exhibitions, running the farm or establishing the property as a thriving wedding venue.[43] All of these activities require 'skill', reflecting the third of Johnson's definitions of a mistress.

It is interesting to note that two of the great champions of the diversification of country-house income in the 1970s and 1980s were women: Lady Cobham at Hagley Hall, and the eleventh duchess of Devonshire (popularly known as Debo), who has been credited with moving Chatsworth into the 'super-league' of visitor attractions.[44] But it is important to appreciate that mistresses have always 'provided' for the house in ways that may seem less directly economic. This would include the political work that women engaged in, as we saw in the examples of Frances Irwin and Louisa Knightley in the eighteenth and nineteenth centuries. It would also include the crucially important estate activities that so many of these women undertook to form close links with the tenancy – whether through directly managing estate workers (as Alice Le Strange did) or hosting garden parties (in the style of Henrietta Bankes). This also connects to the importance of forming friendship networks with other elites, so that they could provide both emotional and practical support (as we see with both the Souls and the bluestockings).

CONCLUSION: DEFENDING THE COUNTRY HOUSE

In performing these activities, many of the women worked in partnership with their spouses, as we saw with the Thynnes, the Boscawens, the Trevelyans, the Lucys and – although they were not married – in the relationship of the Ladies of Llangollen. The idea that a mistress was a 'woman beloved', in Johnson's phrase, can be seen in their lives. There were, of course, some exceptions, and most of these marriages were not equal; even Mary Elcho and Maria Thynne were subject to their husband's choices about estate matters, although they both often found ways to get solutions that worked for them. Also, some women did not derive joy from being 'beloved' by their spouse, and instead found affection in extramarital relationships (as we saw with Mary Elcho) or from siblings or children (as reflected by the relationship Anne Dormer had with her sister, and Brilliana Harley with her son). But this desire to work with others in order to preserve their family home and maintain and enhance their dynastic status is something that connects many elite women who lived in the period that this book has explored. It is this sense of duty to the family and the estate that underpinned the ideal of being a country-house mistress. This role meant that women were able to use this duty positively to 'govern'; it was usually only when male gender ideals were not met that mistresses were, in Fanny Boscawen's phrase, 'reduced to submission'. Therefore, although some of them faced obstacles to the fulfilment of these roles – whether on account of finances, familial discord or external problems – it is because of their commitment to the houses and to their families that we can see that these women were indeed the mistresses of their country houses.

Endnotes

INTRODUCTION

1. Samuel Johnson, *A dictionary of the English language; in which the words are deduced from their originals and illustrated in their different significations by examples from the best writers. To which are prefixed, a history of the language, and an English grammar*, vol. 2 (W. Strahan, 1755).
2. Joanne Begiato, 'A "master-mistress": Revisiting the history of eighteenth-century wives', *Women's History Review*, 32 (2023), pp. 2–3.
3. The Hon. Mrs Boscawen to mrs Delany, Brighton, 20 September 1771, reproduced in Augusta Hall (ed.), *The Autobiography and Correspondence of Mary Granville, Mrs Delany: With interesting reminiscences of King George the Third and Queen Charlotte*, 2nd series, vol. I (R. Bentley, 1861–1862; imprint: AMS Press, 1974), pp. 359–360.
4. The peerage is a term that is often used to mean those who had a right to sit in the House of Lords and their immediate families. The terms aristocracy, nobility, gentry, upper class, elite, etc. are all debated terms, which did not have fixed meanings in the past. For a discussion of this, see Amanda Goodrich, 'Understanding a language of "aristocracy", 1700–1850', *The Historical Journal*, 56 (2013), pp. 369–398.
5. Throughout the book, the spelling in extracts from primary sources has been standardised, and punctuation added, in order to help the reader.
6. Mark Girouard, *Life in the English Country House: A social and architectural history* (Yale University Press, 1978), p. 2.
7. Lawrence Stone and Jeanne C. Fawtier Stone, *An Open Elite? England 1540–1880* (Clarendon, 1984), pp. 361–363; Julian Hoppit, 'The landed interest and the national interest, 1660–1800', in Julian Hoppit (ed.), *Parliaments, Nations and Identities in Britain and Ireland, 1660–1850* (Manchester University Press, 2003), p. 84; J.V. Beckett, *The Aristocracy in England, 1660–1914* (Basil Blackwell, 1986), pp. 44–90.
8. Just some of the texts that highlight this include Rosemary Baird, *Mistress of the House: Great ladies and grand houses, 1670–1830* (Weidenfeld & Nicolson, 2003);

Stephen Bending, *Green Retreats: Women, gardens and eighteenth-century culture* (Cambridge University Press, 2013); Amy Boyington, *Hidden Patrons: Women and architectural patronage in Georgian Britain* (Bloomsbury, 2024); Trevor Lummis and Jan Marsh, *The Woman's Domain: Women and the English country house* (Viking, 1990); Briony McDonagh, *Elite Women and the Agricultural Landscape, 1700–1830* (Taylor & Francis, 2018).

9. Among some of the texts that explore these functions of the country house are Joan Coutu, Jon Stobart and Peter N. Lindfield (eds), *Politics and the English Country House, 1688–1800* (McGill-Queen's University Press, 2023); Dana Arnold (ed.), *The Georgian Country House: Architecture, landscape and society* (Sutton, 2003); Karen Hearn, Giles Waterfield and Robert Upstone, *In Celebration: The art of the country house* (Tate Gallery, 1998); Jon Stobart and Mark Rothery, *Consumption and the Country House* (Oxford University Press, 2016); Pamela Sambrook, *Keeping Their Place: Domestic service in the country house* (Sutton, 2007); James S. Ackerman, *The Villa: Form and ideology of country houses* (Thames & Hudson, 1990), chapter one; Judith S. Lewis, 'When a house is not a home: Elite English women and the eighteenth-century country house', *The Journal of British Studies*, 48.2 (2009), pp. 336–363.

10. Leonore Davidoff and Catherine Hall, *Family Fortunes: Men and women of the English middle class, 1780–1850* (Hutchinson, 1987); Linda K. Kerber, 'Separate spheres, female worlds, woman's place: The rhetoric of women's history', *The Journal of American History*, 75.1 (1988), pp. 9–39; Amanda Vickery, 'Golden age to separate spheres? A review of the categories and chronology of English women's history', *The Historical Journal*, 36.2 (1993), pp. 383–414; Eleanor Gordon and Gordon Nair, *Public Lives: Women, family and society in Victorian Britain* (Yale University Press, 2003).

11. Anne Summers, *Female Lives, Moral States: Women, religion and public life in Britain 1800–1930* (Threshold Press, 2000); Simon Morgan, 'Between public and private: Gender, domesticity, and authority in the long nineteenth century', *The Historical Journal*, 54.4 (2011), pp. 1197–1210.

12. Susan Wiseman, *Conspiracy and Virtue: Women, writing, and politics in seventeenth-century England* (Oxford University Press, 2006), p. 16. This blurring of public and private was also seen in the medieval period. See Heather J. Tanner, Laura L. Gathagan and Lois L. Huneycutt, 'Introduction', in Heather J. Tanner (ed.), *Medieval Elite Women and the Exercise of Power, 1100–1400: Moving beyond the exceptionalist debate* (Palgrave Macmillan, 2019), p. 8.

13. K.D. Reynolds, *Aristocratic Women and Political Society in Victorian Britain* (Clarendon Press, 1998), p. 4.

14. Adrian Wooldridge, *The Aristocracy of Talent: How meritocracy made the modern world* (Allen Lane, 2021), p. 37.

15. T.H. Hollingsworth, 'Demography of the British peerage', *Supplement to Population Studies*, 18.2 (1964), Table 11.

16. Sarah Shields, '"An old maid in a house is the devil": Single women and landed estate management in eighteenth-century England', *Journal for Eighteenth-Century Studies*, 44 (2021), pp. 423–438; Pamela Horn, *Ladies of the Manor: How wives and daughters really lived in country house society over a century ago* (Amberley, 2014), pp. 20–21; McDonagh, *Elite Women and the Agricultural Landscape*, pp. 26–27; Linda Levy Peck, *Women of Fortune: Money, marriage, and murder in early modern England* (Cambridge University Press, 2018), pp. 6–7.

17. Judith Schneid Lewis, *In the Family Way: Childbearing in the British aristocracy, 1760–1860* (Rutgers University Press, 1986), p. 65. Both Alice Stubbe (later Le Strange) and Frances Graham (later Horner) were very close to their fathers (see Chapters 1 and 8).
18. Shulamith Firestone, *The Dialectic of Sex: The case of feminist revolution* (Paladin, 1972), p. 81. See for example: Donna Bassin, Margaret Honey and Meryle Mahrer Kaplan, 'Introduction', in Bassin, Honey and Kaplan (eds), *Representations of Motherhood* (Yale University Press, 1994), pp. 2–3; Ellen Ross, 'New thoughts on "the oldest vocation": Mothers and motherhood in recent feminist scholarship', *Signs: Journal of Women in Culture and Society*, 20 (1995), pp. 397–399.
19. Countess Spencer, cited in Ruby H. Rutter, 'Elite women, emotions, and the lived experience in the eighteenth-century country house, 1700–1830', PhD thesis, University of Manchester, 2022, p. 65.
20. For example, one of the daughters of Sabine and Sir Rowland Winn of Nostell Priory married the family baker. Christopher Todd and Sophie Raikes, 'Love, rebellion and redemption: Three generations of women at Nostell Priory', in Ruth M. Larsen (ed.), *Maids and Mistresses: Celebrating 300 years of women and the Yorkshire country house* (Yorkshire Country House Partnership, 2004), pp. 83–84; Randolph Trumbach, *The Rise of the Egalitarian Family: Aristocratic kinship and domestic relations in eighteenth-century England* (Academic Press, 1978), p. 71; Lewis, *In the Family Way*, p. 18.
21. For a discussion of marriage law, see Tim Stretton and K.J. Kesselring, *Married Women and the Law: Coverture in England and the common law world* (McGill-Queen's University Press, 2013).
22. See, for example, Katie Barclay, *Love, Intimacy and Power: Marriage and patriarchy in Scotland, 1650–1850* (Manchester University Press, 2011) and Ingrid H. Tague, 'Love, honor, and obedience: Fashionable women and the discourse of marriage in the early eighteenth century', *The Journal of British Studies*, 40 (2001), pp. 76–106.
23. Edward Howard Marsh, *A Number of People: A book of reminiscences* (William Heinemann, 1939), p. 176.
24. Lawrence Stone, *The Family, Sex and Marriage in England 1500–1800* (Penguin, 1979); Robert B. Shoemaker, *Gender in English Society 1650–1850: The emergence of separate spheres?* (Routledge, 1998); Anthony Fletcher, *Gender, Sex and Subordination in England, 1500–1800* (Yale University Press, 1995); Sara Heller Mendelson and Patricia Crawford, *Women in Early Modern England, 1550–1720* (Clarendon, 1998).
25. John Cannon, *Aristocratic Century: The peerage of eighteenth-century England* (Cambridge University Press, 1984).
26. Ingrid H. Tague, 'Aristocratic women and the ideas of family in the early eighteenth century', in Helen Berry and Elizabeth Foyster (eds), *The Family in Early Modern England* (Cambridge University Press, 2007), pp. 184–208; Amanda Vickery, *The Gentleman's Daughter: Women's lives in Georgian England* (Yale University Press, 1998); Amanda Vickery, *Behind Closed Doors: At home in Georgian England* (Yale University Press, 2009); Paul Langford, *A Polite and Commercial People: England, 1727–1783* (Clarendon Press, 1998).
27. Hannah Greig, *The Beau Monde: Fashionable society in Georgian London* (Oxford University Press, 2013); J. Mordaunt Crook, *The Rise of the Nouveaux Riches: Style*

and status in Victorian and Edwardian architecture (John Murray, 1999); Stella Margetson, *Victorian High Society* (Batsford, 1980), p. 12.
28. Mark Girouard, *The Return to Camelot: Chivalry and the English gentleman* (Yale University Press, 1981), pp. 275–293.

PART ONE

1. J.A. Sharpe, *Early Modern England: A social history 1550–1760*, 2nd edition (Arnold, 1997), p. 23; Charles Carlton, *Going to the Wars: The experience of the British Civil Wars 1638–1651* (Routledge, 1992), p. 340; Thomas Hobbes, *Leviathan, Or, the Matter, Forme, & Power of a Common-Wealth Ecclesiasticall and Civill* (Andrew Ckooke [sic], 1651), p. 62.
2. W.G. Hoskins, 'The rebuilding of rural England, 1570–1640', *Past & Present*, 4 (1953), pp. 44–59; Felicity Heal and Clive Holmes, *The Gentry in England and Wales, 1500–1700* (Macmillan Press, 1994), p. 298; Stone, *The Family, Sex and Marriage*, pp. 150ff; Matthew Johnson, *An Archaeology of Capitalism* (Blackwell Publishers, 1996), pp. 119–134; Clive Aslet, *The Story of the Country House: A history of places and people* (Yale University Press, 2021), pp. 35–77; Ian Warren, 'The cultural horizons of the seventeenth-century English gentry', in Jacqueline Eales and Andrew Hopper (eds), *The County Community in Seventeenth-Century England and Wales*, Explorations in Local History, vol. 5 (University of Hertfordshire Press, 2012), pp. 59–63; Lyn Boothman and Richard Hyde Parker (eds), *Savage Fortune: An aristocratic family in the early seventeenth century* (Boydell [in association with] Suffolk Records Society, 2006), p. li.
3. Alison D. Wall, *Power and Protest in England, 1525–1640* (Arnold, 2000), pp. 45–61. For example, Anthony Mildmay was involved in conflicts such as the Northern Rising (1569) and a protest by the Levellers in 1607. Kathryn A. Morrison, *Apethorpe: The story of an English country house* (Yale University Press, 2016), pp. 80–81.
4. Sharpe, *Early Modern England*, pp. 10–11, 16–17; Helen Payne, 'Aristocratic women, power, patronage and family networks at Jacobean Court', in James Daybell, *Women and Politics in Early Modern England, 1450–1700* (Ashgate, 2004), pp. 164–180; Clare McManus, 'Introduction: The Queen's Court', in Clare McManus (ed.), *Women and Culture at the Courts of the Stuart Queens* (Palgrave Macmillan, 2003), pp. 1–3.
5. John Broad, 'Gentry finances and the Civil War: The case of the Buckinghamshire Verneys', *The Economic History Review*, 32 (1979), pp. 183–200; Sharpe, *Early Modern England*, p. 30. For example, Hamon Le Strange had to pay compensation to the townspeople of King's Lynn. Anna Keay, *The Restless Republic: Britain without a crown* (William Collins, 2022), pp. 177–181.
6. Shoemaker, *Gender in English Society*, pp. 15–19; Jacqueline Eales, *Women in Early Modern England, 1500–1700* (UCL, 1998), pp. 23–24; Susan D. Amussen, 'Gender, family and the social order, 1560–1725', in Anthony Fletcher and John Stevenson (eds), *Order and Disorder in Early Modern England* (Cambridge University Press, 1985), p. 196.
7. Antonia Fraser, *The Weaker Vessel: Woman's lot in seventeenth-century England* (Phoenix, 2002), p. 4; M.E. Wiesner, *Women and Gender in Early Modern Europe* (Cambridge University Press, 1993), p. 40.
8. Mendelson and Crawford, *Women in Early Modern England*, pp. 37–39.

9. Ramona Wray, *Women Writers of the Seventeenth Century* (Northcote House, 2004), pp. 43, 388.
10. Wiseman, *Conspiracy and Virtue*, p. 5; Fraser, *The Weaker Vessel*, p. 566; Eales, *Women in Early Modern England*, pp. 24, 112.
11. Austin, cited in Fraser, *The Weaker Vessel*, pp. 3–4; Shoemaker, *Gender in English Society*, p. 17; Alan Macfarlane, *Witchcraft in Tudor and Stuart England: A regional and comparative study* (Routledge & Kegan Paul, 1970), pp. 158–166; Marianne Hester, *Lewd Women and Wicked Witches: A study of the dynamics of male domination* (Routledge, 1992), pp. 160–163.
12. Fletcher, *Gender, Sex and Subordination*, pp. 101–125; Shoemaker, *Gender in English Society*, p. 45; Thomas Laqueur, *Making Sex: Body and gender from the Greeks to Freud* (Harvard University Press, 1990), pp. 148–169; Karen Harvey, 'The century of sex? Gender, bodies, and sexuality in the long eighteenth century', *The Historical Journal*, 45.4 (2002), pp. 899–916.
13. Linda A. Pollock, 'Mildmay [née Sharington], Grace, Lady Mildmay (c.1552–1620), memoirist and medical practitioner', *Oxford Dictionary of National Biography*, Oxford University Press, 27 May 2010; Linda A. Pollock, *With Faith and Physic: The life of a Tudor gentlewoman, Lady Grace Mildmay, 1552–1620* (Collins & Brown, 1993).
14. While some writers use the surname L'Estrange, which was the spelling preferred by her son, Le Strange was the version used by Alice and her husband. Elizabeth Griffiths and Jane Whittle, 'L'Estrange [née Stubbe], Alice, Lady L'Estrange (1585–1656), keeper of household and estate accounts', *Oxford Dictionary of National Biography*, Oxford University Press, 24 May 2008; Elizabeth Griffiths (ed.), *Her Price Is Above Pearls: Family and farming records of Alice Le Strange, 1617–1656*, Norfolk Record Society, vol. 79 (Norfolk Record Society, 2015).
15. Alison Wall, 'Thynne [née Touchet], Maria, Lady Thynne (c.1578–1611), gentlewoman', *Oxford Dictionary of National Biography*, Oxford University Press, 27 May 2010; Alison Wall (ed.), *Two Elizabethan Women: Correspondence of Joan and Maria Thynne 1575–1611*, Wiltshire Record Society, vol. 37 (Wiltshire Record Society, 1983); Graham T. Williams, *Women's Epistolary Utterance: A study of the letters of Joan and Maria Thynne, 1575–1611*, Pragmatics & Beyond New Series, vol. 233 (John Benjamins Publishing Company, 2014).
16. Mary Chan, 'Wiseman [née North], Elizabeth, Lady Wiseman [other married name Elizabeth Paston, countess of Yarmouth] (1647–1730), litigant', *Oxford Dictionary of National Biography*, Oxford University Press, 23 September 2004; Mary Chan (ed.), *Life into Story: The courtship of Elizabeth Wiseman* (Ashgate, 1998).
17. Jacqueline Eales, 'Harley [née Conway], Brilliana, Lady Harley (bap. 1598, d. 1643), parliamentarian gentlewoman', *Oxford Dictionary of National Biography*, Oxford University Press, 3 January 2008; Jacqueline Eales, *Puritans and Roundheads: The Harleys of Brampton Bryan and the outbreak of the English Civil War* (Cambridge University Press, 1990); Thomas Taylor Lewis (ed.), *Letters of the Lady Brilliana Harley, Wife of Sir Robert Harley, of Brampton Bryan* (Camden Society, 1853).
18. Mary E. O'Connor, 'Dormer [née Cottrell], Anne (1648?–1695), letter-writer', *Oxford Dictionary of National Biography*, Oxford University Press, 21 May 2009; Sara Mendelson and Mary O'Connor, '"Thy passionately loving sister and

faithful friend": Anne Dormer's letters to her sister Lady Trumbull', in Naomi J. Miller and Naomi Yavneh (eds), *Sibling Relation and Gender in the Early Modern World* (Ashgate, 2006), pp. 206–215; British Library, Additional MS 72516, fos. 157–241 (henceforth BL Add MS).

CHAPTER 1

1. Grace Mildmay, 'Autobiography', in Pollock, *With Faith and Physic*, p. 32.
2. Mildmay, 'Autobiography', pp. 32–33.
3. Pollock, *With Faith and Physic*, p. 97; Mildmay, 'Autobiography', p. 27.
4. Mildmay, 'Autobiography', p. 27.
5. Mildmay, 'Autobiography', pp. 28–29.
6. Grace Mildmay, 'Lady Grace's meditation upon the corpse [of her husband]', in Pollock, *With Faith and Physic*, pp. 41–42.
7. Eales, *Women in Early Modern England*, p. 26.
8. Mildmay, 'Autobiography', pp. 34–35.
9. Will of Sir Hamon Le Strange, proved 7 July 1654, reproduced in Griffiths (ed.), *Her Price Is Above Pearls*, p. 353.
10. Keay, *The Restless Republic*, pp. 180–189. For a discussion of the impact of the work of Hamon and Alice Le Strange, see Elizabeth Griffiths, *Managing for Posterity: The Norfolk gentry and their estates c.1450–1700* (University of Hertfordshire Press, 2022), pp. 33–170.
11. Elizabeth Griffiths, '"A country life": Sir Hamon Le Strange of Hunstanton in Norfolk, 1583–1654', in Richard W. Hoyle (ed.), *Custom, Improvement and the Landscape in Early Modern Britain* (Routledge, 2011), p. 214.
12. N.H. Keeble, *The Cultural Identity of Seventeenth-Century Woman: A reader* (Routledge, 1994), p. 143.
13. Mildmay, 'Autobiography', p. 34.
14. Hamon Le Strange, cited in Jane Whittle and Elizabeth Griffiths, *Consumption and Gender in the Early Seventeenth-Century Household: The world of Alice Le Strange* (Oxford University Press, 2012), p. 33.
15. Sara Heller Mendelson, 'Stuart women's diaries and occasional memoirs', in Mary Prior (ed.), *Women in English Society 1500–1800* (Methuen, 1985), pp. 185–200.
16. William Gouge, *Of Domesticall Duties: Eight treatises* (John Haviland for William Bladen, 1622), p. 367.
17. Wall, *Power and Protest in England*, pp. 84–85.
18. Grace Mildmay, cited in Heal and Holmes, *The Gentry*, p. 59.
19. Walter Mildmay, 1570, cited in Heal and Holmes, *The Gentry*, p. 248.
20. Keeble, *The Cultural Identity of Seventeenth-Century Woman*, p. 143.
21. It was probably written in 1612. Nicole Pohl, '"An emblem of themselves": Early Renaissance country house poetry', in M. Hattaway (ed.), *A New Companion to English Renaissance Literature and Culture*, vol. 1 (Wiley-Blackwell, 2010), p. 370.
22. Hugh Jenkins, 'From common wealth to commonwealth: The alchemy of "To Penshurst"', *Clio*, 25.2 (1996), pp. 165–180.
23. Jonson, 'To Penshurst', lines 82–88, reproduced in Sukanta Chaudhuri (ed.), *Pastoral Poetry of the English Renaissance: An anthology* (Manchester University Press, 2016), pp. 376–377.

24. Morrison, *Apethorpe*, pp. 70–71, 89–93; Pollock, *With Faith and Physic*, pp. 19–20.
25. Cited in Lucy Aikin, *Memoirs of the Court of King James the First*, vol. 1 (Longman & Co., 1822), p. 104. Banquets referred to sweetmeats and other small treats served following a meal. Morrison, *Apethorpe*, p. 86.
26. Pollock, 'Mildmay [née Sharington], Grace', *ODNB*.
27. Whittle and Griffiths, *Consumption and Gender*, p. 37.
28. Mary Abbott, *Family Ties: English families 1540–1920* (Routledge, 1993), p. 60; Keay, *The Restless Republic*, p. 181.
29. Morrison, *Apethorpe*, pp. 80–81; Mildmay, 'Autobiography', p. 34.
30. Heal and Holmes, *The Gentry*, p. 280.
31. Abbott, *Family Ties*, p. 61.
32. Rosemary O'Day, *The Family and Family Relationships, 1500–1900: England, France and the United States of America* (Macmillan, 1994), p. 141.
33. Susan Broomhall, 'Emotions in the household', in Susan Broomhall (ed.), *Emotions in the Household, 1200–1900* (Palgrave Macmillan, 2008), pp. 2–4.
34. Whittle and Griffiths, *Consumption and Gender*, p. 34, Figure 6.1.
35. Tim Meldrum, *Domestic Service and Gender 1660–1750: Life and work in the London household* (Longman, 2000), pp. 22–25; Ann Kussmaul, *Servants in Husbandry in Early Modern England* (Cambridge University Press, 1981), p. 3; Broomhall, 'Emotions in the household', p. 3; Anthony Fletcher, *Growing Up in England: The experience of childhood 1600–1914* (Yale University Press, 2010), pp. 260–261.
36. Whittle and Griffiths, *Consumption and Gender*, pp. 218–219, Table 8.2.
37. Walter Mildmay, 1570, cited in Heal and Holmes, *The Gentry*, p. 102.
38. Whittle and Griffiths, *Consumption and Gender*, pp. 101–102, Table 8.1.
39. Whittle and Griffiths, *Consumption and Gender*, pp. 217–218.
40. McDonagh, *Elite Women and the Agricultural Landscape*, pp. 3–4.
41. Griffiths (ed.), *Her Price Is Above Pearls*, pp. 2, 207–258; Whittle and Griffiths, *Consumption and Gender*, pp. 28–30.
42. Gouge, *Of Domesticall Duties*, p. 367; Whittle and Griffiths, *Consumption and Gender*, pp. 42–43.
43. Barbara Harris, *English Aristocratic Women, 1450–1550: Marriage and family, property and careers* (Oxford University Press, 2002), pp. 64–65.
44. Whittle and Griffiths, *Consumption and Gender*, pp. 29, 64–67, 182, 221–226.
45. John Murdoch, 'Hoskins, John [known as John Hoskins the elder, Old Hoskins] (c.1590–1665), miniature painter', *Oxford Dictionary of National Biography*, Oxford University Press, 23 September 2004; Chris R. Kyle, 'L'Estrange, Sir Hamon (1583–1654), politician', *Oxford Dictionary of National Biography*, Oxford University Press, 22 September 2005.
46. Cited in Keay, *The Restless Republic*, p. 185; Heal and Holmes, *The Gentry*, p. 33; Morrison, *Apethorpe*, p. 81.
47. Stone and Fawtier Stone, *An Open Elite?*, p. 197. There were some wall paintings added to Apethorpe during Anthony Mildmay's period of ownership, but little other building work. Morrison, *Apethorpe*, pp. 61–71, 83; Pete Smith, 'The history of the estate and its owners', in English Heritage Apethorpe Research Team (ed.), *Apethorpe Hall, Apethorpe, Northamptonshire: Survey, research and analysis*, vol. 1: *Report* (English Heritage, 2006), p. 43.

48. Griffiths, *Managing for Posterity*, pp. 93–117; Jennifer S. Alexander and Kathryn A. Morrison, 'Apethorpe Hall and the workshop of Thomas Thorpe, Mason of King's Cliffe: A study in masons' marks', *Architectural History*, 50 (2007), pp. 59–94.
49. Christopher Hussey, 'Country homes and gardens old & new: Hunstanton Hall – I. Norfolk. The seat of Mr Charles Le Strange', *Country Life*, 59.1527 (10 April 1926), p. 559; Whittle and Griffiths, *Consumption and Gender*, p. 29.
50. Malcolm Airs, *The Tudor and Jacobean Country House: A building history* (Bramley, 1998), pp. 14–15.
51. The most famous of the female housebuilders from the sixteenth and seventeenth centuries was Elizabeth, countess of Shrewsbury, who built two houses at Hardwick. Lummis and Marsh, *The Woman's Domain*, pp. 6–33.
52. Mildmay, 'Autobiography', p. 35.
53. Rozsika Parker, *The Subversive Stitch: Embroidery and the making of the feminine*, new edition (I.B. Tauris, 2010), pp. 67–71.
54. Susan Frye, 'Sewing connections. Elizabeth Tudor, Mary Stuart, Elizabeth Talbot and seventeenth-century anonymous needleworkers', in Susan Frye and Kate Robertson (eds), *Maids and Mistresses, Cousins and Queens: Women's alliances in early modern England* (Oxford University Press, 1999), pp. 169–174.
55. Whittle and Griffiths, *Consumption and Gender*, pp. 59, 61, 127, 135, 141, 192–193.
56. Linda Levy Peck, *Consuming Splendor: Society and culture in seventeenth-century England* (Cambridge University Press, 2005), pp. 215–216.
57. Kyle, 'L'Estrange, Sir Hamon', *ODNB*; Whittle and Griffiths, *Consumption and Gender*, pp. 37, 52, 55–64, 194–203; R.W. Ketton-Cremer, *Norfolk in the Civil War: A portrait of a society in conflict* (Faber & Faber, 1969), p. 28; Griffiths, *Managing for Posterity*, pp. 72–75, 87.
58. Whittle and Griffiths, *Consumption and Gender*, p. 139. Less than 3% of households in Kent had a mirror in the period 1600–1629 and less than 1% had a clock, according to inventory records. See Mark Overton, Jane Whittle, Darron Dean and Andrew Hann, *Production and Consumption in English Households, 1600–1750* (Routledge, 2004), p. 111. Also see Tara Hamling, *Decorating the 'Godly' Household: Religious art in post-Reformation Britain* (Yale University Press, 2010), passim; Whittle and Griffiths, *Consumption and Gender*, p. 57.
59. Whittle and Griffiths, *Consumption and Gender*, pp. 82, 191–196.
60. Whittle and Griffiths, *Consumption and Gender*, p. 77, Table 3.7.
61. Whittle and Griffiths, *Consumption and Gender*, p. 83; Jonson, 'To Penshurst', lines 48–60.
62. Felicity Heal, *Hospitality in Early Modern England* (Clarendon, 1990), pp. 76–77; Whittle and Griffiths, *Consumption and Gender*, p. 99; Keay, *The Restless Republic*, pp. 181–183.
63. Felicity Heal, *The Power of Gifts: Gift-exchange in early modern England* (Oxford University Press, 2014), p. 12; Whittle and Griffiths, *Consumption and Gender*, pp. 81–82.
64. Elizabeth bore him six children during a nineteen-year marriage. Spring just outlived his father-in-law by one year in the 1650s. W.A. Shaw and Sean Kelsey, 'L'Estrange, Hamon (1605–1660), theologian and historian', *Oxford Dictionary of National Biography*, Oxford University Press, 3 January 2008.

65. Whittle and Griffiths, *Consumption and Gender*, pp. 132–133. For an account of the replacement of garderobes with these inner chambers, see Nicholas Cooper, *Houses of the Gentry, 1480–1680* (Yale University Press, 1999), pp. 294–299.
66. H.F. Lippincott, '*Merry Passages and Jeasts': A manuscript jestbook of Sir Nicholas Le Strange, 1603–1655*, Salzburg Studies in English Literature, Elizabethan & Renaissance Studies, 29 (Institut für Englische Sprache und Literatur, Universität Salzburg, 1974), pp. 12–14; British Library, Harley Manuscript 6395, *Merry Passages and Jests*, Jest 464, fo. 71 and Jest 358, fo. 56; Keith Thomas, 'Bodily control and social unease: The fart in seventeenth-century England', in Angela McShane and Garthine Walker (eds), *The Extraordinary and the Everyday in Early Modern England*, pp. 9–30; Pamela Allen Brown, *Better a Shrew than a Sheep: Women, drama, and the culture of jest in early modern England* (Cornell University Press, 2003), p. 149; Pamela Allen Brown, 'Jesting rights: Women players in the manuscript jestbook of Sir Nicholas Le Strange', in Pamela Allen Brown and Peter Paolin (eds), *Women Players in England, 1500–1660* (Routledge, 2005), p. 307.
67. Whittle and Griffiths, *Consumption and Gender*, p. 194.
68. Heal, *Hospitality in Early Modern England*, pp. 47, 59–63.
69. L.M. Klein, 'Lady Anne Clifford as mother and matriarch: Domestic and dynastic issues in her life writing', *Journal of Family History*, 26 (2001), p. 21; Boothman and Parker, *Savage Fortune*, p. xxii.
70. Pollock, *With Faith and Physic*, pp. 11, 86.
71. Mendelson and Crawford, *Women in Early Modern England*, pp. 67–68.
72. Naomi J. Miller, 'Mothering others: Caregiving as spectrum and spectacle in the early modern period', in Naomi J. Miller and Naomi Yavneh (eds), *Maternal Measures: Figuring caregiving in the early modern period* (Routledge, 2000), p. 7. For a discussion of the power of women as educators, see M. Myers, 'Impeccable governesses, rational dames, and moral mothers: Mary Wollstonecraft and the female tradition in Georgian children's literature', *Children's Literature*, 14 (1986), pp. 33, 36; Mildmay, cited in Heal and Holmes, *The Gentry*, p. 249; O'Day, *The Family and Family Relationships*, p. 166.
73. Griffiths, *Managing for Posterity*, p. 150; Whittle and Griffiths, *Consumption and Gender*, pp. 28–36.
74. Pollock, *With Faith and Physic*, p. 11.
75. Stone, *The Family, Sex and Marriage*, passim, esp. pp. 405, 449–470; Trumbach, *The Rise of the Egalitarian Family*, esp. pp. 187–190, 238–242. These ideas have been critiqued by, among many others, Ralph A. Houlbrooke, *The English Family, 1450–1700* (Longman, 1984), pp. 127–156; Linda A. Pollock, *Forgotten Children: Parent–child relations from 1500 to 1900* (Cambridge University Press, 1983), passim; Fletcher, *Growing Up in England*, pp. 55–64.
76. Elizabeth Grymeston, cited in Wiesner, *Women and Gender*, p. 73; Mendelson and Crawford, *Women in Early Modern England*, pp. 158–159. See also examples in Patricia Crawford and Laura Gowing (eds), *Women's Worlds in Seventeenth-Century England* (Routledge, 2000), pp. 187ff.
77. Patricia Crawford, *Blood, Bodies and Families in Early Modern England* (Longman, 2004), pp. 148–151; Eales, *Women in Early Modern England*, p. 69; Margaret L. King, *Women of the Renaissance* (University of Chicago Press, 1991), pp. 13–15; Abbott, *Family Ties*, p. 48; Whittle and Griffiths, *Consumption and Gender*, pp. 170–172.
78. Whittle and Griffiths, *Consumption and Gender*, pp. 172–173.

79. Pollock, *With Faith and Physic*, p. 11.
80. Morrison, *Apethorpe*, p. 60.
81. Pollock, *With Faith and Physic*, pp. 11–12, 18.
82. Whittle and Griffiths, *Consumption and Gender*, p. 166.
83. Whittle and Griffiths, *Consumption and Gender*, pp. 99–101.
84. Whittle and Griffiths, *Consumption and Gender*, pp. 166, 171–172.
85. Ann Fanshawe, *Memoirs of Lady Fanshawe: Wife of Sir Richard Fanshawe, Bart., ambassador from Charles the Second to the courts of Portugal and Madrid* (H. Colburn and R. Bentley, 1830), pp. 119–120; Raymond A. Anselment, '"The teares of nature": Seventeenth-century parental bereavement', *Modern Philology*, 91.1 (1993), p. 30.
86. Henry Smith, *A Preparative to Marriage* (1591), reproduced in Kate Aughterson (ed.), *Renaissance Woman: A sourcebook. Constructions of femininity in England* (Routledge, 1995), p. 82.
87. Whittle and Griffiths, *Consumption and Gender*, p. 110.
88. Pollock, *With Faith and Physic*, p. 97.
89. Helen Cox, '"A most precious and excellent balm": The theory and practice of medicine in the papers of Lady Grace Mildmay, 1552–1620', *Midland History*, 43.1 (2018), p. 24.
90. Cox, '"A most precious and excellent balm"', pp. 30–32; Edith Snook, 'English women's writing and indigenous knowledge in the early modern Atlantic world', in Patricia Phillippy (ed.), *A History of Early Modern Women's Writing* (Cambridge University Press, 2018), p. 393.
91. Whittle and Griffiths, *Consumption and Gender*, p. 109; Cox, '"A most precious and excellent balm"', pp. 34–35; Morrison, *Apethorpe*, pp. 85, 418.
92. Anne Stobart, *Household Medicine in Seventeenth-Century England* (Bloomsbury Academic, 2016), p. 115.
93. Whittle and Griffiths, *Consumption and Gender*, p. 109.
94. Whittle and Griffiths, *Consumption and Gender*, pp. 106–107.
95. Abbott, *Family Ties*, p. 61.
96. Pollock, *With Faith and Physic*, p. 140.
97. Richard Banister, cited in Pollock, *With Faith and Physic*, p. 109.
98. Pollock, *With Faith and Physic*, pp. 18–19.
99. Whittle and Griffiths, *Consumption and Gender*, pp. 107–108; Ketton-Cremer, *Norfolk in the Civil War*, p. 41.
100. Mildmay, 'Autobiography', passim.
101. Thanks to Kiffy Stainer-Hutchins for this information.

CHAPTER 2

1. Wall, 'Introduction', in Wall (ed.), *Two Elizabethan Women*, p. xviii.
2. Faramerz Dabhoiwala, *The Origins of Sex: A history of the first sexual revolution* (Oxford University Press, 2012), p. 17.
3. Wall, 'Introduction', pp. xv–xvi.
4. O'Day, *The Family and Family Relationships*, p. 148.
5. Susan E. Whyman, *Sociability and Power in Late-Stuart England: The cultural worlds of the Verneys, 1660–1720* (Oxford University Press, 1999), p. 110.
6. Cissie Fairchilds, *Women in Early Modern Europe, 1500–1700* (Pearson Longman, 2007), pp. 196–197.

7. Mendelson and Crawford, *Women in Early Modern England*, p. 108.
8. Mendelson and Crawford, *Women in Early Modern England*, p. 110; Fairchilds, *Women in Early Modern Europe*, pp. 62–63.
9. Fairchilds, *Women in Early Modern Europe*, pp. 62–63; Wiesner, *Women and Gender*, p. 72.
10. Alice Thornton, cited in David Cressy, *Birth, Marriage, and Death: Ritual, religion and the life-cycle in Tudor and Stuart England* (Oxford University Press, 1997), p. 242.
11. Miriam Slater, 'The weightiest business: Marriage in an upper-gentry family in seventeenth-century England', *Past & Present*, 72 (1976), pp. 31–32.
12. Whittle and Griffiths, *Consumption and Gender*, pp. 20–22.
13. Keay, *The Restless Republic*, p. 178.
14. Houlbrooke, *The English Family*, pp. 65–66.
15. Mary Boyle, cited in Mendelson, 'Stuart women's diaries', p. 192.
16. Hollingsworth, 'Demography of the British peerage', p. 17.
17. Mendelson, 'Stuart women's diaries', pp. 193–194.
18. Elizabeth Foyster, 'Parenting was for life, not just for childhood: The role of parents in the married lives of their children in early modern England', *History*, 86.283 (2001), pp. 313–327.
19. Mendelson, 'Stuart women's diaries', p. 193.
20. 'The Lady Wiseman's relation concerning Mr Spencer, Oct. [1686]', reproduced in Chan (ed.), *Life into Story*, p. 23.
21. Thomas Chute, 'Mr Chute's relation, no date', reproduced in Chan (ed.), *Life into Story*, p. 3.
22. Chan (ed.), *Life into Story*, p. 4.
23. Chan (ed.), *Life into Story*, p. 3.
24. Mary Chan, 'Introduction', in Chan (ed.), *Life into Story*, pp. xiv–xv.
25. 'Copy of Lord N.'s letter to Sir Hen. North 16 Nov. 1686', reproduced in Chan (ed.), *Life into Story*, p. 49; Chan, 'Introduction', pp. xiv–xv.
26. Laura Gowing, *Domestic Dangers: Women, words, and sex in early modern London* (Clarendon Press, 1996), pp. 139–179; Cressy, *Birth, Marriage, and Death*, pp. 272–276.
27. Cressy, *Birth, Marriage, and Death*, pp. 234, 269; Fairchilds, *Women in Early Modern Europe*, p. 64.
28. 'Copy of Lord N.'s letter to Sir Hen. North 16 Nov. 1686', reproduced in Chan (ed.), *Life into Story*, p. 49.
29. Charles North, 'Lord North's letter 20 Nov. 1686', reproduced in Chan (ed.), *Life into Story*, p. 57.
30. 'Copy of Lord N.'s letter', pp. 49–50.
31. Cressy, *Birth, Marriage, and Death*, p. 254.
32. Smith, 'The history of the estate and its owners', p. 44. Pollock, *With Faith and Physic*, p. 12; Morrison, *Apethorpe*, p. 60.
33. Wall (ed.), *Two Elizabethan Women*, p. xxviii; Williams, *Women's Epistolary Utterance*, p. 25. For a discussion of the Touchets' finances, see Cynthia B. Herrup, *A House in Gross Disorder: Sex, law and the second earl of Castlehaven* (Oxford University Press, 1999), pp. 10–13.
34. O'Day, *The Family and Family Relationships*, p. 149.
35. For a discussion of the complex relationship between wealth, status and selfhood, see Alexandra Shepard, *Accounting for Oneself: Worth, status, and*

the social order in early modern England (Oxford University Press, 2015), chapter one.
36. 'Copy of Lord N.'s letter', pp. 50–51.
37. Francis White, 'Mr White Dec 29 [i.e. 26] 1686', reproduced in Chan (ed.), *Life into Story*, p. 94; Chan, 'Introduction', p. xiii.
38. Clement Oxenbridge, 'Oxenbridge's Note 7 Apr. 1687', reproduced in Chan (ed.), *Life into Story*, p. 94–95.
39. Chan, 'Introduction', p. xiii.
40. Chan, 'Introduction', p. xiv. This did not happen due to a belief that a jactitation of marriage case would create more even gossip.
41. 'Sp[encer]'s Release to Mr P. and Mr R. [1687]', reproduced in Chan (ed.), *Life into Story*, p. 99.
42. Mary Chan and Nancy E. Wright, 'Marriage, identity, and the pursuit of property in seventeenth-century England: The cases of Anne Clifford and Elizabeth Wiseman', in Nancy E. Wright, Margaret W. Ferguson and Andrew Buck (eds), *Women, Property, and the Letters of the Law in Early Modern England* (University of Toronto Press, 2004), pp. 162, 179.
43. Whittle and Griffiths, *Consumption and Gender*, pp. 168–169.
44. Cressy, *Birth, Marriage, and Death*, pp. 361–362.
45. Whittle and Griffiths, *Consumption and Gender*, pp. 168–169.
46. O'Day, *The Family and Family Relationships*, p. 148.
47. Wall, 'Introduction', p. xxvi.
48. Alison Wall, 'The feud and Shakespeare's *Romeo and Juliet*: A reconsideration', *Sydney Studies in English*, 5 (1979–1980), p. 90.
49. Wall, 'Introduction', pp. xviii–xxix; Williams, *Women's Epistolary Utterance*, p. 21.
50. Alison Wall, 'For love, money, or politics? A clandestine marriage and the Elizabethan Court of Arches', *The Historical Journal*, 38.3 (1995), p. 513.
51. Wall, 'Introduction', p. xxv.
52. Wall, 'For love, money, or politics?', p. 532. For example, Joan Thynne to John Thynne, 30 May 1595, v, fo. 73, reproduced in Wall (ed.), *Two Elizabethan Women*, pp. 11–12.
53. Cressy, *Birth, Marriage, and Death*, pp. 316–318, 321, 331–333.
54. Rolland White, cited in Williams, *Women's Epistolary Utterance*, p. 25.
55. Williams, *Women's Epistolary Utterance*, p. 26.
56. Wall, 'The feud', pp. 84–95.
57. Wall, 'For love, money, or politics?', p. 521.
58. Wall, 'For love, money, or politics?', pp. 526–528; Wall (ed.), *Two Elizabethan Women*, p. xxvi.
59. Williams, *Women's Epistolary Utterance*, pp. 26–27; Wall, 'For love, money, or politics?', p. 530.
60. Maria Thynne to Joan Thynne, 15 September 1601, viii, fo. 12, reproduced in Wall (ed.), *Two Elizabethan Women*, p. 21.
61. Fletcher, *Gender, Sex and Subordination*, p. 155 and Plate 40; Wall, 'Introduction', p. xxvii.
62. Gary Schneider, *The Culture of Epistolarity: Vernacular letters and letter writing in early modern England, 1500–1700* (University of Delaware Press, 2005), pp. 110–111.
63. Maria Thynne to Joan Thynne, 27 July 1602, viii, fo. 18, reproduced in Wall (ed.), *Two Elizabethan Women*, p. 27.

64. Williams, *Women's Epistolary Utterance*, p. 190.
65. Maria Thynne to Joan Thynne, 13 June 1602, viii, fo. 16 and Lucy Audley to Joan Thynne (Caus Castle), 10 June 1602, vii, fo. 232, reproduced in Wall (ed.), *Two Elizabethan Women*, pp. 26–27. For a discussion of Lucy Audley's letter and Joan Thynne's reply, see Williams, *Women's Epistolary Utterance*, chapter six.
66. Maria Thynne to Joan Thynne, [? 1605], viii, fo. 10, reproduced in Wall (ed.), *Two Elizabethan Women*, pp. 33–35; Williams, *Women's Epistolary Utterance*, pp. 192, 201–206.
67. James Daybell, 'Female literacy and the social conventions of women's letter-writing in England, 1540–1603', in James Daybell (ed.), *Early Modern Women's Letter Writing, 1450–1700* (Palgrave, 2001), p. 62; James Daybell, *Women Letter Writers in Tudor England* (Oxford University Press, 2006), p. 195.
68. Wall (ed.), *Two Elizabethan Women*, p. xxix.
69. Chancery suit by Joan Thynne, cited in Wall, 'For love, money, or politics?', p. 516.
70. For a discussion of the last letter between Joan and Thomas, see Williams, *Women's Epistolary Utterance*, pp. 31–45.
71. Fairchilds, *Women in Early Modern Europe*, p. 199.
72. Elizabeth Egerton, cited in Fletcher, *Gender, Sex and Subordination*, p. 358.
73. Grace Mildmay, 'Autobiography', p. 34.
74. Pollock, *With Faith and Physic*, pp. 23–91.
75. Cressy, *Birth, Marriage, and Death*, p. 343.
76. Mildmay, 'Lady Grace's meditation upon the corpse', pp. 40–42; Fletcher, *Gender, Sex and Subordination*, pp. 152, 167–168, 357–358.
77. Crawford, *Blood, Bodies and Families*, pp. 58–59; Wiesner, *Women and Gender*, p. 57; Thomas A. Foster, 'Deficient husbands: Manhood, sexual incapacity, and male marital sexuality in seventeenth-century New England', *The William and Mary Quarterly*, 56.4 (1999), p. 728.
78. Foster, 'Deficient husbands', p. 728.
79. Gouge, *Of Domesticall Duties*, p. 222; Roy Porter and Lesley Hall, *The Facts of Life: The creation of sexual knowledge in Britain, 1650–1950* (Yale University Press, 1995), pp. 33–34; Crawford, *Blood, Bodies and Families*, p. 56; Foster, 'Deficient husbands', p. 742.
80. Fairchilds, *Women in Early Modern Europe*, pp. 196–197.
81. Crawford, *Blood, Bodies and Families*, p. 56.
82. Houlbrooke, *The English Family*, p. 101.
83. Wall (ed.), *Two Elizabethan Women*, p. 36.
84. Wall, 'Introduction', p. xxx. The letters use the spelling Cannon Row.
85. Maria Thynne to Thomas Thynne [after August 1604], viii, fo. 2, reproduced in Wall (ed.), *Two Elizabethan Women*, p. 33.
86. Maria Thynne to Thomas Thynne [after August 1604], viii, fo. 2, reproduced in Wall (ed.), *Two Elizabethan Women*, pp. 32–33; Williams, *Women's Epistolary Utterance*, pp. 209–210.
87. Fairchilds, *Women in Early Modern Europe*, p. 76; Williams, *Women's Epistolary Utterance*, pp. 209–210.
88. Daybell, *Women Letter Writers*, p. 215.
89. Maria Thynne to Thomas Thynne [after August 1604], viii, fo. 2, reproduced in Wall (ed.), *Two Elizabethan Women*, p. 33.

90. Williams, *Women's Epistolary Utterance*, p. 210; Fletcher, *Gender, Sex and Subordination*, p. 4.
91. Wall, 'Introduction', p. xxx; Williams, *Women's Epistolary Utterance*, p. 24.
92. Daybell, *Women Letter Writers*, pp. 100, 112.
93. Maria Thynne to Thomas Thynne (Cannon Row) [n.d.], vi, fo. 6, reproduced in Wall (ed.), *Two Elizabethan Women*, p. 37.
94. Dabhoiwala, *The Origins of Sex*, p. 17.
95. Williams, *Women's Epistolary Utterance*, pp. 210–211.
96. Shakespeare, *Romeo and Juliet*, Act 2, Scene 5.
97. Dabhoiwala, *The Origins of Sex*, pp. 17–18.
98. Maria Thynne to Thomas Thynne (Cannon Row) [n.d.], vi, fo. 6, reproduced in Wall (ed.), *Two Elizabethan Women*, p. 38.
99. Vicki Kay Price, '"Sche evyr desyryd mor and mor": The appropriation of mercantile language and practice in fifteenth to seventeenth-century English women's writing', Unpublished PhD dissertation, Bangor University, 2021, pp. 108–109.
100. Fairchilds, *Women in Early Modern Europe*, pp. 196–197.
101. Dabhoiwala, *The Origins of Sex*, p. 17.
102. Mildmay, 'Lady Grace's meditation upon the corpse', pp. 41–42; Pollock, *With Faith and Physic*, p. 11.
103. Griffiths, '"A country life"', pp. 213–244; Griffiths, *Managing for Posterity*, pp. 75, 93–117.
104. Fairchilds, *Women in Early Modern Europe*, p. 76.
105. Maria Thynne to Thomas Thynne (Cannon Row) [n.d.], vi, fo. 6, reproduced in Wall (ed.), *Two Elizabethan Women*, p. 37.
106. Wall, 'Introduction', pp. xxx–xxxi; Williams, *Women's Epistolary Utterance*, p. 28.
107. Maria Thynne to Thomas Thynne [c.1604–1606], viii, fo. 1, reproduced in Wall (ed.), *Two Elizabethan Women*, pp. 31–32.
108. Maria Thynne to Thomas Thynne [c.1604–1606], viii, fo. 1, reproduced in Wall (ed.), *Two Elizabethan Women*, p. 32.
109. Maria Thynne to Thomas Thynne [after August 1604], viii, fo. 2, reproduced in Wall (ed.), *Two Elizabethan Women*, p. 33.
110. Maria Thynne to Thomas Thynne (Cannon Row) [? 1607], viii, fo. 4, reproduced in Wall (ed.), *Two Elizabethan Women*, p. 33.
111. Thomas Thynne to Maria Thynne (Longleat) [c. May 1610], xl, fo. 8, reproduced in Wall (ed.), *Two Elizabethan Women*, p. 51.
112. Mary Louisa Boyle, *Biographical Catalogue of the Portraits at Longleat in the County of Wilts, the Seat of the Marquis of Bath* (Elliot Stock, 1881), p. 87.
113. Mendelson and Crawford, *Women in Early Modern England*, p. 120.

CHAPTER 3

1. Margaret Cavendish, cited in Ellayne Fowler, 'Margaret Cavendish and the ideal Commonwealth', *Utopian Studies*, 7.1 (1996), p. 45.
2. Helen Berry and Elizabeth Foyster, 'Childless men in early modern England', in Berry and Foyster (eds), *The Family in Early Modern England*, pp. 166–167.
3. Courtney Erin Thomas, *If I Lose Mine Honour I Lose Myself: Honour among the early modern English elite* (University of Toronto Press, 2017), p. 24.

4. Fanshawe, *Memoirs of Lady Fanshawe*, p. 239.
5. Witold Rybczynski, *Home: A short history of an idea* (Penguin, 1986); Stone, *The Family, Sex and Marriage*, p. 253; Girouard, *Life in the English Country House*, p. 123; Patricia Meyer Spacks, *Privacy: Concealing the eighteenth-century self* (Chicago University Press, 2003), pp. 6–7.
6. Jonson, 'To Penshurst', lines 6–17.
7. O'Day, *The Family and Family Relationships*, p. 151.
8. Mendelson and O'Connor, '"Thy passionately loving sister"', pp. 207–208.
9. Leah Astbury, 'When a woman hates her husband: Love, sex and fruitful marriages in early modern England', *Gender & History*, 32.3 (2020), p. 528.
10. Mendelson and O'Connor, '"Thy passionately loving sister"', p. 208.
11. Sir Charles Cottrell, cited in Mendelson and O'Connor, '"Thy passionately loving sister"', p. 208.
12. These letters are in the BL Add MS 72516, Anne Dormer, Letters, fos. 157–241. These are referred to as 'Anne Dormer, Letters' for the rest of this chapter.
13. Sara H. Mendelson, 'Life-writing as letter-writing: The correspondence of Anne Dormer and Elizabeth Trumbull', in Kaspar von Greyerz (ed.), *Selbstzeugnisse in der Frühen Neuzeit: Individualisierungsweisen in interdisziplinärer Perspektive* (De Gruyter Oldenbourg, 2007), p. 149.
14. Mendelson and O'Connor, '"Thy passionately loving sister"', p. 208.
15. Anne Dormer, cited in Vickery, *Behind Closed Doors*, p. 195.
16. Anne Dormer, cited in Mendelson, 'Life-writing as letter-writing', p. 147.
17. Vickery, *Behind Closed Doors*, p. 195.
18. Anne Dormer, cited in Mendelson, 'Life-writing as letter-writing', p. 150.
19. Mendelson and O'Connor, '"Thy passionately loving sister"', p. 212.
20. Anne Dormer, Letters, fo. 170 r.
21. Anne Dormer, Letters, fos. 195 v–196 r.
22. Anne Dormer, Letters, fo. 196 r.
23. Crawford and Gowing (eds), *Women's Worlds*, p. 180.
24. Linda A. Pollock, 'Honor, gender, and reconciliation in elite culture, 1570–1700', *Journal of British Studies*, 46.1 (2007), p. 21.
25. O'Day, *The Family and Family Relationships*, p. 148.
26. Anne Dormer, cited in Sara Mendelson, 'Neighbourhood as female community in the life of Anne Dormer', in Stephanie Tarbin and Susan Broomhall (eds), *Women, Identities and Communities in Early Modern Europe* (Routledge, 2008), pp. 153–155.
27. Anne Dormer, Letters, fo. 166 r.
28. Wendy Wall, 'Just a spoonful of sugar: Syrup and domesticity in early modern England', *Modern Philology*, 104.2 (2006), pp. 156–159.
29. Anne Dormer, cited in Mendelson, 'Life-writing as letter-writing', p. 144.
30. Anne Dormer, cited in Mendelson, 'Neighbourhood as female community', pp. 153–155.
31. Anne Dormer, cited in Vickery, *Behind Closed Doors*, pp. 196–197.
32. Anne Dormer, Letters, fo. 193 r–193 v.
33. Anne Dormer, cited in Vickery, *Behind Closed Doors*, p. 194.
34. Anne Dormer, Letters, fo. 193 r.
35. Anne Dormer, cited in Mendelson and Crawford, *Women in Early Modern England*, p. 157.
36. Anne Dormer, Letters, fo. 188 v–189 r.

37. Anne Dormer, Letters, fo. 181 r.
38. Anne Dormer, cited in Mendelson, 'Life-writing as letter-writing', p. 151.
39. Anne Dormer, cited in Mendelson and O'Connor, '"Thy passionately loving sister"', p. 209.
40. Joel Swann, 'Reading and writing Frances Howard: "From Katherins Dock There Lanch't a Pinke" in context', *The Seventeenth Century*, 35.2 (2020), p. 165; Tim Stretton, 'Marriage, separation and the common law in England, 1540–1660', in Berry and Foyster (eds), *The Family in Early Modern England*, pp. 19–35; Maureen Waller, *The English Marriage: Tales of love, money and adultery* (John Murray, 2010), pp. 35–47. There was only one example of a divorce through parliament between 1500 and 1670: that of the marquess of Northampton in the mid-sixteenth century. K.J. Kesselring and Tim Stretton, *Marriage, Separation, and Divorce in England, 1500–1700* (Oxford University Press, 2022), pp. 20–21.
41. Gowing, *Domestic Dangers*, p. 180.
42. Anne Dormer, cited in Mendelson and O'Connor, '"Thy passionately loving sister"', p. 209.
43. Gowing, *Domestic Dangers*, pp. 207–209.
44. Mendelson, 'Neighbourhood as female community', pp. 154–160; Anne Dormer, Letters, fo. 194.
45. Anne Dormer, Letters, fos. 165 v–166 r.
46. Mendelson, 'Neighbourhood as female community', pp. 155, 158–160.
47. Anne Dormer, Letters, fos. 176 v–177 r.
48. Anne Dormer, cited in Mendelson, 'Neighbourhood as female community', p. 159.
49. Mendelson, 'Life-writing as letter-writing', p. 144.
50. Mary O'Connor, 'Representations of intimacy in the life-writing of Anne Clifford and Anne Dormer', in Patrick Coleman, Jayne Elizabeth Lewis and Jill Anne Kowalik (eds), *Representations of the Self from the Renaissance to Romanticism* (Cambridge University Press, 2000), p. 88; Anne Dormer, Letters, 10 September, fo. 167.
51. Mendelson and O'Connor, '"Thy passionately loving sister"', p. 212.
52. Astbury, 'When a woman hates her husband', p. 534.
53. Anne Dormer, cited in Astbury, 'When a woman hates her husband', p. 533.
54. Mendelson and O'Connor, '"Thy passionately loving sister"', p. 209.
55. Anne Dormer, cited in Mendelson and O'Connor, '"Thy passionately loving sister"', p. 211.
56. Mendelson and O'Connor, '"Thy passionately loving sister"', p. 212.
57. Anne Dormer, cited in Vickery, *Behind Closed Doors*, p. 197.
58. Vickery, *Behind Closed Doors*; Mendelson and Crawford, *Women in Early Modern England*, pp. 139–140; O'Connor, 'Representations of intimacy', p. 91; Sara Mendelson, 'Anne Dormer and her children', in Naomi Yavneh and Naomi J. Miller (eds), *Gender and Early Modern Constructions of Childhood* (Routledge, 2011), p. 135.
59. Anne Dormer, cited in Vickery, *Behind Closed Doors*, p. 198.
60. Anne Dormer to Jack Dormer, 10 August 1691, reproduced in Crawford and Gowing (eds), *Women's Worlds*, p. 232.
61. Eales, 'Harley [née Conway], Brilliana', *ODNB*.

62. Jacqueline Eales, '"An ancient mother in our Israel": Mary, Lady Vere', in Johanna I. Harris and Elizabeth Scott-Baumann (eds), *The Intellectual Culture of Puritan Women, 1558–1680* (Palgrave Macmillan, 2011), p. 86.
63. Eales, *Puritans and Roundheads*, pp. 42–69 provides a full account of the godly community in Herefordshire.
64. Sara Read, 'A woman of masculine bravery: The life of Brilliana, Lady Harley (1598–1643)', *The Historian*, 151 (2021), pp. 34–37.
65. List of prayers headed 'Matter of Request to God', 17 December 1624, cited in Jacqueline Eales, 'Sir Robert Harley, K.B., (1579–1656) and the "character" of a Puritan', *British Library Journal*, 15.2 (1989), p. 142; Nicholas Tyacke, *Aspects of English Protestantism, c.1530–1700* (Manchester University Press, 2001), pp. 132–159.
66. Eales, 'Sir Robert Harley', pp. 134–157.
67. John Stoughton, cited in Johanna Harris, '"But I thinke and beleeve": Lady Brilliana Harley's puritanism in epistolary community', in Harris and Scott-Baumann (eds), *The Intellectual Culture of Puritan Women*, p. 110.
68. Katharine Gillespie, *Women Writing the English Republic, 1625–1681* (Cambridge University Press, 2017), p. 119.
69. Gillespie, *Women Writing the English Republic*, p. 106; Harris, "'But I thinke and beleeve'", p. 116.
70. Edward, Lord Conway, cited in Harris, "'But I thinke and beleeve'", p. 111.
71. Eales, 'Sir Robert Harley', p. 139.
72. Eales, *Puritans and Roundheads*, p. 47. Brilliana became a common name in the Harley family.
73. Eales, *Puritans and Roundheads*, pp. 24–25.
74. Eales, *Puritans and Roundheads*, p. 24.
75. Brilliana Harley to her husband, 4 December 1629, reproduced in Lewis (ed.), *Letters of the Lady Brilliana Harley*, pp. 4–5.
76. Eales, *Puritans and Roundheads*, p. 23.
77. Eales, 'Sir Robert Harley', pp. 139.
78. Brilliana Harley, cited in Eales, *Puritans and Roundheads*, p. 23.
79. Eales, *Puritans and Roundheads*, p. 23.
80. Wiseman, *Conspiracy and Virtue*, p. 61.
81. Eales, *Puritans and Roundheads*, pp. 24–25.
82. Harris, "'But I thinke and beleeve'", pp. 114–115; BL Add MS 70118, Portland Papers, Correspondence of Sir Edward Harley, vol. CXCIII, 'Brilliana Lady Harley to her son [Sir] Edward Harley', undated; Edith Snook, *Women, Beauty and Power in Early Modern England: A feminist literary history* (Palgrave Macmillan, 2011), p. 87.
83. Gillespie, *Women Writing the English Republic*, pp. 121, 134–137.
84. Eales, *Puritans and Roundheads*, pp. 43–49; Diana G. Barnes, 'Wifely "affection and disposition": Brilliana Harley and Thomas Gataker's *A Wife in Deed* (1623)', *English Studies*, 98.7 (2017), p. 718.
85. Brilliana Harley, Commonplace Book, 1622, cited in Diane Purkiss, *The English Civil War: A people's history* (Harper Perennial, 2006), pp. 144–145.
86. Snook, *Women, Beauty and Power*, p. 105.
87. Eales, *Puritans and Roundheads*, pp. 43, 51.
88. Brilliana Harley, cited in Purkiss, *The English Civil War*, p. 146.

89. Eales, *Puritans and Roundheads*, p. 94. For this period, see David Cressy, *Charles I and the People of England* (Oxford University Press, 2015), pp. 278–30.
90. Brilliana Harley to Ned Harley, 4 May 1640, reproduced in Lewis (ed.), *Letters of the Lady Brilliana Harley*, pp. 92–93.
91. Eales, *Puritans and Roundheads*, p. 52.
92. Eales, *Puritans and Roundheads*, p. 106; Patrick Collinson, *The Religion of Protestants: The Church in English society 1559–1625* (Clarendon Press, 1982), pp. 164–170.
93. Gillespie, *Women Writing the English Republic*, p. 121; Wiseman, *Conspiracy and Virtue*, p. 73.
94. For a discussion of ship money, see Henrik Langelüddecke, '"I finde all men & my officers all soe unwilling": The collection of ship money, 1635–1640', *Journal of British Studies*, 46.3 (2007), pp. 509–542.
95. Eales, 'Sir Robert Harley', p. 140.
96. Gillespie, *Women Writing the English Republic*, p. 102; Eales, 'Sir Robert Harley', p. 138.
97. Eales, *Puritans and Roundheads*, pp. 109–115; John Walter, *Covenanting Citizens: The Protestation oath and popular political culture in the English revolution* (Oxford University Press, 2017), pp. 131–132.
98. 'The Protestation oath', May 1641, cited in Edward Vallance, 'Preaching to the converted: Religious justifications for the English Civil War', *Huntington Library Quarterly*, 65 (2002), p. 402.
99. Eales, *Puritans and Roundheads*, pp. 115–116.
100. After 1646, Wright was made a guardian of the Harley estate and of the young Harley children, as well as becoming the governor of Brampton Bryan Castle. Henry Connor, 'Lady Brilliana Harley (1598–1643): Her medicines and her doctors', *Journal of Medical Biography*, 24.1 (2016), p. 132.
101. Eales, *Puritans and Roundheads*, p. 121.
102. Brilliana Harley, cited in Eales, *Puritans and Roundheads*, p. 122.
103. Wiseman, *Conspiracy and Virtue*, pp. 65–66; Purkiss, *The English Civil War*, p. 150; Jennifer Heller, 'Material goods in Brilliana Harley's letters', *Journal for Early Modern Cultural Studies*, 15.2 (2015), p. 96.
104. Wiseman, *Conspiracy and Virtue*, p. 68.
105. Letter from Brilliana Harley to her husband, Robert, 3 August 1642, reproduced in Historical Manuscripts Commission, *The Manuscripts of His Grace the Duke of Portland, Preserved at Welbeck Abbey*, vol. III (HM Stationery Office, by Eyre and Spottiswoode, 1891), p. 90.
106. Letter from Brilliana Harley to her husband, Robert, 23 February 1643, reproduced in Historical Manuscripts Commission, *Duke of Portland*, vol. III, p. 90.
107. Brilliana Harley to Ned Harley, 20 June 1642, reproduced in Lewis (ed.), *Letters of the Lady Brilliana Harley*, pp. 170–172.
108. Brilliana Harley to Ned Harley, 25 December 1642, reproduced in Lewis (ed.), *Letters of the Lady Brilliana Harley*, pp. 186–187.
109. Purkiss, *The English Civil War*, p. 144.
110. Wiseman, *Conspiracy and Virtue*, p. 67.
111. Brilliana Harley to Ned Harley, July 1642, reproduced in Lewis (ed.), *Letters of the Lady Brilliana Harley*, pp. 182–183.

112. Jennifer Heller, 'Reading "wrecks of history" and the Harley family narrative', *The Seventeenth Century*, 32.2 (2017), p. 141.
113. Brilliana Harley to Ned Harley, 2 July 1642, reproduced in Lewis (ed.), *Letters of the Lady Brilliana Harley*, p. 175.
114. Brilliana Harley to Ned Harley, 5 July 1642, reproduced in Lewis (ed.), *Letters of the Lady Brilliana Harley*, p. 176; Gillespie, *Women Writing the English Republic*, pp. 139–140.
115. Brilliana Harley, cited in Gillespie, *Women Writing the English Republic*, pp. 139–140.
116. Brilliana Harley to Ned Harley, 14 February 1643, reproduced in Lewis (ed.), *Letters of the Lady Brilliana Harley*, pp. 188–189; Wiseman, *Conspiracy and Virtue*, p. 73.
117. Gillespie, *Women Writing the English Republic*, pp. 141–142; Wiseman, *Conspiracy and Virtue*, p. 74.
118. BL Add MS 70110, Brilliana Harley to Robert Harley, 1 April 1643, fo. 80; Diana G. Barnes, 'Emotional debris in early modern letters', in Stephanie Downes, Sally Holloway and Sarah Randle (eds), *Feeling Things: Objects and emotions through history* (Oxford University Press, 2018), p. 124.
119. Brilliana Harley to Ned Harley, 8 July 1642, reproduced in Lewis (ed.), *Letters of the Lady Brilliana Harley*, pp. 176–177; Purkiss, *The English Civil War*, pp. 153–154.
120. Fraser, *The Weaker Vessel*, p. 213.
121. Johanna Harris, '"Scruples and ceremonies": Lady Brilliana Harley's epistolary combat', *Parergon*, 29 (2012), pp. 93–112.
122. Eales, *Puritans and Roundheads*, p. 165.
123. Harris, '"Scruples and ceremonies"', pp. 107–108; Joanne H. Wright, 'Not just dutiful wives and besotted ladies: Epistemic agency in the war writing of Brilliana Harley and Margaret Cavendish', *Early Modern Women*, 4 (2009), p. 10.
124. Wiseman, *Conspiracy and Virtue*, p. 75.
125. Henry Lingen, Sir William Pye and William Smallman to Brilliana Harley, 26 July 1643, reproduced in Historical Manuscripts Commission, *Calendar of the Manuscripts of the Marquis of Bath Preserved at Longleat Wiltshire*, vol. I (HM Stationery Office, by Eyre and Spottiswoode, 1904), p. 8.
126. Harris, '"Scruples and ceremonies"', p. 100.
127. Brilliana Harley to Henry Lingen, Sir William Pye and William Smallman, 26 July 1643, reproduced in Historical Manuscripts Commission, *Calendar of the Manuscripts of the Marquess of Bath*, vol. I, p. 8.
128. Brilliana Harley to Sir William Vavasour, 28 July 1643, reproduced in Historical Manuscripts Commission, *Calendar of the Manuscripts of the Marquess of Bath*, vol. I, p. 9.
129. Harris, '"Scruples and ceremonies"', p. 108.
130. Brilliana Harley to Sir William Vavasour, 31 July 1643, reproduced in Historical Manuscripts Commission, *Calendar of the Manuscripts of the Marquess of Bath*, vol. I, p. 12.
131. Wright, 'Not just dutiful wives', p. 10.
132. Priamus Davis, 'An account of the sieges of Brampton Castle and the massacre of Hopton Castle', reproduced in Historical Manuscripts Commission, *Calendar of the Manuscripts of the Marquess of Bath*, vol. I, p. 27.

133. Carlton, *Going to the Wars*, pp. 154–155.
134. Davis, 'An account of the sieges', p. 26.
135. Davis, 'An account of the sieges', p. 3.
136. Davis, 'An account of the sieges', p. 24. These glasses may have been among those that Ned bought in Oxford on his mother's request. Heller, 'Material goods', p. 96.
137. Fraser, *The Weaker Vessel*, pp. 216–218.
138. Cited in Carlton, *Going to the Wars*, p. 167.
139. BL Add MS 70110, Brilliana Harley to Robert Harley, 24 September 1643, fo. 92 r; Barnes, 'Wifely "affection and disposition"', p. 728.
140. The changing nature of Brilliana's handwriting during the siege can be seen in BL Add MS 70110, fos. 68–92.
141. Eales, *Puritans and Roundheads*, p. 174; Davis, 'An account of the sieges', p. 27.
142. Davis, 'An account of the sieges', p. 27.
143. Gataker, *A Good Wife God's Gift*, p. 32, cited in Barnes, 'Wifely "affection and disposition"', p. 721.
144. O'Connor, 'Dormer [née Cottrell], Anne', *ODNB*.

PART TWO

1. D. Hay and N. Rogers, *Eighteenth-Century English Society: Shuttles and swords* (Oxford University Press, 1997), p. 152; J. Smyth, *The Making of the United Kingdom 1660–1800: State, religion and identity in Britain and Ireland* (Longman, 2001), pp. 190–191. The last time that uninvited troops landed in the British Isles was at the end of the eighteenth century, when the French Republic sent forces to Wales (1797) and Ireland (1798) as part of Napoleon's campaign to invade Britain. Linda Colley, *Britons: Forging the nation, 1707–1837* (Yale University Press, 1992), p. 286.
2. G.W. Jones, 'Introduction: The office of prime minister', in H. Van Thal (ed.), *The Prime Ministers*, vol. 1: *Sir Robert Walpole to Sir Robert Peel* (George Allen & Unwin, 1974), pp. 16–18; Sharpe, *Early Modern England*, pp. 344–355; E. Cruickshanks and J. Black, 'Introduction', in E. Cruickshanks and J. Black (eds), *The Jacobite Challenge* (John Donald, 1988), p. 2; J.C.D. Clark, *Revolution and Rebellion: State and society in England in the seventeenth and eighteenth centuries* (Cambridge University Press, 1986), pp. 120–163; D.A. Baugh, 'Introduction: The social basis of stability', in D.A. Baugh (ed.), *Aristocratic Government and Society in Eighteenth-Century England: The foundations of stability* (New Viewpoints, 1976), p. 3.
3. Stone and Fawtier Stone, *An Open Elite?*, p. 422; Penelope J. Corfield, *Georgians: The deeds and misdeeds of 18th-century Britain* (Yale University Press, 2023), pp. 245–265; C. Brad Faught, *Clive: Founder of British India* (Potomac Books Inc., 2013), chapter five; Roy Porter, *English Society in the Eighteenth Century*, revised edition (Penguin, 1990), p. 80; Paul Langford, 'Introduction: Time and space', in Paul Langford (ed.), *The Eighteenth Century, 1688–1815* (Oxford University Press, 2002), p. 14.
4. Girouard, *Life in the English Country House*, pp. 213–244; Ackerman, *The Villa*, chapter one; Aslet, *The Story of the Country House*, pp. 88–134; John Brewer, *The Pleasures of the Imagination: The emergence of English culture in the eighteenth century* (HarperCollins, 1997), p. 207; Christopher Christie, *The British Country*

House in the Eighteenth Century (Manchester University Press, 2000), pp. 26–97; Dana Arnold, 'The illusion of grandeur? Antiquity, grand tourism and the country house', in Arnold (ed.), *The Georgian Country House*, pp. 100–116.

5. Shoemaker, *Gender in English Society*, p. 35; P. Carter, 'Men about town: Representations of foppery and masculinity in early eighteenth-century urban society', in H. Barker and E. Chalus (eds), *Gender in Eighteenth-Century England: Roles, representations and responsibilities* (Longman, 1997), p. 34; G.J. Barker-Benfield, *The Culture of Sensibility: Sex and society in eighteenth-century Britain* (Chicago University Press, 1992); Dror Wahrman, *The Making of the Modern Self: Identity and culture in eighteenth-century England* (Yale University Press, 2004), pp. 42–44.
6. Hannah Barker and Elaine Chalus, 'Introduction', in Barker and Chalus (eds), *Gender in Eighteenth-Century England*, p. 18; Jane Rendall, 'Women and the public sphere', *Gender & History*, 11 (1999), pp. 475–488; Vickery, *The Gentleman's Daughter*, pp. 288ff.
7. Mary Astell, *Reflections upon marriage. The third edition. To which is added a preface, in answer to some objections* (R. Wilkin, 1706), preface.
8. Elaine Chalus and Fiona Montgomery, 'Women and politics', in Hannah Barker and Elaine Chalus (eds), *Women's History, Britain 1700–1850* (Routledge, 2005), p. 220; Jonah Miller, 'Suffrage and the secret ballot in eighteenth-century London parishes', *The Historical Journal*, 67 (2024), p. 50; McDonagh, *Elite Women and the Agricultural Landscape*, pp. 26–27.
9. Lewis, 'When a house is not a home', pp. 336–363; Ruth Larsen, 'Gender and home', in Colin Edwards (ed.), *A Cultural History of the Home in the Age of Enlightenment* (Bloomsbury Academic, 2021), pp. 131–154; Kate Retford, 'Gender and the marital portrait in eighteenth-century England: "A sort of sex in souls"', *British Journal for Eighteenth-Century Studies*, 27 (2004), pp. 99–120.
10. Although Fanny Boscawen is often known as Frances, in order to differentiate her from Lady Irwin we will use 'Fanny', as this was a name that was used by her family members. Elizabeth Eger, 'Boscawen [née Glanville], Frances Evelyn [Fanny] (1719–1805), letter writer and literary hostess', *Oxford Dictionary of National Biography*, Oxford University Press, 23 September 2004; C.F. Aspinall-Oglander, *Admiral's Wife* (Longmans & Co., 1940); C.F. Aspinall-Oglander, *Admiral's Widow* (Hogarth Press, 1942); Peter Kemp (ed.), 'Boscawen's letters to his wife, 1755–1756', in Christopher Lloyd (ed.), *The Naval Miscellany*, vol. IV (Naval Records Society xcii, 1952), pp. 163–256.
11. E.H. Chalus, 'Ingram [née Shepheard, Gibson], Frances, Viscountess Irwin (1734?–1807), landowner and political manager', *Oxford Dictionary of National Biography*, Oxford University Press, 3 January 2008; Adrian Budge, 'Temple Newsam and "the Good Shepheard's"', *Leeds Art Calendar*, 98 (1986), pp. 8–15; A.F. Hughes and K. Knight, *Hills: Horsham's lost stately home and garden* (Horsham Museum Society, 1999); BL Add MS 89317/4/2, Letters to Lady Susanna Leveson-Gower, marchioness of Stafford from Frances, Viscountess Irwin, fos. 1–110.
12. Arianne Burnette, 'Parker [née Robinson], Theresa (1745–1775), art patron', *Oxford Dictionary of National Biography*, Oxford University Press, 23 September 2004; Ronald Fletcher, *The Parkers at Saltram, 1769–89: Everyday life in an eighteenth-century house* (British Broadcasting Corporation, 1970).

13. For an account of Mary Talbot's life, see Joanna Martin, *Wives and Daughters: Women and children in the Georgian country house* (Hambledon and London, 2004). Some of her letters have been published in Joanna Martin (ed.), *The Penrice Letters 1768–1795* (West Glamorgan County Archives Service, 1993).
14. To distinguish her from the other two Marys in this book, she will be called by the more formal Mary Elizabeth throughout. Mary Elizabeth Lucy, *Mistress of Charlecote: The memoirs of Mary Elizabeth Lucy* (Victor Gollancz, 1983). This drew on some of her earlier published works, including *A Sketch of the Life and Death of Herbert Almeric Lucy* (printed for private circulation, 1841); *The Private Journal of a Tour on the Continent in the Years 1841–1843* (C. Whittingham, 1845); and *Biography of the Lucy Family, of Charlecote Park, in the County of Warwick* (privately printed by Emily Faithfull & Co., 1862).
15. Elizabeth Mavor, *The Ladies of Llangollen: A study in romantic friendship* (Michael Joseph, 1971); G.H. Bell (ed.), *The Hamwood Papers of the Ladies of Llangollen and Caroline Hamilton* (Macmillan & Co., 1930).

CHAPTER 4

1. BL Add MS 89317/4/2, Letter from Frances, Viscountess Irwin to Lady Stafford, 14 June 1795, fos. 109–110.
2. West Yorkshire Archives Service, Leeds (henceforth WYAS), WYL100/F/18/2, Marriage Settlement between Charles Ingram and Frances Shepherd.
3. For a study of the role of the male patron and the relationship with the builder, see Richard Wilson and Alan Mackley, *Creating Paradise: The building of the English country house, 1660–1880* (Bloomsbury Publishing, 2000), pp. 109ff.
4. Amy Boyington, 'The architectural endeavours of the widowed Jemima Yorke, Marchioness Grey', in Terence A.M. Dooley, Maeve O'Riordan and Christopher Ridgway (eds), *Women and the Country House in Ireland and Britain* (Four Courts Press, 2018), pp. 21–32; Arnold (ed.), *The Georgian Country House*, p. 85; Lummis and Marsh, *The Woman's Domain*, pp. 21–22; Alison Wall, 'Elizabethan precept and feminine practice: The Thynne family of Longleat', *History*, 75 (1990), pp. 31–32.
5. Clive Wilkinson, 'Boscawen, Edward (1711–1761), naval officer and politician', *Oxford Dictionary of National Biography*, Oxford University Press, 3 January 2008; Fletcher, *Growing Up in England*, pp. 111–114.
6. Fanny Boscawen's journal, 3 June 1748, cited in Aspinall-Oglander, *Admiral's Wife*, p. 85.
7. Anna Miegon, 'Biographical sketches of principal bluestocking women', *Huntington Library Quarterly*, 65.1/2 (2002), p. 26; Wilkinson, 'Boscawen, Edward (1711–1761)'; Aspinall-Oglander, *Admiral's Wife*, pp. 100, 126, 147, 226; Edward Boscawen, cited in Aspinall-Oglander, *Admiral's Widow*, p. 12.
8. Nicole Reynolds, *Building Romanticism: Literature and architecture in nineteenth-century Britain* (University of Michigan Press, 2010), pp. 85–86.
9. S. Tighe to Mrs Goddard, Woodstock, 2 April 1778, reproduced in Bell (ed.), *The Hamwood Papers*, p. 27.
10. Sarah Ponsonby, 'An account of a journey in Wales, 1778', cited in Mavor, *The Ladies of Llangollen*, p. 53.
11. Lummis and Marsh, *The Woman's Domain*, pp. 63–66; Fletcher, *The Parkers at Saltram*, pp. 14–16; Elizabeth Quarmby Lawrence, '"There is no describing the

library": The Parkers of Saltram and their books', *Library History*, 178.3 (2002), p. 208.
12. Boyington, *Hidden Patrons*, p. 50.
13. Fletcher, *The Parkers at Saltram*, pp. 16–20.
14. Hughes and Knight, *Hills*, p. 31.
15. WYAS, Leeds, Pawson MSS, WYL178/10 (January 1748–December 1776), John Ware to Miss Shepherd, 26 April 1756.
16. Emily, Mrs Meynell Ingram, daughter of Charles, first Viscount Halifax, and widow of Hugo Francis Meynell Ingram, was the fourth female owner of the property, from her husband's death in 1871 until 1904. WYAS, Leeds, WYL100/F/18/2, Marriage Settlement of Charles Irwin and Frances Shepherd; Budge, 'Temple Newsam and "the Good Shepheard's"', p. 12. For further information about marriage settlements, see E.M. Craik, 'Introduction', in E.M. Craik (ed.), *Marriage and Property: Women and marital customs in history* (Aberdeen University Press, 1984), p. 2; Lawrence Stone, 'Marriage among the English nobility in the sixteenth and seventeenth centuries', *Comparative Studies in Society and History*, 3 (1961), p. 187.
17. Fiona Brideoake, *The Ladies of Llangollen: Desire, indeterminacy, and the legacies of criticism* (Bucknell University Press, 2017), p. 11.
18. Brideoake, *The Ladies of Llangollen*, pp. 11–12.
19. Mavor, *The Ladies of Llangollen*, p. 41.
20. Brideoake, *The Ladies of Llangollen*, p. 121; Eleanor Butler, cited in Mavor, *The Ladies of Llangollen*, p. 179.
21. Brideoake, *The Ladies of Llangollen*, p. 48; John Yorke, *Plas Newydd: As it was and as it is. With a catalogue of its contents and a few reminiscences of the 'old ladies'* (Hugh Jones, 1884), p. 8.
22. Wilson and Mackley, *Creating Paradise*, pp. 297ff.; Stephanie Barczewski, *Country Houses and the British Empire 1700–1930* (Manchester University Press, 2014); S.D. Smith, *Slavery, Family, and Gentry Capitalism in the British Atlantic: The world of the Lascelles, 1648–1834* (Cambridge University Press, 2006); S. Seymour, S. Daniels and C. Watkins, 'Estate and empire: Sir George Cornewall's management of Moccas, Herefordshire and La Taste, Grenada, 1771–1819', *Journal of Historical Geography*, 24.3 (1998), pp. 313–351; S. Huxtable, C. Fowler, C. Kefalas and E. Slocombe (eds), *Interim Report on the Connections between Colonialism and Properties Now in the Care of the National Trust, Including Links with Historic Slavery* (National Trust, 2020).
23. Edward Boscawen to Fanny Boscawen, 3 June 1756, reproduced in Kemp (ed.), 'Boscawen's letters', p. 219; Aspinall-Oglander, *Admiral's Wife*, p. 247.
24. Epitaph for Admiral Boscawen, cited in Aspinall-Oglander, *Admiral's Wife*, p. 285.
25. R. Wilson and A. Mackley, '"A pleasure not to be envied": The building of the English country house (1660–1880)', *History Today*, 51.7 (2001), pp. 41–47; Wilson and Mackley, *Creating Paradise*, pp. 109–132.
26. Edward Boscawen to Fanny Boscawen, *Royal George* at sea, 18 August 1756, reproduced in Kemp (ed.), 'Boscawen's letters', p. 246.
27. Kemp (ed.), 'Boscawen's letters', pp. 178, 185; Aspinall-Oglander, *Admiral's Wife*, p. 151; Charles O'Brien, Ian Nairn, Bridget Cherry and Nikolaus Pevsner, *Surrey*, revised edition (Yale University Press, 2022), p. 255.
28. Edward Boscawen to Fanny Boscawen, *Invincible* at sea, 17 May 1756, reproduced in Kemp (ed.), 'Boscawen's letters', p. 209.

29. Edward Boscawen to Fanny Boscawen, *Royal George* at sea, 18 August 1756, reproduced in Kemp (ed.), 'Boscawen's letters', p. 246.
30. Boyington, *Hidden Patrons*, pp. 39–41.
31. Edward Boscawen to Fanny Boscawen, 3 June 1756, reproduced in Kemp (ed.), 'Boscawen's letters', p. 219.
32. Aspinall-Oglander, *Admiral's Wife*, p. 256.
33. Fanny Boscawen's journal, 1 January 1748, cited in Aspinall-Oglander, *Admiral's Wife*, p. 68.
34. O'Brien et al., *Surrey*, p. 258.
35. Edward Boscawen to Fanny Boscawen, *Royal George* at sea, 18 August 1756, reproduced in Kemp (ed.), 'Boscawen's letters', p. 246.
36. Vickery, *Behind Closed Doors*, pp. 12–13; Larsen, 'Gender and home', pp. 149–150.
37. Edward Boscawen to Fanny Boscawen, *Royal George* at sea, 18 August 1756, reproduced in Kemp (ed.), 'Boscawen's letters', p. 246.
38. Eileen Harris, *The Country Houses of Robert Adam* (Aurum Press Limited, 2007), p. 113.
39. Aspinall-Oglander, *Admiral's Wife*, p. 248; O'Brien et al., *Surrey*, pp. 255–256.
40. Harris, *The Country Houses of Robert Adam*, p. 26; Boyington, *Hidden Patrons*, p. 42–43; Barczewski, *Country Houses and the British Empire*, p. 11. The room known as the drawing room during the Boscawens' period of ownership is now the library.
41. See, for example, the case of Betsey Fremantle: Elaine Chalus, '"My dearest Tussy": Coping with separation during the Napoleonic wars (the Fremantle papers, 1800–14)', in Quinton Colville and James Davey (eds), *A New Naval History* (Manchester University Press, 2019), passim; Harris, *The Country Houses of Robert Adam*, p. 25; Boyington, *Hidden Patrons*, p. 41.
42. Lummis and Marsh, *The Woman's Domain*, pp. 66–67.
43. Harris, *The Country Houses of Robert Adam*, p. 25.
44. Fletcher, *The Parkers at Saltram*, p. 75; Baird, *Mistress of the House*, pp. 201–202; John Cornforth, 'Saltram, Devon – II: A property of the National Trust', *Country Life*, 141 (4 May 1967), p. 1068; Nicholas Goodison, 'The king's vases', *Furniture History*, 8 (1972), p. 37.
45. Theresa Parker, cited in Kate Retford, 'Reynolds's portrait of Mrs Theresa Parker: A case study in context', *The British Art Journal*, 4.3 (2003), p. 80.
46. Michael Kassler, 'Queen Charlotte's 1789 account book', *Eighteenth-Century Life*, 43 (2019), p. 91.
47. Diary of Eleanor Butler, 7 October 1785, reproduced in Bell (ed.), *The Hamwood Papers*, p. 58.
48. Reynolds, *Building Romanticism*, pp. 88–91, 96; Diary of Eleanor Butler, 12 October 1785 and 7 October 1785, reproduced in Bell (ed.), *The Hamwood Papers*, p. 58.
49. Seward, cited in Freya Gowrley, *Domestic Space in Britain, 1750–1840: Materiality, sociability and emotion* (Bloomsbury, 2022), p. 139; Martha Vicinus, *Intimate Friends: Women who loved women, 1778–1928* (Chicago University Press, 2004), p. 12.
50. Unattributed, *Temple Newsam* (Leeds, 1999), p. 14; A. Wells-Cole, 'The terrace room at Temple Newsam', *Leeds Art Calendar*, 108 (1991), pp. 15–16; WYAS, Leeds, WYL100/EA/13/70 Building Account for Temple Newsam, 1795–1803.

51. Lewis, 'When a house is not a home', p. 352.
52. For example: Bending, *Green Retreats*; McDonagh, *Elite Women and the Agricultural Landscape*; Boyington, *Hidden Patrons*, chapter four; Susan Groag Bell, 'Women create gardens in male landscapes: A revisionist approach to eighteenth-century English garden history', *Feminist Studies*, 16 (1990), pp. 471–491.
53. Stephen Switzer's *Ichnographia Rustica*, cited in Bending, *Green Retreats*, p. 21; Ann B. Shteir, *Cultivating Women, Cultivating Science: Flora's daughters and botany in England 1760–1860* (Johns Hopkins University Press, 1996), pp. 35–37.
54. Martin, *Wives and Daughters*, pp. 266–269.
55. Lord Ilchester to Mary Fox Strangways, cited in Martin, *Wives and Daughters*, pp. 269–270.
56. Susan O'Brian to Mary Talbot, 1794, cited in Martin, *Wives and Daughters*, p. 259.
57. Martin, *Wives and Daughters*, p. 271.
58. Martin, *Wives and Daughters*, pp. 277–279.
59. Christopher Talbot, cited in Martin, *Wives and Daughters*, pp. 276–277.
60. Mary Talbot, cited in Martin, *Wives and Daughters*, pp. 287–290.
61. Gowrley, *Domestic Space in Britain*, pp. 144–145.
62. Diary of Eleanor Ponsonby, reproduced in Bell (ed.), *The Hamwood Papers*, p. 68.
63. Diary of Eleanor Ponsonby, cited in Mavor, *The Ladies of Llangollen*, p. 65.
64. Gowrley, *Domestic Space in Britain*, pp. 156–157.
65. Mavor, *The Ladies of Llangollen*, pp. 109–110.
66. Henry Phillips, *Sylva Horitera: The shrubbery historically and botanically treated; with observations on the formation of ornamental plantations, and picturesque scenery* (Longman, Hurst & Co., 1823), p. 32.
67. Mavor, *The Ladies of Llangollen*, p. 111.
68. Mavor, *The Ladies of Llangollen*, p. 112.
69. BL Add MS 89317/4/2, Letter from Frances, Viscountess Irwin, to Susan Stafford, 5 February 1767, fo. 46 r.
70. Rebecca Solnit, *Wanderlust: A history of walking* (Verso, 2001), p. 88.
71. Steve Ward, *Tales from the Big House: Temple Newsam: The Hampton Court of the North, 1,000 years of its history and people* (Pen & Sword, 2017), chapter six.
72. BL Add MS 89317/4/2, Letter from Frances, Viscountess Irwin, to Susan Stafford, 14 December 1766, fos. 42–43.
73. BL Add MS 89317/4/2, Letter from Frances, Viscountess Irwin, to Susan Stafford, 8 April 1766, fos. 38–39 v.
74. National Trust, *A Guide to Hatchlands Park* (National Trust and the Cobbe Foundation, 1994), p. 15.
75. Edward Boscawen to Fanny Boscawen, *Invincible* at sea, 25 May 1756, reproduced in Kemp (ed.), 'Boscawen's letters', pp. 212–213.
76. Edward Boscawen to Fanny Boscawen, *Invincible* off Portland, 29 April 1756, reproduced in Kemp (ed.), 'Boscawen's letters', p. 199.
77. Edward Boscawen to Fanny Boscawen, *Invincible* at sea, 16 May 1756, reproduced in Kemp (ed.), 'Boscawen's letters', p. 208.
78. For example: Edward Boscawen to Fanny Boscawen, *Invincible* at sea, 17 May 1756, reproduced in Kemp (ed.), 'Boscawen's letters', p. 209.

79. Theresa Parker to her brother, 29 November 1771, cited in Fletcher, *The Parkers at Saltram*, p. 22.
80. Theresa Parker, cited in Lummis and Marsh, *The Woman's Domain*, p. 73.
81. May Woods and Arete Swartz Warren, *Glass Houses: A history of greenhouses, orangeries and conservatories* (Aurum Press, 1990), p. 76.
82. Letter from Theresa Parker to Lord Grantham, 10 July 1775, cited in Woods and Warren, *Glass Houses*, p. 76.

CHAPTER 5

1. Hester Thrale Piozzi, cited in Mavor, *The Ladies of Llangollen*, p. 139.
2. Ingrid H. Tague, *Women of Quality: Accepting and contesting ideals of femininity in England, 1690–1760* (Boydell & Brewer, 2002), p. 194.
3. This figure is especially notable when one remembers that only 1,003 persons held an English peerage during the whole of the eighteenth century. Cannon, *Aristocratic Century*, pp. 10, 105–112; Hoppit, 'The landed interest and the national interest', p. 84; McDonagh, *Elite Women and the Agricultural Landscape*, p. 123.
4. George Canning, cited in Hannah Greig and Amanda Vickery, 'The political day in London, c.1697–1834', *Past & Present*, 252.1 (2021), p. 105; Tague, *Women of Quality*, p. 195.
5. Anne, Lady Irwin to third earl of Carlisle, 16 Jan 1733, reproduced in R.E.G. Kirk (ed.), *Fifteenth Report, Appendix: Part 6: The Manuscripts of the Earl of Carlisle, formerly preserved at Castle Howard* (Historical Manuscripts Commission, 1897), p. 96.
6. Elaine Chalus, *Elite Women in English Political Life, c.1754–1790* (Clarendon Press, 2005), pp. 171–176.
7. Lady Mary Coke, 1787, cited in Amanda Foreman, *Georgiana, Duchess of Devonshire* (Flamingo, 1999), p. 174; Elaine Chalus, 'Elite women, social politics, and the political world of late eighteenth-century England', *The Historical Journal*, 43.3 (2000), p. 687; Hillary Burlock, 'Party politics: Dancing in London's West End, 1780–9', *London Journal*, 47 (2022), p. 187; Chalus, *Elite Women in English Political Life*, p. 174.
8. Burlock, 'Party politics', passim; Chalus, *Elite Women in English Political Life*, pp. 176–185.
9. Judith S. Lewis, *Sacred to Female Patriotism: Gender, class, and politics in late Georgian Britain* (Routledge, 2003), p. 26; John Brooke, 'Horsham', in L. Namier and J. Brooke (eds), *The History of Parliament: The House of Commons 1754–1790*, 1964, accessed via *History of Parliament Online*: http://www.historyofparliamentonline.org/volume/1754-1790/constituencies/horsham; J.B. Lawson, 'Horsham', in R. Sedgwick (ed.), *The History of Parliament: The House of Commons 1715–1754*, 1970, accessed via *History of Parliament Online*: http://www.historyofparliamentonline.org/volume/1715-1754/constituencies/horsham
10. BL Add MS 89317/4/2, Letter from Frances, Viscountess Irwin, to Susan Stafford, 8 April 1766, fos. 38–39 v; Brooke, 'Horsham'.
11. BL Add MS 89317/4/2, Letter from Frances, Viscountess Irwin to Susan, Lady Gower, fos. 103–104 v.
12. Chalus, *Elite Women in English Political Life*, p. 162; Lawson, 'Horsham'; *Sussex Advertiser*, cited in Lewis, *Sacred to Female Patriotism*, p. 45.

13. Chalus, *Elite Women in English Political Life*, pp. 157–161; McDonagh, *Elite Women and the Agricultural Landscape*, p. 124. For a full discussion of these events, see Elaine Chalus, 'Horsham is Lady Irwin's borough': The power of the 18th century political widow', *History of Parliament Blog*, 2015, accessed via https://historyofparliament.com/2015/04/29/horsham-is-lady-irwins-borough-the-power-of-the-18th-century-political-widow/
14. Elaine Chalus, '"To serve my friends": women and political patronage in eighteenth-century England', in Amanda Vickery (ed.), *Women, Privilege, and Power: British politics, 1750 to the present* (Stanford University Press, 2001), p. 57; Tague, *Women of Quality*, pp. 196–197; Joanne Begiato, 'Favouritism, patronage and the "family system" in England, c.1700–1850', *The English Historical Review*, 139 (2024), p. 810.
15. Chalus, '"To serve my friends"', p. 83.
16. Eric J. Evans, *Political Parties in Britain, 1783–1867* (Routledge, 1985), p. 3.
17. Mary Drummond, 'Ingram, Charles (1727–78), of Templenewsam, Yorks', in Namier and Brooke (eds), *The History of Parliament: the House of Commons 1754–1790*, accessed via *History of Parliament Online*: http://www.historyofparliamentonline.org/volume/1754-1790/member/ingram-charles-1727-78; Chalus, *Elite Women in English Political Life*, p. 164.
18. Chalus, *Elite Women in English Political Life*, p. 143; Tague, *Women of Quality*, p. 215. For the importance of family members in patronage networks, see Begiato, 'Favouritism, patronage and the "family system"', passim.
19. Lewis, *Sacred to Female Patriotism*, p. 75.
20. Chalus, '"To serve my friends"', p. 67; Tague, *Women of Quality*, pp. 198–213; Begiato, 'Favouritism, patronage and the "family system"', passim.
21. Tague, *Women of Quality*, p. 203; E.A. Reitan, 'The Civil List in eighteenth-century British politics: Parliamentary supremacy versus the independence of the Crown', *The Historical Journal*, 9.3 (1966), pp. 318–337.
22. Chalus, '"To serve my friends"', p. 80.
23. Chalus, '"To serve my friends"', p. 76; Brideoake, *The Ladies of Llangollen*, p. 13; Mavor, *The Ladies of Llangollen*, pp. 188–189. This was to replace the income from the pension that was awarded to Eleanor Butler. This had stopped being paid following her death earlier that year.
24. J.C. Sainty, 'The parliamentary role of the royal household', *The Court Historian*, 13.2 (2008), pp. 195–196.
25. Tague, *Women of Quality*, pp. 201–204; Ophelia Field, *The Favourite: Sarah, duchess of Marlborough* (Hodder & Stoughton, 2002), p. 99.
26. Chalus and Montgomery, 'Women and politics', pp. 223–224; Payne, 'Aristocratic women', pp. 164–180.
27. Greig and Vickery, 'The political day in London', pp. 119–120.
28. John Rylands Archive, University of Manchester, The Mary Hamilton Papers, HAM 1/6/1/3 Letter from Fanny Boscawen to Mary Hamilton, 12 March 1785, accessed via *The Mary Hamilton Papers (c.1740–c.1850)*, compiled by David Denison, Nuria Yáñez-Bouza, Tino Oudesluijs, Cassandra Ulph, Christine Wallis, Hannah Barker and Sophie Coulombeau, University of Manchester, in progress, https://doi.org/10.48420/21687809. This was probably in relation to the estate of his grandfather, Hugh, Viscount Falmouth. See: 'An Act, for Vesting Part of the real Estate of the late Hugh Lord Viscount Falmouth, situate in the Borough of Tregony, and Parish of Cuby, in the County of Cornwall, in Trustees, to be sold

and conveyed to Sir Francis Basset, Baronet, and for other Purposes therein-mentioned'. *Private Acts (1702–1727) and Private Bills (1727–1814) A Table of the Statutes Public and Private, George III. Regis: Being the Fifth Session of the Sixteenth Parliament of Great Britain*, 25 October 1787, accessed via *18th Century House of Commons Sessional Papers*, Proquest UK Parliamentary Papers.
29. Greig and Vickery, 'The political day in London', p. 120.
30. Chalus, 'Elite women, social politics', p. 675; Greig and Vickery, 'The political day in London', p. 124.
31. Tague, *Women of Quality*, p. 177.
32. Chalus, '"My dearest Tussy"', pp. 61–62.
33. Amanda Foreman, 'A politician's politician: Georgiana, duchess of Devonshire and the Whig party', in Barker and Chalus (eds), *Gender in Eighteenth-Century England*, p. 187; Foreman, *Georgiana*, p. 157; J.S. Lewis, '1784 and all that: Aristocratic women and electoral politics', in Vickery (ed.), *Women, Privilege, and Power*, pp. 89–122.
34. For a discussion of the political day, see Greig and Vickery, 'The political day in London', passim.
35. Greig and Vickery, 'The political day in London', p. 118.
36. Hannah Smith, 'The court in England, 1714–1760: A declining political institution?', *History*, 90.297 (2005), p. 36.
37. For example, on 24 February 1763, she went to court with the duchess of Leeds. Manuscript memorandum book for 1763 kept by Fanny Boscawen, daughter of William Evelyn Glanville and wife of Admiral Edward Boscawen. Accessed via an electronic reproduction of MS Eng. Misc. fo. 71 in the Bodleian Library by Adam Matthew Digital, for their collection *Defining gender, 1450–1910. Section III, Consumption and leisure* (c.2007); Tague, *Women of Quality*, p. 186; Aspinall-Oglander, *Admiral's Widow*, p. 14.
38. Elizabeth Eger, '"The noblest commerce of mankind": Conversation and community in the bluestocking circle', in S. Knott and B. Taylor (eds), *Women, Gender and Enlightenment* (Palgrave Macmillan, 2005), p. 289; Baird, *Mistress of the House*, p. 169.
39. Nicole Pohl and Betty A. Schellenberg, 'Introduction: A bluestocking historiography', *Reconsidering the Bluestockings. Huntington Library Quarterly*, 65.1/2 (2002), pp. 2–4; Elizabeth Eger, 'Introduction', in Elizabeth Eger (ed.), *Bluestockings Displayed: Portraiture, performance and patronage, 1730–1830* (Cambridge University Press, 2013), p. 3.
40. Pohl and Schellenberg, 'Introduction: A bluestocking historiography', p. 2.
41. Hannah More, *Florio: A Tale, for Fine Gentlemen and Fine Ladies: and, The Bas Bleu: Or, Conversation. Two Poems* (printed for T. Cadell, 1786), pp. 73–95; Eger, '"The noblest commerce of mankind"', pp. 288–289.
42. Eger, '"The noblest commerce of mankind"', pp. 288, 293–294, 297; Elizabeth Eger, 'The bluestocking circle: Friendship, patronage and learning', in Elizabeth Eger and Lucy Peltz, *Brilliant Women: 18th-century Bluestockings* (National Portrait Gallery, 2008), p. 27.
43. Haslett notes that Fanny Boscawen and Elizabeth Vesey were almost alone among the more prominent members of the bluestocking circles in not having their work published. Moyra Haslett, 'Becoming bluestockings: Contextualising Hannah More's "The Bas Bleu"', *Journal for Eighteenth-Century Studies*, 33.1 (2010), pp. 90–91.

44. Letter from Fanny Boscawen to Elizabeth (Robinson) Montagu, (September) 1753, The Huntingdon Library, Elizabeth Robinson Montagu papers, MS MO495, accessed via https://hdl.huntington.org/digital/collection/p16003coll18/id/10682/rec/2
45. Lucy Peltz, 'Living muses: Constructing and celebrating the professional woman in literature and the arts', in Eger and Peltz, *Brilliant Women*, pp. 59–63.
46. Aspinall-Oglander, *Admiral's Widow*, p. 73. Among those who enjoyed de Sévigné's works were Eleanor Butler, George Eliot and Elizabeth Gaskell. Mavor, *The Ladies of Llangollen*, p. 60; Alain Jumeau, 'Elizabeth Gaskell on French literary ladies of the seventeenth century: Madame de Sablé and Madame de Sévigné', *The Gaskell Society Journal*, 13 (1999), pp. 19–24.
47. George Selwyn to Lady Carlisle, 1789, reproduced in Kirk (ed.), *The Manuscripts of the Earl of Carlisle*, p. 676.
48. Haslett, 'Becoming bluestockings', p. 104.
49. S.J. Skedd, 'More, Hannah (1745–1833), writer and philanthropist', *Oxford Dictionary of National Biography*, Oxford University Press, 25 September 2014; Aspinall-Oglander, *Admiral's Widow*, p. 71; Eger, 'Boscawen [née Glanville], Frances', *ODNB*.
50. Hannah More, 1774, cited in Aspinall-Oglander, *Admiral's Widow*, p. 71.
51. Hannah More, 1775, cited in Aspinall-Oglander, *Admiral's Widow*, p. 72; Anne Stott, *Hannah More: The first Victorian* (Oxford University Press, 2003), p. 30; Hannah More, *The Inflexible Captive: A tragedy* (S. Farley and T. Cadell, 1774), dedication (no page numbers).
52. Hannah More, cited in Aspinall-Oglander, *Admiral's Widow*, p. 72.
53. Aspinall-Oglander, *Admiral's Widow*, pp. 72–73.
54. Aspinall-Oglander, *Admiral's Widow*, p. 72.
55. Aspinall-Oglander, *Admiral's Widow*, pp. 72–73; Barbara Brandon Schnorrenberg, 'Delany [née Granville; other married name Pendarves], Mary (1700–1788), court favourite and artist', *Oxford Dictionary of National Biography*, Oxford University Press, 4 October 2008; Letters from Fanny Boscawen to Mrs Delany, reproduced in Hall (ed.), *The Autobiography and Correspondence of Mary Granville*, 2nd series, vol. I, pp. 338–340, 343–345.
56. The Hon. Mrs Boscawen to Mrs Delany, Glan Villa, 7 June 1777, in Hall (ed.), *The Autobiography and Correspondence of Mary Granville*, 2nd series, vol. II, p. 297.
57. Haslett, 'Becoming bluestockings', p. 99.
58. Kerri Andrews, *Ann Yearsley and Hannah More, Patronage and Poetry: The story of a literary relationship* (Routledge, 2015), pp. 56–57.
59. Susan Staves, '"Books without which I cannot write": How did eighteenth-century women writers get the books they read?', in J. Batchelor and C. Kaplan (eds), *Women and Material Culture, 1660–1830* (Palgrave Macmillan, 2007), p. 203.
60. Clarissa Campbell-Orr, 'The queen of the blues, the bluestocking queen, and bluestocking masculinity', in Eger (ed.), *Bluestockings Displayed*, pp. 222–225.
61. Letter from Fanny Boscawen to Elizabeth (Robinson) Montagu, (September) 1753, The Huntingdon Library; Letter from Fanny Boscawen to Elizabeth (Robinson) Montagu, 11 November [1790], The Huntingdon Library, Elizabeth Robinson Montagu papers, MS MO550, accessed via https://hdl.huntington.org/digital/collection/p16003coll18/id/47861/rec/57; Emma Major, *Madam Britannia: Women, church, and nation 1712–1812* (Oxford University Press, 2012), p. 248.

62. Letter from Fanny Boscawen to Elizabeth (Robinson) Montagu, Hatchlands, 22 and 25 November 1754, The Huntingdon Library, Elizabeth Robinson Montagu papers, MS MO499, accessed via https://hdl.huntington.org/digital/collection/p16003coll18/id/11776/rec/6
63. WYAS, Leeds, WYL100/EA/12/18 Bills for Books, stationery, etc.
64. A. Gomersall, *Eleonora, a Novel, in a Series of Letters; Written by a Female Inhabitant of Leeds in Yorkshire*, vol. 1 (Literary Society at the Logographic Press, 1789), pp. iii–iv. For a discussion of Mrs Gomersall's career, see James Raven, *Judging New Wealth: Popular publishing and responses to commerce in England, 1750–1800* (Oxford University Press, 1992), chapter six.
65. Brewer, *Pleasures of the Imagination*, p. 606.
66. Mavor, *The Ladies of Llangollen*, p. 69; WYAS, Leeds, WYL100/EA/12/18 Bills for Books, stationery, etc., Bill to Mrs Ingram from William Randall, 2 January 1761.
67. Mavor, *The Ladies of Llangollen*, pp. 183–184; Gowrley, *Domestic Space in Britain*, p. 144.
68. Anna Seward, cited in Brideoake, *The Ladies of Llangollen*, p. 201.
69. Brewer, *Pleasures of the Imagination*, pp. 606–607; Reynolds, *Building Romanticism*, p. 102; Brideoake, *The Ladies of Llangollen*, pp. 204–208; Gowrley, *Domestic Space in Britain*, pp. 161–162.
70. Reynolds, *Building Romanticism*, p. 96.
71. Gowrley, *Domestic Space in Britain*, p. 144, 152; Yorke, *Plas Newydd*, p. 18.
72. Frances Ann Crewe, cited in Gowrley, *Domestic Space in Britain*, p. 151.
73. Yorke, *Plas Newydd*, p. 34; Gowrley, *Domestic Space in Britain*, pp. 151–152; Staves, '"Books without which I cannot write"', pp. 205–206.
74. Stott, *Hannah More*, p. 266; Amy Solomons, 'Fragments and traces: Uncovering Sabine Winn's reading experiences, 1734–1798', *Women's History Review*, July 2024 (online), pp. 3–10.
75. Staves, '"Books without which I cannot write"', p. 193.
76. For a discussion of these issues, see Melanie Bigold, 'Women's book collecting in the eighteenth century: The libraries of the countess of Hertford and the duchess of Northumberland', *Huntington Library Quarterly*, 84.1 (2021), pp. 139–150.
77. Susie West, 'The development of libraries in Norfolk country houses, 1660–1830', PhD thesis, University of East Anglia, 2000, p. 470; Abigail Williams, *The Social Life of Books: Reading together in the eighteenth-century home* (Yale University Press, 2017), pp. 50–51; Colin Cunningham, '"An Italian house my lady": Some aspects of the definition of women's role in the architecture of Robert Adam', in Gill Perry and M. Rossington (eds), *Femininity and Masculinity in Eighteenth-Century Art and Culture* (Manchester University Press, 1994), p. 67.
78. Lawrence, '"There is no describing the library"', pp. 209, 211–213.
79. Baird, *Mistress of the House*, p. 178; Barbara Brandon Schnorrenberg, 'Montagu [née Robinson], Elizabeth (1718–1800), author and literary hostess', *Oxford Dictionary of National Biography*, Oxford University Press, 21 May 2009.
80. Nicole Reynolds, 'Cottage industry: The Ladies of Llangollen and the symbolic capital of the "cottage ornée"', *The Eighteenth Century*, 51.1/2 (2010), p. 218; Mavor, *The Ladies of Llangollen*, p. 108.
81. Eger, 'The bluestocking circle', p. 22.

82. Hannah More to Fanny Boscawen, 1787, reproduced in Hannah More, *The Letters of Hannah More* (selected with an introduction by R. Brimley Johnson), (John Lane the Bodley Head, 1925), p. 115.
83. Prince Pückler-Muskau, cited in Freya Gowrley, 'Plas Newydd's poetics of exchange: Portraiture, poetry, and the intermediality of eighteenth-century gift culture', *Word & Image*, 39.4 (2023), p. 459; Gowrley, *Domestic Space in Britain*, pp. 146–147, 153–156.
84. BL Add MS 89317/4/2, Letter from Frances, Viscountess Irwin to Lady Susan Stewart, 16 September 1767, fos. 46–47 v. We know that this picture was in a bedchamber in the early twentieth century: W. Wheater, *Temple Newsam: Its history and antiquities*, 3rd edition (Goodall & Suddick, Cookridge, 1889), p. 123; Chalus, 'Elite women, social politics', p. 683.
85. Ellis Waterhouse, 'Reynolds, Angelica Kauffman and Lord Boringdon', *Apollo*, 122.284 (1985), p. 273; David H. Solkin, *Painting for Money: The visual arts and the public sphere in eighteenth-century England* (Yale University Press, 1993), pp. 240, 254.
86. Baird, *Mistress of the House*, p. 204.
87. For example, John Gore, 'A patron of portrait and landscape: The picture collection at Saltram House, Devon', *Country Life*, 139.3613 (1966), pp. 1386–1388; Wendy Roworth, 'Kauffman and the art of painting in England', in Wendy Roworth (ed.), *Angelica Kauffman: A continental artist in Georgian England* (Reaktion Books, 1992), pp. 11–95.
88. Nicholas Penny (ed.), *Reynolds* (Royal Academy and Weidenfeld & Nicolson, 1986), p. 283; Gore, 'A patron of portrait and landscape', p. 1386; Baird, *Mistress of the House*, p. 205.
89. Retford, 'Reynolds's portrait of Mrs Theresa Parker', pp. 80, 85; Kate Retford, *The Art of Domestic Life: Family portraiture in eighteenth-century England* (Yale University Press, 2006), pp. 157–158.
90. Retford, 'Reynolds's portrait of Mrs Theresa Parker', pp. 81–82.
91. Lord Grantham, cited in Retford, 'Reynolds's portrait of Mrs Theresa Parker', pp. 81–82.
92. Theresa Parker, cited in Baird, *Mistress of the House*, p. 206.
93. Lummis and Marsh, *The Woman's Domain*, p. 71.
94. Anon, 'Character of the late Hon. Mrs Parker, promised in our last Magazine', *Gentleman's Magazine*, XLVI (February 1776), p. 75.
95. Waterhouse, 'Reynolds, Angelica Kauffman and Lord Boringdon', p. 274; Theresa Parker, cited in Maureen Cross and Sophie Brummitt, 'Gilbert Stuart in Britain (1775–1787): A technical study of selected works from Saltram House, National Trust property, Devon', *Journal of the American Institute for Conservation*, 50.2 (2011), p. 89.
96. Baird, *Mistress of the House*, p. 204.
97. Theresa Parker, 1771, cited in Baird, *Mistress of the House*.
98. Waterhouse, 'Reynolds, Angelica Kauffman and Lord Boringdon', p. 274; Lummis and Marsh, *The Woman's Domain*, p. 71.
99. Angela Rosenthal, *Angelica Kauffman: Art and sensibility* (Yale University Press, 2006), p. 166.
100. Waterhouse, 'Reynolds, Angelica Kauffman and Lord Boringdon', pp. 272–273. Adam also worked on the London property. See: F.H.W. Sheppard (ed.), 'Sackville Street', *Survey of London: Volumes 31 and 32, St James Westminster,*

Part 2 (London County Council, 1963), pp. 342–366. *British History Online*, 15 August 2023. http://www.british-history.ac.uk/survey-london/vols31-2/pt2/pp342-366

101. Theresa Parker, cited in Rosenthal, *Angelica Kauffman*, p. 166. Some of these remain at Saltram, such as *Hector Taking Leave of Andromache* (1768) and *Ulysses Discovering Achilles* (1769). See the National Trust Collections website: https://www.nationaltrustcollections.org.uk/object/872177 and https://www.nationaltrustcollections.org.uk/object/872174
102. Rosenthal, *Angelica Kauffman*, p. 167.
103. Chalus, '"My dearest Tussy"', pp. 61–62.
104. Aspinall-Oglander, *Admiral's Widow*, pp. 14–15.
105. For example, Letter from Fanny Boscawen to Elizabeth (Robinson) Montagu, 7 July [1754], The Huntingdon Library, Elizabeth Robinson Montagu papers, MS MO501, https://hdl.huntington.org/digital/collection/p16003coll18/id/11714/rec/8
106. Devoney Looser, 'The blues gone grey: Portraits of bluestocking women in old age', in Eger (ed.), *Bluestockings Displayed*, p. 100.
107. Letter from Fanny Boscawen to Elizabeth (Robinson) Montagu, 6 August 1794, The Huntingdon Library, Elizabeth Robinson Montagu papers, MS MO556, accessed via https://hdl.huntington.org/digital/collection/p16003coll18/id/49535/rec/63
108. Letter from Fanny Boscawen to Elizabeth (Robinson) Montagu, Rosedale (Surrey) 11 November 1798, The Huntingdon Library, Elizabeth Robinson Montagu papers, MS MO563, accessed via https://hdl.huntington.org/digital/collection/p16003coll18/id/50510/rec/70
109. Diary of Eleanor Butler, 18 November 1785, reproduced in Bell (ed.), *The Hamwood Papers*, pp. 63, 70, 75.
110. Mavor, *The Ladies of Llangollen*, p. 64.
111. Ian McIntyre, *Hester: The remarkable life of Dr Johnson's 'Dear Mistress'* (Constable, 2008), pp. 317–318.
112. Mavor, *The Ladies of Llangollen*, p. 129.
113. Mavor, *The Ladies of Llangollen*, p. 170.
114. Mavor, *The Ladies of Llangollen*, p. 155.
115. Carole Fabricant, 'The literature of domestic tourism and the public consumption of private property', in Felicity Nussbaum and Laura Brown (eds), *The New Eighteenth Century: Theory, politics, English literature* (Methuen, 1987), p. 265; Jonson, 'To Penshurst'.

CHAPTER 6

1. BL Add MS 89317/4/2, Letter from Frances, Lady Ingram to Susan Stafford, 16 March [?], fo. 3 r.
2. Theresa Parker to Lord Grantham, cited in Fletcher, *The Parkers at Saltram*, p. 23.
3. Ackerman, *The Villa*, pp. 12–13.
4. Lucy, *Mistress of Charlecote*, pp. 15–31.
5. Lewis, 'When a house is not a home', pp. 336–363; Larsen, 'Gender and home', pp. 131–154.

6. E. Shorter, *The Making of the Modern Family* (Collins, 1976); Stone, *The Family, Sex and Marriage*; Trumbach, *The Rise of the Egalitarian Family*; Vickery, *The Gentleman's Daughter*, p. 285; Barclay, *Love, Intimacy and Power*, passim. For a brief survey of the study of romantic love, see Katie Barclay and Sally Holloway, 'Interrogating romantic love', *Cultural and Social History*, 17.3 (2020), pp. 271–277. For a study of love among elites in the eighteenth century, see Tague, 'Love, honor, and obedience', pp. 76–106.
7. Fanny Boscawen to Edward Boscawen, 12 August 1748, reproduced in Aspinall-Oglander, *Admiral's Wife*, p. 101.
8. R.B. Outhwaite, 'Introduction: Problems and perspectives in the history of marriage', in R.B. Outhwaite (ed.), *Marriage and Society: Studies in the social history of marriage* (Europa, 1981), pp. 15–16.
9. Tague, 'Love, honor, and obedience', pp. 85, 105.
10. Anon, *The Ladies Complete Letter-Writer; Teaching the Art of Inditing Letters ... Being a collection of letters, written by ladies* (T. Lownds, 1763), p. 126.
11. V. Brodsky Elliot, 'Single women in the London marriage market: Age, status and mobility, 1598–1619', in Outhwaite (ed.), *Marriage and Society*, pp. 81–100; Whyman, *Sociability and Power*, pp. 124–125; Kristen Richardson, *The Season: A history of the debutante* (W.W. Norton & Company, 2020), pp. 31–35; Lewis, *In the Family Way*, p. 20.
12. Martin, *Wives and Daughters*, p. 60.
13. Martin, *Wives and Daughters*, pp. 56–59.
14. Extracts from the pocketbook of Mary Fox Strangways, 1792, reproduced in Martin (ed.), *Penrice Letters*, pp. 113–114.
15. Martin, *Wives and Daughters*, pp. 60–61; Jane Austen, *Pride and Prejudice* (1813) (Macmillan & Co., 1895), chapter forty-three.
16. Martin (ed.), *Penrice Letters*, p. 129.
17. Thomas Mansel Talbot to Mary Fox Strangways, 18 December 1793, reproduced in Martin (ed.), *Penrice Letters*, p. 129.
18. Mary Fox Strangways' letters to her sister Harriot Fox Strangways, January 1792–January 1794, reproduced in Martin (ed.), *Penrice Letters*, pp. 113–132.
19. Lucy, *Mistress of Charlecote*, p. 27.
20. Lucy, *Mistress of Charlecote*, p. 27.
21. Lucy, *Mistress of Charlecote*, pp. 24–25.
22. Lucy, *Mistress of Charlecote*, pp. 25–28.
23. Lucy, *Mistress of Charlecote*, pp. 25–28.
24. Lewis, *In the Family Way*, pp. 19–20.
25. Mary Fox Strangways to Harriot Fox Strangways, 23 January 1794, reproduced in Martin (ed.), *Penrice Letters*, p. 139.
26. Lucy, *Mistress of Charlecote*, p. 29.
27. Sally Holloway, *The Game of Love in Georgian England: Courtship, emotions, and material culture* (Oxford University Press, 2019), p. 56.
28. Lucy, *Mistress of Charlecote*, p. 30.
29. L. Davidoff, M. Doolittle, J. Fink and K. Holden, *The Family Story: Blood, contract and intimacy 1830–1960* (Longman, 1999), p. 61.
30. Letter from Mary Fox Strangways to Harriot Fox Strangways, 6 January 1794, reproduced in Martin (ed.), *Penrice Letters*, p. 131.
31. Letter from Mary Fox Strangways to Harriot Fox Strangways, 13 January 1794, reproduced in Martin (ed.), *Penrice Letters*, p. 132.

32. Letter from Mary Fox Strangways to Harriot Fox Strangways, 20 January 1794, reproduced in Martin (ed.), *Penrice Letters*, p. 135.
33. Letter from Mary Fox Strangways to Harriot Fox Strangways, 20 January 1794, reproduced in Martin (ed.), *Penrice Letters*, p. 135.
34. Letter from Mary Fox Strangways to Harriot Fox Strangways, 20 January 1794, reproduced in Martin (ed.), *Penrice Letters*, p. 135.
35. Lucy, *Mistress of Charlecote*, pp. 30–31.
36. J.R. Gillis, *For Better, For Worse: British marriages, 1600 to the present* (Oxford University Press, 1985), p. 138; Stone, *The Family, Sex and Marriage*, p. 335.
37. Letter from Mary Fox Strangways to Harriot Fox Strangways, 5 February 1794, reproduced in Martin (ed.), *Penrice Letters*, p. 142.
38. Lucy, *Mistress of Charlecote*, p. 32.
39. Lady Williams, cited in Lucy, *Mistress of Charlecote*, p. 34.
40. WYAS, Leeds, WYL100/C/23/33, Isabella Ingram, London, to Mrs Charles Ingram, 18 November [1758].
41. WYAS, Leeds, WYL100/C/23/133, John Waple, Ripley, to Mrs Charles Ingram, 30 November 1759.
42. Fanny Boscawen to Edward Boscawen, 23 December 1756, reproduced in Aspinall-Oglander, *Admiral's Wife*, pp. 243–244.
43. Tague, 'Love, honor, and obedience', p. 94.
44. Anon, *The Ladies Complete Letter-Writer*, p. 126.
45. Stone, *The Family, Sex and Marriage*, passim; Tague, 'Love, honor, and obedience', pp. 84ff.
46. Lucy, *Mistress of Charlecote*, p. 33.
47. Lucy, *Mistress of Charlecote*, pp. 36–37.
48. For a discussion of the notion of the incorporated wife, see: H. Callan, 'Introduction', in H. Callan and S. Ardener (eds), *The Incorporated Wife* (Croom Helm, 1984); Reynolds, *Aristocratic Women*, pp. 6–7.
49. Lucy, *Mistress of Charlecote*, p. 33.
50. Fanny Boscawen to Edward Boscawen, 23 December 1756, cited in Aspinall-Oglander, *Admiral's Wife*, pp. 243–244.
51. Letter from Edward Boscawen to Fanny Boscawen, *Invincible* off Portland, 29 April, reproduced in Kemp (ed.), 'Boscawen's letters', p. 199.
52. Fanny Boscawen's journal, 21 July 1748, cited in Aspinall-Oglander, *Admiral's Wife*, p. 96.
53. Aspinall-Oglander, *Admiral's Wife*, pp. 283–284.
54. Boyington, *Hidden Patrons*, p. 42; Epitaph for Admiral Boscawen, cited in Aspinall-Oglander, *Admiral's Wife*, p. 285.
55. O. Hufton, 'Women without men: Widows and spinsters in Britain and France in the eighteenth century', *Journal of Family History*, 9 (1984), p. 359; Hollingsworth, 'Demography of the British peerage', p. 20.
56. Ruth Larsen, 'For want of a good fortune: Elite single women's experiences in Yorkshire, 1730–1860', *Women's History Review*, 16.3 (2007), pp. 393–395; Helena Whitbread, *I Know My Own Heart: The diaries of Anne Lister, 1791–1840* (Virago, 1988); Jill Liddington, *Female Fortune: Land, gender and authority – The Anne Lister diaries and other writings 1833–36* (Rivers Oram, 1998).
57. Rebecca Jennings, *A Lesbian History of Britain: Love and sex between women since 1500* (Greenwood World, 2007), p. 40; Vicinus, *Intimate Friends*, p. xvii.
58. Vicinus, *Intimate Friends*, pp. xii–xiii.

59. Diary of Eleanor Butler, reproduced in Bell (ed.), *The Hamwood Papers*, p. 27; Mavor, *The Ladies of Llangollen*, p. 66.
60. Mavor, *The Ladies of Llangollen*, p. 66.
61. Mavor, *The Ladies of Llangollen*.
62. Rictor Norton, 'Extraordinary female affection, 1790', *Homosexuality in Eighteenth-Century England: A Sourcebook*, 22 April 2005, updated 15 June 2005, accessed via http://rictornorton.co.uk/eighteen/1790extr.htm
63. 'Extraordinary female affection', *St James's Chronicle or the British Evening Post*, 17 July 1790–20 July 1790, p. 4.
64. Mavor, *The Ladies of Llangollen*, pp. 72–77; Vicinus, *Intimate Friends*, p. 15.
65. Martha Vicinus, '"They wonder to which sex I belong": The historical roots of the modern lesbian identity', in Dennis Altman (ed.), *Homosexuality, Which Homosexuality?: International Conference on Gay and Lesbian Studies* (An Dekker/Schorer and GMP Publishers, 1989), p. 183.
66. Jennings, *Lesbian History*, p. 46.
67. Lillian Faderman, *Surpassing the Love of Men* (Women's Press, 1985), p. 125.
68. Vicinus, *Intimate Friends*, p. 12.
69. Katherine Kittridge, 'Proto-butch or temporally-challenged trans?: Considering female masculinities in eighteenth-century Britain', in Chris Mounsey (ed.), *Developments in the Histories of Sexualities 1400–1900* (Bucknell University Press, 2012), p. 187.
70. Kittridge, 'Proto-butch or temporally-challenged trans?', pp. 187, 194; Mavor, *The Ladies of Llangollen*, p. 195.
71. Lucy, *Mistress of Charlecote*, pp. 19–20.
72. Anne Lister, 1822, cited in Jennings, *Lesbian History*, p. 45.
73. Eleanor Butler's diary, cited in Mavor, *The Ladies of Llangollen*, p. 104.
74. For example, Katherine Binhammer, 'The "singular propensity" of sensibility's extremities: Female same-sex desire and the eroticization of pain in late-eighteenth-century British culture', *GLQ: A Journal of Lesbian and Gay Studies*, 9.4 (2003), p. 489; Mavor, *The Ladies of Llangollen*, p. 105.
75. Sally Holloway, '"You know I am all on fire": Writing the adulterous affair in England, c.1740–1830', *Historical Research: The Bulletin of the Institute of Historical Research*, 89 (2016), pp. 317–339.
76. Sarah Ponsonby, cited in Mavor, *The Ladies of Llangollen*, p. 188.
77. Olwen Hufton, *The Prospect Before Her: A history of women in western Europe*, vol. 1 (Harper Collins, 1995), p. 145.
78. Mary Elizabeth Lucy Talbot to Harriot Fox Strangways, c.10 February 1794, reproduced in Martin (ed.), *Penrice Letters*, pp. 143–144.
79. Sydney Smith, cited in Martin, *Wives and Daughters*, p. 62.
80. Martin, *Wives and Daughters*, p. 62.
81. Lewis, *In the Family Way*, p. 218.
82. Lucy, *Biography of the Lucy Family*, p. 135.
83. WYAS, Leeds, WYL100/C/23/33, Isabella Ingram, London, to Mrs Charles Ingram, 18 November [1758]; WYAS, Leeds, WYL100/C/19/23, Mrs Isabella Ramsden to Isabella Irwin, 1 December 1761.
84. BL Add MS 89317/4/2, Letter from Frances, Lady Ingram to Susan Stafford, 16 March [?], fo. 3 v.
85. WYAS, Leeds, WYL100/C/23/231, Isabella Ingram to Mrs Charles Ingram, 6 March [1760?].

86. Frances was the illegitimate daughter of an MP, and although there is some evidence that money was paid to her mother from her Drummond's bank account, this is the only evidence of contact in her adult life. Julie Day, personal communication.
87. For discussions of the changing nature of medical responses to childbirth, see: Lisa Forman Cody, 'The politics of reproduction: From midwives' alternative public sphere to the public spectacle of man-midwifery', *Eighteenth-Century Studies*, 32 (1999), pp. 477–495; B. Blackwell, 'Tristram Shandy and the theater of the mechanical mother', *English Literary History*, 68 (2001), pp. 81–133; Adrian Wilson, *Ritual and Conflict: The social relations of childbirth in early modern England* (Routledge, 2016), pp. 153–210; Lewis, *In the Family Way*, chapter three.
88. Martin, *Wives and Daughters*, pp. 182–183.
89. BL Add MS 89317/4/2, Letter from Frances, Lady Ingram to Countess Susan Gower, 4 October 1762, fos. 16–18.
90. Sarah Fox, *Giving Birth in Eighteenth-Century England* (University of London, 2022), p. 24; Patricia Crawford, 'The construction and experience of maternity', in Valerie Fildes (ed.), *Women as Mothers in Pre-Industrial England* (Routledge, 1990), p. 22; Ann Dally, *Inventing Motherhood: The consequences of an ideal* (Burnett Books, 1982), p. 38.
91. For example, Lady Jersey wrote three such letters in as many years; she lived to be eighty-two years old. Lewis, *In the Family Way*, pp. 75–76.
92. Aspinall-Oglander, *Admiral's Wife*, p. 147.
93. Theresa Parker, cited in Lummis and Marsh, *A Woman's Domain*, pp. 75–76.
94. Fanny Boscawen to her husband, 19 October 1747, reproduced in Aspinall-Oglander, *Admiral's Wife*, p. 54.
95. Fanny Boscawen to her husband, 6 January 1748, reproduced in Aspinall-Oglander, *Admiral's Wife*, p. 69.
96. See, for example, James Gillray, *The Fashionable Mamma – or – The Convenience of Modern Dress*, coloured print, 15 February 1796, Victoria and Albert Museum Collection; Mary Wollstonecraft, *A Vindication of the Rights of Woman: With strictures on political and moral subjects* (London, 1792), pp. 343–348; William Cadogan, *An Essay upon Nursing and the Management of Children from their Birth to Three Years of Age* (1743), reprinted in Morwenna and John Rendle-Short, *The Father of Child Care: Life of William Cadogan (1711–97)* (Bristol, 1966), p. 7.
97. Wollstonecraft, *Vindication*, p. 59.
98. BL Add MS 89317/4/2, Letter from Frances, Viscountess Irwin, to Susan Stafford, 5 February 1767, fo. 46 r.
99. Theresa Parker, cited in Fletcher, *The Parkers at Saltram*, p. 113.
100. Charlotte Traherne, cited in Martin, *Wives and Daughters*, p. 62.
101. Trumbach, *The Rise of the Egalitarian Family*, chapter five.
102. See for examples WYAS, Leeds, WYL100/C/19/87, Sam Keeling, Temple Newsam, to Isabella Irwin, 15 July 1763; WYAS, Leeds, WYL100/C/19/117, Isabella Ramsden to Isabella Irwin, 16 May 1764; Letters from Edward Boscawen to Fanny Boscawen, *Torbay* at sea, 4 May and 11 May 1755, reproduced in Kemp (ed.), 'Boscawen's letters', pp. 179–182.
103. Letter from Fanny Boscawen to her husband, 9 June 1755, reproduced in Aspinall-Oglander, *Admiral's Wife*, p. 180.

104. Martin, *Wives and Daughters*, pp. 170, 173, 189–190, 195–196, 206–209.
105. For a discussion of the range of texts which explored childcare, see Myers, 'Impeccable governesses', pp. 31–32.
106. WYAS, Leeds, WYL100/EA/12/18 Bills for Books, stationery, etc., Bill to Mrs Ingram from William Randall, 2 January 1761.
107. Joanna Martin (ed.), *A Governess in the Age of Jane Austen: The journals and letters of Agnes Porter* (Hambledon Press, 1998), p. 53.
108. Martin, *A Governess in the Age of Jane Austen*, pp. 43, 54–63.
109. Mary Talbot, cited in Martin, *A Governess in the Age of Jane Austen*, p. 44.
110. Martin, *A Governess in the Age of Jane Austen*, p. 262.
111. Letter from Lady Mary Talbot to Henrietta Maria Hicksville Beach, c.1806, cited in Martin, *Wives and Daughters*, p. 223.
112. Martin, *Wives and Daughters*, p. 225.
113. Myers, 'Impeccable governesses', p. 35. In Mary Wollstonecraft's work women were only given an intellectual voice when they fulfilled the role of pedagogue. Barbara Taylor, *Mary Wollstonecraft and the Feminist Imagination* (Cambridge, 2003), p. 34.
114. Fanny Boscawen, cited in Aspinall-Oglander, *Admiral's Wife*, p. 229.
115. See, for example, Fanny Boscawen's journal, 20 July 1748 and 13 October 1748, reproduced in Aspinall-Oglander, *Admiral's Wife*, pp. 94, 117–118.
116. For example, in 1803 Captain Thomas Fremantle implored his wife not to 'mollycoddle' their sons. Chalus, '"My dearest Tussy"', p. 51.
117. Letter from Fanny Boscawen to her husband, Portsmouth, 30 August 1755, reproduced in Aspinall-Oglander, *Admiral's Wife*, pp. 192–193.
118. Fanny Boscawen's journal, 17 November 1748, reproduced in Aspinall-Oglander, *Admiral's Wife*, p. 124. The servant was given the name of Tom Pride and stayed with the family for a number of years. It is not clear whether he was a freeman, but the fact that he was 'presented' to the family suggests that he was treated as property. Aspinall-Oglander, *Admiral's Wife*, pp. 149, 166, 247.
119. Baird, *Mistress of the House*, p. 222.
120. Reynolds, *Aristocratic Women*, p. 21.
121. Isabella, countess of Carlisle, *Thoughts in the Form of Maxims Addressed to Young Ladies on Their First Establishment in the World* (T. Cornell, 1789), p. 32.
122. Mrs Hamilton, cited in Bell (ed.), *The Hamwood Papers*, p. 42.
123. Mavor, *The Ladies of Llangollen*, p. 71.
124. Letter from Edward Boscawen to Fanny Boscawen, 15 June 1756, reproduced in Kemp (ed.), 'Boscawen's letters', pp. 224–225.
125. Letter from Edward Boscawen to Fanny Boscawen, 2 August 1756, reproduced in Kemp (ed.), 'Boscawen's letters', p. 244.
126. Mavor, *The Ladies of Llangollen*, pp. 151–152.
127. J. Dwyer, *Virtuous Discourse: Sensibility and community in late eighteenth-century Scotland* (Edinburgh, 1987), p. 95.
128. Mavor, *The Ladies of Llangollen*, pp. 152–153.
129. Julie Day, 'Household management and domestic structure at Temple Newsam House near Leeds, in the second half of the eighteenth century', unpublished MA dissertation, University of Leeds, 2001, p. 7.

PART THREE

1. Lytton Strachey, *Eminent Victorians: Cardinal Manning, Florence Nightingale, Dr Arnold, General Gordon* (Chatto & Windus, 1918). The best guides to the 'alternative' Victorians are Matthew Sweet, *Inventing the Victorians* (Faber, 2002) and Susie L. Steinbach, *Understanding the Victorians: Politics, culture and society in nineteenth-century Britain*, 3rd edition (Taylor & Francis, 2023).
2. Edward Royle, *Modern Britain: A social history 1750–2011*, 3rd edition (Bloomsbury Academic, 2012); Colin Matthew, 'Introduction: The United Kingdom and the Victorian century', in Colin Matthew (ed.), *The Nineteenth Century* (Oxford University Press, 2000), pp. 1–40; John M. MacKenzie (ed.), *The Victorian Vision: Inventing New Britain* (V&A, 2001), passim; Steinbach, *Understanding the Victorians*, pp. 72–80, 92–104.
3. Crook, *The Rise of the Nouveaux Riches*, pp. 7–35; Heather A. Clemenson, *English Country Houses and Landed Estates* (Croom Helm, 1982), pp. 96–106; Beckett, *The Aristocracy in England*, pp. 206–228; Adrian Tinniswood, *The Power and the Glory: The country house before the Great War* (Jonathan Cape, 2024), pp. 21–38.
4. Ellis Archer Wasson, 'The House of Commons, 1660–1945: Parliamentary families and the political elite', *The English Historical Review*, 106.420 (1991), pp. 635–651; Beckett, *The Aristocracy in England*, pp. 456–467; David Cannadine, *The Decline and Fall of the British Aristocracy* (Yale University Press, 1990), pp. 35–54.
5. Jarlath Killeen, *History of the Gothic: Gothic literature 1825–1914* (University of Wales Press, 2009), pp. 2–3; Mark Girouard, *The Victorian Country House* (Yale University Press, 1979), p. 66.
6. Michael C.C. Adams, *The Great Adventure: Male desire and the coming of World War I* (Indiana University Press, 1990), p. 45; David M. Wilson, 'The roots of medievalism in north-west Europe: National romanticism, architecture, literature', in Patrick J. Geary and Gábor Klaniczay (eds), *Manufacturing Middle Ages: Entangled history of medievalism in nineteenth-century Europe* (Brill, 2013), pp. 112, 116–117; Girouard, *The Victorian Country House*, pp. 46–53; Roy C. Strong, *Painting the Past: The Victorian Painter and British History*, revised edition (Pimlico, 2004), pp. 8–9, 21, 56.
7. David Peters Corbett, *The World in Paint: Modern art and visuality in England, 1848–1914* (Manchester University Press, 2004), pp. 37–42.
8. Ayla Lepine, 'The Pre-Raphaelites: Medievalism and Victorian visual culture', in Joanne Parker and Corinna Wagner (eds), *The Oxford Handbook of Victorian Medievalism* (Oxford University Press, 2020), pp. 488–491. For a discussion of the conservative model of medievalism, see Rosemary Jann, 'Democratic myths in Victorian medievalism', *Browning Institute Studies*, 8 (1980), pp. 129–149.
9. Tinniswood, *The Power and the Glory*, pp. 130–133.
10. Cited in Horn, *Ladies of the Manor*, p. 9; Catherine Hall, *White, Male and Middle Class: Explorations in feminism and history* (Polity Press, 1992), chapter three; Nancy Armstrong, *Desire and Domestic Fiction: A political history of the novel* (Oxford University Press, 1989), passim; Susan Kingsley Kent, *Gender and Power in Britain, 1640–1990* (Routledge, 1999), pp. 151–178.
11. Martin J. Weiner, 'Domesticity: A legal discipline for men?', in Martin Hewitt (ed.), *An Age of Equipoise?: Reassessing mid-Victorian Britain* (Ashgate, 2000), pp. 155–157.

12. Patricia Hollis, *Ladies Elect: Women in English local government, 1865–1914* (Clarendon, 1987); pp. 6–9; Jon Lawrence, 'Contesting the male polity: The suffragettes and the politics of disruption in Edwardian Britain', in Vickery (ed.), *Women, Privilege, and Power*, pp. 203–204.
13. Maria Quirk, *Women, Art and Money in Late Victorian and Edwardian England: The hustle and the scramble* (Bloomsbury Visual Arts, 2019), pp. 75–88.
14. Steinbach, *Understanding the Victorians*, pp. 202–207; Barbara Caine, *Victorian Feminists* (Oxford University Press, 1992), passim; Jane Rendall, *The Origins of Modern Feminism: Women in Britain, France and the United States, 1780–1860* (Macmillan, 1985), pp. 307–320.
15. Raleigh Trevelyan, 'Trevelyan, Paulina Jermyn [Pauline] [née Paulina Jermyn], Lady Trevelyan (1816–1866), art patron and critic', *Oxford Dictionary of National Biography*, Oxford University Press, 23 September 2004; John Batchelor, *Lady Trevelyan and the Pre-Raphaelite Brotherhood* (Chatto & Windus, 2006); Raleigh Trevelyan, *A Pre-Raphaelite Circle* (Chatto & Windus, 1978); Virginia Surtees (ed.), *Reflections of a Friendship: John Ruskin's Letters to Pauline Trevelyan, 1848–1866* (George Allen & Unwin, 1979).
16. K.D. Reynolds, 'Horner [née Graham], Frances Jane, Lady Horner (1854–1940), hostess and patron of the arts', *Oxford Dictionary of National Biography*, Oxford University Press, 12 November 2020; Frances Horner, *Time Remembered* (Heinemann, 1933); Andrew Gailey, *Portrait of a Muse: Frances Graham, Edward Burne-Jones and the Pre-Raphaelite dream* (Bitter Lemon Press, 2020).
17. Robert Gathorne-Hardy (ed.), *Ottoline: The early memoirs of Lady Ottoline Morrell* (Faber & Faber, 1963), p. 178.
18. Angela Lambert, *Unquiet Souls: The Indian summer of the British aristocracy, 1880–1918* (Macmillan, 1984); Jane Dismore, *Tangled Souls: Love and scandal among the Victorian aristocracy* (History Press Limited, 2023).
19. Jane Ridley and Clayre Percy, 'Charteris [née Wyndham], Mary Constance, countess of Wemyss (1862–1937), hostess', *Oxford Dictionary of National Biography*, Oxford University Press, 22 September 2005; Claudia Renton, *Those Wild Wyndhams: Three sisters at the heart of power* (William Collins, 2014); Jane Ridley and Clayre Percy (eds), *The Letters of Arthur Balfour and Lady Elcho 1885–1917* (H. Hamilton, 1992); Mary Charteris, countess of Wemyss, *A Family Record* (Curwen Press, 1932). For reasons of clarity, she will be known as Mary Elcho throughout this book; this was her preferred name in her letters to Balfour, even after she became countess of Wemyss in 1914.
20. Pamela Watkin, *A Kingston Lacy Childhood: Reminiscences of Viola Bankes* (Dovecote, 1987); Geoffrey Brown, *To Partake of Tea: The last ladies of Kingston Lacy* (Hobnob Press, 2006).
21. Peter Gordon, 'Knightley [née Bowater], Louisa Mary, Lady Knightley (1842–1913), churchwoman and women's activist', *Oxford Dictionary of National Biography*, Oxford University Press, 23 September 2004; Julia Cartwright (ed.), *The Journals of Lady Knightley of Fawsley: 1856–1884* (John Murray, 1915); Peter Gordon (ed.), *Politics and Society: The journals of Lady Knightley of Fawsley 1885–1913* (Taylor & Francis Group, 2005).

CHAPTER 7

1. Beckett, *The Aristocracy in England*, pp. 202–204.

2. John Wolffe, 'Cooper, Anthony Ashley-, seventh earl of Shaftesbury (1801–1885), philanthropist and politician', *Oxford Dictionary of National Biography*, Oxford University Press, 3 January 2008.
3. Reynolds, *Aristocratic Women*, p. 5.
4. For example, Patricia Jalland, *Women, Marriage and Politics 1860–1914* (Oxford University Press, 1988); Sarah Richardson, *The Political Worlds of Women: Gender and politics in nineteenth century Britain* (Routledge, 2013); Simon Morgan, *A Victorian Woman's Place: Public culture in the nineteenth century* (Tauris Academic Studies, 2006); Robert Lee and Sari Mäenpää, 'Intersecting worlds: Women, the family, and merchant culture', in Robert Lee (ed.), *Networks of Influence and Power: Business, culture, and identity in Liverpool's merchant community, c.1800 to 1914* (Routledge, 2024), pp. 165–209; Reynolds, *Aristocratic Women*.
5. Jessica Gerard, *Country House Life: Family and servants, 1815–1914* (Blackwell, 1994), p. 118.
6. Margot Finn and Kate Smith, 'Introduction', in Margot Finn and Kate Smith (eds), *East India Company at Home, 1757–1857* (UCL Press, 2018), pp. 4–7.
7. J.M. Bourne, *Patronage and Society in Nineteenth-Century England* (Edward Arnold, 1986), p. 57.
8. David Roberts, *Paternalism in Early Victorian England* (Croom Helm, 1979), pp. 129–148; E.P. Thompson, *Customs in Common* (Penguin, 1993), pp. 1–64; Amanda Goodrich, *Debating England's Aristocracy in the 1790s: Pamphlets, polemic, and political ideas* (Boydell Press, 2005), passim; Jonathan Powis, *Aristocracy* (Blackwell, 1984), pp. 81–98; John E. Archer, 'The nineteenth-century allotment: Half an acre and a row', *The Economic History Review*, 50 (1997), pp. 26–27.
9. McDonagh, *Elite Women and the Agricultural Landscape*; Emma Purcell, 'Inheritance and influence: Heiresses and the Montagu property network, circa 1749–1827', *Journal for Eighteenth-Century Studies*, 44 (2021), pp. 439–451.
10. Reynolds, *Aristocratic Women*, pp. 42–44.
11. Louisa Knightley, cited in Cartwright (ed.), *Journals of Lady Knightley*, pp. 2–3.
12. Reynolds, *Aristocratic Women*, pp. 45–46.
13. Lady Knightley's journal, 18 November 1869, reproduced in Cartwright (ed.), *Journals of Lady Knightley*, p. 175.
14. Cartwright (ed.), *Journals of Lady Knightley*, pp. 175–176.
15. Watkin, *A Kingston Lacy Childhood*, pp. 34–36.
16. Clemenson, *English Country Houses*, pp. 87–88; Reynolds, *Aristocratic Women*, pp. 45–46.
17. Brown, *To Partake of Tea*, p. 24; Watkin, *A Kingston Lacy Childhood*, pp. 36–40.
18. Archer, 'The nineteenth-century allotment', p. 25.
19. Reynolds, *Aristocratic Women*, p. 91; Peter Mandler, 'Cain and Abel: Two aristocrats and the early Victorian factory acts', *The Historical Journal*, 27 (1984), pp. 83–109; Anne Hattersley, 'Paternalism and education on landed estates in rural Northumberland, 1850–1900', *Northern History*, 44.1 (2007), pp. 111–131.
20. Reynolds, *Aristocratic Women*, pp. 13, 71, 101–102; Horn, *Ladies of the Manor*, pp. 102–141; Jessica Gerard, 'Lady Bountiful: Women of the landed classes and rural philanthropy', *Victorian Studies*, 30.2 (1987), pp. 183–210; Carrie Howse, 'From Lady Bountiful to Lady Administrator: Women and the administration of rural district nursing in England, 1880–1925', *Women's History Review*, 15 (2006), pp. 423–441.

21. Hattersley, 'Paternalism and education', pp. 117, 122; Batchelor, *Lady Trevelyan*, p. 169; H.J. Yallop, *The History of the Honiton Lace Industry* (University of Exeter Press, 1992), pp. 210–212. For a wider discussion of the role of elites supporting artisan traders in rural communities, see Stana Nenadic and Sally Tuckett, 'Artisans and aristocrats in nineteenth-century Scotland', *The Scottish Historical Review*, 95.241 (2016), pp. 203–229.
22. Anon, *The English Matron: A practical manual for young wives*, 3rd edition (James Hogg & Sons, 1861), pp. 106–108.
23. Louisa Knightley, cited in Cartwright (ed.), *Journals of Lady Knightley*, p. 241.
24. Gerard, 'Lady Bountiful', p. 186.
25. Brown, *To Partake of Tea*, p. 29.
26. Neil Armstrong, *Christmas in Nineteenth-Century England* (Manchester University Press, 2010), chapter five.
27. Brown, *To Partake of Tea*, pp. 28–29.
28. Lady Knightley's journal, 23 December 1869, in Cartwright (ed.), *Journals of Lady Knightley*, p. 177.
29. Cartwright (ed.), *Journals of Lady Knightley*, pp. 179–180.
30. Beckett, *The Aristocracy in England*, p. 344.
31. Lucy, *Biography of the Lucy Family*, p. 174; Lucy, *Mistress of Charlecote*, pp. 80–81.
32. Watkin, *A Kingston Lacy Childhood*, p. 8.
33. *Western Gazette*, 18 July 1902, cited in Brown, *To Partake of Tea*, pp. 27–28.
34. Rev. Thomas Green to his wife, 12 July 1820, reproduced in Anon, 'A Fawsley christening', *Northamptonshire Past and Present*, 1.2 (1949), p. 41.
35. Howard Newby, 'The deferential dialectic', *Comparative Studies in Society and History*, 17 (1975), pp. 156–157.
36. Beckett, *The Aristocracy in England*, p. 344.
37. Jeanne MacKenzie, *The Children of the Souls: A tragedy of the First World War* (Chatto & Windus, 1986), p. 75; Wemyss, *A Family Record*, p. 89.
38. For a discussion about the ways in which Victorian elites used deference to maintain their power, see Newby, 'The deferential dialectic', passim.
39. Watkin, *A Kingston Lacy Childhood*, pp. 7–8; Brown, *To Partake of Tea*, pp. 23–25.
40. Jon Stobart and Mark Rothery, *Consumption and the Country House* (Oxford University Press, 2016), p. 176.
41. Mark Girouard, *A Country House Companion* (Century, 1987), p. 183.
42. Beckett, *The Aristocracy in England*, p. 345.
43. Brown, *To Partake of Tea*, p. 34.
44. Patricia Jalland, *Death in War and Peace: A history of loss and grief in England, 1914–1970* (Oxford University Press, 2012), p. 102. It remained unusual through the start of the First World War, but among those who elected for cremation was Percy Wyndham, Lady Mary Elcho's father, who died in 1911. Renton, *Those Wild Wyndhams*, p. 279.
45. Patricia Jalland, *Death in the Victorian Family* (Oxford University Press, 1996), p. 223; Peter C. Jupp, *From Dust to Ashes: Cremation and the British way of death* (Palgrave Macmillan, 2006), p. 74.
46. Brown, *To Partake of Tea*, pp. 34–35.
47. Albert Bankes diary, 24 November 1904, cited in Brown, *To Partake of Tea*, p. 35.
48. Jalland, *Women, Marriage and Politics*, pp. 35–37; Waller, *The English Marriage*, pp. 320–323.

49. Brown, *To Partake of Tea*, pp. 15–17.
50. *Sunday Times*, cited in Brown, *To Partake of Tea*, p. 23.
51. Girouard, *Life in the English Country House*, pp. 64, 145–146.
52. Tinniswood, *The Power and the Glory*, pp. 243–262; Pamela Horn, *High Society: The English social élite, 1880–1914* (Alan Sutton, 1993), pp. 58–59.
53. Anon, 'Court circular', *The Times*, 8 December 1905, p. 8; Anon, 'Court circular', *The Times*, 9 December 1907, p. 9.
54. Watkin, *A Kingston Lacy Childhood*, pp. 79–87.
55. Fletcher, *Growing Up in England*, p. 296.
56. Anon, 'Prince Leopold at Cannes', *Examiner*, 2813, 18 December 1861, p. 826.
57. Peter Gordon, 'Introduction', in Gordon (ed.), *Politics and Society*, p. 2; Peter Gordon, 'Louisa Knightley and the royal household', *Northamptonshire Past and Present*, 62 (2009), pp. 91–94.
58. Gordon, 'Louisa Knightley and the royal household', pp. 90–91, 97.
59. Reynolds, *Aristocratic Women*, p. 128; R.J. Olney, 'The politics of land', in G.E. Mingay (ed.), *The Victorian Countryside*, vol. 1 (Routledge & Kegan Paul, 1981), pp. 58–70.
60. Elaine Chalus, ' "That epidemical Madness": women and electoral politics in the late eighteenth century', in Barker and Chalus (eds), *Gender in Eighteenth-Century England*, pp. 151–178; S. Richardson, 'The role of women in electoral politics in Yorkshire during the eighteen-thirties', *Northern History*, 32 (1996), pp. 133–151; Peter Mandler, 'From Almack's to Willis's: Aristocratic women and politics 1815–1867', in Vickery (ed.), *Women, Privilege, and Power*, pp. 152–167; Sumiao Li, ' "Arabian Nights Entertainment": The rule of fashion and the public roles of aristocratic women in Britain 1820–1860', *Nineteenth-Century Gender Studies*, 6 (2010), passim; Amanda Vickery, 'Introduction', in Vickery (ed.), *Women, Privilege, and Power*, pp. 53–54.
61. Reynolds, *Aristocratic Women*, p. 141; Diana Urquhart, *Ladies of Londonderry: Women and political patronage* (I.B. Tauris, 2007), pp. 9–69.
62. Frances Evelyn Maynard Greville Warwick, *Afterthoughts* (Cassell & Company, 1931), p. 45.
63. Urquhart, *Ladies of Londonderry*, p. 7; Horn, *High Society*, p. 159; Jalland, *Women, Marriage and Politics*, p. 190.
64. Jalland, *Women, Marriage and Politics*, pp. 193–194.
65. Gailey, *Portrait of a Muse*, pp. 176–180.
66. Girouard, *The Return to Camelot*, pp. 208–209.
67. Nancy W. Ellenberger, *Balfour's World: Aristocracy and political culture at the fin de siècle* (Boydell Press, 2015), pp. 160–164.
68. Letter from Mary Elcho to Arthur Balfour, 19 January 1904, reproduced in Ridley and Percy (eds), *Letters of Arthur Balfour*, p. 210.
69. Peter Gordon, 'Lady Knightley and the South Northamptonshire election of 1885', *Northamptonshire Past and Present*, 6 (1981), pp. 265–266.
70. Matthew Cragoe, *An Anglican Aristocracy: The moral economy of the landed estate in Carmarthenshire, 1832–1895* (Clarendon, 1996), pp. 129–130, 144–150.
71. Gordon, 'Lady Knightley and the South Northamptonshire election', p. 267; J. Howarth, 'Liberal revival in Northamptonshire, 1880–1895: Case study in late nineteenth century elections', *The Historical Journal*, 12 (1969), p. 83; Olney, 'The politics of land', p. 60.
72. Lady Knightley's journal, 29 July 1885, cited in Linda Walker, 'Party political women: A comparative study of Liberal women and the Primrose League, 1890–

1914', in Jane Rendall (ed.), *Equal or Different: Women's politics 1800–1914* (Basil Blackwell, 1987), p. 172.
73. Lady Knightley's journal, 12 October 1885, reproduced in Gordon (ed.), *Politics and Society*, p. 9.
74. Gordon, 'Lady Knightley and the South Northamptonshire election', p. 269.
75. Lady Knightley's journal, 12 October 1885, reproduced in Gordon (ed.), *Politics and Society*, p. 9.
76. Lady Knightley's journal, 2 November 1885, reproduced in Gordon (ed.), *Politics and Society*, p. 78.
77. Gordon, 'Lady Knightley and the South Northamptonshire election', pp. 271–272; Gordon, 'Introduction', pp. 9–10. For a brief discussion of the 1784 election, see Chapter 5. A fuller survey can be found in Lewis, '1784 and all that', pp. 89–122.
78. Lady Knightley's journal, 19 October 1885, reproduced in Gordon (ed.), *Politics and Society*, pp. 90–91; Gordon, 'Lady Knightley and the South Northamptonshire election', p. 272.
79. Lady Knightley's journal, 12 October 1885, reproduced in Gordon (ed.), *Politics and Society*, p. 89; Howarth, 'Liberal revival in Northamptonshire', p. 83; Gordon, 'Introduction', p. 12.
80. Olney, 'The politics of land', p. 68.
81. Reynolds, *Aristocratic Women*, pp. 148–149; Jalland, *Women, Marriage and Politics*, p. 206.
82. Walker, 'Party political women', p. 164, 170; Christopher Ridgway, 'Rosalind Howard, the contradictory countess of Carlisle', in Dooley, O'Riordan and Ridgway (eds), *Women and the Country House*, p. 215; Ben Griffin, *The Politics of Gender in Victorian Britain: Masculinity, political culture, and the struggle for women's rights* (Cambridge University Press, 2012), p. 265.
83. Walker, 'Party political women', p. 166; Gordon, 'Lady Knightley and the South Northamptonshire election', p. 270; Vickery, 'Introduction', p. 33. Women were not able to join the Conservative or Liberal parties on the same terms as men until after the First World War.
84. Lady Knightley's journal, 12 May 1885, reproduced in Gordon (ed.), *Politics and Society*, p. 62.
85. Lady Knightley's journal, 5 August 1888, cited in Walker, 'Party political women', p. 172.
86. Walker, 'Party political women', pp. 171–172, 178; Vickery, 'Introduction', p. 16.
87. Walker, 'Party political women', p. 172; Horn, *High Society*, p. 162.
88. Sophia van Wingerden, *The Women's Suffrage Movement in Britain, 1866–1928* (Palgrave Macmillan, 1999), p. 57.
89. Walker, 'Party political women', p. 185; Brian Harrison, *Separate Spheres: The opposition to women's suffrage in Britain* (Croom Helm, 1978), p. 76.
90. Jalland, *Women, Marriage and Politics*, p. 210.
91. Edith Castlereagh, 'Lady Castlereagh's views', *The Times*, 1 April 1912, p. 6; A. Susan Williams, *Ladies of Influence: Women of the elite in interwar Britain* (Allen Lane, 2000), p. 2.
92. Louisa Knightley, Speech in Northampton, 1893, cited in Gordon, 'Introduction', p. 18.
93. *Votes For Women*, II.36, 12 November 1908, p. 111.

94. Jalland, *Women, Marriage and Politics*, p. 215; Horn, *High Society*, p. 163; Ridgway, 'Rosalind Howard', pp. 215–216.
95. Hollis, *Ladies Elect*, pp. 6–9; Lawrence, 'Contesting the male polity', p. 206.
96. Gordon, 'Knightley [née Bowater], Louisa', *ODNB*.
97. Of the first eight women who took their seats in the House of Commons, three had titles (Nancy, Viscountess Astor, Katharine, duchess of Atholl, and Lady Vera Terrington). House of Commons Information Office, *Women in the House of Commons*. Factsheet M4: Members Series. Revised June 2010, Appendix B, accessed via https://www.parliament.uk/globalassets/documents/commons-information-office/m04b.pdf
98. Thomas Adam, *Buying Respectability: Philanthropy and urban society in transnational perspective, 1840s to 1930s* (Indiana University Press, 2009), pp. 127–128; Olwen Claire Niessen, *Aristocracy, Temperance and Social Reform: The life of Lady Henry Somerset* (Tauris Academic Studies, 2007), pp. 1, 12; Andrea Geddes Poole, *Philanthropy and the Construction of Victorian Women's Citizenship: Lady Frederick Cavendish and Miss Emma Cons* (University of Toronto Press, 2014), pp. 10–11, 13, 16–58.
99. Mandler, 'From Almack's to Willis's', pp. 157, 161–164; Reynolds, *Aristocratic Women*, pp. 111–119.
100. Brian Harrison, 'For Church, queen and family: The Girls' Friendly Society 1874–1920', *Past & Present*, 61 (1973), pp. 107–108; Vivienne Richmond, '"It is not a society for human beings but for virgins": the Girls' Friendly Society membership eligibility dispute 1875–1936', *Journal of Historical Sociology*, 20 (2007), pp. 304–305.
101. Cartwright (ed.), *Journals of Lady Knightley*, p. 287.
102. Lady Knightley's journal, 11 June 1878, reproduced in Cartwright (ed.), *Journals of Lady Knightley*, p. 289; F.K. Prochaska, *Women and Philanthropy in Nineteenth-Century England* (Clarendon Press, 1980), pp. 118–121.
103. Julia Cartwright, 'Introduction', in Cartwright (ed.), *Journals of Lady Knightley*, p. xiv; Gordon, 'Knightley [née Bowater], Louisa', *ODNB*; Jalland, *Women, Marriage and Politics*, pp. 211–212.
104. Peter Grant, *Philanthropy and Voluntary Action in the First World War: Mobilizing charity* (Routledge, 2014), pp. 2–3.
105. Frances Horner, cited in Caroline Dakers, *The Countryside at War, 1914–1918* (Constable, 1987), p. 35.
106. Dakers, *The Countryside at War*, p. 36.
107. Edward Bujak, *English Landed Society in the Great War: Defending the realm* (Bloomsbury Academic, 2019), p. 96; Lady Carnarvon, *The Earl and the Pharaoh* (William Collins, 2023), pp. 226, 247; Dakers, *The Countryside at War*, p. 36.
108. Gerald Gliddon, *The Aristocracy and the Great War* (Gliddon Books, 2002), p. 132; Dakers, *The Countryside at War*, p. 37.
109. Dakers, *The Countryside at War*, pp. 37, 198–199.
110. Frances Horner, cited in Dakers, *The Countryside at War*, p. 193.
111. Brown, *To Partake of Tea*, p. 48.
112. E.L. Pugh, 'Women and slavery: Julia Gardiner Tyler and the duchess of Sutherland', *The Virginia Magazine of History and Biography*, 88 (1980), pp. 188–193; Mandler, 'From Almack's to Willis's', p. 164; Reynolds, *Aristocratic Women*, pp. 122–127.
113. See Julia Bush, *Edwardian Ladies and Imperial Power* (Leicester University Press, 2000).

114. Cited in Bush, *Edwardian Ladies*, pp. 50–51.
115. Cartwright, 'Introduction', p. xii; Lisa Chilton, *Agents of Empire: British female migration to Canada and Australia, 1860s–1930* (University of Toronto Press, 2007), p. 61; Lisa Chilton, 'A new class of women for the colonies: The imperial colonist and the construction of empire', *Journal of Imperial and Commonwealth History*, 31 (2003), p. 36; Julia Bush, '"The right sort of woman": Female emigrators and emigration to the British Empire, 1890–1910', *Women's History Review*, 3.3 (1994), p. 398.
116. Gordon, 'Introduction', pp. 31–34.
117. Brown, *To Partake of Tea*, p. 6.
118. Oliver Garnett, 'The letters and collection of William Graham – Pre-Raphaelite patron and Pre-Raphael collector', *The Volume of the Walpole Society*, 62 (2000), p. 148. For a discussion of how 'new money' became landowners in the mid-nineteenth century, see David Brown, 'Equipoise and the myth of an open élite: New men of wealth and the purchase of land in the equipoise decades, 1850–69', in Hewitt (ed.), *An Age of Equipoise?*, pp. 122–154.
119. Bourne, *Patronage and Society*, p. 181.
120. Wemyss, *A Family Record*, p. 35.
121. David Cannadine, *Ornamentalism: How the British saw their empire* (Oxford University Press, 2001), p. 28.
122. Bourne, *Patronage and Society*, p. 181.
123. Lucy, *Mistress of Charlecote*, p. 108. The spelling is also to be found as Powlett Lane.
124. Carry Pawlett Lane to her mother, Mary Elizabeth Lucy, August 1861/2, reproduced in Lucy, *Mistress of Charlecote*, p. 108. The narrative in this section of the autobiography is a little confused, and so it is not clear whether this letter is from 1861 (as noted) or 1862 (which fits the narrative of the text).
125. Finn and Smith, 'Introduction', pp. 3–7, 13.
126. Lucy, *Mistress of Charlecote*, p. 122; N.J. Thomas, 'Embodying imperial spectacle: Dressing Lady Curzon, Vicereine of India 1899–1905', *Cultural Geographies*, 14.3 (2007), p. 391; E.A. Coleman, *The Opulent Era: Fashions of Worth, Doucet and Pingat* (Thames & Hudson, 1989), p. 101.
127. Lucy, *Mistress of Charlecote*, p. 122.
128. Lucy, *Biography of the Lucy Family*, pp. 198–201; Corinne Fowler, *Green Unpleasant Land: Creative responses to rural Britain's colonial connections* (Peepal Tree Press, 2021), p. 133; Lucy Porten, 'The East India Company', in Huxtable et al. (eds), *Interim Report*, p. 46.
129. Barczewski, *Country Houses and the British Empire*, p. 214.
130. Barczewski, *Country Houses and the British Empire*, Appendices.
131. Girouard, *The Return to Camelot*, p. 209.
132. For a full discussion of Balfour and international politics, see Denis Judd, *Balfour and the British Empire: A study in imperial evolution 1874–1932* (Macmillan, 1968).
133. Wemyss, *A Family Record*, pp. 35, 101, 105–106, 117.
134. Bush, *Edwardian Ladies*, p. 25; Eliza Riedi, 'Women, gender, and the promotion of empire: The Victoria League, 1901–1914', *The Historical Journal*, 45 (2002), pp. 569–599.
135. Nicola J. Thomas, 'Mary Curzon: "American Queen of India"', in David Lambert and Alan Lester (eds), *Colonial Lives across the British Empire: Imperial*

careering in the long nineteenth century (Cambridge University Press, 2006), pp. 287–291.
136. Dana Cooper, *Informal Ambassadors: American women, transatlantic marriages, and Anglo-American relations, 1865–1945* (Kent State University Press, 2014), p. 122; David Gilmour, *Curzon: Imperial statesman* (Penguin Books, 2019), p. 222. While Curzon was foreign secretary between 1919 and 1924, he never became prime minister.
137. Bruce Redford, *Venice and the Grand Tour* (Yale University Press, 1996), pp. 10–11; Jeremy Black, *The British Abroad: The Grand Tour in the eighteenth century* (Alan Sutton, 1992), pp. 4–13; Rosemary Sweet, *Cities and the Grand Tour: The British in Italy, c.1690–1820* (Cambridge University Press, 2012), pp. 3, 7–8, 10–13; Dory Agazarian, 'Victorian roads to Rome: Historical travel in the wake of the Grand Tour', *Nineteenth-Century Contexts*, 37 (2015), pp. 391–394; James Buzard, *The Beaten Track: European tourism, literature, and the ways to culture, 1800–1918* (Clarendon Press, 1993), pp. 5–7.
138. Lucy, *Mistress of Charlecote*, pp. 60–61.
139. Lucy, *The Private Journal*, pp. 2, 17–21; Lucy, *Biography of the Lucy Family*, p. 146 (author's own emphasis).
140. Lucy, *Mistress of Charlecote*, p. 63; Lucy, *Biography of the Lucy Family*, p. 146.
141. Lucy, *Mistress of Charlecote*, p. 67.
142. Lucy, *The Private Journal*, pp. 43, 72–80, 97–99.
143. Lucy, *The Private Journal*, pp. 122–129; Lucy, *Mistress of Charlecote*, pp. 68–69, 72. The date is incorrectly given as 1842 in the latter text.
144. Robert Aldrich, *The Seduction of the Mediterranean: Writing, art, and homosexual fantasy* (Routledge, 1993), pp. 70–74; Anne Sebba, *The Exiled Collector: William Bankes and the making of an English country house* (Dovecote Press, 2009), pp. 149–185.
145. Gregory Claeys, *Imperial Sceptics: British critics of empire, 1850–1920* (Cambridge University Press, 2010), pp. 36–43; James Mitchell, 'The imprisonment of Wilfrid Scawen Blunt in Galway: Cause and consequence', *Journal of the Galway Archaeological and Historical Society*, 46 (1994), pp. 65–110; Cannadine, *Ornamentalism*, p. 72.
146. Elizabeth Longford, 'Blunt, Wilfrid Scawen (1840–1922), hedonist, poet, and breeder of Arab horses', *Oxford Dictionary of National Biography*, Oxford University Press, 3 January 2008; Elizabeth Longford, *A Pilgrimage of Passion: The life of Wilfrid Scawen Blunt* (Weidenfeld & Nicolson, 1979), pp. 308–309.
147. Blunt's diary, cited in Longford, *Pilgrimage of Passion*, p. 311.
148. Blunt's diary, cited in Longford, *Pilgrimage of Passion*, pp. 310–311.
149. Blunt's diary, cited in Longford, *Pilgrimage of Passion*, p. 312.
150. Tinniswood, *The Power and the Glory*, p. 264.
151. Blunt's diary, cited in Longford, *Pilgrimage of Passion*, p. 313.
152. Longford, *Pilgrimage of Passion*, p. 314. For a discussion of orientalism, see Edward W. Said, *Orientalism* (Vintage Books, 1979), passim, esp. p. 257.

CHAPTER 8

1. Horner, *Time Remembered*, p. 181.
2. Renton, *The Wild Wyndhams*, p. 22.
3. Horner, *Time Remembered*, p. 1; Kathryn Hughes, *The Victorian Governess* (Hambledon Press, 1993), p. 70.

4. Gailey, *Portrait of a Muse*, p. 18; L. Wolff, 'When I imagine a child: The idea of childhood and the philosophy of memory in the Enlightenment', *Eighteenth-Century Studies*, 31 (1998), p. 391.
5. Ridley and Percy, 'Charteris, Mary', *ODNB*; Renton, *Those Wild Wyndhams*, p. 7; Caroline Dakers, *Clouds: The biography of a house* (Yale University Press, 1993), pp. 147–152.
6. Renton, *Those Wild Wyndhams*, pp. 8–9.
7. Barbara Bryant, 'The Grosvenor Gallery, patronage and the aesthetic portrait', in Stephen Calloway and Lynn Federle Orr (eds), *The Cult of Beauty: The aesthetic movement, 1860–1900* (V&A, 2011), p. 160; Fiona MacCarthy, *The Last Pre-Raphaelite: Edward Burne-Jones and the Victorian Imagination* (Faber, 2011), p. 337; Renton, *Those Wild Wyndhams*, p. 34.
8. MacCarthy, *The Last Pre-Raphaelite*, pp. 109, 276–277; Mackenzie, *Children of the Souls*, p. 18; Edward Coley Burne-Jones, *The Golden Stairs*, oil paint on canvas, 1880, Tate Britain, London.
9. Barbara Leighton, 'Jones, Sir Edward Coley Burne-, first baronet (1833–1898)', *Oxford Dictionary of National Biography*, Oxford University Press, 23 September 2004; Horner, *Time Remembered*, p. 26.
10. Gailey, *Portrait of a Muse*, pp. 28–29, 42, 58.
11. Batchelor, *Lady Trevelyan*, pp. 24, 31.
12. Gailey, *Portrait of a Muse*, pp. 77–81.
13. Horner, *Time Remembered*, pp. 65–67.
14. Horner, *Time Remembered*, p. 66; Gailey, *Portrait of a Muse*, pp. 102–104; Dakers, *Clouds*, passim.
15. Renton, *Those Wild Wyndhams*, p. 53; Letter from Edwin Lutyens to Lady Emily Lutyens, 2 January 1902, reproduced in Clayre Percy and Jane Ridley (eds), *The Letters of Edwin Lutyens: To his wife Lady Emily* (Collins, 1985), p. 96.
16. Ridley and Percy, 'Charteris, Mary', *ODNB*.
17. Renton, *Those Wild Wyndhams*, p. 57.
18. Marsh, *A Number of People*, p. 200.
19. Wemyss, *A Family Record*, p. 37.
20. Cartwright (ed.), *Journals of Lady Knightley*, p. 181.
21. Gordon, 'Introduction', p. 3.
22. Lucy, *Biography of the Lucy Family*, p. 134; Clive Wainwright, *The Romantic Interior: The British collector at home, 1750–1850* (Yale University Press, 1989), pp. 213–215.
23. Lucy, *Biography of the Lucy Family*, pp. 135–136; Lucy, *Mistress of Charlecote*, pp. 33, 47–50.
24. Wainwright, *The Romantic Interior*, pp. 219–232; Lucy, *Mistress of Charlecote*, pp. 51, 73.
25. Lucy, *Mistress of Charlecote*, p. 33.
26. Lucy, *Mistress of Charlecote*, pp. 42, 47.
27. Nickianne Moody, 'Gardening in print: Profession, instruction and reform', *Nineteenth-Century Gender Studies*, 5 (2009); Brent Elliott, *Victorian Gardens* (Batsford, 1990), pp. 236–237; Gailey, *Portrait of a Muse*, p. xvi.
28. Trevelyan, *A Pre-Raphaelite Circle*, p. 69.
29. William Bell Scott, *Autobiographical Notes of the Life of W.B. Scott and Notices of His Artistic and Poetic Circle of Friends 1830 to 1882*, ed. W. Minto, vol. 2 (J.R. Osgood, 1892), pp. 3–4.

30. Horner, *Time Remembered*, p. 81.
31. Horner, *Time Remembered*, p. 82.
32. Horner, *Time Remembered*, pp. 195–196; Gathorne-Hardy (ed.), *Ottoline*, p. 176.
33. Watkin, *A Kingston Lacy Childhood*, pp. 36–39.
34. Brown, *To Partake of Tea*, pp. 41, 47, 50.
35. Lucy, *The Private Journal*, passim; Lucy, *Biography of the Lucy Family*, pp. 144–157.
36. S. Huxtable, 'Wealth, power and the global country house', in Huxtable et al. (eds), *Interim Report*, p. 9; Wainwright, *The Romantic Interior*, pp. 215–217.
37. Jon Stobart, 'Making a home: Family, memory and domestic objects in England, c.1750–1830', in Jon Stobart (ed.), *The Comforts of Home in Western Europe: 1700–1900* (Bloomsbury Academic, 2020), pp. 216–217.
38. Annabelle Gilmore and Jon Stobart, 'Suite of ebony furniture inlaid with ivory, Charlecote Park', in Jon Stobart (ed.), *Global Goods and the Country House: Comparative perspectives, 1650–1800* (UCL Press, 2023), p. 134; Wainwright, *The Romantic Interior*, p. 209; Barczewski, *Country Houses and the British Empire*, p. 138.
39. Wainwright, *The Romantic Interior*, p. 219.
40. Lucy, *Mistress of Charlecote*, p. 84.
41. Lucy, *Biography of the Lucy Family*.
42. Lucy, *Mistress of Charlecote*, pp. 73–75.
43. Wainwright, *The Romantic Interior*, pp. 234–235.
44. Nathaniel Hawthorne's journal, reproduced in Bryan Homer, *An American Liaison: Leamington Spa and the Hawthornes, 1855–1864* (Fairleigh Dickinson University Press, 1998), pp. 55–56.
45. Batchelor, *Lady Trevelyan*, p. 82; Ruskin, cited in Trevelyan, *A Pre-Raphaelite Circle*, p. 35.
46. Tony Tanner, *Venice Desired* (Blackwell, 1992), pp. 67–156; Batchelor, *Lady Trevelyan and the Pre-Raphaelite Brotherhood*, p. 40. Their letters can be found in Surtees (ed.), *Reflections of a Friendship*.
47. Lucy West, '"She enclosed & decorated this hall on the advice of John Ruskin": Pauline, Lady Trevelyan and the creation of Wallington Hall's Central Hall', *Journal of Art Historiography*, 22.1 (2020), p. 2.
48. West, '"She enclosed & decorated this hall"', passim.
49. Batchelor, *Lady Trevelyan and the Pre-Raphaelite Brotherhood*, p. 82; Trevelyan, *A Pre-Raphaelite Circle*, p. 120; West, '"She enclosed & decorated this hall"', p. 8.
50. Trevelyan, *A Pre-Raphaelite Circle*, p. 120; Dianne Sachko Macleod, 'Private and public patronage in Victorian Newcastle', *Journal of the Warburg and Courtauld Institutes*, 52 (1989), pp. 189–190; Jan Marsh, *The Pre-Raphaelite Sisterhood* (Quartet Books, 1985), pp. 67, 234, 259.
51. Pauline Trevelyan, cited in Batchelor, *Lady Trevelyan and the Pre-Raphaelite Brotherhood*, p. 101.
52. West, '"She enclosed & decorated this hall"', p. 5; Jeremy Maas, *The Victorian Art World in Photographs* (Barrie & Jenkins, 1984), pp. 115–116.
53. Letter from John Ruskin to Pauline Trevelyan, 17 May 1856, reproduced in Surtees (ed.), *Reflections of a Friendship*, p. 112.
54. Batchelor, *Lady Trevelyan*, p. 127; West, '"She enclosed & decorated this hall"', pp. 16–17.

55. Batchelor, *Lady Trevelyan*, pp. 125–144.
56. Batchelor, *Lady Trevelyan*, pp. 135–139; West, '"She enclosed & decorated this hall"', p. 19.
57. Jonah Siegel, *Desire and Excess: The nineteenth-century culture of art* (Princeton University Press, 2000), pp. 215–217.
58. Trevelyan, *A Pre-Raphaelite Circle*, p. 132; Surtees (ed.), *Reflections of a Friendship*, p. 128.
59. Batchelor, *Lady Trevelyan*, p. 112; Trevelyan, *A Pre-Raphaelite Circle*, p. 122.
60. Batchelor, *Lady Trevelyan*, pp. 58–69; West, '"She enclosed & decorated this hall"', pp. 11–13.
61. Letter from John Ruskin to Pauline Trevelyan, c.December 1854, reproduced in Surtees (ed.), *Reflections of a Friendship*, pp. 94–95.
62. West, '"She enclosed & decorated this hall"', pp. 11–13.
63. Trevelyan, *A Pre-Raphaelite Circle*, p. 12; Paul Barlow, 'Grotesque obscenities: Thomas Woolner's *Civilization* and its discontents', in Colin Trodd, Paul Barlow and David Amigoni (eds), *Routledge Revivals: Victorian culture and the idea of the grotesque* (Taylor & Francis Group, 2018), pp. 97–98.
64. Woolner, cited in Barlow, 'Grotesque obscenities', p. 100.
65. Woolner, cited in West, '"She enclosed & decorated this hall"', p. 25.
66. West, '"She enclosed & decorated this hall"', pp. 22–23.
67. David Wooster (ed.), *Selections from the Literary and Artistic Remains of Paulina Jermyn Trevelyan, First Wife of Sir W.C. Trevelyan* (Longmans, Green & Co., 1879), pp. iii–iv.
68. Batchelor, *Lady Trevelyan*, pp. 193–194; Trevelyan, *A Pre-Raphaelite Circle*, p. 133; Catherine Maxwell, 'Algernon Charles Swinburne (1837–1909)', in Elizabeth Prettejohn (ed.), *The Cambridge Companion to the Pre-Raphaelites* (Cambridge University Press, 2012), pp. 236–237.
69. Larry J. Schaaf, '"Splendid calotypes" and "hideous men": Photography in the diaries of Lady Pauline Trevelyan', *History of Photography*, 34.4 (2010), pp. 326, 338–340.
70. Trevelyan, *A Pre-Raphaelite Circle*, p. 126.
71. Gilmour, *Curzon*, pp. 100–104; Lambert, *Unquiet Souls*, pp. 8–15.
72. Gailey, *Portrait of a Muse*, pp. 19–21, 128–133.
73. Roger Bowdler, 'Memorials at Mells: An emerging story of remembrance', *Art and the Country House* website, Paul Mellon Centre, accessed via https://doi.org/10.17658/ACH/MME589; MacCarthy, *The Last Pre-Raphaelite*, pp. 339–340.
74. Max Egremont, *Balfour: A life of Arthur James Balfour* (Collins, 1980), pp. 47–53; Penelope Fitzgerald, *Edward Burne-Jones: A biography* (Joseph, 1975), pp. 160–161, 226.
75. Frances Horner, cited in Caroline Dakers, 'Frances Horner and Mells: Model, muse, hostess, friend, patron, collector', *Art and the Country House* website, Paul Mellon Centre, accessed via https://doi.org/10.17658/ACH/MME585
76. Burne-Jones, cited in Gailey, *Portrait of a Muse*, pp. 258–259.
77. Stanley Olson, *John Singer Sargent: His portrait* (Macmillan, 1986), p. 133; Richard Ormond, Elaine Kilmurray and John Singer Sargent, *John Singer Sargent: Complete paintings*, vol. II: *Portraits of the 1890s* (Yale University Press, 1998), p. 156.
78. Olson, *John Singer Sargent*, p. 219.

79. 'The Royal Academy', *The Times*, 5 May 1900, p. 14.
80. Olson, *John Singer Sargent*, p. 219; Evan Edward, Vernon Lee Charteris and John Singer Sargent, *John Sargent* (William Heinemann, 1927).
81. Jane Brown, *Lutyens and the Edwardians: An English architect and his clients* (Viking, 1996), pp. 109–110.
82. Brown, *Lutyens and the Edwardians*, pp. 107, 114, 223–224; David Frazer Lewis, 'Lutyens's designs for Campion Hall, Oxford', *Twentieth Century Architecture*, 11 (2013), p. 55.
83. Percy and Ridley (eds), *The Letters of Edwin Lutyens*, p. 55; Alex King, *Memorials of the Great War in Britain: The symbolism and politics of remembrance* (Berg, 1998), pp. 143–145.
84. Horn, *High Society*, pp. 3–4.
85. Lambert, *Unquiet Souls*, pp. 133–134; Adeline R. Tintner, 'Consuelo Vanderbilt and "The Buccaneers"', *Edith Wharton Review*, 10.2 (1993), p. 18.
86. Lambert, *Unquiet Souls*, pp. 134–135.
87. Margot Tennant, cited in Lambert, *Unquiet Souls*, p. 134.
88. Lambert, *Unquiet Souls*, p. 136; Ellenberger, *Balfour's World*, p. 181.
89. Horner, *Time Remembered*, pp. 72–80; Gailey, *Portrait of a Muse*, p. 140.
90. R.W.B. Lewis, *Edith Wharton: A biography* (Vintage, 1993), p. 243.
91. Betty Balfour, cited in Ellenberger, *Balfour's World*, p. 144.
92. Ellenberger, *Balfour's World*, p. 184.
93. Laura Tennant, cited in Renton, *Those Wild Wyndhams*, pp. 58–59.
94. Ellenberger, *Balfour's World*, pp. 73–77.
95. From an essay by Mary Elcho on the Souls, cited in Dismore, *Tangled Souls*, p. 40.
96. Gailey, *Portrait of a Muse*, p. 133.
97. Diary of Emily Lytton (later Lutyens), 5 December 1892, reproduced in Emily Lutyens, *A Blessed Girl: Memoirs of a Victorian girlhood* (Heinemann, 1989), p. 182.
98. Cynthia, Lady Asquith, *Remember and Be Glad* (John Barrie, 1952), pp. 4–5.
99. Asquith, *Remember and Be Glad*, p. 8.
100. Letter from Mary Elcho to Arthur Balfour, 15 October 1907, reproduced in Ridley and Percy (eds), *Letters of Arthur Balfour*, p. 242.
101. Marsh, *A Number of People*, p. 203. Marsh thought this criticism was unfair.
102. Asquith, *Remember and Be Glad*, pp. 4–5.
103. Wemyss, *A Family Record*, p. 38.
104. From an essay by Mary Elcho on the Souls, cited in Dismore, *Tangled Souls*, p. 251.
105. Ellenberger, *Balfour's World*, p. 238.
106. Asquith, *Remember and Be Glad*, p. 6.
107. Letter from Mary Elcho to Arthur Balfour, 12 September 1912, reproduced in Ridley and Percy (eds), *Letters of Arthur Balfour*, p. 287.
108. Marsh, *A Number of People*, p. 204.

CHAPTER 9

1. Pauline Trevelyan, 'Wedded love', in Wooster (ed.), *Selections from the Literary and Artistic Remains of Paulina Jermyn Trevelyan*, p. 6.
2. Louisa Knightley's diary, 19 December 1895, reproduced in Gordon, *Politics and Society*, p. 319.

3. Bush, '"The right sort of woman"', p. 398.
4. Lucy, *A Sketch of the Life and Death of Herbert Almeric Lucy*; Lucy, *The Private Journal*.
5. Batchelor, *Lady Trevelyan and the Pre-Raphaelite Brotherhood*, pp. 107, 134, 231–232.
6. Bowdler, 'Memorials at Mells'.
7. David Thomas, 'The social origins of marriage partners of the British peerage in the eighteenth and nineteenth centuries', *Population Studies*, 26.1 (1972), pp. 99–111; Horn, *Ladies of the Manor*, pp. 61–62.
8. Maureen E. Montgomery, *'Gilded Prostitution': Status, money, and transatlantic marriages, 1870–1914* (Routledge, 1989), pp. 113–114.
9. Carnarvon, *The Earl and the Pharaoh*, pp. 74ff.
10. Renton, *Those Wild Wyndhams*, p. 42.
11. Nicola Beauman, *Cynthia Asquith* (Hamish Hamilton, 1987), p. 10.
12. Renton, *Those Wild Wyndhams*, pp. 40–41; Beauman, *Cynthia Asquith*, p. 14.
13. Renton, *Those Wild Wyndhams*, pp. 39–53; Ridley and Percy, 'Charteris, Mary', *ODNB*.
14. Renton, *Those Wild Wyndhams*, p. 45.
15. Mary Wyndham, cited in Ellenberger, *Balfour's World*, p. 67.
16. Mary Wyndham, cited in Renton, *Those Wild Wyndhams*, p. 47.
17. Renton, *Those Wild Wyndhams*, pp. 47–49.
18. Mary Elcho, cited in Ellenberger, *Balfour's World*, p. 68.
19. Ellenberger, *Balfour's World*, p. 295.
20. Gailey, *Portrait of a Muse*, pp. 94–95.
21. Helena Michie, 'Victorian honeymoons: Sexual reorientations and the "sights" of Europe', *Victorian Studies*, 43 (2001), pp. 229–251; Stephanie Coontz, *Marriage, a History: From obedience to intimacy, or, how love conquered marriage* (Viking, 2005), p. 190.
22. Renton, *The Wild Wyndhams*, pp. 48–53.
23. Lambert, *Unquiet Souls*, pp. 136, 142.
24. For a discussion of her management of her flirtations with H.H. Asquith and Edward Burne-Jones in 1892, see Gailey, *Portrait of a Muse*, pp. 150–181.
25. Ellenberger, *Balfour's World*, p. 200.
26. Renton, *Those Wild Wyndhams*, pp. 125–126.
27. Ellenberger, *Balfour's World*, pp. 196, 201–202; Tinniswood, *The Power and the Glory*, pp. 265–266.
28. Renton, *Those Wild Wyndhams*, p. 296.
29. Watkin, *A Kingston Lacy Childhood*, p. 34.
30. Watkin, *A Kingston Lacy Childhood*, pp. 8, 34–35.
31. Brown, *To Partake of Tea*, pp. 37–38.
32. Jennifer Aston and Frances Hamilton, 'On the development of marital law', *Journal of Legal History*, 43 (2022), p. 131.
33. For Minnie Benson's life, see: Betty Askwith, *Two Victorian Families* (Chatto & Windus, 1971), pp. 127–181; Rodney Bolt, *As Good as God, as Clever as the Devil: The impossible life of Mary Benson* (Atlantic Books, 2011).
34. Renton, *Those Wild Wyndhams*, pp. 160–177; Longford, *A Pilgrimage of Passion*, p. 132; Tinniswood, *The Power and the Glory*, p. 256.
35. Hugo Elcho, cited in Renton, *Those Wild Wyndhams*, p. 185.
36. Renton, *Those Wild Wyndhams*, pp. 185–186.
37. Mary Elcho, cited in Longford, *Pilgrimage of Passion*, p. 419.

38. Renton, *Those Wild Wyndhams*, p. 30; Ridley and Percy (eds), *Letters of Arthur Balfour*, p. xi.
39. Egremont, *Balfour*, p. 31; Ellenberger, *Balfour's World*, p. 26.
40. Mary Gladstone, cited in Renton, *Those Wild Wyndhams*, p. 31.
41. H.G. Wells, cited in Beauman, *Cynthia Asquith*, p. 15; Ruddock F. Mackay, *Balfour, Intellectual Statesman* (Oxford University Press, 1985), p. 8.
42. Egremont, *Balfour*, p. 69.
43. Blunt, cited in Egremont, *Balfour*, p. 118.
44. Mary Elcho, cited in Egremont, *Balfour*, p. 119. Their letters have been published in Ridley and Percy (eds), *Letters of Arthur Balfour*.
45. Mary Elcho, cited in Ridley and Percy (eds), *Letters of Arthur Balfour*, p. 353.
46. Letter from Mary Elcho to Arthur Balfour, 7 March 1929, reproduced in Ridley and Percy (eds), *Letters of Arthur Balfour*, pp. 353–354.
47. Letter from Arthur Balfour to Frances Balfour, 6 March 1887, reproduced in Ridley and Percy (eds), *Letters of Arthur Balfour*, pp. 33–34.
48. Egremont, *Balfour*, p. 69.
49. Letter from Arthur Balfour to Frances Balfour, 6 March 1887, reproduced in Ridley and Percy (eds), *Letters of Arthur Balfour*, pp. 33–34.
50. Holloway, '"You know I am all on fire"', pp. 323, 338.
51. Renton, *Those Wild Wyndhams*, p. 185.
52. Mary Elcho to Arthur Balfour, 13 August 1890, reproduced in Ridley and Percy (eds), *Letters of Arthur Balfour*, p. 71.
53. Renton, *Those Wild Wyndhams*, pp. 66–69.
54. Gailey, *Portrait of a Muse*, p. 146.
55. Ellenberger, *Balfour's World*, p. 159.
56. Kenneth Young, *Arthur James Balfour: The happy life of the politician, prime minister, statesman and philosopher, 1848–1930* (Bell, 1963), p. 135.
57. Letter from Mary Elcho to Arthur Balfour, 1 February 1906, reproduced in Ridley and Percy (eds), *Letters of Arthur Balfour*, p. 231.
58. Ridley and Percy (eds), *Letters of Arthur Balfour*, p. 22.
59. Letter from Mary Elcho to Arthur Balfour, 1 February 1906, reproduced in Ridley and Percy (eds), *Letters of Arthur Balfour*, p. 231.
60. Letter from Mary Elcho to Arthur Balfour, 16 January 1906, reproduced in Ridley and Percy (eds), *Letters of Arthur Balfour*, p. 231.
61. Beauman, *Cynthia Asquith*, pp. 1–6; R.J.Q. Adams, *Balfour: The last grandee* (John Murray, 2007), p. 48.
62. Letter from Arthur Balfour to Mary Elcho, 20 November 1887, reproduced in Ridley and Percy (eds), *Letters of Arthur Balfour*, p. 44.
63. Letter from Arthur Balfour to Mary Elcho, 21 January 1888, reproduced in Ridley and Percy (eds), *Letters of Arthur Balfour*, p. 46.
64. Ridley and Percy (eds), *Letters of Arthur Balfour*, p. 208. This is a different view from that held by Kenneth Young, who suggests that their physical relationship primarily took place during the late 1880s. Young, *Arthur James Balfour*, pp. 135–138.
65. Letter from Mary Elcho to Arthur Balfour, 19 January 1904, reproduced in Ridley and Percy (eds), *Letters of Arthur Balfour*, pp. 209–211.
66. Letter from Mary Elcho to Arthur Balfour, 30 October 1903, reproduced in Ridley and Percy (eds), *Letters of Arthur Balfour*, p. 209; Letter from Mary Elcho to Arthur Balfour, 25 June 1905, reproduced in Ridley and Percy (eds), *Letters of Arthur Balfour*, pp. 223–224; Mary Elcho, cited in Egremont, *Balfour*, p. 199.

67. Letter from Mary Elcho to Arthur Balfour, 14 February 1905, and Letter from Mary Elcho to Arthur Balfour, February 1906, reproduced in Ridley and Percy (eds), *Letters of Arthur Balfour*, pp. 217, 231–233.
68. Letter from Mary Elcho to Arthur Balfour, 14 February 1907, reproduced in Ridley and Percy (eds), *Letters of Arthur Balfour*, p. 236.
69. Annebella Pollen, '"The Valentine has fallen upon evil days": Mocking Victorian Valentines and the ambivalent laughter of the carnivalesque', *Early Popular Visual Culture*, 12 (2014), pp. 127–173.
70. Letter from Mary Elcho to Arthur Balfour, 25 June 1905, reproduced in Ridley and Percy (eds), *Letters of Arthur Balfour*, pp. 223–224.
71. For example, Egremont, *Balfour*, p. 121; Ellenberger, *Balfour's World*, pp. 160, 290–291.
72. Marsh, *A Number of People*, p. 203.
73. Ellenberger, *Balfour's World*, p. 293.
74. Adams, *Balfour*, p. 46.
75. Letter from Mary Elcho to Arthur Balfour, 7 March 1929, reproduced in Ridley and Percy (eds), *Letters of Arthur Balfour*, pp. 353–354.
76. Adams, *The Great Adventure*, p. 67.
77. Ridley and Percy (eds), *Letters of Arthur Balfour*, p. 354.
78. Hollingsworth, 'Demography of the British peerage', p. 24.
79. Asquith, *Remember and Be Glad*, pp. 16–19.
80. Asquith, *Remember and Be Glad*, p. 20.
81. Renton, *Those Wild Wyndhams*, pp. 125–127, 139.
82. Wemyss, *A Family Record*, preface.
83. Watkin, *A Kingston Lacy Childhood*, p. 48.
84. Watkin, *A Kingston Lacy Childhood*, p. 25.
85. Watkin, *A Kingston Lacy Childhood*, pp. 24–26.
86. Adeline Hartcup, *Children of the Great Country Houses* (Sidgwick & Jackson, 1986), pp. 1–27.
87. Watkin, *A Kingston Lacy Childhood*, pp. 116–118.
88. Watkin, *A Kingston Lacy Childhood*, pp. 126–128.
89. Mackenzie, *Children of the Souls*, pp. 19, 21.
90. Frances Horner, cited in Gailey, *Portrait of a Muse*, p. 279.
91. Frances Horner, cited in Mackenzie, *Children of the Souls*, p. 36.
92. Gailey, *Portrait of a Muse*, p. 280.
93. Mackenzie, *Children of the Souls*, p. 78.
94. Gathorne-Hardy (ed.), *Ottoline*, pp. 176–177; Gailey, *Portrait of a Muse*, pp. 283, 286–287.
95. Mackenzie, *Children of the Souls*, pp. 79, 107–108.
96. Marsh, *A Number of People*, p. 177; Frances Horner, cited in Mackenzie, *Children of the Souls*, p. 79.
97. Gailey, *Portrait of a Muse*, pp. 295–297.
98. Patrick Shaw Stewart, cited in Mackenzie, *Children of the Souls*, p. 129.
99. Bujak, *English Landed Society*, p. 27.
100. Adams, *The Great Adventure*, pp. 63–65; Stefan Goebel, *The Great War and Medieval Memory: War, remembrance and medievalism in Britain and Germany, 1914–1940* (Cambridge University Press, 2007), p. 194; Mackenzie, *Children of the Souls*, p. 142; Allen J. Frantzen, *Bloody Good: Chivalry, sacrifice, and the Great War* (University of Chicago Press, 2004), p. 129.

101. For a description of the efforts of the duchess of Rutland to protect her son from active service, see Catherine Bailey, *The Secret Rooms* (Penguin, 2013), pp. 235ff.
102. Gailey, *Portrait of a Muse*, p. 301.
103. Edward Horner, cited in Dakers, *The Countryside at War*, p. 25; Marsh, *A Number of People*, p. 179.
104. Edward Horner, cited in *Children of the Souls*, p. 167.
105. Mackenzie, *Children of the Souls*, p. 168.
106. Gailey, *Portrait of a Muse*, p. 305.
107. Mackenzie, *Children of the Souls*, pp. 220–221, 249–254.
108. Edward Horner, cited in Mackenzie, *Children of the Souls*, p. 254.
109. Gailey, *Portrait of a Muse*, pp. 321–322; Anthony Fletcher, *Life, Death and Growing Up on the Western Front* (Yale University Press, 2013), pp. 268–269.
110. Gailey, *Portrait of a Muse*, pp. 316–317.
111. Wemyss, *Family Record*, p. 304.
112. Wemyss, *Family Record*, p. 337.
113. Lambert, *Unquiet Souls*, p. 190. For Yvo's death in battle, see Fletcher, *Life, Death and Growing Up*, pp. 262–264.
114. Lambert, *Unquiet Souls*, pp. 193–194; Wemyss, *Family Record*, pp. 372–376.
115. Mary Elcho to Arthur Balfour, 12 September 1916, reproduced in Ridley and Percy (eds), *Letters of Arthur Balfour*, p. 341.
116. Frances Horner, cited in Fletcher, *Life, Death and Growing Up*, p. 269.
117. Cynthia Asquith's diary, 11 November 1915, reproduced in Cynthia Asquith, *Diaries: 1915–18* (Hutchinson, 1968), p. 97.
118. Cynthia Asquith's diary, 23 November 1917, reproduced in Asquith, *Diaries*, p. 370.
119. Bujak, *English Landed Society*, pp. 13–15.
120. Letter from Mary Elcho to Arthur Balfour, August 1914, reproduced in Ridley and Percy (eds), *Letters of Arthur Balfour*, pp. 311–312.
121. Cited in Ridley and Percy (eds), *Letters of Arthur Balfour*, p. 312.
122. Fletcher, *Life, Death and Growing Up*, p. 36.
123. Dakers, *Countryside at War*, p. 81.
124. Bujak, *English Landed Society*, pp. 33–34.
125. Alun Howkins, *The Death of Rural England: A social history of the countryside since 1900* (Routledge, 2003), pp. 27–36; Bujak, *English Landed Society*, pp. 59–62.
126. Frances Horner to Edward Horner, cited in Mackenzie, *Children of the Souls*, p. 255.
127. Historic England, 'Stanway War Memorial: Official list entry', National Heritage List for England, accessed via https://historicengland.org.uk/listing/the-list/list-entry/1154209
128. Fletcher, *Life, Death and Growing Up*, p. 255; Percy and Ridley (eds), *The Letters of Edwin Lutyens*, p. 371.
129. Letter from Edwin Lutyens to Lady Emily Lutyens, 4 August 1919, reproduced in Percy and Ridley (eds), *The Letters of Edwin Lutyens*, p. 371.
130. Kate Tiller, *Remembrance and Community: War memorials and local history* (British Association for Local History, 2013), p. 38; Fletcher, *Life, Death and Growing Up*, p. 256.
131. Goebel, *The Great War and Medieval Memory*, pp. 1, 39.
132. King, *Memorials of the Great War*, pp. 145–146; Goebel, *The Great War and Medieval Memory*, p. 32.

133. Goebel, *The Great War and Medieval Memory*, p. 32.
134. Argha Banerjee, 'Memory and remembrance: Women's elegies of the First World War (1914–18)', in Abbes Maazoui (ed.), *The Arts of Memory and the Poetics of Remembering* (Cambridge Scholars, 2016), pp. 5–7.
135. Mary Elcho to Arthur Balfour, 21 January 1917, reproduced in Ridley and Percy (eds), *Letters of Arthur Balfour*, p. 343.
136. Renton, *Those Wild Wyndhams*, p. 342.
137. Mary Elcho, cited in Renton, *Those Wild Wyndhams*, pp. 342–343.
138. Wemyss, *A Family Record*, pp. 40–41.

CONCLUSION

1. Ettie Desborough, cited in Pamela Horn, *Country House Society: The private lives of England's upper class after the First World War* (Amberley, 2015), p. 50.
2. Charles F.G. Masterman, *England after War: A study* (Harcourt, Brace & Co., 1923), pp. 45–46.
3. J.M. Winter, 'Britain's "lost generation" of the First World War', *Population Studies*, 31.3 (1977), p. 464.
4. Gailey, *Portrait of a Muse*, p. 376.
5. Roughly four fifths of British and Irish peers and their sons who joined up returned home alive. Cannadine, *The Decline and Fall of the British Aristocracy*, p. 82. One of the few titles that were extinguished by the Great War was that of Baron Desborough, the title Ettie's husband held. Bujak, *English Landed Society*, p. 116.
6. Randolph Churchill, cited in Madeleine Beard, *English Landed Society in the Twentieth Century* (Routledge, 1989), p. 9.
7. Smith, 'The history of the estate and its owners'.
8. Gordon, 'Introduction', p. 23.
9. Marie M. Fletcher, 'Death and taxes: Estate duty – a neglected factor in changes to British business structure after World War Two', *Business History*, 65 (2023), pp. 191–193.
10. Cynthia Asquith's diary, 23 August 1915, reproduced in Asquith, *Diaries*, p. 71; Dakers, *Countryside at War*, p. 79.
11. Horn, *Ladies of the Manor*, p. 224; Bujak, *English Landed Society*, pp. 111–112; F.M.L. Thompson, 'Presidential address: English landed society in the twentieth century I. Property: collapse and survival', *Transactions of the Royal Historical Society*, 40 (1990), p. 13.
12. Alison Oram, 'Going on an outing: The historic house and queer public history', *Rethinking History*, 15.2 (2011), pp. 189–207.
13. Masterman, *England after War*, p. 49.
14. Peter Mandler, 'Nationalising the country house', in M. Hunter (ed.), *Preserving the Past: The rise of heritage in modern Britain* (Sutton, 1996), pp. 99–100.
15. Dakers, *Countryside at War*, p. 203.
16. Gordon, 'Introduction', p. 21; Mandler, 'Nationalising the country house', p. 101; Howkins, *The Death of Rural England*, pp. 58–61.
17. Brown, *To Partake of Tea*, p. 64.
18. Renton, *Those Wild Wyndhams*, p. 352.
19. Dakers, *Countryside at War*, p. 190; Dakers, *Clouds*, p. 156.
20. Horner, *Time Remembered*, p. 228; Brown, *Lutyens and the Edwardians*, p. 219; Gailey, *Portrait of a Muse*, pp. 344–345.

21. Adrian Tinniswood, *The Long Weekend: Life in the English country house between the wars* (Jonathan Cape, 2016), pp. 11, 127–135; Beard, *English Landed Society*, pp. 70–72; Horn, *Country House Society*, pp. 105–127.
22. Brown, *To Partake of Tea*, pp. 66–69.
23. Marsh, *A Number of People*, p. 202.
24. Brown, *To Partake of Tea*, pp. 86–87.
25. Brown, *To Partake of Tea*, pp. 83–87; Ruth Larsen, 'The British country house, 1939–1945', *Everyone's War*, 15 (2007), pp. 50–55; Caroline Seebohm, *The Country House: A wartime history, 1939–45* (Weidenfeld & Nicolson, 1989), pp. 69–73; Adrian Tinniswood, *Noble Ambitions: The fall and rise of the post-war country house* (Jonathan Cape, 2021), pp. 11–12.
26. Peter Mandler, *The Fall and Rise of the Stately Home* (Yale University Press, 1997), p. 315.
27. David Littlejohn, *The Fate of the English Country House* (Oxford University Press, 1997), p. 55.
28. Historic England, 'Hunstanton Hall: Official list entry', National Heritage List for England, accessed via https://historicengland.org.uk/listing/the-list/list-entry/1001006
29. Historic England, 'Fawsley Hall: Official list entry', National Heritage List for England, accessed via https://historicengland.org.uk/listing/the-list/list-entry/1075281; Anon, 'History of Fawsley Hall', Fawsley Hall Hotel, accessed via https://www.handpickedhotels.co.uk/fawsleyhall/welcome/inspirations/our-heritage
30. Thomas Methuen-Campbell, 'Penrice estate history', Penrice Castle Cottages, accessed via https://penricecastle.co.uk/penrice-estate-history
31. Mandler, 'Nationalising the country house', p. 104.
32. Littlejohn, *The Fate of the English Country House*, pp. 58–59.
33. John Cornforth, *The Country Houses of England, 1948–1998* (Constable, 1998), p. 74; Lummis and Marsh, *The Woman's Domain*, pp. 180–181; Tinniswood, *Long Weekend*, pp. 341–342; Littlejohn, *The Fate of the English Country House*, pp. 59–61. After another change in the law, the Trust was able to purchase some of the contents of Hatchlands with government support.
34. Mandler, 'Nationalising the country house', p. 109.
35. Tinniswood, *Noble Ambitions*, pp. 223–224.
36. Ruth Adams, 'The V&A, the destruction of the country house and the creation of "English Heritage"', *Museum & Society*, 11.1 (2015), pp. 1–18.
37. Watkin, *A Kingston Lacy Childhood*, p. 34.
38. Historic England, 'Rousham House: Official list entry', National Heritage List for England, accessed via https://historicengland.org.uk/listing/the-list/list-entry/1052944; Heller, 'Reading "wrecks of history"', p. 145; Anon, 'Historic Houses president', *Country Life Magazine*, 19 March 2009, accessed via https://www.countrylife.co.uk/out-and-about/theatre-film-music/historic-houses-president-30272#part2; Anon, 'Stanway House and fountain', accessed via https://www.stanwayfountain.co.uk/
39. For an excellent survey of the recent history of the country house, see Ben Cowell, *The British Country House Revival* (Boydell Press, 2024).
40. Harriet Quick, 'Eastnor's Eden', HTSI magazine, *Financial Times*, 7 December 2024, pp. 60–65.
41. Cowell, *The British Country House Revival*, pp. 79–81.

42. Heather Evennett, 'Women, hereditary peerages and gender inequality in the line of succession', House of Lords Library, 2022, accessed via https://lordslibrary.parliament.uk/women-hereditary-peerages-and-gender-inequality-in-the-line-of-succession/
43. For example, the importance of the daughter and granddaughter of the sixth marquess of Exeter, Lady Victoria Leatham and Miranda Rock, to the management and promotion of the collections at Burghley House, Lincolnshire. See Charles Spencer, 'Line of duty', *FT Wealth*, 86 (December 2024), p. 8. The work of Sarah Callander Beckett at Combermere Abbey, Cheshire, is discussed in Cowell, *The British Country House Revival*, pp. 163–165.
44. Cowell, *The British Country House Revival*, pp. 152–153, 156.

Index

Adam, Robert 104–5, 130, 131, 149, *Plate 9*
adultery and extramarital relationships 70, 77, 153, 197–8, 225–34
Aesop, *Fables* 128
affection *see* children; marriage
Aitchison, George 202
Albert, Prince 181
Amisfield (East Lothian) 242, 248
Anne, Queen 91, 117, 121
Apethorpe Palace (Northamptonshire) 16, 18, 20, 22–3, 27, 34, 36–7, 38, 46, 247, *Plate 3*
art collections *see* country houses
Asquith, Lady Cynthia 191, 218, 231, 234–5, 241, 249
Asquith, Herbert 183
Asquith, Katharine 242, 246
Asquith, Margot (née Tennant) 183, 216
Austen, Jane, *Pride and Prejudice* 142

Bagot, Margaret 48
Balfour, Arthur, first earl of 194, 215, 216; and Mary Elcho 170, 183–4, 228–34, *Plate 23*
Balfour, Elizabeth (Betty), second countess of 217
Balfour, Lady Frances 229
Banister, Richard 37
Bankes, Daphne 181, 235, *Plate 25*
Bankes, Henrietta 'Jenny' 170, 179–80, 181, 192, 222, 249, 254; and estate management, 175, 248; and gardens 208; and marriage 226–7; and motherhood 235–6, *Plate 25*; and philanthropic activities 176–7; and her wedding 180–1, *Plate 24*
Bankes, (Henry John) Ralph 175, 178, 248, 249–50
Bankes, Hilary 250
Bankes, Viola 175, 181, 235–6
Bankes, Walter 170, 175, 176–7, 179–80, 199, 222, 226, 235–6
Bankes, William 197
Barrett Browning, Elizabeth 214
Barrie, James 249
Beaufort, Elizabeth, fifth duchess of 108
Bell Scott, William 207, 211–12, *Plate 20*
Benson, Mary (Minnie) 227
Beresford, Lord Charles 217
Bill of Rights (1689) 89
bluestockings 124–7, 134, 136, 254, 283 n.43
Blunt, Wilfrid Scawen 197–8, 216, 220, 227, 228, 230
Bodelwyddan Castle (Denbighshire) 93, 139, 143, 145, 206
Boreman, Thomas, *A Description of Three Hundred Animals* 128

INDEX

Boscawen, Admiral Hon. Edward 92, 95, 100, 124, 157; and his career in the navy 96, 100–1, 123; and his death 134, 149; and Hatchlands Park 96, 101–5, 112–13; and marriage 148–9; and servants 162

Boscawen, Edward (Ned) 160–1

Boscawen, Frances (Fanny) 1–2, 92, 95–6, 116, 122, 123, 129, 130, 162, 251, 255, 276 n.10; and the bluestockings 124, 125–7, 136, 283 n.43; and courting 140; and Hatchlands Park 96, 101–5, 112–13; and marriage 147, 148–9; and motherhood 156, 157, 159, 160–1; and relationship with Elizabeth Montagu 125, 134–5

Boulton, Matthew 106

Bowater, Major-General Sir Edward 171, 181

Brampton Bryan Castle (Herefordshire) 17, 63, 78–84, 252, 273 n.100, *Plate 6*

Bridgewater, Elizabeth, countess of 52

Brown, Lancelot 'Capability' 112, 206

Burke, Edmund 151; *Reflections on the Revolution in France*, 127

Burne-Jones, Sir Edward 170, 202–3, 215, 218, *Plate 26*; *The Golden Stairs* 202

Burton, Robert, *Anatomy of Melancholy* 54

Butler, Lady Eleanor 93, 96, 115–16, 131, 135–6, 162–3, 248, 253, 255, *Plate 13*; death of 153; and finances 99–100; and Plas Newydd 97, 106–7, 128–9; and relationship with Sarah Ponsonby 97, 149–153; and servants 100, 163

Carlisle, Isabella, fourth countess of 161, 163

Carnarvon, Almina, fifth countess of 190, 223

Carnarvon, George, fifth earl of 223

Carryl, Mary 100, 162

Carter, Elizabeth 125

Cartwright, Julia 177, 190

Castle Howard (North Yorkshire) 163

Castlereagh, Edith *see* Londonderry, Edith, seventh marchioness of

Caus Castle (Shropshire) 95

Cavendish, Lucy 189

Cavendish, Margaret, duchess of Newcastle upon Tyne 62

celebration of family events 177–9, 180, 249

Chapone, Hester 124

charity and philanthropic activities 5, 8, 37–8, 124, 172, 175–7, 188–90, 191–2, 217, 242

Charlecote Park (Warwickshire) 93, 146, 194, 196, 205–7, 209–10, 251, *Plate 17*

Charles I 17, 84

Charlotte, Princess 156

Charlotte, Queen (consort of George III) 106, 130

Charteris, Ego (Hugo) 178, 194, 240, 243–4

Charteris, Yvo 240, 243–4

Chatsworth (Derbyshire) 118, 184, 254

childbirth *see* motherhood

children: conflict with parents 50–2, 68–9, 96, 235–8; education and care of 2, 7, 18–19, 24–5, 32–4, 35, 37, 56, 68, 76–7, 128, 157–61, 201–2, 253; illegitimate 98, 226, 227, 291 n.86; parental affection for 33–4, 157–8, 234; *see also* death; servants

chivalry *see* medievalism

christenings 29, 34–5, 178

Christmas 30, 79, 148, 176–7

Churchill, Randolph 247

Civil List 99, 120–1

Civil Wars, British 13, 14, 17, 20, 63, 73, 76, 81–4

Clive, Robert, first Baron Clive of Plassey 89–90

Clouds House (Wiltshire) 204, 223, 235, 241

Cobham, Penelope, ninth Viscountess 254

colonialism *see* empire

commemoration: memorial monuments 38–9, 100, 149, 209, 215, 242–3; obituaries and memorial writings 85, 132–3, 222, 243–4

INDEX

conduct literature *see* didactic literature
Conservative Party 182, 183, 184–5, 186–7, 298 n.83; Conservative and Unionist Women's Franchise Association 187–8; Primrose League 186–7
consumption 6, 24, 29, 48, 79, 80, 161, 194, 254; of clothes 34, 47, 145, 181; of food 25, 31, 110
cookery *see* food production and preparation
Corfe Castle (Dorset) 178
Corrupt Practices Act (1883) 186
Coterie, the Corrupt 237, 238, 239
Cottrell, Sir Charles 17, 64, 65, 66, 67, 72
country houses: and their art collections 130–4, 203, 211–13; and their construction/rebuilding 4, 13–14, 90, 95–6, 100–6, 168–9, 204, 205, 216, 249; destruction of 248, 250, 252; and their drawing rooms 104, 107, 110, 130, 210, 279 n.40; and their gardens 108–14, 206–9; as homes 4, 9, 63, 67–8, 73, 79, 80, 83, 91, 93, 97, 100, 107–8, 114, 138–40, 142, 154, 163, 200, 203, 204–5, 209; as hospitals and convalescent homes 190, 249–50; and their interior decoration 28–9, 30–1, 103–7, 203, 204, 210–13; and their libraries 4, 29, 35, 105, 128–30, 205; purpose of 3–4, 13–14, 27, 63, 90, 96, 106–7, 117, 118, 139, 172, 200; royal visits to 181–2; weekends at 216–19
court, royal 2, 14, 27, 40, 49, 55, 73, 115, 117, 120, 121, 123, 141, 172, 181–2, 195, 283 n.37
courting 16, 41–2, 43–7, 64, 99, 140, 141, 143, 144–5, 223; and the role of parents 7, 18, 40–3, 65, 141–4, 223–4
cremation 179
Curzon, George Nathaniel, Marquess 183, 195, 216
Curzon, Mary 183, 195

Davies, Priamus 83–5
death: in childbirth 60, 156–7, 215; of children 34–5, 171, 196, 237, 240–1, 242–4; of spouses/partners 63, 72, 123, 134, 149, 153, 195, 221; *see also* commemoration
death duties *see* taxation
Delany, Mary 2, 126
Dent-Brocklehurst, Elizabeth 253
Desborough, Lady *see* Grenfell, Ethel (Ettie), Lady Desborough
Devonshire, Deborah (Debo), eleventh duchess of 254
Devonshire, Georgiana, fifth duchess of 117–18, 122–3, *Plate 14*
didactic literature 15, 76, 90–1, 128, 160, 169, 176; and household management 4, 20–1; and marriage 44, 52–3, 54, 140, 147–8; *see also* Gouge, William
Dilke, Emilia Francis, Lady 214
divorce, annulment and separation 48, 69–70, 131, 169, 227, 234, 271 n.40
Dobson, John 211, 212
domesticity, idea of 63, 73, 85, 91, 139–40, 154, 159, 169, 203; *see also* country houses; household management
Dormer, Anne 17, 63, 79, 85, 227, 255; and her children 68–9, 72–3; and her father 65, 72; and her husband 64–72; and her servants 66; and her sister 64, 71–2; as a widow 72–3
Dormer, Clement 68–9
Dormer, Fanny 68
Dormer, Jack 72–3
Dormer, Robert 17, 63, 64–73
drawing rooms *see* country houses
dynasty, concept of 5–6, 10, 32, 42, 62–3, 90, 93, 123, 164, 208–9, 255

Eastnor Castle (Herefordshire) 253
education *see* children
Edward VII 181, 208, 215
Egypt 197–8, 228, 239
Elcho, Hugo (later eleventh earl of Wemyss) 170, 190, 198, 205, 228, 230, 241–2, 247, 248; and courting 223–4; and his extramarital relationships 198, 225–6, 234; and his honeymoon 225

315

INDEX

Elcho, Mary (later eleventh countess of Wemyss) 170, 194, 215, 216, 242, 248–9, 252, 255, *Plate 21*; and Arthur Balfour 183–4, 228–34, *Plate 23*; and Wilfrid Scawen Blunt 197–8, 227–8; and charitable activities 190–1; childhood of 201–2; and her children 234–5, 240–1; and courting 223–4; *A Family Record* 235, 243–5; and her honeymoon 225; as a hostess 217–20; and married life 225–6, 230; and servants 241; and Stanway 204–5
electioneering 117–19, 133, 184–6
Elizabeth I 27, 49, 55, 209
Elliot, Sir Gilbert, of Minto, third baronet 104
embroidery 28, 203, 209
empire 9, 89, 100–1, 161, 167, 172, 191–5, 197
Essex, Lady 101–2
estate management 4, 6, 16, 20, 25–6, 39, 55, 57, 58–60, 99, 112–13, 172, 174–6, 254
Eton College (Berkshire) 236–7, 240
extramarital relationships *see* adultery

family events *see* celebration
Fanshawe, Ann, Lady Fanshawe 35, 63, 135
fathers, relationship between children and 33, 65, 68 108–9, 154, 160–1, 202, 203, 214, 235–6, 258 n.17
Fawsley Hall (Northamptonshire) 171, 174, 175, 177, 178, 182, 189, 200, 205, 247, 250
femininity *see* gender ideals
feudalism *see* medievalism
Fielding, Sarah 124
First World War 190–1, 222, 238–44
Fisher, Alexander 242
food production and preparation 8, 16, 22, 67, 162, 193, 262 n.25
Forbes, Lady Angela 226, 234
Fothergill, John 106
Fownes, Elizabeth 97
Fownes, Sir William 97
Fox Talbot, Henry 214

French, Field Marshal Sir John 239
friendship 70–2, 79, 84, 107, 111, 121, 129, 130, 133, 134–6, 144, 183, 202–3, 210, 214, 228–30, 233; *see also* bluestockings; romantic friendships; Souls, the
funerals 34–5, 179–80

gardens *see* country houses
gender ideals 9, 10, 15, 24, 33, 55, 70, 84, 90–1, 137, 151–3, 169, 254, 255; femininity 15, 21, 67, 82, 90–1, 93, 120, 124, 163; masculinity 70–1, 90–1; and separate spheres 5, 91, 169, 188
George II 120
George III 2, 106, 121
gifts 29–30, 131, 155, 176, 194, 249; and courting 44–5, 50, 145; and the Ladies of Llangollen 99, 106, 129, 130–1, 135–6; to servants 25, 159–60; and weddings 47, 177, 205
Gill, Eric 242
Girls' Friendly Society (GFS) 189, 191, 222
Gladstone, William Ewart 183
Gledstone Hall (North Yorkshire) 249
Godolphin, Sidney, first earl of 121
Gomersall, Ann 128
Gosford House (East Lothian) 204, 231, 234, 240, 241
Gothic revival 206, 209, 210–11, 243
Gouge, William 54, 76; *Of Domesticall Duties* 21–2, 24, 26, 28, 29, 33, 253
Grafton, Anne, duchess of 131
Graham, Jane Catherine 204, 208
Graham, William 170, 192, 195–6, 214, 258 n.17
Grand Tour 90, 172, 209
Great Reform Act (1832) *see* Representation of the People Act
Grenfell, Ethel (Ettie), Lady Desborough 229, 243, 246, 310 n.5
Grey, Marchioness *see* Yorke, Jemima, Marchioness Grey

Hagley Hall (Worcestershire) 254
Hamilton, Mary 122
Hardwick, Bess of 28, 95, 263 n.51

316

INDEX

Hardwick Hall (Derbyshire) 95
Harewood House (West Yorkshire) 190
Harley, Brilliana, Lady Harley 16–17, 63, 252, 255, *Plate 5*; and death 84–5; and defence of Brampton Bryan Castle 78–84; and marriage 73, 75, 85; and motherhood 76; and religious beliefs 73–5, 76–8, 78; and support for the parliamentarian cause 77–8, 80
Harley, Sir Edward (Ned) 75, 76, 77, 79–8, 255
Harley, Sir Robert 17, 73–80, 84, 85, 140
Harvey, Dr William 37
Hatchlands Park (Surrey) 92, 96, 100–5, 106, 112–13, 114, 148–9, 162, 251, 253, 311 n.33, *Plate 9*
Hawthorne, Nathaniel 210
Helen, Princess (duchess of Albany) 182, *Plate 18*
Hervey-Bathurst, Imogen 253
Highclere Castle (Hampshire) 190
homes *see* country houses
honeymoons 224–5
Honiton lace industry 176
Horner, Edward 236–9, 240–1, 242, *Plate 28*
Horner, Frances, Lady Horner 8, 170, 200, 216, 230, 246; and Edward Burne-Jones 202–3, 215, *Plate 26*; and charitable activities 190, 191; and childhood 201–2; and gardens 207–8; as a hostess 214, 217–18; and Sir Edwin Lutyens 216, 242; and marriage 224; and Mells Park 203–4, 249; and politics 183; and relationship with her father 202, 214, 258 n.17; and relationship with her son 236–8, 239, 240–1
Horner, Sir John (Jack) 170, 203–4, 208, 224, 236–8, 246
Horsham, Sussex (parliamentary constituency) 116, 118–20
Hoskins, John 27
hospitality 22–3, 29–30, 32, 38, 53, 136, 151, 176
household management 4, 9, 10, 20–6, 58–9, 76, 78, 80–2, 84, 139–40, 151, 161–3, 193, 198, 214; *see also* servants

housewifery *see* household management
Hunstanton Hall (Norfolk) 16, 20, 24–5, 26, 27–9, 30–2, 36, 38, 47, 136, 250

Ilchester, Elizabeth, countess of 108, 110
ill health 36, 65, 152, 158–9, 193, 222, 234
Imperial Colonist (periodical) 192
India 89, 192, 193–4, 195, 209, 235
industrialisation 9, 89, 167, 189–90, 200, 212
inheritance 6, 26, 43, 98–9, 246, 253–4; problems with 34, 48, 52, 99
interior decoration *see* country houses
Irving, Washington 205–6
Irwin, Arthur, third viscount of 118
Irwin, Charles, ninth viscount of 92, 98–9, 119, 147, 156
Irwin, Frances, ninth viscountess of 92, 131, 157, 163, 247, 254, *Plate 8*; and courting 98–9; and married life 138–9, 147; and motherhood 127–8, 154–5, 156, 159; and politics 118–20; and Temple Newsam 94, 107–8, 111–12
Irwin, Isabella, third viscountess of 118, 155

James VI and I 22, 42
Jekyll, Gertrude 207, 249
Jersey, Margaret, seventh countess of 187
jests 16, 31, 38, 85
Jocelin, Elizabeth, *The Mothers Legacie* 15
Johnson, Samuel 124; *Dictionary of the English Language* 1, 4, 6, 8, 253, 254, 255
Jonson, Ben, 'To Penshurst' 22, 30, 31, 63, 136

Kauffman, Angelica 133–4, 136, 169
King's Lynn, 26, 29, 259 n.5
Kingsley, Rev. Charles 169
Kingston Lacy (Dorset) 170, 175, 176–7, 178, 179, 181, 191, 197, 208, 235–6, 248, 252

INDEX

Knightley, Louisa, Lady Knightley 170–1, 181, 247, 248, 250, 254, *Plate 18*; and estate management 174; and marriage 221–2; and philanthropic activities 175, 176, 189–90, 191–2; and politics 184–8; and the royal family 181–2

Knightley, Sir Rainald 171, 174, 178, 205, 247; and marriage 221–2; and politics 184–5

Ladies of Llangollen *see* Butler, Lady Eleanor; gifts; Ponsonby, Sarah

Lassels, Richard, *The Voyage of Italy* 195

Le Strange, Lady Alice 16, 27, 28–9, 38–9, 47, 53, 62, 254, 258 n.17, 260 n.14, *Plate 1*; and the building of Hunstanton Hall 27–8; and estate management 26; and hospitality 29–32; and household management 24–5; and married life 19–20, 23, 53, 58; and medical knowledge 36–7; and motherhood 32–5; and relationship with servants 24–5

Le Strange, Elizabeth 31

Le Strange, Sir Hamon 16, 19–20, 23, 24–5, 27–32, 38, 42, 53, 58

Le Strange, Jane 34

Le Strange, Mary 34–5

Le Strange, Sir Nicholas 31, 34, 47

Leadbetter, Stiff 102

Lees-Milne, James 251

Leighton, Frederic, Baron Leighton 202; home of 228

Leinster, Hermoine, sixth duchess of 197, 225–6, 227

Leopold, Prince 181–2

letters 50–1, 54, 55–6, 64, 70, 71–2, 73, 75–6, 81–3, 125, 127, 128, 139, 147–8; burning of 203, 229–30, 232; collating of 243

Liberal Party 185, 186, 187, 298 n.83; Women's Liberal Federation, 186–7

libraries *see* country houses

Lister, Anne 150, 152

Llangollen (Denbighshire) 136, 162; Dinas Brân, 97; *see also* Plas Newydd

London 27, 28, 29, 55, 95–6, 103, 109, 124, 125, 134, 141, 143, 156, 200, 202; Admiralty Screen 104; fashionable society in 9, 123, 135, 138–9, 167–8, 180, 228; French Gallery (Pall Mall) 211; New Gallery 203; Palace of Westminster 121–2, 123; Westminster (parliamentary constituency) 123, 185, *Plate 14*; Westminster Abbey 243

Londonderry, Edith, seventh marchioness of 187

Londonderry, Frances, third marchioness of 182

Longleat (Wiltshire) 16, 51, 54, 55, 56–7, 58, 250, 252

Longniddry, Scottish Veterans' Garden City of 191

Lorrain, Claude 109, 112

Loudon, Jane 207

Lucy, Caroline (Carry) 193–4

Lucy, George 93, 143, 144–5, 148, 196, 205–7, 209, 221

Lucy, Mary Elizabeth 93, 139, 152, 177, 194, 243, 253, 277 n.14, *Plate 16*; and Charlecote 205–6, 209–10, 251, 253; and courting 143, 144–5; and gardening 206–7; and marriage 148; and motherhood 154, 222; and relationship with her parents 143–4, 146–7; and travel 196; and her wedding 146

Lutyens, Lady Emily (née Lytton) 218

Lutyens, Sir Edwin 204, 207, 216, 242–3, 249

Lyttelton, Laura (née Tennant) 215, 217, 229, 230

Manners, Lady Diana 237, 239

Marie Antoinette (queen consort of Louis XVI of France) 151

marital cruelty 64–72

Marlborough, Consuelo, ninth duchess of 181

Marlborough, Sarah, first duchess of 95, 121

marriage 5–6, 7–8, 16, 18, 40–61, 63–72, 92, 109, 140–9, 222–7, 255; and affection 7, 41–2, 44, 52–3, 54, 60–1, 75, 139–40, 144, 147–9, 221;

318

INDEX

clandestine 48–9; and physical intimacy 53–8, 65, 145–6, 225, 227; *see also* divorce; marital cruelty

marriage settlements 45–6, 52, 94, 99, 146

Marsh, Edward 233, 249, 305 n.101

Marshall, Elizabeth 226–7

Marvin, Sir James 40, 48

medical knowledge, women and 8, 18, 35–8, 254

medievalism 202, 206, 243, *Plate 29*; and feudalism 171, 177, 189, 200; and ideals of chivalry 9, 177, 234, 238, 243

Mells (Somerset) 222, 224, 239, 242, 246; Mells Manor 208, 216, 236; Mells Park 203–4, 207–8, 215, 218, 236, 242, 249, *Plate 27*; St Andrew's church 215, 242, *Plate 28*

Middleton Park (Oxfordshire) 249

Mildmay, Sir Anthony 16, 18, 23, 25, 32, 34, 38, 46, 53, 58

Mildmay, Lady Grace 16, 20, 28, 38, 45–6, 61, 148, 253, 254, *Plate 2*; and charitable activities 37–8; and childhood 18–19; and courting 18; and hospitality 22; and household management 21, 23; and marriage 19, 53, 58; and medical knowledge 35–7; and motherhood 32–3, 34; and her spiritual memoirs 19, 20–1, 37, 53, 62

Mildmay, Sir Walter 18, 21, 23, 25, 27, 45

Mildmay Fane, Mary (countess of Westmorland) 32, 34, 247

mistress: definition of 1; expected roles of 2–8, 10, 20–1, 253–5

Montagu, Elizabeth 112, 124–5, 127, 130, 134–5

More, Hannah 116, 125–7, 129, 130, 136; 'Bas Bleu, or Conversation' 124; *Inflexible Captive* 126; 'Sensibility', 127

Morrell, Ottoline 170, 208, *Plate 23*

motherhood 6–7, 21, 32–4, 51, 68–9, 72–3, 132, 154–61; childbirth 155–6; childlessness 8, 32, 54, 62, 64; pregnancy 154–5, 193, 225; *see also* death

Munnings, Sir Alfred 242

National Trust 251–2

National Union of Women Workers 189

Newcastle upon Tyne 211

Norfolk, Charles, eleventh duke of 118–19

Norfolk, Edward, ninth duke of 117

North, Charles, fifth Baron 43–6

North, Roger 44, 46

Norwich, 26, 29, 38, 47

Nostell Priory (West Yorkshire) 129, 258 n.20

Ormond family, 129, 150

Oxford 76, 79, 213, 237; Campion Hall 216; Corpus Christi College 40; Oxford Museum 213

Palladio, Andrea 90

Parker, Catherine 98, 131

Parker, George 98

Parker, Jack 158

Parker, John 92, 98, 105–6, 131–4, 156–7

Parker, Theresa 92, 95, 113, 131–4, 136, 139, 253; and death 113, 132–3, 157; and Angelica Kauffman 133–4; and marriage 98; and motherhood 156–7, 158; and Sir Joshua Reynolds 131–3, *Plate 11*; and Saltram 105–6, 133

Parliament Act (1911) 168

paternalism 9, 37, 173–4, 213

patriarchy 1, 8–9, 15, 22, 58, 61, 140

Pawlett Lane, Captain 193–4

Pennington, Sarah, *Unfortunate Mother's Advice to her Absent Daughters* 159

Penrice Castle (Glamorganshire) 92, 109–10, 141–2, 154, 163, 250, *Plate 15*

philanthropy *see* charity

Phillips, Henry 111

Piozzi, Hester Thrale 115, 129, 135

Plas Newydd (Denbighshire) 93, 97, 100, 106–7, 110–11, 128–31, 136, 139, 152, 162–3, 248, 253, *Plate 12*

INDEX

Plaw, John, *Rural Architecture* 106
Pless, Prince and Princess Henry of 180
politics 4, 5, 6, 8, 10, 42, 89, 90, 91, 115–23, 131, 132, 136–7, 171, 182–8, 194–5, 200, 248; and entertaining 117–19, 122–3, 182–4; local 5, 169, 188; parliamentary 5, 14, 74, 77, 116, 119, 121–2, 168, 182, 188; *see also* electioneering
Ponsonby, Sarah 93, 96, 115–16, 130, 135–6, 248, 253, 255, *Plate 13*; and finances 100, 121; and Plas Newydd 97, 106–7, 128–9; and relationship with Lady Eleanor Butler 97, 149–53; and servants 100, 162–3
poor law boards 188, 190
Pope, Alexander 127
Porter, Agnes 159–60
Pre-Raphaelite art 168, 170, 201, 202, 210–11, 212, 213, 215; *see also* Burne-Jones, Sir Edward; Rossetti, Dante Gabriel; Ruskin, John
Pride, Tom 161, 292 n.118
primogeniture 6, 253
Primrose League *see* Conservative Party
Pückler-Muskau, Prince 130
puritanism 17, 35, 73–5, 78

Red Cross 190
Redlynch Park (Somerset) 92, 108–9, 142, 156
religious beliefs 10, 19, 20–1, 23, 37, 53, 77, 79, 117, 129, 156; *see also* puritanism
Representation of the People Act (Great Reform Act) (1832) 91, 169, 182
Reynolds, Sir Joshua 92, 116, 131–3, 136
Richardson, Samuel 140; *Clarissa: Or the History of a Young Lady* 231; *The History of Sir Charles Grandison* 127
Robinson, Frederick 133–4
Robinson, Thomas, Baron Grantham 92, 105
Robinson, Thomas, second Baron Grantham 106, 113, 132, 133, 158

romantic friendships 97, 150–1
Rome 196, 209
Rossetti, Christina 214
Rossetti, Dante Gabriel 202, 211
Rousham House (Oxfordshire) 17, 63, 64, 65, 66, 67–8, 73, 252
Rousseau, Jean-Jacques 128; *Julie, ou la nouvelle Heloise* 128, 150
Royal Academy of Arts 131–2, 133, 169, 215
Ruskin, John 201, 210–13
Russell Farm (Hertfordshire) 101
Rutland, Elizabeth, fifth duchess of 179
Rutland, Violet, eighth duchess of 309 n.101

St Valentine's Day 233
Saltram House (Devon) 92, 98, 105–6, 113–14, 130, 131–4, 161, *Plate 10*
Salvin, Anthony 205
same-sex relationships 6, 149–53, 197; *see also* romantic friendships
Samuel, Richard, *The Nine Living Muses of Great Britain* 125
Scott, Sir Walter 128, 206
Seaton (Devon) 213
Second World War 249–50
sensibility 9, 91, 108, 128, 138–9, 163
servants, 4, 14, 21, 23–5, 27, 31, 37, 59, 66–7, 71, 79, 81, 161–3, 169, 179, 193, 218, 231, 240; butlers 163, 242; gardeners 109, 112, 208; governesses and nannies 18, 159–60, 197, 201–2, 236, 253; housekeepers 37, 100, 162; stewards 24, 58, 101; wet nurses 33, 35; *see also* Carryl, Mary; Porter, Agnes; Pride, Tom
Seward, Anna 107, 111, 135; 'Llangollen Vale' 128
Shaftesbury, Anthony, third earl of 124
Shaftesbury, Anthony, seventh earl of 172
Shakespeare, William 127, 206, 209; *Much Ado About Nothing* 58; *Romeo and Juliet* 49, 57, 233
Shrewsbury, Bess countess of *see* Hardwick, Bess of
Singer Sargent, John 215, *Wyndham Sisters* 215, *Plate 21*

INDEX

single women 6, 149
slavery, views on 120, 125, 191
Smith, Rev. Sydney 154
social reform 9, 172, 175
Society for the Propagation of the Gospel in Foreign Parts 191
Somerset, Lady Henry 189
Souls, the 170, 183, 194–5, 201, 214–18, 230–1, 243, 246, 254
South African Colonisation Society 192
South Northamptonshire (constituency) 184–5, 186
Southey, Robert 128
Spencer, Georgiana, Countess Spencer 7
Spencer, Robert 43–7
Stanway (Gloucestershire) 215, 242
Stanway House (Gloucestershire) 170, 190, 204, 231, 234, 241, 244–5, 248–9, 252, *Plate 22*; guests at 216, 217, 218–20, 249; rearrangement of interior of 205
Stott, Philip Sidney 242
Strangways, Harriot Fox 109, 145–6
Strangways, Henry Fox, second earl of Ilchester 92, 108–9, 141–3, 144
Stuart, Gilbert 133
Stuart, Katherine, Lady d'Aubigny 82
Stubbe, Richard 16, 26, 42
Studland (Dorset) 179, 226–7
Sudeley (Gloucester) 253
suffrage, female 91, 117, 173, 187–8
Swinburne, Algernon 214
Switzer, Stephen, *Ichnographia Rustica* 108

Talbot, Caroline 189
Talbot, Christopher (Kit) 109
Talbot, Mary 92, 144, 253; and courting 141–3; and gardening 108–10; and married life 153–4; and motherhood 156, 158, 159–60; and her wedding 145–6
Talbot, Thomas Mansel 92, 141–3, 144, 153–4, 159, 163
taxation 14, 77, 241, 247, 250, 252; death duties 247, 251
Temple Newsam (West Yorkshire) 92, 94, 99, 107–8, 111–12, 138, 247–8, *Plate 7*, *Plate 29*

Tennant, Pamela, *Edward Wyndham Tennant* 243
Thornton, Alice 42
Thynne, Joan, Lady Thynne 46, 48, 49, 50–2, 59, 60, 95
Thynne, John 46, 48, 49, 52
Thynne, Maria, Lady Thynne 16, 41, 61, 62, 152, 254, 255, *Plate 4*; and estate management 58–60; and expression of sexual desire 56–8; and marriage 40, 48–50, 54–5, 60; and Joan Thynne 50–2
Thynne, Sir Thomas 16, 40, 41, 48–50, 51, 52, 54–61, 62, 255
Tighe, Sarah 135
Torlonia, Prince 196
Touchet, Lucy 40, 48, 51
Towcester (Northamptonshire) 185
Trevelyan, Pauline, Lady Trevelyan 170, 176, 203, 213–14, 219, 220, 221–2, 251, 253, *Plate 20*; and William Bell Scott 211–12; and death 213; and gardening 207; and the interior decoration of Wallington Hall 210–14; and John Ruskin 210–11, 212
Trevelyan, Sir Walter 170, 203, 211–13, 220, 221–2, 251
Trumbull, Lady Elizabeth 64, 71–72, 255
Trumbull, Sir William 64

Vavasour, Sir William 81–3
Venice 210
Vernon, Elizabeth (Betty) 69
Vesey, Elizabeth 124
Victoria, Queen 181
Victoria League 194

Walker, Ann 150
Wallington Hall (Northumbria) 170, 194, 201, 203, 207, 210–14, 219, 220, 251, *Plate 19*
Walpole, Horace 127
Warwick, Frances (Daisy), fifth countess of 182–3, 216
Webb, Beatrice 219
wedding rings 53

INDEX

weddings 31, 40, 47–8, 142–3, 145–6, 177–8, 180–1, *Plate 24*
Wellington, Arthur, duke of 121, 129
Wells, H.G. 216, 219, 228; *The New Machiavelli* 216
Wemyss, Anne (Annie), tenth countess of 230
Wemyss, Francis, tenth earl of 204, 205
Wemyss, Hugo, eleventh earl of *see* Elcho, Hugo
Wemyss, Mary, eleventh countess of *see* Elcho, Mary
Wharton, Edith 216, *The Buccaneers* 216
Whig party 122–3
Whistler, James McNeill 202
William IV 181
Williams, Sir John 93, 143
Williams, Lady Margaret 93, 143–4, 146–7
Wilton House (Wiltshire) 217, 223
Wimborne (Dorset) 176, 179
Winn, Sabine 129, 258 n.20
Wiseman, Lady Elizabeth 41, 43–7, 61
Wollstonecraft, Mary 157
Women's Institutes 191
women's suffrage *see* suffrage, female
Woodstock House (County Kilkenny) 96–7, 162
Woolner, Thomas 213; *Civilisation* 213, *Plate 19*
Working Ladies' Guild 189
Wortley Montagu, Lady Mary 129
Wright, Dr Nathaniel 78, 84, 273 n.100
Wyndham, Madeline 170, 197, 201, 202, 223
Wyndham, Percy 170, 197, 201, 202, 215

Yarmouth, Amalie, countess of 120–1
Yearsley, Ann 127
Yorke, Jemima, Marchioness Grey 95